THE HISTORICAL MIND

THE HISTORICAL MIND

Humanistic Renewal in a Post-Constitutional Age

Edited by Justin D. Garrison
and Ryan R. Holston

Published by State University of New York Press, Albany

©2020 State University of New York Press

All rights reserved

No part of this book may be used or reproduced in any manner whatsoever without written permission. No part of this book may be stored in a retrieval system or transmitted in any form or by any means including electronic, electrostatic, magnetic tape, mechanical, photocopying, recording, or otherwise without the prior permission in writing of the publisher.

For information, contact State University of New York Press, Albany, NY
www.sunypress.edu

Library of Congress Cataloging-in-Publication Data

Names: Garrison, Justin D., editor. | Holston, Ryan R., 1973- editor.
Title: The historical mind : humanistic renewal in a post-constitutional age / Edited by Justin D. Garrison and Ryan R. Holston.
Description: Albany : State University of New York Press, [2020] | Includes bibliographical references and index.
Identifiers: LCCN 2019049054 (print) | LCCN 2019049055 (ebook) | ISBN 9781438478432 (hardcover : alk. paper) | ISBN 9781438478449 (ebook) | ISBN 9781438478425 (pbk. : alk. paper)
Subjects: LCSH: Political science—Philosophy. | Constitutional law—Philosophy. | Constitutional law—United States. | Humanism—United States. | United States—Politics and government—Philosophy.
Classification: LCC JK31 .H56 2020 (print) | LCC JK31 (ebook) | DDC 320.01—dc23
LC record available at https://lccn.loc.gov/2019049054
LC ebook record available at https://lccn.loc.gov/2019049055

10 9 8 7 6 5 4 3 2 1

For Timothy and Hermione. Become who you are.
    —J.D.G.

For Kate and Ben, who are never short on imagination.
    —R.R.H.

History is life's teacher.
—Marcus Tullius Cicero

To the several perversities of the day a man should always oppose only the great masses of universal history.
—Johann Wolfgang von Goethe

The past is never dead. It's not even past.
—William Faulkner

Contents

Acknowledgments ix
Introduction xi

Part I. The New Humanism

ONE What I Believe: Rousseau and Religion 5
Irving Babbitt

TWO Power without Limits: The Allure of Political Idealism and the Crumbling of American Constitutionalism 19
Claes G. Ryn

Part II. Culture and Imagination

THREE Russell Kirk and the Romance of Babbittianism 45
Bradley J. Birzer

FOUR The Pillars of Hercules: Babbitt, Warren, and the Dangers of Scientific Naturalism 61
Justin D. Garrison

FIVE Luminosity, Imagination, Truth: On Voegelin and Ryn 89
S. F. McGuire

Part III. Ethics and Character

SIX Politics, Moral Judgment, and the Enlightenment Project 109
William F. Byrne

SEVEN   Natural Law, the Moral Imagination, and Prudent Exceptions   127
           Robert C. Koons

EIGHT   Irving Babbitt and Christianity: A Response to T. S. Eliot   145
           Ryan R. Holston

Part IV. America and Constitutional Spirit

NINE   Can Constitutions Preserve the Engendering Experiences
           of Order?   173
           Michael P. Federici

TEN   On the Moral Necessity of Constitutionalism:
           Claes Ryn and Ethical Democracy   201
           Bruce P. Frohnen

Part V. America, Humanism, and the World

ELEVEN   "Let Things Be Called by Their Right Names":
           Difference as Constraint in American Exceptionalism   225
           Richard M. Gamble

TWELVE   A Little Place and a Big Idea: The Temptation to Imperialism
           and the Loss of Republicanism   241
           Justin B. Litke

THIRTEEN   Resistance and Renewal: Irving Babbitt and China   257
           Zhang Yuan and Justin D. Garrison

Conclusion   273
Contributors   277
Index   281

Acknowledgments

The editors would like to acknowledge the following as reprinted materials and to thank the content owners for granting reprint permission: Chapter 1 was originally published by Irving Babbitt in *The Forum* 83, no. 2 (February 1930): 80–87. Reprinted with permission of Current History Magazine INC. © 2018 Current History, Inc. Chapter 2 was originally published by Claes G. Ryn in *Humanitas* 26, nos. 1–2 (2013): 5–27. Reprinted with permission of *Humanitas*. Lyrics appearing in the introduction from "The Levee's Gonna Break," Bob Dylan, author, copyright © 2006 by Special Rider Music. All rights reserved. International copyright secured. Reprinted by permission.

Justin Garrison would like to acknowledge Roanoke College and the summer research grant it provided to facilitate completion of this volume. He would also like to thank Ms. Judi Pinckney and Mr. Kasey F. Reese for assistance in preparing in preparing portions of the manuscript. Ryan Holston would like to extend his appreciation to Jim Hentz (RIP), who provided valuable guidance along the way. He would also like to thank Spencer Bakich for his insight into the contemporary literature on democratic peace theory. Additionally, he wishes to express his deep gratitude to Bruce Frohnen, whose early dedication to this volume provided it with needed support and momentum.

Finally, both editors would like to extend their sincere appreciation to Michael Federici for his mentorship throughout the process; without him this book certainly would not have come to fruition.

Introduction

> If it keep on rainin' the levee gonna break
> —Bob Dylan

POST-CONSTITUTIONAL AMERICA

The temperature is hovering around freezing. The clouds intermittently disburse noonday sunlight into a leaden sky. On the western front of the Capitol, President George W. Bush strides to a podium to take his second oath of office as president of the United States. In his second inaugural address, he seeks to explain the true meaning of this axial moment in human history. According to his view, since the Founding, Americans have furthered history's purpose of promoting freedom, individual rights, and self-government at home and abroad. In his time as president, the United States has acted in Afghanistan and Iraq in accordance with the country's "great liberating tradition" and has thereby kindled anew "a fire in the minds of men."[1] Much work remains to be done. The process of converting the globe to principles that are "eternally right" will be done through diplomacy, if possible; it will be done through force, if necessary.[2] The United States, too, is in need of substantial change. More home ownership, better health care, greater investment in education, and stronger retirement programs are vital to providing the American people with "greater freedom from want and fear," while making "our society more prosperous and just and equal."[3] Returning to his universal focus, Bush channels the Prophet Isaiah and concludes his remarks, stating, "America, in this young century, proclaims liberty throughout all the world and to all the inhabitants thereof."[4]

Four years later, the United States has a new president. The temperature is below freezing when Barack Obama begins his first inaugural address. Most of his remarks touch upon domestic areas of concern and anxiety. He explains that failing infrastructure must be repaired. A recommitment to science and technological investment is needed because it will lower health-care costs and allow Americans to "harness the sun and the winds and the soil to fuel our cars and run our factories."⁵ The national government will play a decisive role in these efforts. He devotes some of his time to discussing the broader world. Rejecting as false a choice between security and idealism, he warns terrorists and others who might harm the United States, "We will not apologize for our way of life, nor will we waver in its defense."⁶ He says the United States is a friend to all who desire "peace and dignity."⁷ He offers America's help to nations suffering from conflict and poverty. He admonishes countries with wealth to be more generous. Reflecting on the essence of American history and the realization of his vision for the future, Obama articulates his convictions that "the lines of tribe shall soon dissolve; that as the world grows smaller, our common humanity shall reveal itself, and that America must play its role in ushering in a new era of peace."⁸

Despite differences in ideology and party affiliation, there are some striking similarities in these remarks from Bush and Obama. Although they place different degrees of emphasis on involvement of the federal government in American life, they both believe it has a crucial role to play in numerous policy areas and on various social scales. Both presidents share the belief that the United States is a special nation called to spread human rights and self-government to the ends of the earth; they differ over tactics rather than vision. Both of them invite Americans to pursue the realization of a domestic paradise of freedom and equality and a world at peace made possible through unflagging optimism and robust American action. Each president argues that he is stating nothing new but is reminding Americans of what they have always believed, have always been. They see their presidencies as continuations of the best in the American tradition.

In his speech, Bush asked younger Americans who might be suspicious of the truth of his remarks to "believe the evidence of your eyes."⁹ A number of the things those eyes would see would be troubling. Among other things, the Bush years included failed wars in Afghanistan and Iraq, widespread and illegal surveillance of citizens, signing statements reflecting disregard for limitations on executive power, torture, a Great Recession, almost six trillion dollars in new national debt, and diminishing job prospects for large swaths of the population. In most respects, Obama followed in Bush's footsteps. Torture stopped, but Guantanamo Bay remained open. The Iraq War (sort of) ended, but Afghanistan continued to deteriorate. A new war in Libya was launched and failed. Drone attacks on suspected terrorists increased, as did resulting civilian deaths. Unemployment was at one point the highest in a generation.

A proliferation of executive orders reflected contempt for the rule of law, as did the expansion of illegal surveillance of Americans. Another nearly eight trillion dollars was added to the national debt. In 2011, America's AAA credit rating was lost. In his inaugural address, Obama paraphrased St. Paul and told Americans, "The time has come to set aside childish things," imploring us to end the "petty grievances" of ordinary politics so that we may recommit ourselves to "the God-given promise that all are equal, all are free, and all deserve a chance to pursue their full measure of human happiness."[10] These are strong words, but in light of the romantic and idealistic dreams associated with both of these presidencies, so many of the political priorities of Bush and Obama seem, well, childish.

Thinking about human nature, the eighteenth-century German humanist Johann Wolfgang von Goethe writes, "Truth is contrary to our nature, not so error, and this for a very simple reason: truth demands that we should recognize ourselves as limited, error flatters us that, in one way or another, we are unlimited."[11] For Goethe, truth is very much something worth living by, but individuals and societies must make strenuous moral effort for it to take hold. Such labor cannot be profitable without a broad and deep knowledge of the normative power of human historical experience. In contrast, the relative ease of ethical and intellectual indolence can be very appealing. With this in mind, it is not entirely surprising that Bush and Obama often ignored constitutional and moral constraints on their abilities to pursue allegedly noble ends. Many other American leaders and Americans in general seem to chafe under even the most modest legal barriers or ethical limitations standing between them and the realization of their momentary desires. Despite the appearance of stark divisions within the United States, the extent to which living in the error of the unlimited has come to define American politics and life in the twenty-first century is astonishing. This has serious implications for the continued existence of the United States as a constitutional republic in any meaningful sense.

John Adams once described republican government as the best form of government, because it makes possible an "empire of laws, and not of men."[12] He and many of his fellow Framers understood that free government works only when a people possesses a level of virtue and self-control sufficient not only to make laws, but to *govern* themselves by them. Human history confirms this view, they believed. In his second inaugural, even Bush acknowledges as much, saying, "Self-government relies, in the end, on the governing of the self."[13] Unfortunately, when the words and deeds of many contemporary political figures and ordinary citizens are weighed, it is clear that the ethical wisdom of history on which Adams and his contemporaries relied for guidance and inspiration has lost a great deal of its normative authority. When leaders and citizens will not enforce and live according to self-imposed limits, both constitutional and moral, Adams believes, history teaches that "the people, when they have been unchecked, have been just as unjust, tyrannical, brutal, barbarous, and cruel, as any king or senate possessed of uncontrollable power."[14] In other words, political institutions ultimately cannot function without the presence of ethically sensible citizens. The degree to which the United States of the present reflects Adams's description of an unprincipled people reveling in the exercise of unrestrained power is the degree to which America has transitioned from a constitutional republic to what may be described as a post-constitutional government and society.

Americans do seem to have an inkling that something is wrong in the United States. Sadly, the sources of the problems they sense are often overlooked. It is true that Americans frequently and vigorously complain about transgressions by this leader or that party, but such protests seem often motivated by rank partisanship, toxic ideology, or perceived electoral advantages. Principled concerns about ethical character, institutional durability, or fidelity to the Constitution are rarely raised or taken seriously. Countless politicians, public intellectuals, political operatives, business leaders, and others routinely invoke various aspects of the American past to justify any number of policy, electoral, or social goals. The vagueness and inaccuracy of many such claims exposes how unhistorical, how dreamlike, the American understanding of its own past has become. Further, it betrays an ignorance of the cultural foundations that once supported America's historical institutions and policy choices. Conventional political activities including campaigning, voting, promoting policies, and legislating remain important, but no amount of success or reform in these areas can adequately address the more fundamental crisis of post-constitutionalism in the United States.

To get to the heart of the predicament felt but misunderstood by many, the deeper problem of America's deteriorating constitutional culture must be confronted. A genuine revival of America's constitutional spirit is possible only if a revitalized historical consciousness and renewed emphasis on moral character become socially authoritative. Scholarship has a role to play in facilitating such rejuvenation, insofar as it provides essential intellectual elucidation and the rationale for prescribed changes. That is the purpose of this volume. At the same time, it is worth acknowledging at the outset that more than sound thinking is needed to address the current crisis. Historical consciousness and moral character are ultimately grounded in the customs and habits that define the ways in which Americans *live* as well as reason. Therefore, such intellectual arguments, while essential, will not by themselves suffice but must be accompanied by changes in these concrete ways of living.

The Historical Mind engages with the intellectual dimensions of this broader cultural challenge in a number of ways. It draws together scholars from disciplines such as political theory, philosophy, law, and history. Regardless of each scholar's field of study, their chapters take seriously the truths derived from historical human experience. In so doing, many contributions illuminate the complexity and richness of the past, what Edmund Burke called "the general bank and capital of nations and of ages."[15] For readers disoriented by the omnipresent unreality of the present, this book can help them gain clearer understanding of different problems, thereby awakening their senses of history as a living force. This is especially true of what historical experience has to say about human nature, that is, that we are self-interested as well as capable of acquiring wisdom and self-control, and that sound institutions will be insufficient for thriving regimes, which also require ethically mature individuals. Beyond identifying what the past can impart about politics and the human condition, much of this text actually demonstrates how this sort of historical awareness can inform one's approach to politics and culture.

A HISTORICAL HUMANISM

Addressing areas including imagination and culture, moral philosophy, constitutionalism, and foreign policy, the following chapters are engaged to varying degrees with ideas from Irving Babbitt, the twentieth-century pioneer of the American New Humanism movement, and Claes G. Ryn, a political theorist and Babbitt's foremost interpreter. The humanism of Babbitt and Ryn has been incorporated into this book, because it strives to provide greater conceptual clarity regarding universal truths of life's moral order without resorting to ahistorical thinking or ideological assertions about politics and human nature.[16] Though neither thinker uses the term *post-constitutional*, they repeatedly bring their philosophical, aesthetic, and ethical insights to bear on analyses of threats to the constitutional spirit needed to make American democracy serve its proper political and moral ends. Whether or not each contributing scholar is wholly aligned with Ryn and Babbitt, and, indeed, some would politely decline being described as humanist, each is similarly aware of how much a flourishing society depends on a culture steeped in historical knowledge and the attendant ethical character that defines the human being of ethical proportion or measure. These concerns are at the very heart of Babbitt and Ryn's thinking.

In *Literature and the American College*, Babbitt draws inspiration from Socrates and explains that especially in an age in which much philosophical, political, aesthetic, and moral confusion reigns, one task in which society in general and scholars in particular must engage is that of "right defining."[17] Heeding Babbitt's words, the reader must be given a perspective from which to observe the unity of this volume's thoughtful contributions. A brief orientation to Ryn and Babbitt's major ideas and areas of interest, especially those related to their thoughts on American constitutionalism in the deepest sense, must be offered. In the course of these remarks, it will be made clearer precisely how this historically informed variety of humanism will be helpful in promoting the constitutional spirit that is seen as no longer supporting American political life.

Like democracy and liberty, humanism is a term with various meanings and representatives. Ancient Greek and Roman philosophers such as Plato, Aristotle, Cicero, and Seneca have been described as classical humanists. Christians too have a kind of humanism—one that is present in the writings of figures, including Justin Martyr, Clement of Alexandria, Thomas More, and John Paul II. More recently, a secular type of humanism has emerged in the West as a conscious alternative to theistic religions, especially Christianity, and can be traced from the Renaissance thinker, Niccolò Machiavelli, through Enlightenment liberals such as Thomas Paine, and more recently to popular intellectuals, such as Richard Dawkins and Sam Harris. All of these humanisms are united in the belief that conceptualization of human experience illuminates the nature of human beings and the structure of reality. Further, these types of humanism are in agreement that their theoretical insights *ought* to shape the ways in which people conduct their lives as individuals and as members of societies. Hence, each has descriptive and normative dimensions. At the same time, these humanisms produce diverging accounts of human nature, the world, ethics, and politics because they place different emphases on the importance of and relationships among philosophy, religion, and science.

The humanism of Ryn and Babbitt intersects with elements in each of these traditions mentioned above, but it has more in common with the classical and Christian humanisms than with the modern varieties. Both thinkers see humanism as occupying a philosophical and experiential middle ground between scientific rationalism and materialism, on the one hand, and counterfeit spirituality, either of a rigidly doctrinal or sentimental variety, on the other hand. Ryn and Babbitt find much to admire in traditional religions of the East and West, as well as in the methods and fruits of modern positive science. Still, they see their kind of humanism as *more* "positive" than most conventional approaches because it realizes the full meaning of the positivist project by giving spiritual (nonmaterial) experiences conceptual elucidation without reducing such occurrences to epiphenomena of material being. At the same time, by refusing to prioritize social uplift or dogmatic disputation, by focusing on the commands to undertake a journey of moral discipline found in the shared insights of Jesus, the Buddha, and others, Babbitt and Ryn see their type of humanism as *more* religious than the sham spiritualities that have been ascendant in the West, particularly in the United States, since the early twentieth century. While never claiming humanism can or should replace various religions, Babbitt and Ryn see humanism as entirely compatible with and a manifestation of the truths about human life found in Judaism, Christianity, Buddhism, and Confucianism.

Such truths, Babbitt would say, are made manifest in the historical experience of each of these great traditions, which provide evidence of our universal human nature. For Babbitt, synthesizing such experience of the human species means nothing less than bringing the past to life in the present. Benedetto Croce, a twentieth-century Italian philosopher known to Babbitt and much admired by Ryn, writes, "Man is a microcosm, not in the natural sense, but in the historical sense, a compendium of universal history."[18] Think of how we might get by on a daily basis. We set an alarm to wake up in the morning. We dress, eat breakfast, go to work, and engage others in conversation. Similar actions are taken throughout the day. Most of these routine activities would seem to be done almost unconsciously, but we are making decisions all the time, deciding what and what not to will. For moments that can be too brief to recognize, the present is giving us obstacles to overcome. Waking, grooming, cooking, walking, eating, speaking, and so forth are not discovered anew each day and relearned. At the same time, every day is not quite the same as any other. Thus our need to act in the circumstances of each day can be satisfied only by synthesizing our past and our present. Whether or not we recognize it, our ability to live as coherent beings over time is possible only because we are our living history. Our history, in turn, is shaped in ways we do and do not know by the history of our country, civilization, and humanity as a whole.

When confronted with unusual situations, including those involving great political change and civilizational crises, we become acutely aware of our need for more knowledge. We may feel compelled to spend a great deal of time discovering and thinking about those things that dwell in the deep of the past. In a general sense, history is the record of various things that have been done by and happened to people. In a more meaningful sense, history is embedded with knowledge of how different peoples and ages conceptualized and lived goodness, truth, and beauty, as well as their opposites. Taken together, history has wisdom to impart about relationships between unique circumstances and recurring "oughts" and "ought nots." People in search of this kind of knowledge are not looking for ahistorical principles that can be grafted on to the present. The normative dimension of history can no more be severed from the diverse experiences that generates it than a trunk can be removed from the branches without killing the tree. Inspiration for creative action in the distinct present, not identifying for transplantation allegedly unchanging ideas from the past, is what we seek. In ordinary and extraordinary circumstances, this process of bringing the past to bear on the present is the same. In other words, human beings are historical creatures. The knowledge people carry and act on is always and unavoidably historical knowledge.

The more we develop our sense of the past, that is, our historical consciousness, the more we understand a seemingly contradictory truth: the universal manifests itself and is known to human beings in the diverse particulars to which it is inextricably linked. Truth, goodness, and beauty are present in but are never consumed by historical examples. There are no fixed models for philosophy, ethics, politics, or art. There are only diverse instances of universality that stand on their own and stand ready as inspiration for new acts in each of these areas. Every instance of universality simultaneously brings forward and remains distinct from the past. Specifically with regard to truths in philosophical ideas, Ryn argues, "Knowledge is carried by concepts that can be forever improved. Cognition is a dialectical straining towards, never the achievement of, perfect clarity."[19]

The idea that universality and particularity exist in a relationship of fruitful tension will likely meet with some misgivings. Historical relativists might be pleased to see attention called to the diversity of historical experiences, but they will likely bristle under the notion that the past can be more than one thing after another, something greater than random beads on a meaningless string. Babbitt sees the Romantic movement's reaction to scientific rationalism as an understandable reassertion of the particularity of human life. However, what philosophers such as Friedrich Nietzsche and Henri Bergson miss in the "philosophy of the flux" is the Oneness that unites all of human existence—the abiding and eternal order that brings coherence and deep satisfaction (*eudaimonia*) to a life well-lived.²⁰ While these thinkers correctly recognize life's undeniable historical dimension, the novelty that characterizes each particular person and moment, they fail to appreciate its permanent, higher potential. The moral, intellectual, and aesthetic standards internal to human life are thus not arbitrary, for Babbitt and Ryn, but reveal themselves in all their objectivity in human experience through the ages. While it is possible to ignore these standards and live according to the romantic's dream of idiosyncrasy and eccentricity, "the person who flees from their authority is left no peace."²¹

Abstract rationalists might applaud this embrace of universality, but they will probably become apprehensive when it is not tied to celebrations of "universal values" raised above or somehow separate from the dangerous flow of history. However, for both Babbitt and Ryn, several problems emerge with regard to this strain of antihistorical philosophy going back to Plato, which actually hinders rather than promotes, universal values. In the first place, by identifying the standards by which human conduct is to be judged with some abstract, noetic realm, severed from concrete, historical life, such thinkers create fixed intellectual precepts, whose rigidity renders them unable to meet the moral needs of historically diverse circumstances.²² Consequently, in the name of moral universality, these philosophers impose principles on a changing reality toward which they are insensitive and for which they are entirely inappropriate, paradoxically bringing about an unjust states of affairs.²³ In the second place, invocations of abstract principles of "natural right" often serve as cover for evading moral responsibility, insofar as they use the perfect nature of their ideals as a pretext for shunning the messiness of the ethical life and foregoing difficult but necessary decisions. In the name of noble principles, moral idealists often reject discriminating between "shades of gray" as mere relativism or as compromising one's principles, effectively preaching abstention from moral and political life in the name of remaining pure.²⁴

In the development of Babbitt's idea of a "oneness that is always changing," or what Ryn calls "value centered historicism," their historically conscious humanism recognizes both the persistence of the universal moral order as well as the historical life within which it always resides and operates. In various writings, Babbitt argues that all philosophers must eventually confront the relationship between universality and particularity, what he describes as the Platonic problem of the One and the Many. Often in Western philosophy, this relationship has been seen as adversarial or illusory. Different thinkers, including many of the great philosophers in the Western tradition, have eventually sided with one and discounted or rejected the other. Babbitt and Ryn see the choice that is often presented between history and universality as ultimately false. In truth, both elements are always present, always making life possible. The satisfaction to be derived from the simplicity of relativism, on the one hand, and absolutism, on the other, does not change the barrenness of each of these views. Such theories are gray, but historical life, in all its splendor and paradox, is green.

IMAGINATION, CHARACTER, AND CULTURE

A person's knowledge of the relationship between the universal and the particular described above does not rest exclusively on the possession of a sophisticated intellect. Most people are not philosophers. How then can we come to know what we know? For Babbitt and Ryn, people experience universality first and most potently through the mutually reinforcing relationship between imagination and will. Every person has a host of impulses seeking translation into action. Whether the needs are mundane or extraordinary, the stirrings of will in an individual become known to the extent that those desires take on the immediacy and texture provided by the imagination. The images generated by the intuition intensify the power of growing volitions, giving us a preconceptual awareness of what we might do. As this occurs, the will rejects some invitations to act and accepts others, according to habits developed over the course of a life. When confronted with elaborate and comprehensive imaginings, the reason can also become involved in the process, seeking the truth of an intuition by scrutinizing its constituent parts, testing them against reality. The development of historical consciousness is the growth of imagination and will as well as reason.

The imagination always gives a unity, but it does not always give one that is real, which is to say, it is not always commensurate with the concrete, historical experience of human life. To distinguish between intuitions grounded in reality and those of pure fantasy, Ryn and Babbitt, and others such as Peter Viereck and Russell Kirk, dichotomize qualities or types of imagination into moral and romantic. The moral imagination is nourished by the experience of daily life as well as encounters with works of philosophy, history, theology, and literature. A person who has this quality of imagination sees human nature as dualistic, that is, as comprised not merely of various desires but of impulses both ethical and unethical. The will works along with moral imagination to restrain the latter while allowing itself to become realized in concrete action.

Over time, repeated exercise of the ethical will produces habits of true moral character in an individual. With moral imaginative vision, one sees politics as capable of providing some level of justice and space for human flourishing, but expectations of what can be accomplished through such activity are modest. A morally imaginative conception of politics accounts for both the best and the worst of which people are capable.

Romantic imagination is also formed through experience and learning, but the results are quite different. For someone attached to such intuitions, human beings are not seen as suffering from a chronic moral weakness that can be mitigated to some extent through protracted effort. People are either held to be so naturally good or rational that injustice and unhappiness are attributed to ignorance or, more commonly, to the machinations of malevolent external forces. With no need to work on the self, the romantic imagination focuses a person's attention on the reconfiguration of social, economic, and governmental institutions. The possibilities of politics are felt to be unlimited with the attainment of sufficient knowledge and the power to reform institutions. Through a mixture of technical sophistication and a deep if ultimately vague sense of sympathy for other human beings, those who have this quality of imagination believe problems that have afflicted humanity for generations can be completely and permanently resolved. In the language of T. S. Eliot, those who have this sense of the world dream "of systems so perfect that no one will need to be good."[25] In the event that things do not go as planned, it is rare that the alleged nobility of romantic vision itself is called into question. Something or someone else often takes the blame for disappointment or failure.

Mention was made above of the relationship between historical consciousness and universality and of the connections between will, reason, and imagination. Ryn writes, "Only an imagination which is sensitive to possibilities of experience in their relation to what is ultimately real—exercise of the ethical will and the happiness it brings—can express the essence of the human condition."[26] To be more specific, historical consciousness is acquired through and part of moral imagination. It is only under the guidance of this type of imagination that the will can act as an "ethical check," to use Babbitt's language. Rationalism and dreaminess, unaware of or uninterested in the normative aspects of history, are not shaped by such intuitions. Moral imagination is where true universality is most intensely experienced. In contrast, romantic imagination seduces its possessor into denials or distortions of genuine universals. Reason is capable of distinguishing qualities of imagination, but in a practical sense this is only possible in a person of moral imagination. For one who thrills to romantic intuitions, will, and imagination often undermine the proper functioning of reason precisely because that is what the individual desires.

One of these forms of imagination tends to predominate in the individual, defining one's character as sober or frenzied, humble or hubristic, moral or licentious. One leads to happiness, the other does not. What is true about the imagination of an individual is true about the representative quality of imagination in a nation. A society's intuitive disposition is reflected in its laws, customs, religions, economic arrangements, and understandings of leisure, architecture, music, and so forth. The presence of moral imagination in these areas provides the bonds of community and civility that make not merely for life but for good, peaceful living. When romantic imagination permeates these areas, a society tends toward fragmentation and division. Suspicion, opportunism, deceit, vulgarity, cravenness, and violence are common features of a country in which this type of imagination prevails. Nations can get by, for a time, on such impoverished vision, but not much more than that. Moral imagination is the lodestone of civilization; romantic imagination is the engine of decadence.

DEMOCRACIES AND AMERICA

In *Democracy and the Ethical Life*, Ryn argues the word *democracy* is so frequently used and variously defined as to make the concept appear meaningless.[27] To bring theoretical weight to bear on meanings of democracy, both he and Babbitt dichotomize the idea into two types: constitutional democracy and direct democracy. For both thinkers, a constitutional democracy is one in which laws, decentralized power, and social customs all act together as the ethical check writ large. About this kind of democracy Ryn writes, it "is the political dimension of ethical self-restraint and hence the necessary political condition for the furtherance of the ethical life."[28] In contrast, a direct or plebiscitary democracy is one in which popular sovereignty is conceived of as the exercise of undiluted power by an undifferentiated mass in the pursuit of the political whim of the moment. Despite their shared use of the term "democracy," Babbitt and Ryn do not see these as variations on a similar theme. About the distinction between the two, Babbitt explains, "There is an opposition of first principles between those who maintain that the popular will should prevail, but only after it has been purified of what is merely impulsive and ephemeral, and those who maintain that this will should prevail immediately and unrestrictedly."[29] The difference, one might say, between such first principles is the presence or absence of the constitutional spirit.

The idea of a constitutional democracy, it is worth noting, abounded in the minds of many leading figures in the American Framing, whose view of human nature was clearly aligned with the humanistic priority of restraint and placing checks on impulse. In Federalist No. 71, Alexander Hamilton explains the very notion of a republic carries with it a commitment to popular sovereignty, but "it does not require an unqualified complaisance to every sudden breeze of passion."[30] In some instances, the people need government to protect them from suffering the consequences of mass exercises of the lower will. But government itself also needs to be restrained. An essential purpose of a constitution is to establish durable institutions and procedures by which the ends of government can be pursued to the benefit of all and the threat of factious political movements and legislation can be minimized to the most realistic extent.

As important as a written constitution can be, it ultimately fails without a corresponding constitutional character predominant in politics and the broader society. In Federalist No. 55, Madison draws on historical wisdom and the moral imagination, arguing, "As there is a degree of depravity in mankind, which requires a certain degree of circumspection and distrust: so there are other qualities in human nature, which justify a certain proportion of esteem and confidence. Republican government presupposes the existence of these qualities in a higher degree than any other form."[31] The best relationship between constraint and freedom cannot be determined in the abstract. In a society in which ethical maturity is in short supply, government tends to use a heavy hand to establish some degree of order. In a constitutional democracy, as Madison and many others at the time knew, citizens must assume the primary responsibility for exercising the moral self-discipline that distinguishes true freedom from license.

For most of those who drafted, debated, and implemented the Philadelphia Constitution, commitments to federalism, separation of powers, popular sovereignty under law, and limited government grew out of concrete experience and varying degrees of historical understanding of human nature and politics. In this light, the Constitution's purpose of forming "a more perfect union" is in continuity with colonial aims such as promoting "orderly and decent government" found in the "Fundamental Orders of Connecticut" over a century earlier.[32] John Adams had an especially keen sense of America's historical indebtedness, explaining how much its political thought and practice owed to the broader

Western past, especially America's English heritage. In a letter to John Taylor of Caroline, Adams flatly rejects the idea that in the late eighteenth century the United States invented a novel approach to politics, stating, "America has made no discoveries of principles of government that have not been long known."[33] In other words, the basic constitutional disposition of many Framers was not informed by doctrinaire adherence to untested ideas from the Enlightenment.[34]

Though it was a minority view during the Framing, what Babbitt and Ryn call direct democracy had notable advocates. Like others, Thomas Jefferson and Thomas Paine were proponents of a very different type of constitutionalism. For each, a constitution was a deliberate, written expression of the rational consensus of a people. In *The Rights of Man*, Paine argues that the formation of a social contract "is the only mode in which governments have a right to arise, and the only principle on which they have a right to exist."[35] For Jefferson, a constitution is necessary because government has a natural tendency toward tyranny; it must be bound in manacles of legal iron to protect the rights of the people. About the people themselves, both he and Paine see them as a group that can do little wrong by accident—and nothing intentionally dishonest. The majority in such a democracy should prevail over the minority. In public remarks upon accepting his appointment as secretary of State, Jefferson intones, "Let us, then, my dear friends, for ever bow down to the general reason of society."[36] For Jefferson and Paine, a dichotomy exists between the people, naturally good and reasonable, and government, naturally inclined toward despotism.

Whereas Adams sees continuity between the American past and present, even after July 4, 1776, Jefferson observes a fresh start for Americans and the rest of the world as the fruits of the independence movement. Finding the principles of the American Revolution "engraved in our hearts," Jefferson feels no need to "investigate the laws and institutions of a semi-barbarous ancestry."[37] In *Common Sense*, Paine also dismisses the normative importance of history, stating the following about the then impending American separation from England: "We have it in our power to begin the world over again."[38] Reflecting on the fiftieth anniversary of the Declaration of Independence, Jefferson expresses his hope for the future significance of the American Revolution, writing, "May it be to the world, what I believe it will be ... the signal of arousing men to burst the chains under which monkish ignorance and superstition had persuaded them to bind themselves, and to assume the blessings and security of self-government."[39] For Jefferson and Paine, visions of the American independence movement grounded in aspirations more modest than global transformation are contemptible.

Especially since the turn of the twentieth century, this mixture of belief in natural human goodness and rationality, combined with a disposition to ignore or reject history as a source of inspiration and wisdom in the present, has gained ascendency in the US. As a thinker and president, Woodrow Wilson exemplifies this development. He dismisses much of what the Framers believe about government and human nature as the unfortunate product of applying the imagery of Newtonian physics to politics. Impressed by Darwinism and an evolutionary conception of societies, he seeks to redirect the American mind and imagination away from cultivating moral and legal restraints on rash, unchecked action and toward harnessing power to provide humanitarian service to all. Because Wilson sees his responsibilities as shepherding popular opinion and translating the desires of the people into action, he disparages the diversity of views found in Congress as provincial and inefficient. About the American presidency, he states, "The president is at liberty, both in law and conscience, to be as big a man as he can. His capacity will set the limit."[40] Under benevolent leadership, and provided the results are approved by the people, traditional concerns about constitutionalism recede into the background.

Despite having a number of things in common with Wilson, both Jefferson and Paine would likely be dismayed over the lack of suspicion of government and political power found in Wilson's political thought. At the same time, Jefferson and Paine make explicit room for each generation to determine for itself how to govern and by what beliefs it wants to live. Both figures celebrate the nobility of the people and place great faith in their common sense. That Americans would end up embracing a presidentially centered and increasingly centralized national government of the kind admired by Wilson and many of his successors is not the inexorable outcome of Jefferson and Paine's way of thinking, but neither is it a bizarre result. Unmoored from the historical, the romantic imaginative dimensions of the ideas of Jefferson, Paine, and Wilson retain their potency and have an increased field on which to act. Babbitt appears to be right when he claims that the differences between constitutional and direct democracy are existential rather than trivial. They are incompatible approaches to politics and reflect irreconcilable philosophical anthropologies.

AMERICA AND THE WORLD

These very different types of democracies, Babbitt and Ryn agree, also generate distinct approaches to American foreign policy. In many instances, the spirit of constitutional democracy is manifest in a foreign policy of restraint that finds the roots of international disorder to be the same as those that cause strife at home: human moral failing. Such a foreign policy does not avoid using force to defend national sovereignty and other legitimate interests, but neither does it resort to such means without careful ethical consideration and submission to the relevant constitutional and other legal decision-making procedures. Peace among nations is a goal, but hopes for anything approaching such an achievement must be grounded in a sober understanding of the human condition, as well as knowledge of and respect for international cultural and political diversity. On this view, the good society and the democratic society are not always synonymous. Rather, historical wisdom is the essential prerequisite for formulating such a vision, which may be properly described as that of moral realism. As Ryn writes, "Only on the basis of intimate familiarity with the highest achievements of one's own society is it possible to have more than shallow appreciation for the corresponding highest achievements of other societies."[41] Such a sense of a nation's past, along with the unique traditions of others, is essential to cultivating relationships with other countries that are both informed and circumspect, open and restrained.

The passion that drives plebiscitary democracy, in contrast, tends to produce a foreign policy prone to dreamy and abstract thinking. On this view, human beings are more or less the same wherever they live. People are good and want more or less the same things in life. Their cultural and historical differences are deemed superficial and ultimately unimportant, if they are acknowledged at all. International disorder is attributed to many external causes. Peace remains a goal, but it is believed to be achievable—even on a permanent basis—through the establishment of liberal democratic political, economic, and other institutions. War can still be fought for traditional reasons, but it is more common to use force as a means of delivering economic uplift and democratic progress around the world. About the international relations of such a democracy, Babbitt draws a startling conclusion, writing that such a regime "is likely to be idealistic in its feelings about itself, but imperialistic in its practice." This observation probably sounds illogical to those who equate democracy with goodness and interpret this kind of foreign policy as the model of moral service to the world. However, because Babbitt can distinguish types of democracy, he believes he is on firm historical ground in claiming a connection between this romantic kind of democracy and imperialism.[42]

Both strains of thought can be found in the American foreign policy tradition. In his Farewell Address, George Washington speaks as a moral realist when he reminds Americans that "religion and morality" are vital to domestic harmony and recommends the following to them: "The great rule of conduct for us, in regard to foreign nations is in extending our commercial relations to have with them as little *political* connection as possible."⁴³ In a similar spirit, John Quincy Adams admonishes Americans not to allow their successes with self-government to tempt them into benevolent empire, scanning the world for "monsters to destroy," because it would mean the end of their constitutional republic.⁴⁴ The nineteenth-century American thinker Orestes Brownson writes at length about the relationship between culture, what he calls the unwritten constitution, and government, successful examples of which he believes emerge out of distinct national unwritten constitutions. In this way, he makes ample theoretical room in American foreign policy for respecting the distinct ways of life prevailing in many nations. For him, the pursuit of peace needs humane understanding of other cultures, not demands to implement a universal political template. These and other American moral realists held such views because they were attuned to the ethical center of existence that comes with historical insight.

What Babbitt describes as a type of democratic imperialism has been ascendant in the United States since the early twentieth century. Woodrow Wilson sees America as the most unselfish of nations, charged with a divine mission to share its ways with everyone. "The world must be made safe for democracy," he tells Congress in April 1917, and the US bears primary responsibility for making this come true.⁴⁵ In 1941, Franklin Roosevelt announces America's obligation to promote free speech, religious liberty, economic prosperity, and peace "everywhere in the world."⁴⁶ Four decades later, Ronald Reagan makes a similar commitment, stating that under his guidance the United States will "foster the infrastructure of democracy, the system of a free press, unions, political parties, [and] universities" around the globe.⁴⁷ To those who resist joining the League of Nations, Wilson says they run the risk of breaking "the heart of the world."⁴⁸ Roosevelt cites America itself, a nation "engaged in change, in a perpetual, peaceful revolution" since its inception, as proof that his foreign policy is "no vision of a distant millennium."⁴⁹ Reagan rejects the idea that his proposals amount to "cultural imperialism," accusing opponents of engaging in "cultural condescension, or worse."⁵⁰ This kind of American foreign policy inclines toward expansiveness, sentimentality, ahistorical thought, and avoidance of serious debate.

These visions assign different levels of importance to respecting the rule of law when operating in the realm of foreign affairs. In the early republican period, the norm in making foreign policy was close adherence to constitutional procedures. Presidents felt legally and morally obligated to submit to Congress in deciding questions of war. Congress appropriated funds to raise an army and navy as circumstances required, made Washington's Neutrality Proclamation enforceable, set clear limits on Adams and his conduct of the Quasi-War with France, and circumscribed the American response to the Barbary pirates during the Jefferson and Madison presidencies. Political leaders saw participating in this process as vital to maintaining popular control over government on such issues. However, American constitutionalism has suffered much harm from foreign policy practice since the early twentieth century. From Korea, to Grenada, to Serbia, to Libya, American wars both great and small have been conducted with increasing executive mendacity, as well as impatience with and avoidance of constitutional requirements. Congress and the American people have largely shirked their responsibility to hold presidents accountable for their actions. Perhaps Dean Acheson, Harry Truman's Secretary of State, expressed best this new attitude when he told Congress in 1951: "If we could all agree on the fact that something should be done, we will perform a much greater role in the world, than by quarreling about who ought to do it."[51]

Dubious ideas and indifference to law are not the only reasons one can accurately categorize this latter foreign policy as democratic imperialism. To pursue the visions of Wilson, Roosevelt, Truman, Reagan, Clinton, Bush, Obama, and other like-minded leaders, substantial power must be harnessed and expended. Such policies would require much of what has actually happened in American national politics since the early 1900s. Political, economic, and administrative power has moved away from states and localities toward the national government. Defense expenditures in the US are often the same as those of the next dozen countries combined. The US leads a number of permanent military treaties and alliances. American soldiers are deployed around the world. All of this requires staggering budgetary expenditures, and these funds are derived from a combination of high taxation and the increasing accumulation of debt. In *Democracy and Leadership*, Babbitt writes, "The humanitarian would, of course, have us meddle in foreign affairs as part of his program of world service. Unfortunately, it is more difficult than he supposes to engage in such a program without getting involved in a program of world empire."[52] The historical record of US foreign policy over the last century appears to support this claim.

Despite its many costs and failures, democratic empire remains appealing for American leaders and ordinary citizens. In *America the Virtuous*, Ryn argues,

"As the United States is called to bestow its high principles and general benevolence on all of humanity, it must of course have power over all of humanity. Since communism, no ideology has provided so much stimulation for the will to power, and many of America's leading policymakers are embracing this doctrine."[53] As is the case with qualities of imagination and types of democracy, the differences between moral realism and democratic imperialism come down to character. Just as constitutional democracy informed by moral realism hinges on the socially authoritative presence of the constitutional personality, democratic empire cannot function without a corresponding imperial personality at its core. Possessing self-control, historical wisdom, and a desire to pursue the common good, the constitutional spirit can live on peaceful terms with other nations. At war with itself and others, the imperial soul, even of the sentimental variety, cannot make good on its promises to provide peace and justice. According to Babbitt and Ryn, such a person's lust for power and misunderstanding of the world is too great.

HUMANISTIC RENEWAL

The foundation of the American constitutional way of life has been seriously weakened, especially over the last few decades, but the authors here do not despair. Like Babbitt and Ryn, they value historical thinking, or "the historical mind," because the past matters now. History is a well that never runs dry. It invites those attuned to it to draw to the surface the wisdom of human experience and to use such resources to make the best of given circumstances, however bleak they may seem. Considered in this light, historical consciousness actually yields cautious optimism about the future—even in situations as dire as those indicating the arrival of "post-constitutionalism" in America. Insofar as the contributors to this volume share this experiential (some might say Burkean) orientation of Babbitt's New Humanism, they may correctly be described as seeking a truly *humanistic* renewal of the constitutional spirit.

While these scholars are thus working in a frame similar to that of Babbitt and Ryn, it should be understood that this collection of essays does not constitute a single "argument," according to which its contributors march in predictable and bland lockstep. In *The Politics*, Aristotle criticizes Plato for desiring too much unity among the people who form the ideal city depicted in *The Republic*: "Socrates thinks that if all unanimously say 'mine' and 'not mine,' this is an indication of the state's complete unity. But the word 'all' is used in two senses: 'all separately' and 'all together.' Used in the former sense this might better bring about what Socrates wants."⁵⁴ The unity in the present volume, it might be said, has the sort of harmonious diversity that would be appreciated by Aristotle if not necessarily by Plato. To elaborate on a musical metaphor Aristotle uses in the same section of *The Politics*, the "sound" of these chapters is polyphonic harmonious rather than monophonic excessive unity or atonal excessive diversity. Thus, the reader is invited to enter into a conversation in which meaningful affinities as well as differences are identified among the individual authors and the two humanists that are its focal point. As with any conversation, the agreements and objections that arise among interlocutors move the dialogue forward and help clarify many of the fundamental issues at stake.

The first section of the book provides representative illustrations of the work of Babbitt and Ryn. It serves as a linchpin of sorts, orienting those who may be unfamiliar with either thinker to the central ideas in this volume. It also conveys the broader context within which the cultural, moral, and political needs of Western civilization are contemplated and discussed by each of the book's contributors. This section begins with a piece of Babbitt's, which is a synoptic statement of what he thinks is needed to save the West from the cultural decay or anomie into which it has been declining since the late eighteenth century. In the second essay, Ryn gives Babbittian scrutiny to contemporary American understandings of "idealism." The troubling idealism Ryn has in his sights is one that uses highly moralistic terms such as "justice" and "fairness," not only for American citizens but also for those of all nations, as a means for expanding governmental power and eroding the capacity of Americans to govern themselves. Such claims, palpably demonstrated in the rhetoric of Bush and Obama above, betray what Ryn calls a "new morality," one that is fundamentally incompatible with the "old" or traditional morality that underpins America's constitutional order.

In the next section, three authors focus specifically on the cultural element, each reflecting on the priority of the aesthetic or imaginative dimension of human life. Bradley Birzer, who has elsewhere written extensively on twentieth-century luminary and cultural critic Russell Kirk, examines the influence of Babbitt on Kirk and exposes a subtle but important difference between them—their distinctive attitudes toward romanticism. In calling our attention to this, Birzer implicitly raises the important question for anyone influenced by Babbitt, which is whether there may be cultural circumstances in which the romantic spirit actually needs to be stoked in order to confront the scientific rationalism against which Babbitt himself rails. Justin Garrison's chapter also deals with Babbitt's concern with the scientific or "Baconian" spirit, particularly the modern danger that the "law for thing," or laws of physical nature, may altogether eclipse the "law for man" in the aspiration to achieve progress in human affairs. In his analysis of *All the King's Men*, Garrison unpacks Robert Penn Warren's imaginative portrayal of this impulse, along with his remarkably Babbittian account of the easy, dangerous slippage from scientism into humanitarianism in the human personality. Steve McGuire puts Ryn's account of the ethical quality of the imagination into a conversation with that of the influential mid-twentieth century political philosopher, Eric Voegelin, who was well-known for his diagnosis of pseudo-religious ideology. While acknowledging Ryn's critique of Voegelin as insufficiently attuned to the imagination, McGuire objects, identifying Voegelin's latent intimations of the concept, principally in his work on symbolizations and the important role that Voegelin—echoing Ryn himself—sees in their orienting human beings toward reality.

The cultural formation of individual character must ultimately issue in concrete, ethical conduct of some type, which on the humanist's account is its principal purpose. This is the subject of the next section. Drawing on Burke, Babbitt, and Ryn, William Byrne distills several implications of ethical judgment being "downstream" from the culture's shaping of the imagination. Significantly, he believes this calls into question the Enlightenment idea, still predominant in contemporary political thought, that reason holds the ultimate seat of moral authority in the ethical decision-maker. This, Byrne shows, sheds significant light on problems with contemporary moral discourse and the difficulty of bringing about meaningful social change. In the next essay, Robert Koons responds to this sort of antirationalism associated with the thinking of Babbitt and Ryn from a Neo-Thomist perspective. While Koons agrees wholeheartedly with Ryn on the "indispensable role of both experience and imagination in right moral judgment," he argues that Ryn's criticisms with regard to the rigidity of the intellect are misplaced in the case of the natural law tradition, whose emphasis on practical wisdom (*phronesis, prudentia*) obviates most of the "exceptionless moral rules" of which Ryn accuses it. In the third chapter of this section, Ryan Holston takes on a challenge to Babbitt's humanism from one of Babbitt's most famous students, T. S. Eliot. The criticism against which Holston defends Babbitt is that humanism actually tries to replace, not restore, the traditional morality of Christianity, which Holston contends fails to appreciate not only their compatibility but the ways in which Christianity is actually bolstered by humanism.

The third and fourth sections of the volume consider the more overtly political implications of the presence (or absence) of the constitutional personality. The third section deals with constitutional government. In his chapter, Michael Federici places Babbitt once more in a fruitful dialogue with Voegelin. Only here, one sees the further implications of changes in imaginative symbolizations on action within the political order. Through a literary analysis of Edward Bellamy's utopian novel, *Looking Backward*, Federici relates the philosophical anthropology of progressivism to the latent assumptions in early-twentieth-century sociological jurisprudence, along with its progeny, contemporary legal realism and the theory of the "living constitution." Bruce Frohnen's chapter deals with the related idea of "plebiscitary democracy," which is the target of Ryn's seminal work on constitutionalism, *Democracy and the Ethical Life*. In his analysis, Frohnen identifies a number of affinities between what he, together with the late George W. Carey, has termed "constitutional morality" and Ryn's conception of the "constitutional personality" discussed above. However, Frohnen raises a cautionary note. While he is sympathetic to Ryn's Aristotelian critique of liberalism as failing to take into account the ethical character of political actors, he fears that Ryn asserts too strong an identification between morality and law, and Frohnen stresses the importance of small-scale groups and associations having sufficient moral and political autonomy from the state.

The fourth and final section of the book continues the discussion of the political element, turning from domestic to international politics. Richard Gamble's essay argues that those who champion the trope that "American exceptionalism" implies that America is (and ought to be) a "dangerous nation" gloss the complexity of this long-disputed idea. Echoing Ryn's distinction between the "old" and "new" morality, Gamble reveals that there have, in reality, been two opposing American exceptionalisms. There is an "old school" exceptionalism defended by those such as William Graham Sumner, which emphasizes America's "constraint" in contrast to the old European empires, and a "new school" exceptionalism touted by the likes of Woodrow Wilson, which avows the divine purpose of American global dominion. Gamble concludes by embracing Walter McDougall's recent call for American "self-containment," and he sees in this the potential to reinvigorate that older, more chastened tradition. Justin Litke's essay, which returns our attention to the question of the imagination, focuses on the latter's implications for American foreign policy and is similarly concerned with American empire. Drawing on Wendell Berry's novel, *Jayber Crow*, Litke argues that the large-scale killing required for empire is only conceivable when citizens see their identities as bound up with the comparably "large" idea of the nation. The pivotal moment of imaginative reconceptualization Litke points to is Lincoln's Civil War rhetoric—particularly, the Gettysburg Address. Litke suggests that the reinvigoration of a sense of place and quotidian politics might be a useful antidote to this ideological predisposition that fuels the expansionist impulse.

Yuan Zhang, together with Justin Garrison, authors the final chapter of the volume, which is fitting on a number of levels. A Chinese professor of classical literature, Zhang is the intellectual descendent of Chinese students who studied with Babbitt at Harvard in the early 1900s and then returned to China as disciples of his New Humanism. Prominent in Babbitt's thinking is an acknowledgment that the traditional wisdom of Confucius and Buddha in the East have paralleled that of Aristotle and Christ in the West in remarkable ways—that the great Eastern philosophical and religious traditions have discovered the same universal truths regarding the higher will and the life of proportion as their Western counterparts. Zhang and Garrison detail the tumultuous history of Babbitt in China, due to mistranslations and misinterpretations, while demonstrating along the way Babbitt's substantial resonance with Confucian thinking. Previous generations of "cultural conservatives" in China, who navigated between radical reformists on the left and intransigent reactionaries on the right, have seen Babbitt's thinking as a way of "integrating the best elements of Chinese culture with Western insights." There is, in other words, what might be described as a Burkean sensibility in China, which seeks cultural preservation through discriminating change, insofar as it properly applies the past to the circumstances of the present. The resurgent interest in Babbitt's thinking in China and the common ground that is shared with Americans of a humanistic bent may hold out the promise of peaceful relations among nations, insofar as they come to an awareness of their mutual commitment to the same universal truths that have a deep historical lineage in both the Eastern and Western traditions.

These aspirations for cross-cultural understanding are more than just a romantic dream. In 2012 Zhang became the Executive Director of a new Humanities Institute, Renwen Yanjiusuo, whose work has been inspired by Babbitt's humanism and is housed within the prestigious Beijing Normal University (BNU) in China. That same year, Zhang became a visiting scholar at The Catholic University of America, where she studied with Ryn, who himself was made an honorary professor at BNU. Alongside these hopeful developments, it is important to note that, as with the case of the American scholars above, such cross-cultural engagement and collaboration must be seen as laying the groundwork for a conversation, not as working toward the spread of a doctrine or fixed set of ideas. Indeed, the past is not self-interpreting, and although it is "a well that never runs dry," it takes great intellectual labor and dialogue to distill its insights into the human condition, which must be gleaned from centuries of human experience. As with the history of Babbitt's ideas in China themselves, there are often disagreements and misinterpretations. Therefore, it is worth repeating that any optimism must always be tempered with sobriety, understanding both the difficulty of the task at hand and that one must, in this instance, take the long view of human affairs. It will, in short, take the same sustained effort and ethical striving that Babbitt believes defines the moral personality if we are to achieve, collectively, an improvement in the relationship of these peoples and great traditions.

NOTES

1. George W. Bush, "Inaugural Address, January 20, 2005," in *Public Papers of the Presidents of the United States: George W. Bush, 2005, Book I—January 1 to June 30, 2005* (Washington, DC: U.S. Government Printing Office, 2007), 67.
2. Bush, "Inaugural Address," 67.
3. Bush, "Inaugural Address," 68.
4. Bush, "Inaugural Address," 69.
5. Barack Obama, "Inaugural Address, January 20, 2009," in *Public Papers of the Presidents of the United States: Barack Obama, 2009, Book I—January 20 to June 30, 2009* (Washington, DC: U.S. Government Printing Office, 2010), 2.
6. Obama, "Inaugural Address," 2.
7. Obama, "Inaugural Address," 2.
8. Obama, "Inaugural Address," 3.
9. Bush, "Inaugural Address," 68.
10. Obama, "Inaugural Address," 1.
11. Johann Wolfgang von Goethe, *Maxims and Reflections*, trans. Elisabeth Stopp, ed. Peter Hutchison (New York: Penguin, 1998), 37.
12. John Adams, "Thoughts on Government," in *The Portable John Adams*, ed. John Patrick Diggins (New York: Penguin, 2004), 235.
13. Bush, "Inaugural Address," 68.
14. John Adams, *A Defense of the Constitutions of the Government of the United States of America*, in *The Political Writings of John Adams*, ed. George W. Carey (Washington, DC: Regnery Publishing, 2000), 231.

15. Edmund Burke, *Reflections on the Revolution in France*, ed. J. G. A. Pocock (Indianapolis, IN: Hackett, 1987), 76.

16. Ryn's interest in Babbitt's humanism is based, to a large degree, on Babbitt's view that universal moral truths are embedded in concrete historical experience. Ryn's own moral philosophy, which he has described as "value-centered historicism," is ultimately grounded in a synthesis of moral universality and historical particularity, which he argues can be identified in the thinking of both Babbitt and the Italian Hegelian philosopher Benedetto Croce. An article length exposition of this theory can be found in Ryn, "Universality and History: the Concrete as Normative," *Humanitas* 6, no. 1 (1992/93): 10–39.

17. Irving Babbitt, *Literature and the American College: Essays in Defense of the Humanities* (Washington, DC: National Humanities Institute, 1986), 72.

18. Benedetto Croce, *History as the Story of Liberty*, rev. trans. Sylvia Sprigge (Indianapolis, IN: Liberty Fund, 2000), 9.

19. Claes G. Ryn, *Will, Imagination and Reason: Irving Babbitt and the Problem of Reality* (Washington, DC: Regnery Books, 1986), 120.

20. Following Babbitt, Ryn draws on Aristotle for the idea that the ultimate standard for the life well-lived is the superior quality of certain types of experience, typically connected with the life of measure or proportion, which ultimately issue in the harmony of a well-ordered soul. See Claes G. Ryn, "Universality and History: the Concrete as Normative," *Humanitas* 6, no. 1 (1992/3): 10–39.

21. Ibid., 31.

22. This critique of abstract rationalism has obvious affinities with Aristotle's critique of Plato. Although demonstrating a much more penetrating historical consciousness than Aristotle, Ryn has similarly shown the contemporary philosopher, Leo Strauss, to be guilty of this same tendency in his invocation of an abstract standard of "natural right." See Ryn, "History and the Moral Order," in *The Ethical Dimension of Political Life*, ed. Francis J. Canavan (Durham, NC: Duke University Press, 1983).

23. For both Babbitt and Ryn, the paradigmatic instance of this error of moral idealism in the realm of politics is the French Revolution's extolling of the principles of "liberty, equality, and fraternity."

24. See Claes G. Ryn, "The Politics of Transcendence: The Pretentious Passivity of Platonic Idealism," *Humanitas* 12, no. 2 (1999): 4–26.

25. T. S. Eliot, "Choruses From 'The Rock,'" in *Collected Poems 1909–1962* (London: Faber and Faber, 2002), 164.

26. Ryn, *Will, Imagination and Reason*, 152.

27. Claes G. Ryn, *Democracy and the Ethical Life: A Philosophy of Politics and Community* (Washington, DC: CUA Press, 1990), 7–8.

28. Ryn, *Democracy and the Ethical Life*, 15.

29. Irving Babbitt, *Democracy and Leadership* (Indianapolis, IN: Liberty Fund, 1979), 273.

30. Alexander Hamilton, Federalist No. 71, in *The Federalist*, the Gideon Edition, Alexander Hamilton, John Jay, and James Madison, ed. George W. Carey (Indianapolis, IN: Liberty Fund, 2001), 370.

31. James Madison, Federalist No. 55, in *The Federalist*, the Gideon Edition, Alexander Hamilton, John Jay, and James Madison, ed. George W. Carey (Indianapolis, IN: Liberty Fund, 2001), 291.

32. See Willmoore Kendall and George W. Carey, *The Basic Symbols of the American Political Tradition* (Baton Rouge: Louisiana State University Press, 1970).

33. John Adams, "Letter XV to John Taylor of Caroline," in *The Political Writings of John Adams*, ed. George W. Carey (Washington, DC: Regnery Publishing, 2000), 398.

34. John Dickinson might have been even more suspicious of ideological political thinking than John Adams. Dickinson's understanding of the legal and moral claims surrounding the disputes between Britain and the American colonies during the 1760s and 1770s, and his arguments defending the just grievances of the Americans against their parent country, are shaped almost entirely by the concrete ideas and legal precedents of Britain's unique, unwritten constitution. Perhaps the most famous example of Dickinson's historical mind at work is his *Letters from a Farmer in Pennsylvania*.

35. Thomas Paine, *The Rights of Man* in *The Thomas Paine Reader*, eds. Michael Foot and Isaac Kramnick (New York: Penguin, 1987), 220.

36. Thomas Jefferson, "Response to the Citizens of Albemarle," in *The Portable Thomas Jefferson*, ed. Merrill D. Peterson (New York: Penguin, 1977), 260.

37. Thomas Jefferson, "Letter to Major John Cartwright, June 5, 1824," in *The Portable Thomas Jefferson*, ed. Merrill D. Peterson (New York: Penguin, 1977), 578.

38. Thomas Paine, *Common Sense* in *The Thomas Paine Reader*, eds. Michael Foot and Isaac Kramnick (New York: Penguin, 1987), 109.

39. Thomas Jefferson, "Letter to Roger C. Weightman, June 24, 1826," in *The Portable Thomas Jefferson*, ed. Merrill D. Peterson (New York: Penguin, 1977), 585.

40. Woodrow Wilson, *Constitutional Government in the United States* in *The Politics of Woodrow Wilson: Selections from His Speeches and Writings*, ed. August Heckscher (New York: Books for Libraries Press, 1956), 23.

41. Claes G. Ryn, *A Common Human Ground: Universality and Particularity in a Multicultural World* (Columbia: University of Missouri Press, 2003), 21.

42. Babbitt, *Democracy and Leadership*, 293–94, 296. This assumption of mutual exclusiveness between democracy and foreign policy imperialism can be observed in various contemporary theories of international relations, especially in a concept such as "democratic peace theory." With origins in the political thought of Immanuel Kant, this theory employs empirical evidence to show that democracies do not fight one another, which is sometimes attributed to the value it places on the moral dignity shown to its citizens and other times based on its institutional structures. For the former line of argument, see Michael Doyle, *Ways of War and Peace* (New York: W.W. Norton, 1997), and for a combination of these two strands of argument, see John M. Owen IV, *Liberal Peace, Liberal War* (Ithaca, NY: Cornell University Press, 1997). Regardless of whether such behavior is explained by "Normative" or "Structural" Democratic Peace Theory, the normative conclusion ostensibly supported by these theories is that all nations *should* embrace liberal democracy as a means to peace.

Babbitt would draw attention to the following regarding the normative inference that is often made from this theory. Even if one were to assume for the sake of argument that democracies do not fight other democracies, it must strike some as strange that various democratic governments, especially the United States after World War II, are so frequently, even perpetually, at war. A response to this observation might be that such a state of affairs is a regrettable but unavoidable step toward lasting peace. If that is true, then it really must take a global empire to realize the dream of a democratic peace. In "America's Illiberal Liberalism: The Ideological Origins of Overreaction in U.S. Foreign Policy" (*International Security* 32, no. 3, Winter 2007/2008), Michael C. Desch analyzes George W. Bush's foreign policy in terms similar to those here described. Whether one is talking about a foreign policy of democratic unilateralism in the mode of Bush or a foreign policy of humanitarian multilateralism in the mode of Barack Obama, to realize the type of peace at the core of this concept, warfare and violence are inescapable and even a moral necessity. The combination of liberalism and imperialism might sound paradoxical to some, but it would not sound that way to Babbitt, or for that matter, George Orwell. To reconstruct the world along the lines desired by sentimental imperialists, war really is peace.

43. George Washington, "Farewell Address, September 19, 1796," in *The American Republic*, ed. Bruce Frohnen (Indianapolis, IN: Liberty Fund, 2002), 76, 78.

44. John Quincy Adams, "Address of July 4, 1821," in *John Quincy Adams and American Continental Empire: Letters, Speeches & Papers*, ed. Walter Lafeber (Chicago, IL: Quadrangle Books, 1965), 45.

45. Woodrow Wilson, "Address to the Senate, April 2, 1917," in *The American Nation*, ed. Bruce Frohnen (Indianapolis, IN: Liberty Fund, 2008), 511.

46. Franklin Delano Roosevelt, "The Four Freedoms, January 6, 1941," in *The American Nation*, ed. Bruce Frohnen (Indianapolis, IN: Liberty Fund, 2008), 568.

47. Ronald Reagan, "Address to Members of the British Parliament, Palace of Westminster, June 8, 1982," in *Speaking My Mind: Selected Speeches* (New York: Simon and Schuster, 1989), 116–17.

48. Woodrow Wilson, "Address to the Senate, Washington, July 10, 1919," in *The Politics of Woodrow Wilson: Selections from His Speeches and Writings*, ed. August Heckscher (New York: Books for Libraries Press, 1956), 367–68.

49. Roosevelt, "The Four Freedoms," 568.

50. Ronald Reagan, "Address to Members of the British Parliament," 116–17.

51. Louis Fisher, *Presidential War Power*, 3d. ed. (Lawrence, KS: University Press of Kansas, 2013), 111.

52. Babbitt, *Democracy and Leadership*, 296.

53. Claes G. Ryn, *America the Virtuous: The Crisis of Democracy and the Quest for Empire* (New Brunswick, NJ: Transaction, 2003), 8.

54. Aristotle, *The Politics*, trans. T. A. Sinclair, rev. trans. Trevor A. Saunders (1981; repr., New York: Penguin, 1992), 107.

BIBLIOGRAPHY

Adams, John. *The Political Writings of John Adams*. Edited by George W. Carey. Washington, DC: Regnery Publishing, 2000.

Adams, John Quincy. *John Quincy Adams and American Continental Empire: Letters, Speeches and Papers*. Edited by Walter Lafeber. Chicago, IL: Quadrangle Books, 1965.

Aristotle. *The Politics*. Translated by T. A. Sinclair. 1962. Revised Translation by Trevor A. Saunders. 1981. Reprint, New York, Penguin, 1992.

Babbitt, Irving. *Democracy and Leadership*. Indianapolis, IN: Liberty Fund, 1979.

———. *Literature and the American College: Essays in Defense of the Humanities*. Washington, DC: National Humanities Institute, 1986.

Burke, Edmund. *Reflections on the Revolution in France*. Edited by J. G. A. Pocock. Indianapolis, IN: Hackett, 1987.

Bush, George W. *Public Papers of the Presidents of the United States: George W. Bush, 2005, Book I—January 1 to June 30, 2005*. Washington, DC: Government Printing Office, 2007.

Croce, Benedetto. *History as the Story of Liberty*. Translated by Sylvia Sprigge. 1941. Revised Translation. Reprint, Indianapolis, IN: Liberty Fund, 2000.

Desch, Michael C. "America's Illiberal Liberalism: The Ideological Origins of Overreaction in U.S. Foreign Policy." *International Security* 32, no. 3 (Winter 2007–2008): 7–43. Project Muse.

Doyle, Michael. *Ways of War and Peace*. New York: W. W. Norton, 1997.

Eliot, T. S. *Collected Poems 1909–1962*. London, Faber and Faber, 2002.

Fisher, Louis. *Presidential War Power*, 3d Edition. Lawrence, KS: University Press of Kansas, 2013.

Frohnen, Bruce, ed. *The American Republic*. Indianapolis, IN: Liberty Fund, 2002.

———. *The American Nation*. Indianapolis, IN: Liberty Fund, 2008.

von Goethe, Johann Wolfgang. *Maxims and Reflections*. Translated by Elisabeth Stopp. Edited by Peter Hutchison. New York: Penguin, 1998.

Hamilton, Alexander, John Jay, and James Madison. *The Federalist*. The Gideon Edition. Edited by George W. Carey and James McClellan. Indianapolis, IN: Liberty Fund, 2001.

Jefferson, Thomas. *The Portable Thomas Jefferson*. Edited by Merrill D. Peterson. New York: Viking Press, 1975.

Kendall, Willmoore, and George W. Carey. *The Basic Symbols of the American Political Tradition*. Baton Rouge: Louisiana State University Press, 1970.

Obama, Barack. *Public Papers of the Presidents of the United States: Barack Obama, 2009, Book I—January 20 to June 30, 2009*. Washington, DC: U.S. Government Printing Office, 2010.

Owen IV, John M. *Liberal Peace, Liberal War*. Ithaca, NY: Cornell University Press, 1997.

Paine, Thomas. *The Thomas Paine Reader*. Edited by Michael Foot and Isaac Kramnick. New York: Penguin Putnam, 1987.

Reagan, Ronald. *Speaking My Mind: Selected Speeches*. New York: Simon and Schuster, 1989.

Ryn, Claes G. *America the Virtuous: The Crisis of Democracy and the Quest for Empire*. New Brunswick, NJ: Transaction, 2003.

———. *A Common Human Ground: Universality and Particularity in a Multicultural World*. Columbia: University of Missouri Press, 2003.

———. *Democracy and the Ethical Life: A Philosophy of Politics and Community*. 2d ed. Washington, DC: CUA Press, 1990.

———. "Universality and History: The Concrete as Normative." *Humanitas* 6, no. 1 (1992/1993): 10–39.

———. *Will, Imagination, and Reason: Irving Babbitt and the Problem of Reality*. Washington, DC: Regnery Books, 1986.

Wilson, Woodrow. *The Politics of Woodrow Wilson: Selections from His Speeches and Writings*. Edited by August Heckscher. New York: Harper & Row, 1970.

Part I
The New Humanism

The two essays in this section serve as representative illustrations of the humanism developed by Babbitt and Ryn. In "What I Believe: Rousseau and Romanticism," Babbitt begins by explaining the profound influence Jean-Jacques Rousseau's writings have had over the last two centuries in virtually every area of study. At the center of Rousseau's new vision of the world, Babbitt argues, is a fundamental assertion in the *Discourse on the Origin of Inequality* that it is not humans themselves who are fundamentally responsible for their social ills, but their institutions. In identifying this sentiment as such a pivotal moment in modern thinking, Babbitt first establishes the importance of what, in the broadest sense, might be termed *historical consciousness*. For, it is Rousseau's understanding of Western institutions as irredeemably corrupt, and worsening all the time, that has exercised a revolutionary influence on subsequent generations.

By "revolutionary," one need not think only of the Jacobins, Robespierre, and the immediate political fallout of Rousseau's writing. For Babbitt, what is revolutionary in Rousseau's philosophy is the dramatic change in thinking about human nature and our relationship to the past. Under attack, Babbitt claims, are the truths of the inner life—the struggle between good and evil within the human soul. Once preserved by traditional religion, these truths are now undermined by what Babbitt calls "sentimental humanitarianism," an ideology that follows Rousseau in replacing "theological" with "sociological" explanations of our social ills. This spirit of Romantic idealism, Babbitt further argues, combines in the modern era with the spirit of utilitarian rationalism to demand radical social reform in the most moralistic of terms. In order to combat this tendency, Babbitt appeals to the concrete evidence of historical human experience at the levels of both the individual and society. Thereby he attempts to rebuild the traditional meanings of moral concepts such as "virtue" and "justice," which now apply mainly to the arrangement of social institutions, through a "keen discrimination" of the intellect. Babbitt's effort to recover the wisdom of traditional morality demands the recognition that there are some human experiences that never go away, particularly the happiness (*eudaimonia*) that accompanies the life of measure and the corresponding misery and suffering attendant to sensual indulgence. It is only by restoring our belief in the importance of "the war within the cave"—the ethical struggle for self-restraint within human beings—that Babbitt believes we can hope to survive the civilizational crisis wrought by Rousseau and humanitarianism.

In "Power without Limits: The Allure of Political Idealism and the Crumbling of American Constitutionalism," Ryn examines the ideological trend Babbitt identifies after nearly one hundred years of its ascendancy. Why is it, Ryn begins, that the Framers of the American Constitution were concerned, above all other objectives, with putting limitations on the powers of those in government? An older view of human nature prevailed, he explains, which the Framers inherited from the classical and Christian tradition—one that was fearful of the social consequences of original sin. On their account, human beings are unable to be trusted with unrestrained political power. The needs of good government point not only to the formal, institutional controls or restraints on official power from without, so often identified with the U.S. Constitution, but also to the idea that a less formal system of internal restraints or "checks" must be relied on to control the selfishness and ambition of leaders, as well. In other words, as conceived by the Framers, the American constitutional system depends not only on institutional limits on political power, but also on what Ryn calls the "constitutional personality" of its members, that is, the character type that disciplines selfish appetite so that one may live harmoniously in community with others.

Essential to the formation of this personality in the early republic, Ryn continues, was the "unwritten constitution"—the traditional morality and customs that habituated self-control and made acceptance of the Constitution's "parchment barriers" possible. Without this, even Madison's famous "ambition counteracting ambition" would have meant very little when faced with human beings who would indulge their will to power. Drawing on Babbitt's critique of humanitarianism, Ryn proceeds to demonstrate how the mendacious flattery of Rousseauistic idealism has fueled a rejection of these customary or traditional restraints on our appetitive selves and justified increasing governmental power. Having reimagined human beings as naturally good, Rousseau's new conception of human nature supports the claims of various elites as well as leaders in both major US political parties who demand centralized political power in the name of promoting "freedom," "equality," and "democracy." It is just such power grabs the Framers most feared. Vindicating Babbitt's prescient warnings, Ryn concludes that a revival of "the constitutional personality" is all that can save America and its people from those whose idyllic imaginations ultimately turn diabolical as they demand unlimited power for the realization of their allegedly incontestable ideals.

CHAPTER ONE

What I Believe

Rousseau and Religion

Irving Babbitt

I

Rousseau is commonly accounted the most influential writer of the past two hundred years. Lord Acton, indeed, is reported to have said, with a touch of exaggeration, that "Rousseau produced more effect with his pen than Aristotle or Cicero or Saint Augustine or Saint Thomas Aquinas or any other man who ever lived." At all events, this saying needs to be interpreted in the light of the saying of Madame de Staël that "Rousseau invented nothing but set everything on fire." His leading ideas were abundantly anticipated, especially in England. These ideas made their chief appeal to a middle class which, in the eighteenth century, was gaining rapidly in power and prestige, and has been dominant ever since.

The Rousseauistic outlook on life has also persisted, with many surface modifications, to be sure, but without any serious questioning on the part of most men of its underlying assumptions. To debate Rousseau is really to debate the main issues of our contemporary life in literature, politics, education, and above all, religion. It is not surprising, therefore, that his reputation and writings have from the outset to the present day been a sort of international battleground. One cannot afford to be merely partisan in this strife, to be blind to Rousseau's numerous merits—for example, to all he did to quicken man's sense of the beauties of nature, especially wild nature. Neither should one forget that there is involved in all the strife a central issue toward which one must finally assume a clear-cut attitude.

Regarding this central issue—the source of the fundamental clash between Rousseauist and anti-Rousseauist—there has been and continues to be much confusion. A chief source of this confusion has been the fact that in Rousseau as in other great writers, and more than in most, there are elements that run counter to the main tendency. Rousseau has, for example, his rationalistic side. On the basis of this fact one professor of French[1] has just set out to prove that, instead of being the arch-sentimentalist he has usually been taken to be, "the real Rousseau is at bottom a rationalist in his ethics, politics, and theology."

Again, there are utterances in Rousseau quite in line with traditional morality. Another American scholar has therefore set out to show that it is a mistake to make Rousseau responsible for a revolution in ethics. Still another of our scholars has managed to convince himself on similar lines that Rousseau is not primarily a primitivist in his *Discourse on Inequality*.

Most remarkable of all is a book that has just appeared,[2] the author of which covers with contumely practically all his predecessors in this field on the ground that they have been blinded by partisanship, and promises to give us at last the true meaning of Rousseau. Yet this writer does not even cite the passage that, as Rousseau himself correctly tells us, gives the key to his major writings. It is to this passage that every interpreter of Rousseau who is not academic in the bad sense will give prominence: for the thesis it sums up has actually wrought mightily upon the world. It has thus wrought because it has behind it an imaginative and emotional drive not found behind other passages of Rousseau that might in themselves have served to correct it.

The passage to which I refer is one that occurs in Rousseau's account of the sudden vision that came to him by the roadside on a hot summer day in 1749 in the course of a walk from Paris to Vincennes. This vision has an importance for the main modern movement comparable to that of Saint Paul's vision on the road to Damascus for the future development of Christianity. Among the multitude of "truths" that flashed upon Rousseau in the sort of trance into which he was rapt at this moment, the truth of overshadowing importance was, in his own words, that "man is naturally good and that it is by our institutions alone that men become wicked."

The consequences that have flowed from this new "myth" of man's natural goodness have been almost incommensurable. Its first effect was to discredit the theological view of human nature, with its insistence that man has fallen, not from Nature as Rousseau asserts, but from God, and that the chief virtue it behooves man to cultivate in this fallen state is humility. According to the Christian, the true opposition between good and evil is in the heart of the individual: the law of the spirit can scarcely prevail, he holds, over the law of the members without a greater or lesser degree of succor in the form of divine grace. The new dualism which Rousseau sets up—that between man naturally good and his institutions—has tended not only to substitute sociology for theology, but to discredit the older dualism in any form whatsoever.

Practically, the warfare of the Rousseauistic crusader has been even less against institutions than against those who control and administer them—kings and priests in the earlier stages of the movement, capitalists in our own day. "We are approaching," Rousseau declared, "the era of crises, and the age of revolutions." He not only made the prophecy but did more than any other one man to insure its fulfillment. There are conservative and even timid elements in his writings; but as a result of the superior imaginative appeal of the new dualism based on the myth of man's natural goodness, the role he has actually played has been that of arch-radical. In one of the best-balanced estimates that have appeared, the French critic, Gustave Lanson, after doing justice to the various minor trends in Rousseau's work, sums up accurately its major influence: "It exasperates and inspires revolt and fires enthusiasms and irritates hatreds; it is the mother of violence, the source of all that is uncompromising; it launches the simple souls who give themselves up to its strange virtue upon the desperate quest of the absolute, an absolute to be realized now by anarchy and now by social despotism."

I have said that there has been in connection with this Rousseauistic influence a steady yielding of the theological to the sociological or, as it may also be termed, the humanitarian view of life. One should add that there enters into the total philosophy of humanitarianism an ingredient that antedates Rousseau and that may be defined as utilitarian. Utilitarianism already had its prophet in Francis Bacon. Very diverse elements enter into the writings of Bacon as into those of Rousseau, but, like those of Rousseau, they have a central drive: they always have encouraged and, one may safely say, always will encourage the substitution of a kingdom of man for the traditional Kingdom of God—the exaltation of material over spiritual "comfort," the glorification of man's increasing control over the forces of nature under the name of progress.

Rousseauist and Baconian, though often superficially at odds with one another, have cooperated in undermining, not merely religious tradition, but another tradition which in the Occident goes back finally, not to Judea, but to ancient Greece. This older tradition may be defined as humanistic. The goal of the humanist is poised and proportionate living. This he hopes to accomplish by observing the law of measure. Anyone who has bridged successfully the gap between this general precept and some specific emergency has to that extent achieved the fitting and the decorous. Decorum is supreme for the humanist even as humility takes precedence over all other virtues in the eyes of the Christian. Traditionally the idea of decorum has been associated, often with a considerable admixture of mere formalism, with the idea of the gentleman. Humanism and religion in their various forms have at times conflicted, but have more often been in alliance with one another. As Burke says in a well-known passage: "Nothing is more certain than that our manners, our civilisation, and all the good things that are connected with manners and with civilisation, have, in this European world of ours, depended for ages upon two principles; and were indeed the result of both combined; I mean the spirit of a gentleman and the spirit of religion."

II

All the points of view I have been distinguishing—Baconian, Rousseauist, Christian, humanistic—often mingle confusedly. From all the confusion, however, there finally emerges a clear-cut issue—namely, whether humanitarianism, or, if one prefers, the utilitarian-sentimental movement, has supplied any effective equivalent for Burke's two principles. As for the "spirit of a gentleman," its decline is so obvious as scarcely to admit of argument. It has even been maintained that in America, the country in which the collapse of traditional standards has been most complete, the gentleman is at a positive disadvantage in the world of practical affairs; he is likely to get on more quickly if he assumes the "mucker pose."[3] According to William James, usually taken to be the representative American philosopher, the very idea of the gentleman has about it something slightly satanic. "The prince of darkness," says James, "may be a gentleman, as we are told he is, but, whatever the God of earth and heaven is, he can surely be no gentleman."

As to the spirit of religion, though its decline has in my opinion been at least as great as that of the spirit of a gentleman, it is far from being so obvious. In any case, everything in our modern substitutes for religion—whether Baconian or Rousseauistic—will be found to converge upon the idea of service. The crucial question is whether one is safe in assuming that the immense machinery of power that has resulted from activity of the utilitarian type can be made, on anything like present lines, to serve disinterested ends; whether it will not rather minister to the egoistic aims either of national groups or of individuals.

One's answer to this question will depend on one's view of the Rousseauistic theory of brotherhood. It is at this point, if anywhere, that the whole movement is pseudo-religious. I can give only in barest outline the reasons for my own conviction that it *is* pseudo-religious. It can be shown that the nature from which man has fallen, according to Rousseau, does not correspond to anything real, but is a projection of the idyllic imagination. To assert that man in a state of nature, or some similar state thus projected, is good, is to discredit the traditional controls in the actual world. Humility, conversion, decorum—all go by the board in favor of free temperamental overflow. Does man thus emancipated exude spontaneously an affection for his fellows that will be an effective counterpoise to the sheer expansion of his egoistic impulses? If so, one may safely side with all the altruists from the Third Earl of Shaftesbury to John Dewey. One may then assume that there has been no vital omission in the passage from the service of God to the service of man, from salvation by divine grace to salvation by the grace of nature.

Unfortunately, the facts have persistently refused to conform to humanitarian theory. There has been an ever-growing body of evidence from the eighteenth century to the Great War that in the natural man, as he exists in the real world and not in some romantic dreamland, the will to power is, on the whole, more than a match for the will to service. To be sure, many remain unconvinced by this evidence. Stubborn facts, it has been rightly remarked, are as nothing compared with a stubborn theory. Altruistic theory is likely to prove peculiarly stubborn, because, probably more than any other theory ever conceived, it is flattering: it holds out the hope of the highest spiritual benefits—for example, peace and fraternal union—without any corresponding spiritual effort.

If we conclude that humanitarian service cannot take the place of the spirit of religion and that of a gentleman—Burke's "two principles"—what then? One should at least be able to understand the point of view of those who simply reject the modern movement and revert to a more or less purely traditionalist attitude. Dogmatic and revealed Christianity, they hold, has in it a supernatural element for which altruism is no equivalent. Religion of this type, they argue, alone availed to save the ancient world from a decadent naturalism; it alone can cope with a similar situation that confronts the world today.

But does it follow, because one's choice between the religious-humanistic and the utilitarian-sentimental view of life should, as I have said, be clear-cut, one is therefore forced to choose between being a pure traditionalist or a mere modernist? At bottom the issue involved is that of individualism. The Roman Catholic, the typical traditionalist, has in matters religious simply repudiated individualism. In this domain at least, he submits to an authority that is "anterior, superior, and exterior" to the individual. The opposite case is that of the man who has emancipated himself from outer authority in the name of the critical spirit (which will be found to be identical with the modern spirit), but has made use of his emancipation, not to work out standards, but to fall into sheer spiritual anarchy. Anyone, on the other hand, who worked out standards critically would be a sound individualist and at the same time a thoroughgoing modern. He would run the risk, to be sure, of antagonizing both traditionalists and modernists; of suffering, in short, the fate of Mr. Pickwick when he intervened between the two angry combatants. This hostility, at least so far as the traditionalist is concerned, would seem to be ill-advised. The true modern, as I am seeking to define him, is prepared to go no small distance with him in the defense of tradition.

At all events, anyone who seeks to deal in modern fashion—in other words, critically—with the religious problem, will be brought back at once to Rousseau. He will have to make his clear-cut choice, not between dogmatic and revealed religion, on the one hand, and mere modernism, on the other, but between a dualism that affirms a struggle between good and evil in the heart of the individual and a dualism which, like that of Rousseau, transfers the struggle to society.

Let us ask ourselves what it is the modern man has tended to lose with the decline of the older dualism. According to Mr. Walter Lippmann, the belief the modern man has lost is "that there is an immortal essence presiding like a king over his appetites." This immortal essence of which Mr. Lippmann speaks is, judged experimentally and by its fruits, a higher will. But why leave the affirmation of such a will to the pure traditionalist? Why not affirm it first of all as a psychological fact, one of the immediate data of consciousness, a perception so primordial that, compared with it, the denial of man's moral freedom by the determinist is only a metaphysical dream? The way would thus be open, as I pointed out in my *Forum* review of *A Preface to Morals*, for a swift flanking movement on the behaviorists and other naturalistic psychologists, who are to be accounted at present among the chief enemies of human nature.

This transcendent quality of will—which is the source of humility and is, at the same time, immediate and intuitive—has often been associated traditionally with the operation of God's will in the form of grace. For this higher immediacy, Rousseau—at least the Rousseau who has influenced the world—

tended to substitute the lower immediacy of feeling, thus setting up a sort of subrational parody of grace. In order to make this substitution plausible, he—and, in his wake, the sentimentalists—have resorted to the usual arts of the sophist, chief among which are a juggling with halftruths and a tampering with general terms. For example, in their use of words like 'virtue' and 'conscience,' they have eliminated more or less completely, in favor of vital impulse (*élan vital*), the equally vital principle of control (*frein vital*)—in short, the dualistic element that both religion and humanism require.

The halftruth that has been used to compromise religion in particular is that, though religion is in itself something quite distinct from emotion, it is in its ordinary manifestations very much mixed up with emotion. I give an example of this error in its latest and fashionable form. In a very learned and, in some respects, able book,[4] the Reverend N. P. Williams seeks to show that Saint Augustine's experience of grace or, what amounts to the same thing, his love of God, was only a "sublimation" of his "lust." Saint Augustine was a very passionate man and his passionateness no doubt entered into his love of God. But if it could be shown that the love of God was in Saint Augustine or any other of the major saints merely emotion, sublimated or unsublimated, religion would be only the "illusion" that Freud himself has declared it to be. The psychoanalytical divine, who is, I am told, a fairly frequent type in England, is about the worst *mélange des genres* that has appeared even in the present age of confusion.

Another example of prevailing misapprehensions in this field, and that not merely from the point of view of dogma but of keen psychological observation, is the standard treatment of Rousseau's religion by P. M. Masson, a work which has been almost universally acclaimed by scholars and which has, as a matter of fact, distinguished merits as a historical investigation. M. Masson admits that this religion is "without redemption or repentance or sense of sin," and then proceeds to speak of Rousseau's "profound Christianity"!

Religion has suffered not only from the Rousseauist but also from the pseudo-scientist. If the Rousseauist gives to emotion a primacy that does not belong to it, the pseudo-scientist claims for physical science a hegemony to which it is not entitled. A science that has thus aspired out of its due place runs the risk of becoming not only a "wild Pallas from the brain" but, in connection with its use in war, "procuress to the Lords of Hell." Mr. Walter Lippmann seeks to persuade us in his *Preface to Morals* that if one becomes "disinterested" after the fashion of the scientific investigator, one will have the equivalent not only of "humanism" but of "high religion." Certain scientific investigators are busy in their laboratories at this very moment devising poison gases of formidable potency. What proof is there that, so far as the scientific type of "disinterestedness" is concerned, these gases will not be pressed into the service of the will to power? In seeking to base ethics on monistic postulates, Mr. Lippmann has simply revived the error of Spinoza, who himself revived the error of the Stoics. This error becomes not less but more dangerous when associated with the methods of science. The question involved is at all events that of the will and finally of dualism. One cannot insist too often that "the immortal essence presiding like a king over man's appetites" is transcendent—in other words, set above "nature," not only in Rousseau's sense, but also in the sense that is given to the term by the man of science.

This higher will is felt in its relation to the impressions and impulses and expansive desires of the natural man as a will to refrain. In the great traditional religions, notably in Christianity and Buddhism, the will to refrain has been pushed to the point of renunciation. The modern movement, on the other hand, has been marked since the eighteenth century and in some respects since the Renaissance by a growing discredit of the will to refrain. The very word "renunciation" has been rarely pronounced by those who have entered into the movement. The chief exception that occurs to one is Goethe (echoed at times by Carlyle). Anyone who thinks of the series of Goethe's love affairs prolonged into the seventies is scarcely likely to maintain that his *Entsagung* was of a very austere character even for the man of the world, not to speak of the saint.

III

One must admit that genuine renunciation was none too common even in the ages of faith. As for the typical modern, he is not only at an infinite remove from anything resembling renunciation, but is increasingly unable to accept the will to refrain or anything else on a basis of mere tradition and authority. Yet the failure to exercise the will to refrain in some form or degree means spiritual anarchy. A combination such as we are getting more and more at present of spiritual anarchy with an ever-increasing material efficiency—power without wisdom, as one is tempted to put it—is not likely to work either for the happiness of the individual or for the welfare of society. That the drift toward spiritual anarchy has been largely a result of the decline of dogmatic and revealed religion is scarcely open to question. It does not follow that the only hope of recovering spiritual discipline is in a return to this type of religion.

Both naturalists and supernaturalists have been too prone to underestimate the value of the third possible attitude toward life which I have defined as the humanistic.

The humanist exercises the will to refrain, but the end that he has in view is not the renunciation of the expansive desires but the subduing of them to the law of measure. The humanistic virtues—moderation, common sense, and common decency—though much more accessible than those of the saint, still go against the grain of the natural man—terribly against the grain, one is forced to conclude from a cool survey of the facts of history. Such, indeed, is the difficulty of getting men to practice even humanistic control that one is led, not necessarily to revive the dogma of original sin, but to suspect that the humanitarians, both Baconian and Rousseauistic, are hopelessly superficial in their treatment of the problem of evil. The social dualism they have set up tends in its ultimate development to substitute the class war for what Diderot termed in his denunciation of the older dualism the "civil war in the cave."

One reason that Rousseau gave for his abandonment of his five children was that he had been robbed by the rich of the wherewithal to feed them. The ease with which multitudes have been persuaded to follow Rousseau in this evasion of moral responsibility puts one on the track of a human trait that one may actually observe in oneself and others, and that gives some positive justification to the theological emphasis on the old Adam. This trait may be defined as spiritual indolence, a disinclination to oppose to one's expansive desires any will to refrain, and then to shift the blame on something or somebody else for the unpleasant consequences.

It is evident that in the eyes of anyone who believes in the existence in man of a higher will, with reference to which he may be a responsible moral agent, the characteristic modern malady is not plain and unvarnished materialism but sham spirituality. The remedy would seem to be in a reaffirmation in some form of the true dualism rather than in the merely cynical and "hard-boiled" attitude so prevalent nowadays among those who have become convinced of the final inanity of the humanitarian type of idealism. Joubert wrote over a century ago: "To all tender, ardent, and elevated natures, I say: Only Rousseau can detach you from religion, and only true religion can cure you of Rousseau." I have already made plain that in my judgment one may not only oppose Rousseau on humanistic as well as religious grounds, but that, while making abundant use of the wisdom of the past, one may come at humanism itself in a more positive and critical fashion than has been customary heretofore.

IV

I can scarcely hope, within the limits of an article, to make entirely clear what I mean by a positive and critical humanism. This, to judge by certain current misunderstandings of my position, is a feat I have been unable to accomplish in a series of volumes. I may, however, touch briefly on a few of the main issues. A consideration of Rousseau and his influence will be found to converge on two main problems—the problem of the will, of which I have already spoken, and, of lesser though still major importance, the problem of the intellect. That Rousseau is at the headwaters of an anti-intellectualist trend extending down to James and Bergson and beyond is generally recognized. This trend is prefigured in his saying that "the man who thinks is a depraved animal." At bottom the protest of this type of anti-intellectualist is against the mechanizing of the world by a scientific or pseudo-scientific rationalism. He seeks to escape from mechanism by the pathway of romantic spontaneity. This means practically that he is ready to surrender to the naturalistic flux in the hope of thus becoming "creative." Unfortunately this surrender involves a sacrifice of the standards and the conscious control that are needed to give to creation genuine human significance.

It is above all in dealing with the problems of the intellect and the will that I have sought to be positive and critical. As against the Rousseauistic emotionalist, it seems to me imperative to reestablish the true dualism—that between vital impulse and vital control—and to this end to affirm the higher will first of all as a psychological fact. The individual needs, however, to go beyond this fact if he is to decide how far he is to exercise control in any particular instance with a primary view to his own happiness: in short, he needs standards. To secure standards, at least critically, he cannot afford, like the Rousseauist, to disparage the intellect. One needs to turn its keen power of analysis to an entirely different order of experience from that envisaged by physical science.

To have standards means practically to have some principle of unity with which to measure mere manifoldness and change. There is a power in man, often termed imagination, that reaches out and seizes likenesses and analogies and so tends to establish unity. The unity thus apprehended needs, however, to be tested from the point of view of its reality by the analytical intellect—the power that discriminates—working not abstractly but on the actual data of experience. The fraternal union that the Rousseauist would establish among men on the basis of expansive emotion is found, when tested in this way, to involve an imaginative flight from the reality of both the human and the natural order, and so to exist only in dreamland. An inspection of all the facts of human experience, past and present, would seem to show that what unity a man may achieve either within himself or with his fellow men must be based primarily, not upon feeling, but upon an exercise of the higher will.

One's conception of the constant and unifying factor in life will appear in one's use of general terms. It is plain that the humanist and the Rousseauist clash radically in their definitions. As a result of his elimination of the dualistic element, the Rousseauist has, as I have remarked, set up a "virtue" that, in the eyes of the humanist, is not true virtue; and so likewise for such terms as "justice" and "liberty," and above all (at least in its application to man) "nature." If there is to be a reintegration of the dualistic element into these words, there would seem to be needed an art of inductive defining somewhat similar to that which Socrates brought to bear upon the sophists. It is precisely at this point that the keen discrimination of which I have spoken would have its fullest play. At all events one may say that the standards that result from the cooperation of the imagination and the analytical intellect, and that are reflected in one's definitions, are finally pressed by the humanist into the service of the higher will with a view to imposing a right direction upon the impulses and expansive desires of the natural man.

The humanist is rather distrustful of sudden conversions and pistol-shot transformations of human nature. Hence his supreme emphasis on education. If the humanistic goal is to be attained, if the adult is to like and dislike the things he should—according to Plato, the ultimate aim of ethical endeavor—he must be trained in the appropriate habits almost from infancy. Occasional humanists may appear under present conditions, but if there is to be anything resembling a humanistic movement, the first stage would, as I have said, be that of Socratic definition; the second stage would be the coming together of a group of persons on the basis of this definition—the working out, in short, in the literal sense of that unjustly discredited word, of a convention; the third stage would almost inevitably be the attempt to make this convention effective through education.

V

The mention of education brings the whole discussion home to America. Our educators are more completely and more naively Rousseauistic than those of almost any other country. For example, there is an important survival of the religious-humanistic conception of education in France and Germany and, above all, England; whereas the assumption is all but universal among those who control our educational policies from the elementary grades to the university that anything that sets bounds to the free unfolding of the temperamental proclivities of the young, to their right of self-expression, as one may say, is outworn prejudice. Discipline, so far as it exists, is not of the humanistic or the religious type, but of the kind that one gets in training for a vocation or a specialty. The standards of a genuinely liberal education, as they have been understood, more or less from the time of Aristotle, are being progressively undermined by the utilitarians and the sentimentalists. If the Baconian-Rousseauistic formula is as unsound in certain of its postulates as I myself believe, we are in danger of witnessing in this country one of the great cultural tragedies of the ages.

Moreover Rousseauism not only dominates our education but has been eating into the very vitals of the Protestant religion. Practically, this means that Protestantism is ceasing to be a religion of the inner life and is becoming more and more a religion of "uplift." The result of the attempt to deal with evil socially rather than at its source in the individual, to substitute an outer for an inner control of appetite, has been a monstrous legalism, of which the Eighteenth Amendment is only the most notable example. Those Protestants who have allied themselves with an organization like the Anti-Saloon League have been violating one of the most necessary of Christian precepts—that which warns against confounding the things of God with the things of Caesar.

The multiplication of laws, attended by a growing lawlessness—the present situation in this country—is, as every student of history knows, a very sinister symptom. It may mean that our democratic experiment is, like similar experiments in the past, to end in a decadent imperialism. Nothing is farther from my thought than to suggest that we are on a fatal descending curve. I do not believe in any such fatality, and am in general skeptical of every possible philosophy of history—of the Spenglerian variety most of all. The all-important factor that the Spenglers are wont to overlook or deny in favor of collective tendencies is the moral choices of individuals. For example, the majority in the United States seems just now to be careless of the higher cultural values, to desire nothing better than a continuation of the present type of material prosperity based on the miracles of mass production. Individuals, however, are already standing aside from the majority and assuming a critical attitude toward its "ideals."

Whether this remnant will become sufficiently large to make itself felt in an important way, remains of course a question. At all events, there is an increasing number of persons in this country who can at least see the point of view of the rest of the world. This point of view may be defined as a curious blend of admiration for our efficiency and of disdain for our materialism. The foreigner is, however, far too prone to make America the universal scapegoat for the present domination of man by the machine.

Though the utilitarian-sentimental movement may have triumphed more completely in America than elsewhere, it has been extending its conquests over the whole of the Occident and is now invading the Orient. The issues it raises are, in short, international. That the peripheral merits of this movement are almost innumerable I should be the first to admit: indeed, almost everything in it seems plausible until one penetrates to its very center, and then one discovers an omission that unless corrected vitiates all the rest—the omission, namely, as I have been trying to show, of any reference to a higher will or power of control.

Without making any pretense to a prophetic role for which I am not qualified, I am yet willing to express the conviction that unless there is a recovery of the true dualism or, what amounts to the same thing, a reaffirmation of the truths of the inner life in some form—traditional or critical, religious or humanistic—civilization in any sense that has been attached to that term hitherto is threatened at its base. I speak of the interests of civilization, though my own prime objection to Rousseauism is that it is found finally not to make for the happiness of the individual.

NOTES

1. *La Pensée de Jean-Jacques Rousseau par Albert Schinz*, 2 vols., Smith College, 1929.
2. Ernest Hunter Wright, *The Meaning of Rousseau*, Oxford University Press, 1929.
3. See James Truslow Adams, "The Mucker Pose," *Harper's*, November 1928.
4. *The Ideas of the Fall and of Original Sin* (Bampton Lectures for 1924). See p. 331.

BIBLIOGRAPHY

Adams, James Truslow. "The Mucker Pose." *Harper's*, November 1928.
Schinz, Albert. *La Pensée de Jean-Jacques Rousseau*. Paris: Falcon, 1929.
Williams, Norman Powell. *The Ideas of the Fall and of Original Sin*. New York: Longmans, Green, 1927.
Wright, Ernest Hunter. *The Meaning of Rousseau*. London: Oxford University Press, 1929.

CHAPTER TWO

Power without Limits

The Allure of Political Idealism and the Crumbling of American Constitutionalism

Claes G. Ryn

For the framers of the U.S. Constitution no task seemed more important than to limit and tame power. The chief reason why they established a government of divided powers and checks and balances was their view of human nature, which was primarily Christian and classical. It seemed to them self-evident that human beings are morally cleft. They are potentially decent, even admirable, but also have darker inclinations that pose a great threat to themselves and others. Human beings cannot be trusted with unrestricted power. The constitutionalism of the framers assumed that the drive for power had to be contained first of all through the self-discipline of individuals, but corresponding external restraints, including constitutional checks, were necessary to protect the public.

Since the adoption of the Constitution American government and society have changed radically. The Constitution still enjoys a kind of ceremonial respect. It is cited as if it possessed an august authority. In actuality, political practice is today so different from the intent of the framers that, in substance, the original Constitution has been virtually suspended. Over the years sometimes tortuous and highly tendentious constitutional interpretation has combined with powerful political and intellectual trends to produce an enormous expansion and centralization of the federal government and a concomitant erosion of checks and balances. The claim that these developments have realized the hopes of Alexander Hamilton is blatantly anachronistic. The American federal National Security and Welfare State with its presidential system bears little resemblance to the scheme of the framers.

The reasons for the change are many and complex. They include the effects of wars, economic and scientific developments, and globalization. The change can also be traced to moral, cultural, and social developments that have had profound, transformative consequences. Briefly put, the way in which Americans today view themselves and the world is very different from what was the case at the time of the framing of the Constitution. That change is far-reaching and goes a long way toward explaining the mentioned political change. One major consequence is a muting of the old American fear of power and the creation of vast new opportunities for politicians who desire more power. Although these developments have distinctively American characteristics, they reflect trends throughout the Western world. Those trends have, in fact, been even more pronounced in Europe.

Although traditional religion and morality have long been in retreat, moralistic language seems more pervasive in American politics today than ever. Few public policy stands are advanced that are not said to be demanded by "justice" or "fairness." To oppose them is to be "greedy," "callous" or "intolerant"—to be morally inferior, even despicable. Moral indignation is, it seems, the favored posture of politicians and pressure groups.

But the moralism of today is very different from the notion of morality prevalent at the time of the writing of the Constitution. The purpose of this article is to identify a powerful strain within this new moralism and to elucidate its role in engendering the transformation of American society and politics. While sharply lessening the old American fear of power, the change has facilitated and even stimulated a desire for power. According to the new conception of morality, it is virtuous to want government, almost always the federal government, to expand its reach. In foreign policy, it is common for American leaders to claim, sometimes with great ideological fervor, that America is exceptional and has a moral mission in the world. American leadership is needed to remake insufficiently "free" and "democratic" countries. According to assertive nationalists, neoconservatives, and liberal interventionists in both parties, America should seek armed global hegemony—not, of course, to indulge a desire to dominate but to fulfill a morally noble destiny. The advocates of uncontested hegemony will deny that they *desire*, for its own sake, the enormous military power that would be necessary to achieving the stated goal; the need to wield enhanced American power is only *incidental* to the moral imperative of creating a better world. In domestic politics, many politicians similarly assume that their wish greatly to expand the scope and functions of government has solely moral motives. Here, too, the need to accumulate power at the political center is viewed as merely *incidental* to wanting a more just society. Yet one might wonder why the desire for moral public policy rarely, if ever, issues in calls for *reducing* the power of political leaders. So striking is this pattern that it raises the question whether the moralism in question and the wish to expand and centralize power might somehow be integrally connected. Whatever else this moralism might be, is it a subtle way of justifying a desire to rule others?

The purpose of this article is to analyze the "idealism" that has helped transform America and, in particular, to demonstrate that its moral-imaginative dynamic is quite different from its reputation. It would appear that indistinguishable from its ostensible caring for the welfare of others is a desire to direct their lives. Indeed, the deepest source of idealism's appeal may be that it is a sense of moral superiority that implies a right to dominate.

To argue this thesis it will be necessary to revisit points that this author has made in other contexts and to recast, combine, and supplement them for the present purpose.

THE OLD MORALITY AND ITS SOCIAL AND POLITICAL ENTAILMENTS

The traditional Western view of man's moral predicament carried with it a deep ambivalence about power. On the one hand, no political objectives could be achieved without the exercise of power. On the other hand, the prominent lower proclivities of human beings made power potentially dangerous, so that people in political authority had to be subjected to restraint. Both in personal and political life, it was important to foster moderation and a sense of limits. Even the political theory of Thomas Hobbes (1588–1679), which *breaks* with the Western tradition with regard to both moral philosophy and the idea of restraints on power, offers a kind of confirmation of an older sense that governments must recognize limits. It never occurs to this advocate of supposedly absolute political rule to extend the sphere of sovereignty beyond matters touching law and order. He is in this respect a kind of forerunner of classical liberalism. In his view of human beings Hobbes rejects much of the older heritage, but in stressing man's wholly egocentric nature he might be said to advocate a simplified and extreme Augustinianism.

Representatives of the dominant modern notion of political morality do not much worry about possible egotism and ruthlessness in people who seem to them to have the right ideals. They tend to place any dark inclinations outside of the supposedly idealistic and hence benevolent politician, place it among those, especially, who oppose the supposedly moral cause. One of the reasons why virtuous politicians are thought to need great power is to be able to overcome the opposition of recalcitrants.

The framers of the U.S. Constitution were acutely aware that the responsible exercise of power had moral preconditions. They feared original sin in themselves as well as others. They hoped that in personal life moral character would restrain the desire for self-aggrandizement, just as in national political life the checks and balances of the U.S. Constitution would contain and domesticate the all-too-human desire for power as an end in itself. Personal self-control and constitutionalism were but different aspects of the need to subdue the voracious ego. Freedom and rule of law required republican virtue. They had to be achieved by the members of society over time through protracted inner and outer moral struggle. Freedom and rule of law could not be bestowed as a gift on a people that had not undertaken any of this work. Constitutionalism could be safeguarded in America only through the continuation of the kind of culture that fostered it.[1]

The framers assumed that for the Constitution to work its institutions had to be manned by individuals who embodied its spirit of restraint. That spirit stemmed from America's *unwritten* constitution, that is, from the religious, moral, cultural, and social life that had inclined Americans to constitutionalism. To be capable of sustaining the constitutional order those working under its provisions had to be predisposed to virtues like moderation, respect for law, and readiness to compromise. They had to have what this author calls the constitutional personality. The main reason why the U.S. Constitution has become a mere shadow of its old self is that it cannot function as intended without the aforementioned personality traits.[2]

It is important to understand that the moral character that the framers saw as the ultimate protection against arbitrary power and as the source of the constitutional temperament also generated a society of a certain type. Most Americans will vaguely remember that at the heart of Christian morality is the admonition to "love neighbor as thyself." What is commonly forgotten or is not very well understood are the far-reaching social implications of that moral vision. By "neighbor" is meant individuals within the person's own sphere of life, people of flesh and blood with names and faces. We are to treat them as we would like to have them treat us. Note carefully that traditional Christianity does not call on us to love "mankind" or "humanity," which, by modern, idealistic standards, looks more generous and ambitious. What sounds so nice in modern ears—loving "humanity"—is very different from loving "neighbor" in that its object is not some particular person in the here and now. "Humanity" is highly amorphous and distant. Humanity is not here, in our way, where it might inconvenience us. By the standards of traditional morality, which are down to earth and rather crusty, loving mankind does not engage us where we live. It does not interfere with our ordinary lives and require acts of self-sacrifice. It takes place chiefly in the imagination. For that reason, it does not represent any moral challenge. All it requires is having supposedly noble sentiments, "feeling the pain" of a diffuse suffering collective somewhere far away. The proof to you and others that you are morally noble is that thinking about those who suffer puts a tear in your eye. Moral virtue is not, as for Christianity, charitable action toward particular people up close, but having warm feelings for nobody in particular. Those in trouble are not actually present, making uncomfortable demands. From the point of view of traditional Western morality, the sentimental notion of virtue has little to do with real morality, which is to shoulder responsibility for persons, for "neighbors." That older morality presupposes the ability to overcome our native egotism and laziness. It requires strength of *character*. To be up to the task, the individual must have already learned to moderate his self-indulgence and callousness and to make the needs of others his own. It is because the problems of actual persons are concrete and nearby that loving neighbor can be very demanding. It may take up much of our time and energy. To compound the difficulty, neighbor may not even be likable. Yet love him we should, not by emoting nobly and walking away, but by taking concrete, perhaps greatly inconvenient action. Without strength of will we may shrink from acting. Loving "mankind" does not require character. It takes place in the imagination and is to that extent morality made comfortable and easy.

People who believe that loving neighbor will give meaning to life will be prone to give their best in settings that are near and intimate—families, neighborhoods, schools, churches, and workplaces. There are many reasons why such groups and associations will be for most people the main sphere of life, but it is crucial to understand that it is here more than elsewhere that traditional morality has its center and primary outlet. Note that in small, intimate associations the person must repeatedly take others into account. There he cannot indulge his native self-indulgence and slothfulness without inviting immediate censure. In families and small groups where relations of mutual dependence are dense and numerous, the person is taught to behave with the well-being of others in mind. You cannot always have your own way. Each member must learn to perform little acts of self-denial. The person is habituated to doing his part, assisting others, and compromising. Character is bred and repeatedly tested. Where life is personal and up close no one can get away with portraying himself as morally better than he is. Others will be quick to see through mere posturing. Never mind some conceited self-image of being a deeply caring friend of humanity; it is your actions toward real people that reveal who you really are, and they decide your reputation. To the extent that moral character is fostered through life in groups, the will is honed for the responsibilities of the larger society. The more people learn to restrain their lower natures and take others into account, the greater the likelihood that ties of community will be fostered and strengthened.

Traditional Western morality does not assume that people up close will be the only beneficiaries of moral responsibility. It assumes merely that genuine morality will originate in and be nurtured in intimate settings. Thus formed, moral character will have an effect wherever a person directs his attention. Some people will concern themselves with a world far beyond local associations and issues, but they will have learned from life in their groups and communities that what makes for a better society is not some nebulous warm sentiment, but a readiness to act responsibly in and to understand the world as it is, full not least of human weakness.

To be able to understand moral "idealism" and its various entailments it is important to recognize first the social and political ramifications of the rather different traditional ethic just described. The latter generates certain priorities. Love of neighbor is not for exceptional, grandiose circumstances but for the concrete life of the here and now. It shapes and enhances day-to-day relationships. Because it emphasizes that doing right by persons up close is essential to human well-being, it encourages people to give their best within their own groups, neighborhoods, businesses, associations, and local communities. From this understanding of man's higher calling is derived the old principle of subsidiarity, central not least to Roman Catholic social thought, which says that problems should be addressed, as far as possible, by those immediately concerned. Only if people cannot manage on their own should they seek assistance elsewhere, and then, again, as near to themselves as possible. This sense of moral responsibility will let them attain their full stature as human beings. It is not difficult to see that the traditional understanding of morality encouraged and built energetic, strong communities. What people felt that they should handle personally, privately, and locally minimized the need for government. This morality was a powerful decentralizing force.

It was in the 1830s that Alexis de Tocqueville commented at length on the vitality and proliferation of private and local associations in America. Americans had a strong inclination to collaborate and to address their needs within their own groups. Tocqueville was particularly struck by the active role of members of churches. He noted the great reluctance of Americans to part with any authority over their own lives. Except perhaps for the *prominence* of these observations in *Democracy in America*, they should not be very surprising. Although there was no single reason for these social patterns, it should be easy to see the connection between a highly decentralized, group-oriented society and America's moral roots.

The same moral heritage that fostered cooperation, self-reliance, mutual assistance, self-restraint, modesty, respect for law, and a willingness to compromise helped shape the constitutional personality. These traits formed the mentioned unwritten constitution, which gave life and direction to the written one. Just as the traditional views and habits of Americans made them impose internal checks on themselves, so did they make them willing to accept and respect external legal constraints. Had these personality traits not been strong and widespread, nothing like the U.S. Constitution could have been conceived or made to work.

That the American form of government today bears little resemblance to the constitutional design of 1787 reflects a change in America's unwritten constitution, in the basic self-understanding and priorities of Americans. There can be no question here of attempting a comprehensive summary of what brought about the present state of affairs. The emphasis will have to be on how the change in the understanding of morality and society helped produce a new attitude towards power and government. It is necessary to take account of an aspect of so-called modernity that has had profound and far-reaching effects but that is still poorly understood.

IDEALISM: MORALITY RECONCEIVED

Not all strains of modernity are incompatible with the older moral tradition, but special attention needs to be paid to the explicitly stated desire for liberation from earlier beliefs and ways of life that is most commonly called modernity. Two seemingly disparate but intimately connected currents have given that part of modernity its distinctive flavor and dynamic: one is a belief in rational enlightenment; the other is entertaining "idealistic" dreams of human existence transformed. Both currents assume the coming of a new, superior world, an era of liberty, harmony, and general well-being.

Modern idealism follows no single path, but one may discern a central, enduring pattern. The philosopher who gives the clearest and most thoroughgoing expression to the dream of a new world and who comes closest to being paradigmatic for this idealism is probably Jean-Jacques Rousseau (1712–1778). More than anybody else he inspired the kind of imagination that has, in more or less extreme form, exerted enormous influence in the Western world, first of all in literature, art, philosophy, and religion, but soon also in politics. *Idealism* as a term for the moral-political force that Rousseau helped create should not be confused with the nineteenth-century school of German philosophy that is often given the same name.

Rousseau flatly rejects the ancient Western belief that human beings are morally torn between higher and lower potentialities and that they are their own worst enemies. Human beings have nothing to fear from themselves. They are naturally good, but traditional societies pervert and imprison their true nature. The way to a better life is to liberate man's natural goodness from inner and outer restraint. Rousseau dreams himself away from what he considers a dark and intolerable present. He starts the modern theme of estrangement from existing society—alienation, indeed, from all of life as it currently exists. He imagines a long lost idyllic past and a corresponding glorious future. Employing a new form of the imagination, he becomes the great pioneer in the West for envisioning a society wholly different from anything known in history.

The term *imagination* has been carefully defined by this author in other places. Here the context should provide sufficient definition.[3]

Human beings are dreamers. They often dream themselves far away. Capable of imagining something quite different from the present, they are free in a way that animals are not. But this power presents humanity with a big problem. They can use it to imagine and long for what simply cannot be, dream the impossible dream. The dream may become so captivating that they will try to enact it, which may bring disaster upon themselves and others.

A central feature of what used to be known as civilization is *not* letting human beings escape too far into dreamworld. They need to tether their visions of a better life to what humanity has found to lie in the realm of the possible. Civilization protects people against frivolous dreaming not least through its moral teachings and great works of art and literature, which seek to anchor the imagination in the world in which human beings have to act. More often than not experience in the world of action shows dreams to be mere wishful thinking. Civilization teaches that we cannot have the world just as we would like it. Children dream endlessly of what cannot be, but to mature as a human being means giving up childish things. Adults must face the facts of life, most importantly the limits imposed by man's moral predicament.

Yet in the last 250 years Western men and women became more and more reluctant to accept a world that limits their hopes. They did not want to remain imperfect creatures torn in the depths of their being between high and low, condemned to struggle against dark inclinations in themselves and others. Idealistic dreaming let them set aside the uncomfortable traditional claims about human nature. Leading idealistic artists, philosophers, and politicians nurtured their hope for a marvelous new world, free of the old restrictions.

Just where the imagination crosses over the line from contemplating real possibilities for improvement to dreaming the impossible dream we cannot say for certain ahead of time, but the mature person knows to adjust his aspirations to what historical experience has shown to be unavoidable facts of life. The dreamer of the impossible dream, by contrast, is not willing to let evidence from the world of human practice—the historical world—put a damper on his dreaming. For mature persons, daydreams are never more than momentary departures from life as it is, but for idealists dreams of a radically different, wonderful world are a permanent accompaniment of daily life, a vantage point from which the present can be seen to be all the more disappointing.

Rousseau represents the idealistic imagination in a particularly thoroughgoing form, but in one version or another, this kind of dreaminess has continued to reverberate. It may indeed be the dominant moral sensibility of the contemporary Western world.

Rousseau declared that everything was the opposite of how it had seemed. Traditional civilization is not a support for making the best of life. It enslaves the goodness that belonged to man in a pre-civil state of nature. Evil is not in human beings but is due to wicked social norms and institutions. "Man is born free, and everywhere he is in chains." Even the works of culture helped enslave human beings. "The sciences, letters and the arts . . . spread garlands of flowers over the iron chains with which they are burdened."[4]

Returning to the primitive state of natural goodness is neither possible nor desirable, Rousseau averred, but the unimpeded spontaneity of the natural man can be restored in a radically reconstituted society. Doing away with inequality and dependence on others will create virtuous unity. Though Rousseau did not propose returning into the woods, the natural, uninhibited man was for him the standard for revolutionizing society. Rousseau gave a detailed account of the goodness of man in his original state. It is when most unaffected by civilization that men are at their best. To create a new society man must repair to the natural man, the child within, as it were, and make a fresh start.

Rousseau's dreams were greatly pleasing to many in that they seemed to free human beings from the hard, unending work of disciplining dark forces in themselves. He directed the blame for evil away from the individual onto the institutions of existing society. Human beings are the *victims* of perverse circumstance. But they can make a wonderful new existence for themselves by revolutionizing the social and political exterior.

From the perspective of the classical and Christian view of man this is not a story for adults. It flies in the face of human experience. It is an elaborate fantasy. But it enthused Western readers. They *wanted* to believe this dream. How wonderful to be relieved of the never-ending struggle to improve self, to hear that man is already what he should be—that nature made him such! The vision promised a short-cut to fulfillment.

It should be carefully noted that the Rousseauistic dream of a transformed human existence involved from the very beginning an element of conscious or semiconscious self-deception. It offered a striking example of an imagination of escape. Significantly, Rousseau was not wholly unaware of disregarding actual human experience. He *admitted* to wondering at times if there was not something frivolous and unreal about his own flights of fancy. It was, he said, as if his "heart," his dreamy imagination, did not belong to the same person as his "head," his moments of critical reflection. Yet he could not, *would* not, resist his dream. In the *Second Discourse* he introduced his elaborate survey of the state of nature and the origins of the corrupt civilized society by saying that his account should not be regarded as an historical narrative. He wrote: "Let us . . . begin by putting aside all the facts, for they have no bearing on the question." His "investigations" should not "be taken for historical truths, but only for hypothetical and conditional reasonings."[5] In other words, he asked his readers to follow him into an imaginary history and to find there the true nature of man and the inspiration for remaking society. Countless political activists have engaged in this kind of dreaming and pushed a political agenda of liberation.

It is important to realize that what Rousseau understands as natural and fulfilling is conceived as incompatible with trying to make the best of the historically known world. He does not employ his imagination to help us live to advantage in a world in which man is divided against himself and has to contend with various other impediments. He simply rejects what he considers an unacceptable human existence. He imagines life on wholly different terms. It is not possible here to explore why something that looks to the traditional Christian like a children's tale should have had such deep and enduring appeal. The time must have been ripe in the West for something like romantic escape and revolt. Rousseau offered happiness and enchantment without difficult moral striving. Fulfillment would be a free gift of nature.

It is relevant to the issue of morality and power that Rousseau found in human beings a natural inclination to sympathize with those who suffer. He pioneered a new notion of caring. Charity does not, as in Christianity, develop through character formation but is a spontaneous impulse. For Rousseau, the measure of being a good person is not to exhibit decency in practical conduct, but to have warm feelings, a supposedly benevolent "heart." The new caring takes place not in the world of action, but in the imagination of the caring person. Replacing the traditional understanding of love with teary-eyed sentiment became a powerful trend in Western morality. The new morality was appealing not only in that it did not require an effort of will, but in that it was inherently self-applauding, giving the sympathizing person a nice feeling of nobility.

Dreaming the impossible dream had dramatic social and political consequences. It inspired the French Jacobins and the French Revolution. Later it inspired socialism and communism. Even when modern idealism did not accept the Rousseauistic premise of man's natural goodness, it assumed a sharp contrast between a diseased present and a future of radiant health. Even National Socialism had its dream of a glorious time to come, the thousand-year *Reich*. In recent decades many have fantasized about global peace and democracy.

Rousseau himself did not much care for Enlightenment rationalism, but idealistic imagination formed in the West an antitraditional alliance with rationalism. What the two currents had in common was that they rejected the old stress on moral character as the key to a satisfying life. All over the Western world this informal alliance exhibited a "head" that was narrowly technocratic and instrumentalist and a "heart" that was full of dreamy sensibility. The quintessentially modern Westerner combines with sophisticated technical ideas and equipment a sentimental imagination. Politicians of this type feel the pain of suffering collectives and dare to share that they care. They also have elaborate plans for reorganizing society. Their goals are idealistic; their method for enacting them is social engineering. Today the typical idealist espouses a special brand of ecologism and has very ambitious plans for cleaning up the planet. This idealism owes much to the Rousseauistic assumption that civilization has ruined a pure and wholesome nature.

Looking back on what has been said here about modern idealism, it might appear incongruous that, like Rousseau, persons can at the same time be intellectually brilliant and have imaginations that people of an earlier worldview would consider naïve and utopian. Yet nothing seems more common in the modern Western world. Many employ high intelligence to argue that their cherished dreams for remaking the world are wholly plausible. As already mentioned, there is something willful about Rousseauistic dreaming. It would appear that among those who seem most to need to be persuaded are the idealists themselves.

IDEALISM AND THE DESIRE FOR POWER

There is an aspect of idealism that may explain much of its appeal but that is poorly understood: its connection to the subject of power. Whatever else dreaming of this kind accomplishes for the dreamer, it seems to satisfy a desire to feel superior to others. The person who envisages a life far above the humdrum, routinized present is by this very act, in his own eyes, lifted far above those who are caught within that present and who, by definition, lack his fine, elevated sentiments. See how noble and superior I am, the idealist announces to self and others, words being unnecessary. The putatively benevolent dream is, among other things, a form of self-flattery. The one who thinks of self as committed to a better world for others also feels deserving of their praise. He feels entitled, moreover, to directing their lives. The greater the person's imagined caring for mankind, the greater the power to which the person feels entitled to do good for mankind.

This aspect of the idealistic dream is, it can be argued, no marginal component or hidden implication of the dream. The sense of moral superiority and the corresponding sense of entitlement are parts of what makes the dream what it is and recommends it to the dreamer. It is perhaps the most important source of its allure. To get pleasure from the idealistic dream the person does not have to receive the actual adulation of others or exercise power over them in practice. Short of engaging in politics, the person can experience them in the imagination. He can enjoy them viscerally by identifying with the idealistic political movement or with its virtuous leader whose rhetoric and actions confirm the idealist's moral authority and nobility.

To many admirers of modernity, the twentieth century was the most enlightened in human history. It was an era committed to noble ideals—"equality" and "democracy" prominent among them. Yet in that century far more people died at the hands of other human beings than in any previous century. Some of the biggest idealists, championing a vision of universal brotherhood—Lenin, Trotsky, Stalin, Mao—were also among the greatest killers and murderers. They caused enormous suffering. Yet the Western world seems to have learned very little about idealism from this horrifying experience. Idealists *still* expect, and often receive, admiration for their allegedly noble visions. The *idealism* cannot be blamed for the homicidal mania, idealists tell others. There was nothing wrong with the *ideals*; they are as beautiful as ever. The ruthlessness was the result of practical means somehow getting away from noble ends.

But at this stage of the argument being presented it should be possible to see that there is a connection between the impossible dream and ruthlessness. The problem is not with poorly chosen means but with the impossible dream itself. The dream ignores basic facts of life, specifically the need for moral character. The typical idealistic goals fly in the face of reality. They more or less deliberately *hide* aspects of life that are crucial to any realistic assessment of whether change of a particular kind is desirable or even possible. In particular, the ideals conceal the darker side of human nature, letting it be acknowledged at most among opponents of the dream. To the idealist, issues of character seem trivial or beside the point in comparison with the need to end great social evils and realize great plans. As the champion of a noble cause, the idealistic leader does not need to be shackled. More power to him! The idealistic leader himself sees little need to worry about personal weaknesses of his own, such as an inclination to be ruthless in dealing with opposition. To oppose him is, after all, perverse.

How to explain that in many quarters the view that idealists have of themselves is still considered plausible? People who are not as heavily under the sway of idealism nevertheless sense that to attack its leading representatives is to attack a part of themselves. Idealistic assumptions come up against overwhelming philosophical and historical evidence, but so dependent is the self-worth of millions of people on the purported nobility of the dream that they cannot let it be challenged root and branch. Yet neglecting unwelcome but stubborn and salient facts of human life, as idealists do, is not admirable. Contrary to their reputation, the idealistic goals are not noble and beautiful. They are reprehensible and dangerous. The horrors of the twentieth century were not paradoxical or difficult to explain. In important respects, they emanated directly from a self-deluding, self-applauding moralism and a concomitant dearth of moral character. The brutality of the idealists simply brought the neglect of moral self-control into the open, just as it expressed a hatred of the existing world and a disdain for actual human beings that was contained in the ideal from the beginning. Edmund Burke fully expected violence to flow from the Rousseauistic dreams of the Jacobins.

Irving Babbitt calls Rousseau's imagination "idyllic," and so it is, in part. The term *idyllic* takes note of the fact that from Rousseau's imaginary "nature" all disturbing elements have been removed: life in the state of nature is simple, sunny, and pleasant, a kind of vacation from life as known to history. But the term *idyllic* does not convey the potential for inhumanity that is a basic, if often unrecognized, part of this kind of imagination. Imagination of a reality-defying idealistic kind foreshadows and rather predictably calls forth certain dark practical consequences. These are consonant with the back side of the dream, its disgust with what exists. That disgust is part of what *defines* the dream. The apparent benevolence of the dream may to some extent hide its potential for ruthlessness, hide it even from the dreamer, but it surfaces as soon as the dream is brought into contact with the real world, the world of action, where it is bound to encounter opposition. The true believer's predictable response when others fail to yield unquestioningly is coercion. You are either for him or against him. The dreamer of the impossible dream sees no reason to tolerate opposition. In its assumption of moral superiority the dream is uncompromising. It demands monopoly. Those who do not acknowledge the moral authority of the idealist have to suffer his wrath. His reaction to opposition is not unlike that of the egotistical child: he throws a temper tantrum. Sooner or later idealism brings conflict, whether domestic or international. As the idealist tries to make uncooperative reality conform to the dream, the violence expands and intensifies. Through unbending zeal the dreamer tries to persuade even himself of the sacred nature of his vision. To show mercy for or to compromise with opponents would cast doubt on the moral nobility and necessity of the dream and would, in effect, denigrate self. To give up the dream is unthinkable, for it is the idealist's source of personal worth and pride. It alone legitimizes his power.

To capture idealism's potential for merciless brutality a term like "diabolical" is needed. The idyllic aspect of the ideals of the French Revolution was "freedom, equality and brotherhood." Their diabolical aspect, made evident by their practical entailments, was the guillotine.[6]

It should be possible to see that in its pure form the impossible dream expresses and serves, but also veils, unbridled moral conceit. It extends to the dreamer a right to unlimited power. It serves as a great *stimulant* and *justification* for self-aggrandizement. It is incompatible with traditional modesty, self-restraint, and limits on power. The gist of what has been argued so far about idealism is, then, not merely that "ideas have consequences," but that the dream is inherently, from the beginning, consonant with its practical expression.

To sum up on that point, imagining and advocating unattainable goals is from the point of view of traditional morality not admirable, but perverse and dangerous. It distracts human beings from attainable goals and from the need to deal realistically with the chief obstacles to moral well-being, which are in human beings themselves. Idealists who promise a different world are not sweet and well-intentioned. Their dreams reveal bad *motives*. Contrary to their reputation, their souls are not beautiful, but ugly and ignoble. The imagination through which they view the world is wicked and shoddy. Idealists have pulled entire societies into disaster, and they can do so again.

Many people regard the great suffering of the otherwise progressive and enlightened twentieth century as a terrible aberration, perhaps the birth pangs associated with something glorious coming into being. Surely, mass killings and murder are now a thing of the past. But many people remain greatly susceptible to the lure of political idealism, if not always of the most extreme sort. For example, in the last several decades a powerful political and intellectual movement invested the United States of America with a worldwide mission to spearhead what George W. Bush called a "global democratic revolution." The French Jacobins of the eighteenth century appointed France as the liberator of mankind. The *new* Jacobins appointed America.

It was partly to wean Americans off the traditional fear of unlimited power and the view of life that it implies that the new Jacobins sought to transfer the allegiance of Americans to a *reinvented*, more uninhibited America. They propounded the myth of *America the Virtuous*—the myth of a morally noble America, according to which America should have free rein in transforming the world. The myth provided the moral justification for a great unleashing of power.

Political idealism is no less ravenous for power when applied to domestic politics. There, too, it assumes a monopoly of moral virtue. It feels entitled to mobilizing and directing great power to reshape society. In America it does not care for a small federal government with checks and balances and does not like to share power with states, counties, and localities, to say nothing of citizens in their private capacities. Whether it considers itself "right" or "left," the imagination of political idealism thrills to the dream of maximum energy in the executive, of a virtuous president who overpowers opposition.

It might be objected that power seeking does not need some kind of idealism to give it energy. Most people are perfectly cynical in their pursuit of power. However true that may be, the will to power can hardly present itself as a desire to rule others for its own sake, especially not at a time when moral-sounding motives are expected and there is a need to appeal to democratic majorities. Today that desire routinely wraps itself in idealistic rhetoric. For those in our era who desire expansion and concentration of power idealism is the great enabler. It discovers ever-new reasons for government to act benevolently. The greater the caring for others, the greater the need to place power in the hands of those who care.

If the argument of this article has any validity, it is no coincidence that idealistic benevolence always justifies giving more power to the benevolent— never less. So well does the will to dominate dress itself up in moralistic attire that it may at times deceive even the power seekers themselves.

IDEALISM VERSUS CONSTITUTIONALISM

The old American idea of limited, decentralized government was conceived by people who believed that placing restrictions on self and on government and encouraging strong communities was essential to human well-being. Today, an increasingly common and influential human type espouses grandiose political objectives and correspondingly grandiose moral justifications for a desired expansion of power. The title of a book, *An End to Evil*, written several years ago by two enthusiastic advocates of American global supremacy during the glory days of the New Jacobinism, summed up the moral purpose of the desired reign.[7] America should get rid of dictators and other evil people. *An end to evil*—could any goal appeal more to the will to power? The task is surely the very essence of moral nobility, and because it is at once enormous and endless it requires power to match.

A wish to "end" evil would have been rejected out of hand by the old Americans. It betrays an unwillingness to face the human condition. Evil can be to some extent contained—that the framers of the Constitution did believe—but evil is an inescapable part of human life, hence the great need for character and both internal and external limits on power.

The old Western notion of man's moral and intellectual shortcomings and the accompanying recognition of a need for self-control and humility can be traced back through Christianity to the ancient Greeks. This view of human nature and the political attitudes that it fosters tend to *forestall*, *censure*, and *defuse* an inordinate desire for power. For that reason, it is not pleasing to the ego that wants to dominate other human beings. Idealism has just the opposite effect. It is a potent *stimulant* for the desire for self-aggrandizement. Today idealism is letting a grasping, "imperialistic" ego throw off the old American constitutional personality and related constitutional restraints. It offers powerful support for the transformation of traditional limited, decentralized American government into a national Superstate.

It might be objected that the idealism described in this article is only an "ideal type" in the Weberian sense and that in real life we seldom encounter it in such pure form. In most people it is diluted or balanced by other factors. Also, this idealism is certainly not the only force to have contributed to the expansion and concentration of power. That many seek political power for the wrong reasons also does not mean that government cannot be a beneficial force. Each of these comments is well-grounded, and they are not contradicted by anything that has been argued in this article. It should perhaps be stated explicitly that, needless to say, there are reasons for wanting to expand the role of government that may have nothing to do with idealistic dreaming. The point of what has been argued here is not that political idealism, by itself, has caused the transformation of America, although it has exerted great influence. The main purpose has been to draw attention to a major, but poorly understood, factor in the transformation of America (as well as the rest of Western civilization) and to demonstrate the nature of its influence—to show how idealism changes morality and society and the view of power. In order to lay bare the moral-imaginative core of idealism, this article has examined this phenomenon in full flower, as it were, rather than in the practical politics of a particular society where it inevitably blends with or is balanced by other currents.

The effect of idealism in America as elsewhere has been to trivialize and weaken love of neighbor and thus to undermine the support for traditional decentralized political and social structures. At the same time it has helped inspire a vast accumulation and centralization of state power. In proportion as the moral sensibilities of Americans have become idealistic, Americans have come to expect more and more from government and less and less from themselves, their intimate groups, and communities. Not even the idea of the state as parent, which is far advanced in Europe, is without traction in America. To an extent that the Americans described by Tocqueville would have found hard to fathom, Americans today are willing to rely on a distant central government for their well-being. Idealism has played a key role in undermining the old American distrust of a concentration of power. Wrapping itself in vaguely Christian-sounding rhetoric, idealism has been the Trojan horse for the forces wanting to dismantle traditional American constitutionalism. Most Christian churches, too, have been deeply affected by idealism. To that extent they have gradually abandoned the traditional concern about sin and the need for repentance and adopted a feel-good sentimentalism. As Americans lowered their moral guard, they became increasingly willing to abdicate old responsibilities and local and private autonomy. In practice, if not always in theory, they moved away from the principle of subsidiarity. This has been the case also with many Roman Catholics, whose notion of "social justice" has under the influence of idealism become indistinguishable from that of the centralized and secularized welfare state. Substituting idealism for traditional morality, people were able to persuade themselves that in abdicating personal responsibility they were actually behaving nobly. In fact, the greater their willingness to hand over power to virtuous-sounding leaders and presumed experts, the greater the evidence of having a superior moral sensibility. As government benevolence has replaced traditional morality, people have been freed from sometimes burdensome familial and communal ties and responsibilities and have been spared much inconvenience. Relieved of the need to show character and exercise up-close responsibilities, they can give more attention to their own personal interests and pleasures. Yet by the standard of an *earlier* understanding of man's humanity, their personhood has been greatly diminished.

Though idealism in one form or another has greatly affected all parts of American society, traditional morality is not extinct. It keeps buttressing some old social and political habits and structures. Americans are not of one mind. There is not yet any consensus in favor of the comprehensive, benevolent state. Opposition to it is stronger in America than in Europe. Still, the central power that idealism has done so much to boost is so far-reaching that it would have horrified an earlier type of American. So deeply attracted have Americans become to the idea that a distant central government can be their benign guardian that many of them barely notice or care that the sphere of private, local, and autonomous action is contracting precipitously. In recent decades the centralization and expansion of government has been greatly aided by benevolent-sounding arguments for protecting the American people against threats to its security, specifically terrorism. Already predisposed by idealism to regard federal power as a benign force, Americans have, more or less, invited the creation of an elaborate, massive national security apparatus that employs nothing less than totalitarian methods of surveillance.

Rousseau gave the West the image of the wonderfully natural child, uninfected by civilization. To be natural, men should be more like children. He did not want to consider the evidence that children are *at least* as prone to egotism and cruelty as adults. In partly unrecognized cooperation with rationalists, Rousseauistic idealists have had much success in overturning the ancient civilization of the West, but they have not rid society of egotism, greed, or the will to power. They have only managed greatly to weaken the old moral, intellectual, cultural, and political restraints placed upon them. They have produced, in abundance, immature, ill-behaved, ignorant, erratic egotists. Rationalist modernity has simultaneously placed sophisticated technology, including military and surveillance equipment, at their disposal.

Many defenders of the old American Constitution seem to think that all that would be needed in order to save the Constitution would be to persuade Americans of the correct interpretation of the framers' intent. These "constitutionalists" live in a world of abstractions, a dreamworld of their own. The argument here advanced should have demonstrated that there is only one way to revive American constitutionalism, and that is for Americans, from leaders to people in general, to revive or freshly create something like the older type of morality and to start *living* very differently. Should that not be a likely development, the future of American constitutionalism is bleak.

NOTES

1. The points made in this paragraph are more fully argued and substantiated in Claes G. Ryn, *America the Virtuous: The Crisis of Democracy and the Quest for Empire* (New Brunswick, NJ: Transaction Publishers, 2003) and Claes G. Ryn, *Democracy and the Ethical Life*, 2d exp. ed. (Washington, DC: Catholic University of America Press, 1990; first published in 1978). Regarding the British origins of the American constitutional order, see Russell Kirk, *The Conservative Constitution* (Washington, DC: Regnery, 1990) and *The Roots of American Order* (Wilmington, DE: ISI Books, 2003; first published in 1974). See also, Willmoore

Kendall and George W. Carey, *The Basic Symbols of the American Political Tradition* (Washington, DC: Catholic University of America Press, 1995; first published in 1970).

2. On the relationship between the written Constitution and the unwritten one, including the constitutional personality, see Claes G. Ryn, "Political Philosophy and the Unwritten Constitution," *Modern Age* 34, no. 4 (Summer 1992), available also at http://www.nhinet.org/unwrit.htm.

3. For a systematic analysis of the differences and intimate interconnections among will, imagination and reason, see Claes G. Ryn, *Will, Imagination and Reason: Babbitt, Croce and the Problem of Reality*, 2d exp. ed. (New Brunswick, NJ: Transaction Publishers, 1997; 1986).

4. Jean-Jacques Rousseau, *First Discourse* in *The Basic Political Writings*, trans. and ed. Donald A. Cress (Indianapolis, IN: Hackett, 1987), 3.

5. Ibid., 38.

6. For an in-depth study of the new Jacobinism and how it relates to more traditional American political thought and culture, see Ryn, *America the Virtuous*.

7. David Frum and Richard Perle, *An End to Evil* (New York: Random House, 2003). As a speechwriter for President George W. Bush, Frum coined the phrase "the axis of evil."

BIBLIOGRAPHY

Frum, David, and Richard Perle. *An End to Evil*. New York: Random House, 2003.

Kendall, Willmoore, and George W. Carey. *The Basic Symbols of the American Political Tradition*. Baton Rouge: Louisiana State University Press, 1970. Reprint, Washington, DC: Catholic University of America Press, 1995.

Kirk, Russell. *The Conservative Constitution*. Washington, DC: Regnery Publishing, 1990.

———. *The Roots of American Order*. LaSalle, IL: Open Court, 1974. Reprint, Wilmington, DE: ISI Books, 2003.

Rousseau, Jean-Jacques. *The Basic Political Writings*. Translated and edited by Donald A. Cress. Indianapolis, IN: Hackett, 1987.

Ryn, Claes G. *America the Virtuous: The Crisis of Democracy and the Quest for Empire*. New Brunswick. NJ: Transaction Publishers, 2003.

———. *Democracy and the Ethical Life,* Baton Rouge: Louisiana State University Press, 1978. Reprint, Washington, DC: Catholic University of America Press, 1990.

———. "Political Philosophy and the Unwritten Constitution." *Modern Age* 34, no. 4 (Summer 1992): 303–9.

———. *Will, Imagination and Reason: Babbitt, Croce and the Problem of Reality*, Chicago. IL: Regnery Publishing, 1986, Reprint, New Brunswick, NJ: Transaction Publishers, 1997.

Part II
Culture and Imagination

When a people agree upon and live in community according to specific conceptions of the good, the true, and the beautiful, they are engaged in the process of creating culture. Important artifacts of a culture include its codes of law, systems of education, works of art and imagination, religious beliefs and practices, philosophical achievements, and methods of governance. Genuine culture develops organically over a long period of time, providing order and stability while making room for change. It is both produced by and shapes a people's history. The people who belong to a genuine culture are also active participants in its creation and maintenance. They are engaged in an enduring process of nurturing, revising, and abandoning cultural beliefs and practices based on the degree to which such things increase or diminish the dignity and purpose of human life. Sham culture, in contrast, consists of elements ranging from the shallow, as in the case of popular culture, to the deliberately dehumanizing, as in the case of various twentieth-century ideologies. Such counterfeit culture is often deliberately designed to amuse, distract, or terrorize a people who grudgingly, or even willingly, accept artificial patterns of living that they have had little or no role in creating. The spectral order it imposes on a people is a thin, unsustainable cover over a deep moral and imaginative disorder.

What ought an individual or a people to do when their vibrant culture deteriorates into a more degrading variety? This question is very much on the minds of both Babbitt and Ryn, especially in the context of American politics and culture. Both of these thinkers are engaged with this concern to some degree or another when thinking and writing about historical consciousness, imagination, and culture. In the section that follows, this humanistic approach to the question of a degraded culture is placed in a conversation with three prominent intellectuals and the similar concerns that they have articulated. Though writing in diverse fields, Russell Kirk, Robert Penn Warren, and Eric Voegelin all share the humanistic emphasis on historical consciousness and its importance in shaping the imagination. The authors of each of the chapters in this section have, in various ways, shown these three thinkers are developing and attempting to respond to the same set of cultural concerns and how, in doing so, we might see their concurrence as well as their challenges to humanism as pointing to possibilities for addressing America's post-constitutional crisis.

Russell Kirk was an intellectual historian, social and political critic, and fiction author who wrote with a rare degree of productivity and stylistic elegance from the immediate aftermath of World War II through the end of the Cold War. Deeply influenced by Babbitt, Kirk encouraged American readers to resist the temptations of ahistorical and dreamy ideologies while he reintroduced them to elements of the American political and cultural tradition that had been neglected or undermined during the first half of the twentieth century. In works such as *The Conservative Mind*, *Edmund Burke: A Genius Reconsidered*, and *The Roots of American Order*, Kirk wanted to appeal to the imagination as much as the reason of the reader, gathering together historical "wholes" that would allow a person to see America and its people in a clearer and better light. In "Russell Kirk and the Romance of Babbittianism," Bradley J. Birzer argues that in such instances, Kirk is, somewhat paradoxically given Babbitt's usage, making *moral* use of romantic imagination. Birzer thus provocatively suggests that there might actually be times when the best responses to political and social deterioration will require the cultivation and use of responsible, historically informed romantic imagination.

Robert Penn Warren is one of the most talented and celebrated of American twentieth-century authors. He remains the only American to win Pulitzer prizes for both poetry and fiction. Like Ryn and Babbitt, Warren is interested in questions of cultural stability and decline. In nonfiction works such as *Democracy and Poetry* and *The Legacy of the Civil War*, Warren articulates the proper role of the artist in a democratic regime and decries the dangers of ideological extremism in politics. In novels such as *All the King's Men* and in works of poetry such as *Brother to Dragons*, Warren blends historical insight with artistic perception and explores the ways in which moral blindness and political corruption in America have done much to diminish the human person as a spiritually and physically integrated whole. His thoughts on these topics resonate in several interesting ways with previously examined ideas from Ryn and Babbitt. In "The Pillars of Hercules: Warren, Babbitt, and the Dangers of Scientific Naturalism," Justin D. Garrison focuses on how Warren and Babbitt come to similar conclusions about the dangers of extending the methods of natural science to theorizing and practicing politics, the former using imagination and the latter using reason. Garrison also explains how both Babbitt and Warren think humanistic reforms of culture and politics suffering from "scientific naturalism" can begin. In the case of Warren's novel, Garrison's chapter also identifies a concrete example of a moral imagination, grounded in a particular culture and historical tradition, at work in a nondidactic manner on the overarching problems of political disorder and renewal.

Out of the three authors treated in this section, Eric Voegelin perhaps had the most explicit encounter with the malignant aspects of the twentieth century. Born in Germany in 1901, Voegelin grew up in Vienna, Austria. He and his wife had to flee that country shortly after it was annexed by Nazi Germany, abandoning a teaching position at the University of Vienna. He eventually accepted a position at Louisiana State University, and he spent most of the rest of his life in the United States. His published works include *The New Science of Politics*; *Science, Politics, and Gnosticism*; and five volumes of a series titled *Order and History*. In "Luminosity, Imagination, Truth: On Voegelin and Ryn," S. F. McGuire explains how Voegelin's overarching philosophical project is related to examining historical instances of order and disorder in an effort to comprehend the order of history itself. Although Voegelin comes to the explicit language of imagination very late in his career, McGuire indicates that something like imagination plays an important role in many of Voegelin's earlier writings. Further, McGuire suggests that Voegelin's turn toward imagination includes attention to its "luminous" aspects, that is, the mysterious ways in which imagination serves as a means by which reality actively discloses its structure to individuals waiting to encounter what existence desires to reveal. Ryn would not reject a notion such as "luminous" imagination. Indeed, McGuire provides evidence of Ryn's awareness of it. Still, McGuire wonders if Ryn might strengthen his understanding of imagination as such by devoting more attention to its luminosity.

CHAPTER THREE

Russell Kirk and the Romance of Babbittianism

Bradley J. Birzer

It would be no exaggeration to claim that Russell Kirk's magnum opus, *The Conservative Mind*, was the sequel to Babbitt's magnum opus, *Democracy and Leadership*, though separated by twenty-nine years in terms of publication. Certainly Babbitt, who passed away in 1933, when Kirk was still in high school, had no idea of how devoted a pupil he would have in the young Michiganian. From his earliest memories, though, Kirk had absorbed the ideas of Babbitt, however indirectly and seemingly by osmosis. Indeed, a veritable sponge when it came to reading and influence, few outside of Kirk's family would shape him as much as did the ideas of Irving Babbitt. It was through his maternal grandfather's wisdom and extensive reading, in particular, that Kirk first encountered—albeit it, rather indirectly—the wisdom of Babbitt. "My family shared all the prejudices of Professor Babbitt," Kirk proudly remembered in 1983, "even though we possessed none of his books."[1]

Kirk would not actually encounter anything direct or tangible from Irving Babbitt until his first year as a student at Michigan State College in Lansing. That first year, Kirk met not only his favorite professor, John Abbott Clark, but he also met a group of men in Lansing dedicated to the humanist ideas of Babbitt and Paul Elmer More. Of those men who happily included the young Kirk in their discussions and company, however, none affected him as much as Clark. He was, Kirk remembered, "the best college teacher of literature this writer ever knew." Indeed, Kirk continued, Clark's "students learned more from his courses in critical writing and in the history of criticism than they got from everything else in their undergraduate years, or from graduate studies."[2] And yet, the administration in East Lansing treated Clark with increasing contempt, Kirk bitterly noted, slowly removing from him the classes he loved and taught so well. Kirk would take great issue with the transformations at Michigan State, much to the university's embarrassment, over the next four decades in his regular column for *National Review*, "From the Academy." When Kirk rather publically resigned from Michigan State in the fall of 1953, it was in no small measure due to the mistreatment of Clark, a series of slights Kirk would never forget.

During his first two years of college, under Clark's tutorship, Kirk devoured all six of Babbitt's books and a significant number of his articles and reviews. The young man even joked with one of his closest friends that he bent his knee at the shrine of Babbitt. "When I read Babbitt," Kirk confessed to a crowd in the early 1980s, "a conscience spoke to a conscience," noting especially, a "strong sympathy of mind and character." Even more than Christopher Dawson and T. S. Eliot, Kirk claimed, Babbitt "influenced me more strongly than has any other writer of the twentieth century." *The Conservative Mind* especially was influenced by "Babbitt, as much as Burke," Kirk admitted. As far as Kirk—as a young man and as an elder scholar—was concerned, Irving Babbitt stood with Socrates, Plato, Cicero, Virgil, Confucius, and Horace as one of the greats of world civilization, "one of the sages of antiquity," Kirk proclaimed.[3] Despite the many disparate Occidental and Oriental cultures from which Babbitt drew, "he is one of the most thoroughly native of American writers," Kirk thought.[4] Babbitt never strove to be the leader of a movement, but he found himself as one, the younger Kirk noted, being duly impressed with such an achievement. No one in the twentieth century within Western civilization, Kirk concluded, better exemplified a mature conservatism than did Babbitt.

WHAT HAS BABBITT TO DO WITH KIRK?

Before getting into the heart of the argument for this chapter, it is worth noting a few things about the Babbitt-Kirk connection. First, and importantly, each man was an American original, a true individualist who generally distrusted individualism. Whether one wants to label each as eccentric or quirky, each was certainly his own man. Though both might seem somewhat stuffy given merely what they wrote and published, each lived life as radically as any moral individual ever has. While Kirk viewed Halloween as the highest holiday of the year (in action, if not always in thought), carried a sword-stick with him across North Africa, and sometimes jumped out from under the bed of a house guest, Babbitt often walked or ran during his Harvard office hours, once lived with a New York street gang, and enjoyed whipping rattlesnakes in circles around his head while ranching in Wyoming. After gleefully noting Babbitt's rather unusual life, Kirk claimed with a straight face (presumably) that few men better represented the virtue of charity and the mores of normalness and humility: "He was such a man as even a great university sees but seldom," Kirk enthused. He was "a scholar suffused with the unbought grace of life, a gentleman who feared neither the oligarch nor the mob. One may agree with him, or not," Kirk conceded, "but it is shabby to refuse him his due admiration." The man himself, after all, "rose superior to such jealousies."[5] That Babbitt resisted the pressure of many of his peers and contemporaries—such as Ernest Hemingway, Dorothy Thompson, H. L. Mencken, Oscar Cargill, James Farrell, Henry Hazlett, Edmund Wilson, and Allen Tate—impressed the stalwart Kirk even more.[6] Indeed, Sinclair Lewis's wife in the 1920s, Dorothy Thompson, who would, by the 1930s, become one of the most famous journalists in the world, once commented that "when she was in the hospital at the time her baby was born," reading an article by a Humanist "was worse than having the baby."[7] The famous literary critic, Edmund Wilson, dismissed More as an "old-fashioned Puritan who has lost the Puritan theology without having lost the Puritan dogmatism."[8] On the surface, even those who seemingly should have allied with Babbitt, such as Albert Jay Nock, opposed him. Nock claimed that the Humanists emphasized human will at the expense of human passion. Additionally, Nock believed, the Humanists gave too much credence to the power of culture and possessed too much faith in a natural aristocracy.[9]

Equally important, or so it seems at several levels, each also had a similar religious upbringing. Though generations had passed since each family had embraced New England Puritanism, Babbitt's immediate family as well as Kirk's immediate family had wrapped themselves in radical and mystical forms of late-nineteenth-century spiritualism. For Kirk, this meant séances, levitations, and visiting with ghosts. Only very slowly did Kirk move away from such an upbringing, though he continued to practice reading tarot cards and defending the presence and existence of ghosts well into his later years. Having grown up with the otherworldly phenomena, Kirk delved deeply into and read extensively in the serious literature about the supernatural and the occult.[10] He also investigated a number of claims in the US and in Europe, and he even contributed to at least one serious work of the occult, Brad Steiger's 1969, *Stranger Powers of ESP*. Though he received no authorial credit on the cover of the book, Kirk wrote chapter 2, "A Note on Ghostly Phenomena in Russell Kirk's Old House at Mecosta, Michigan."[11] A belief in the supernatural, he held, served as a marker for our understanding of faith. In an age of faith, the human person took the supernatural as natural. One saw unusual things, and saints radiated, as represented in the "halo" of art. In an age of scientism, the person and the culture dismissed the supernatural event as ridiculous and religion as a whole as superstitious.[12] But as Kirk put it rather humorously, the haunting and haunted spirits of the world, in turn, "simply ignore rationalists."[13] Regardless, he argued, a mass of anecdotal evidences has sprung forth from almost every era and every culture and religion in human history of the appearance of ghosts, revenants, and poltergeists.[14] To ignore all of this, he argued, served as pure obstinacy. "Have I ever seen a ghost? Why, I am one, and so are you—a geist, a spirit, in a mortal envelope," he wrote in 1979.[15]

In ways unlike Kirk, Babbitt developed a rigorous rationalism and aestheticism. Like Kirk, though, he remained open to the idea of the supernatural in the world of reality. "He had been immersed in childhood in an atmosphere of spiritualism, and had absolutely none of the common inhibitions as to believe in what transcends ordinary experience. He would talk in the most matter-of-fact manner of having seen tables, nay, even pianos, float in the air, and used to laugh away my doubts," an undergraduate friend remembered of Babbitt. He "professed himself so inured to the idea of supernatural apparitions as to be quite prepared to see, any night, without the slightest tremor of surprise, a ghost standing at his bedside."[16] Babbitt's father, Edwin Dwight Babbitt (1828–1905), described by one person as a "crackpot," had peddled bizarre occultism and pseudoscience in a number of works in the nineteenth century.[17] Perhaps most famously, he had authored and self-published *The Principles of Light and Color: Including among Other Things, The Harmonic Laws of the Universe, the Etherio-Atomic Philosophy of Force, Chromo Chemistry, Chromo Therapeutics, and the General Philosophy of the Fine Force, Together with Numerous Discoveries and Practical Applications* in 1878. He followed up this book with a number of New Age titles dealing with the "other world" and the use of light to manipulate the physical world, including *The Wonders of Light and Color* (1879), *Religion as Revealed by the Material and Spiritual Universe* (1881), and *Health and Power* (1893). He had become a spiritualist in 1869 and, in addition to writing and publishing, opened a medical-business practice as a "psychophysician."[18]

Second, as mentioned above, Kirk wrote *The Conservative Mind* as much as anything as a sequel to Babbitt's 1924, *Democracy and Leadership*. As such, Kirk borrowed such terms and phrases as "the flies of summer" and the "moral imagination" and his concepts of "private judgment" and the integration of all elements of society—from Babbitt, even as Babbitt took several of these from thinkers he admired such as Edmund Burke. One of Kirk's later books, 1978's *Decadence and Renewal in Higher Education*, originally suggested to him by T. S. Eliot, also reflected Babbitt's ideas, sometimes exactly.[19]

Third, however, no one should consider Kirk a clone of Babbitt, either. Kirk was no man's clone, though he rather proudly and openly expressed his admiration of those from whom he borrowed and learned. At the same time that Kirk was reading and devouring Babbitt, he was equally attracted to the anarchist Albert Jay Nock and extreme constitutionalist, Isabel Patterson. When it came to the humanists, Kirk, for example, never embraced Asian philosophy and theology to the extent that Babbitt did, and, perhaps connected to this, Kirk remained firmly Occidental in this thought, migrating eventually to Roman Catholicism and always possessing a spontaneous and romantic streak in his life and writings, fiction and nonfiction alike. While Babbitt also grew in appreciation of the Roman Catholic tradition, he also wielded many of the prejudices of the Protestants of his era. "The more the neoclassical movement is studied, the more one whole side of it is seen to be merely the expression in matters artistic and literary of the Jesuitical spirit," Babbitt argued in 1910. "Just as the Jesuits, in order to strengthen and centralize the principle of author, were ready to multiply their minute rulings on moral 'cases' even at the risk of suppressing spontaneity in the religious life and arriving at a pure formalism, so the Aristotelian commentators exercised a centralizing influence on literature and tended to substitute purely formal precepts for spontaneous opinions."[20]

Where Babbitt ended on the question of faith remains a mystery, perhaps a critically vital one when understanding the very history of Babbittian humanism. Toward the end of his life, Babbitt had the following comments and conversation on religion. " ' Oh, god is very great and a man is a worm.' After a silence, I said, 'But the God whom men worship is not just a Will, as in your writings, but a Being, a complete Being, who—' 'Yes, yes,' he broke in with humorous impatience, 'but that is beyond my province as a writer. Why do you keep wishing me to be a theologian? I am merely a critic.' "[21] This is a considerably different end than that experienced by either Paul Elmer More or T. S. Eliot, each of whom had come to a rough form of Christian orthodoxy.

ROMANTICISM AND ITS MYSTERIOUS ORIGINS

As to romanticism, it must be noted that Kirk did not share Babbitt's nearly wholesale condemnation of the movement. "It was in France, in the writings of Rousseau, that certain romantic and naturalistic points of view first found powerful expression," Babbitt had lamented.[22] As the charitable David Hume found out to his chagrin, Jean-Jacques Rousseau was certainly not the equal morally to the manner he had presented himself intellectually. Often referred to as the "insane Socrates" of the French Revolution, Rousseau very much lived in the clouds, "dreaming of systems so perfect that no one will need be good," as Eliot would later put it. In his most famous writing, *Of the Social Contract*, Rousseau contemplated a society in which "each of us puts his person and his full power in common under the supreme direction of the general will; and in a body we receive each member as an indivisible part of the whole."[23] From this primitivism, Babbitt feared, creativity and imagination became something spontaneous and disordered, a mere novelty, rather than something that was universally true, wrapped in the particular.[24]

Kirk certainly had no fondness for Jean Jacques Rousseau—the bête noire of almost all of Babbitt's books—but he found in Edmund Burke not just classicism, Whiggism, and tradition, but the very beginnings of romanticism as well. It's difficult to know exactly where the Romantic movement started, as many conservatives have recognized, though most historians and literary scholars would give the nod to Edmund Burke and his second great work, *A Philosophical Enquiry into the Origin of our Ideas of the Sublime and the Beautiful*. Certainly, from Burke's treatise, much of modern Romantic thought arose, especially in the English-speaking world. Burke's presence is at times implicit, and at times it is blatant in the works of such critical figures as William Wordsworth and Samuel Coleridge; but it can be found throughout most of the romantic poetry and art of the early nineteenth century.[25] As of the first half of the twenty-first century, it is certainly not hard even to imagine Burke's shadow lingering over Beethoven's Sixth Symphony, the Pastoral, for example.

In his own writings on Western civilization, Christian humanist Dawson argued that the rise of Romanticism, whatever its excesses and failings, was as important to Western civilization, as the rediscovery of Hellenic thought in the Renaissance. Whatever its original and essential intent, Romanticism successfully saved Christianity from the utilitarianism and rationalism of the eighteenth century, Dawson continued. In its recovery of medieval Christianity in the early nineteenth century, the Anglo-Welsh Roman Catholic scholar asserted, the Romantics actually discovered "a new kind of beauty."[26] Importantly, Dawson had written this for the Babbittian-influenced journal, *The Criterion*, founded and edited by Eliot. Elsewhere, Dawson developed this theme in his many histories of Europe. In his 1952 book *Understanding Europe*, importantly, he wrote: "The conception of a society which should be the earthly embodiment of the Spirit—a Spirit-created and Spirit-filled organism—was no invention of the Romantics: it was a common possession of the whole Christian past."[27]

Even before Dawson had made this argument, however, Lord Acton had stated this even more bluntly.

> The romantic reaction which began with the invasion of 1794 was the revolt of outraged history. The nation fortified itself against the new ideas by calling up the old, and made the ages of faith and of imagination a defence from the age of reason. Whereas the pagan Renaissance was the artificial resurrection of a world long buried, the romantic Renaissance revived the natural order and restored the broken links from end to end. It inculcated sympathy with what is past, unlovable, indefensible, especially with the age of twilight and scenes favourable to the faculties which the calculators despised. The romantic writers relieved present need with all the abounding treasure of other times, subjecting thereby the will and the conscience of the living to the will and conscience of the dead.[28]

While Kirk did not always appreciate the writings and legacy of Lord Acton—believing him too influenced by abstraction and liberalism—he certainly sounds far closer to Acton than he does to Babbitt on the issue of the origins of romanticism.

Certainly Kirk did not believe that one could take Rousseauvian romanticism without criticism or, perhaps where most needed, even plain rejection, but he also recognized from its earliest origins, one can trace Romanticism's history through the nineteenth century and into the early twentieth century through figures as diverse as Friedrich Nietzsche, G. K. Chesterton, and Willa Cather. Perhaps most importantly for Western culture, however, was its manifestation in the vast mythology of J. R. R. Tolkien and the works of Ray Bradbury, both of which Kirk admired profoundly. Not surprisingly, especially given its origins in the thought of Edmund Burke, Romanticism, properly understood, can be deeply conservative in its praise of ancestors, its idealization of the past, and in its admiration of folk customs as a greater wisdom than any one generation or one person can know. Romanticism is also, when understood from a Catholic perspective, deeply sacramental. Like all good things in this world, it can be perverted to varying degrees, as Babbitt so readily illustrated. Its love of the past and one's ancestry can be unthinkingly reactionary, its love of place can become pantheistic, and its love of the folk can become nationalistic and even at times downright fascistic.

AGREEMENT: LIBERAL EDUCATION

During Russell Kirk's freshman year of college, however, it was Babbitt's first book, *Literature and the American College*, that affected him so deeply.[29] Further, it convinced Kirk that this first book of Babbitt's, originally published in 1908, provided the necessary introduction or preface to all of Babbitt's other works and to his understanding of the philosophy of humanism. "All the rest of Babbitt's books enlarged on this topic," the younger Kirk wrote, noting that perhaps Babbitt's most important work was his first chapter in this first book, titled "What is Humanism?"[30] This influence lasted throughout Kirk's life, and in 1956 and 1986, Kirk had the chance to repay the debt he owed to the book and its author by writing two different introductions to each republished edition. While the 1956 introduction is quite good and revealing, it is a standard-length introduction for a republished book. The 1986 introduction, however, exceeds anything even remotely normal in terms of length. Kirk used it not only to express his admiration for his great hero and exemplar, but he also used it as a means to reintroduce the entire humanist program in education to a new generation. Kirk's introduction, which reflects Kirk's views as much as it does Babbitt's, takes up a full one-third of the book. At the time he wrote this 20,000–plus word introduction, Kirk had retired from writing his regular column on education for *National Review*; but he and his wife, Annette, had become intimately involved in educational issues being reconsidered during President Ronald Reagan's two terms in the White House. The Kirks undoubtedly saw the 1980s as a critical moment in the history of education that, if properly understood and explained, could dramatically shape its future.

As Kirk explained it, Babbitt's humanism rested on the time-tested norm that human beings are "distinct" creatures, neither purely spirit as the angels nor purely material as the animals. As such, they share in both the spiritual (the high) and the material (the low). Further, we know all of this, making us self-aware in the way that other creatures simply are not. Being a creature in "the middle" as it were, we must employ our reason to balance the high, the spiritual, with the low, the material. Reason, Kirk contended, channeling and interpreting Babbitt, served as the bridge connecting individuals and generations. With this argument, both Babbitt and Kirk echo the best teachings of the Roman Republican Cicero.

> A human being, [*sic*] was endowed by the supreme god with a grand status at the time of its creation. It alone of all types and varieties of animate creatures has a share in reason and thought, which all the others lack. What is there, not just in humans, but in all heaven and earth, more divine that reason? When it has matured and come to perfection, it is properly named wisdom . . . [R]eason forms the first bond between human and god.[31]

By embracing reason as the language not only between individuals but across generations, humanity can avoid the three great enemies of the modern and postmodern world: the sentimentalist, the pragmatist, and the leveler. Each exaggerates an aspect of human nature while denying the totality and wholeness of human nature. That is, none of the enemies of humanism lie, but they take a truth and move it beyond context and without limits. By following such a wrongheaded course, each of the enemies of humanism would "reduce human differences to collective mediocrity."[32]

Again, sounding very much like the ancient Stoics and Ciceronians, both Babbitt and Kirk focus not on the rights of the individual, but rather on their duties. It is duties, not rights, which define us and help shape and delimit who and what we are. While Babbitt and Kirk were both champions of action, they each believed that the key to a humane, ordered, and stable society rested on the individual's ability to restrain rather than to act or promote. In this, they proclaimed rather loudly and unpopularly that liberty meant little if it was not the liberty to behave and act virtuously. By narrowing and subdividing, modernity endangered the entire history and essence of human beings.

While individuals and associations within society can do a variety of things and employ a number of means to combat and attenuate these dangerous and fallacious counter-humanistic ideas, the hope for stability lies in Western civilization. The greatest potential institutions for the promotion of humanity, order, and stability, however, are educational. And, not just any education, but a liberal education—one that embraces the arts and the humanities. To combat the rampant egoism of the modern world, a liberal education reminds us what it means to be human, that is, failures, successes, and everything in between, and it combats the very generational ideas—such as those embraced in the 1960s—which result in a tyrannical and chronological snobbery. Never utilitarian, real education is, even without intending it, ethical.

For Babbitt as well as Kirk (and Burke, too), therefore, there is always hope in a society, even if it appears that Western civilization is barely breathing. Humanism, after all, understands that there are truths well beyond the human ability or inability to create or to unmake. These truths exist regardless of human action or inaction. The human being must only remember to reclaim the highest of truths. It is worth closing with the ending Kirk wrote for his highly influential 1955 book, *Academic Freedom*, itself a more modern statement of Babbittian principles.

> To what truths, then, ought the Academy to be dedicated? To the proposition that the end of education is the elevation of reason of the human person, for the human person's own sake. To the proposition that the higher imagination is better than the sensate triumph. To the proposition that the fear of God, and not the mastery over man and nature, is the object of learning. To the proposition that quality is worth more than quantity. To the proposition that justice takes precedence over power. To the proposition that order is more lovable than egoism. To the proposition that to believe all things, if the choice must be made, is nobler than to doubt all things. To the proposition that honor outweighs success. To the proposition that tolerance is wiser than ideology. To the proposition, Socratic and Christian, that the unexamined life is not worth living. If the Academy holds by these propositions, not all the force of Caesar can break down its walls; but if the Academy is bent upon sneering at everything in heaven and earth, or upon reforming itself after the model of the market-place, not all the eloquence of the prophets can save it.[33]

There is only one aspect of the above that is not quite Babbittian. While the views expressed are quite in line with Irving Babbitt, its expression is purely Kirk. Far from classical in its manifestation, it is almost utterly romantic. Kirk may not be tilting at windmills, but he certainly is tilting at ivory towers.

For what it's worth, Babbitt did as well. And, frankly, it's worth quite a bit.

NOTES

1. Russell Kirk, "The Enduring Influence of Irving Babbitt," in George A. Panichas and Claes G. Ryn, eds., *Irving Babbitt in Our Time* (Washington, DC: Catholic University of America Press, 1986), 19. See also Kirk, "Babbitt Read Anew," *National Review* (January 19, 1957), 67.

2. Kirk, "John Abbot Clark, RIP," *National Review* (November 16, 1965), 1018. Kirk dedicated his biography of Edmund Burke (New York: Arlington House,

1967) to Clark. On Clark's decline and death, see Warren Fleischauer to Peter Stanlis, September 18, 1965, in Stanlis Papers, Russell Kirk Center for Cultural Renewal; and Peter Stanlis to Warren Fleischauer, September 23, 1965, in Stanlis Papers, Russell Kirk Center for Cultural Renewal, Mecosta, MI.

3. Kirk, "The Enduring Influence of Irving Babbitt," 20. While this might seem hyperbolic, Kirk was certainly not alone in offering Babbitt such praise. In his book, *Great Humanists* (New York: Abingdon-Cokesbury Press, 1952), Lynn Harold Hough placed Babbitt and More on the level with Aristotle, Cicero, and Erasmus. Equally taken with Babbitt—though voiced in much less "over-the-top" praise—is the extraordinary work of Claes Ryn. See especially his *Will, Imagination, and Reason: Irving Babbitt and the Problem of Reality* (Washington, DC: Regnery Books, 1986); and his masterly and lengthy introduction to Irving Babbitt, *Character and Culture: Essays on East and West* (New Brunswick, NJ: Transaction, 1995).

4. Kirk, *The Conservative Mind*, 366. Though I do not explore the topic of Babbitt and the Orient in this brief chapter, the connection is so important that it must be mentioned, even if only in passing. Not only had Babbitt studied deeply the Hindu and Confucian writings, he found himself quite taken with the writings of the Buddha. The ideas of the Buddha come up in almost all of Babbitt's writings, but they are best found in the posthumously published book, Irving Babbitt, *The Dhammapada* (1936; New York: New Directions, 1965).

5. Russell Kirk, "Introduction" to Irving Babbitt, *Literature and the American College* (Chicago, IL: Regnery, 1956), x.

6. The best collection of opposition to Babbitt is found in C. Hartley Grattan, ed., *The Critique of Humanism: A Symposium* (New York: Brewer and Warren, 1930).

7. Seward Collins to PEM, 17 December 1930, in Box 24, Folder 3, PEM Papers (C0054), Princeton University.

8. Edmund Wilson, "Notes on Babbitt and More," in C. Hartley Grattan, ed., *The Critique of Humanism: A Symposium* (New York: Brewer and Warren, 1930), 59. On the influence of the Humanists, see Austin Warren, "The 'New Humanism' Twenty Years After," *Modern Age* (Winter 1958–59): 81–87.

9. Michael Wreszin, *The Superfluous Anarchist: Albert Jay Nock* (Providence, RI: Brown University Press, 1971), 87.

10. Russell Kirk, "A Cautionary Note on the Ghostly Tale," *The Critic* (April–May 1962): 17. The same essay is reprinted as the conclusion to Kirk, *Surly Sullen Bell* (Fleet, 1962), 231–40. Kirk employed the same title for the introduction to his 1984 collection, *Watchers at the Strait Gate* (Sauk City, WI: Arkham House, 1984),

ix–xiv. By 1984, however, Kirk had radically altered this piece. While the themes remain similar, the examples used to illustrate his points are quite different. Vigen Guroian's edited collection, Kirk, *Ancestral Shadows: An Anthology of Ghostly Tales* (Eerdmans, 2004), 402–6, reprints the 1984 version. Also important is Kirk, "Prologue," to *The Princess of All Lands* (Sauk City, WI: Arkham House, 1979), vii–viii; as well as his "The Canon of the Ghostly Tales," introduction to Canon Basil A. Smith, *The Scallion Stone* (Chapel Hill, NC: Whispers Press, 1980), xi–xv.

11. Kirk, "A Note on Ghostly Phenomena in Russell Kirk's Old House at Mecosta, Michigan," in Brad Steiger, *Strange Power of ESP* (New York: Belmont Books, 1969), 20–27. A note on page 20 reads: "This chapter was written for this book by Russell Kirk." I am indebted to Mr. Steiger for sharing his views on Kirk via correspondence. Kirk even started to explore the veracity of UFO sightings in the 1960s. See Kirk, "The Unexpected Visitors," To the Point column, *Ada Evening News* (April 5, 1966), 4.

12. Kirk, "A Cautionary Note," 17. See also, Kirk's 1954 book, *St. Andrews*. It should be noted, Kirk especially disliked the literary genre of science fiction, seeing it, in general, as banal and meaningless," a superficial mirroring of the works of H. G. Wells. This is surprising, given how thoughtful writers such as Walter Miller, James Blish, or Kingsley Amis could be, and how much in line they would be with Kirk's own understanding of the world. The best science fiction, to Kirk's mind, was that of Ray Bradbury and C. S. Lewis, the kind that is far more fantasy set in space, rather than what might be termed hard science fiction. These are, essentially, what literary critic and biographer Joseph Pearce would call "theological thrillers."

13. Kirk, "Racketing Spirits," *Ada Evening News* (February 13, 1966), 4.

14. Kirk, "A Cautionary Note," 18.

15. Kirk, "Prologue," to *The Princess of All Lands*, viii.

16. Giese, "IB, Undergraduate," *American Review*, 74.

17. "Crackpot" taken from Milton Hindus, *Essays: Personal and Impersonal* (Santa Rosa, CA: Black Sparrow Press, 1988), 108–9.

18. See entry, "Edwin Dwight Babbitt," in *Ohio Authors*, 22–23.

19. Kirk admitted the connection between Decadence and Renewal to Babbitt's humanism in Kirk, "The Enduring Influence," 22.

20. Irving Babbitt, *The New Laokoon* (Boston, MA: Houghton Mifflin, 1910), 7.

21. G. R. Elliott, "Irving Babbitt as I Knew Him," *American Review* 8 (1936–1937): 59–60.

22. Babbitt, *New Laokoon*, xii. Babbitt's most complete expression of his thoughts on Rousseau can be found in what is arguably his best book, *Rousseau and Romanticism* (Boston, MA: Houghton Mifflin, 1919), but especially chapter 5. See also, Babbitt, *The Masters of Modern French Criticism* (1912; New York: Farrar, Straus and Company, 1963), 352–53.

23. Jean-Jacques Rousseau, *The Social Contract and Other Later Political Writings*, ed. by Victor Gourevitch (New York: Cambridge University Press, 1997), 50.

24. Babbitt, *On Being Creative*, 5.

25. Kirk addressed the connection of Burke to the Romantics in his 1967 biography, *Edmund Burke: A Genius Reconsidered* (1967; Wilmington, DE: ISI Books, 1997), 9, 21, 155, 167–69. See also the works of Owen Barfield, but, especially, Barfield, *What Coleridge Thought* (Middletown, CT: Wesleyan University Press, 1971); and Barfield, *Romanticism Comes of Age: Essays on the Creative Imagination* (Oxford, UK: Barfield Press, 2012), pp. 209–10. To be fair, Babbitt recognized that there was much more to Wordsworth than a primitive Rousseauvianism. See Babbitt, *Rousseau and Romanticism*, xvii; and Babbitt, "The Primitivism of Wordsworth," in *On Being Creative* (Boston, MA: Houghton Mifflin, 1932), chapter 2.

26. Christopher Dawson, "The Origins of the Romantic Tradition," *The Criterion* 11 (1932): 223. See also, Dawson, "Religion and Romanticism," *Christendom* 1 (Summer 1936): 577–92; Dawson, *Understanding Europe* (New York: Sheed and Ward, 1952), 201–2; and Dawson, *The Gods of Revolution* (New York: New York University Press, 1972), 129–45.

27. Dawson, *Understanding Europe*, 201.

28. Lord Acton, "German Schools of History," in *Essays in the Study and Writing of History*, ed. by J. Rufus Fears (Indianapolis, IN: Liberty Fund, 1986), 326–27. See also, Tim Blanning, *The Romantic Revolution: A History* (New York: Modern Library, 2012), 126–27.

29. Kirk, "Enduring Influence," 20.

30. Kirk, "Introduction," to *Literature and the American College* (1956), xi.

31. Cicero, "On the Laws," in *On the Commonwealth and On the Laws*, edited and translated by James E. G. Zetzel (New York: Cambridge University Press),113.

32. Kirk, "Introduction" to Babbitt, *Literature and the American College* (1986), 7.

33. Kirk, *Academic Freedom* (Chicago, IL: Regnery, 1955), 190–91.

BIBLIOGRAPHY

Acton, Lord. "German Schools of History." *Essays in the Study and Writing of History*, ed. J. Rufus Fears. Indianapolis, IN: Liberty Fund, 1986.

Babbitt, Irving. *The Dhammapada*. New York: Oxford University Press, 1936. Reprint, New York: New Directions, 1965.

———. *Literature and the American College*. Chicago, IL: Regnery Publishers, 1956.

———. *The Masters of Modern French Criticism*. New York: Houghton Mifflin Company, 1912. Reprint, New York: Farrar, Straus, and Company, 1963.

———. *The New Laokoon*. Boston, MA: Houghton Mifflin, 1910.

———. *On Being Creative*. Boston, MA: Houghton Mifflin, 1932.

———. *Rousseau and Romanticism*. Boston, MA: Houghton Mifflin, 1919.

Barfield, Owen. *Romanticism Comes of Age: Essays on the Creative Imagination*. 3d ed. Oxford: Barfield Press, 2012.

———. *What Coleridge Thought*. Middletown, CT: Wesleyan University Press, 1971.

Blanning, Tim. *The Romantic Revolution: A History*. New York: Modern Library, 2012.

Cicero, Marcus Tullius. "On the Laws," in *On the Commonwealth and On the Laws*. Edited and translated by James E. G. Zetzel. New York: Cambridge University Press, 1999.

Coyle, William. "Edwin Dwight Babbitt," in *Ohio Authors and Their Books*. Cleveland, OH: World Publishing Company, 1962.

The Critique of Humanism: A Symposium. Edited by C. Hartley Grattan. New York: Brewer and Warren, 1930.

Dawson, Christopher. *The Gods of Revolution* (New York: New York University Press, 1972), 129–45.

———. "The Origins of the Romantic Tradition," *Criterion* 11, no. 43 (January 1932): 222–48.

———. "Religion and Romanticism," *Christendom* 1 (Summer 1936): 577–92.

———. *Understanding Europe*. New York: Sheed and Ward, 1952.

Elliott, G. R. "Irving Babbitt as I Knew Him." *American Review* 8 (1936–1937): 36–60.

Giese, W. F. "Irving Babbitt, Undergraduate," *American Review* 6 (1935): 65–94.

Hindus, Milton. *Essays: Personal and Impersonal*. Santa Rosa, CA: Black Sparrow Press, 1988.

Hough, Lynn Harold. *Great Humanists*. New York: Abingdon-Cokesbury Press, 1952.
Kirk, Russell. *Academic Freedom*. Chicago, IL: Regnery, 1955.
———. *Ancestral Shadows: An Anthology of Ghostly Tales*. Edited by Vigen Guroian. Grand Rapids, MI: Eerdmans Publishing Company, 2004.
———. "Babbitt Read Anew." *National Review*, January 19, 1957.
———. "The Canon of the Ghostly Tales." Introduction to *The Scallion Stone*, by Canon Basil A. Smith. Chapel Hill, NC: Whispers Press, 1980.
———. *The Conservative Mind*. Chicago, IL: Regnery, 1953.
———. "A Cautionary Note on the Ghostly Tale." *The Critic* (April–May 1962): 17–19.
———. "John Abbot Clark, RIP." *National Review*, November 16, 1965.
———. *Edmund Burke: A Genius Reconsidered*. New Rochelle, NY: Arlington House, 1967. Reprint, Wilmington, DE: ISI Books, 1997.
———. "The Enduring Influence of Irving Babbitt," in *Irving Babbitt in Our Time*. Edited by George A. Panichas and Claes G. Ryn. Washington, DC: Catholic University of America Press.
———. Introduction to *Literature and the American College*, by Irving Babbitt. Chicago, IL: Regnery, 1986.
———. "A Note on Ghostly Phenomena in Russell Kirk's Old House at Mecosta, Michigan," in *Strange Power of ESP* by Brad Steiger. New York: Belmont Books, 1969.
———. Prologue to *The Princess of All Lands*. Sauk City, WI: Arkham House, 1979.
———. "Racketing Spirits." *Ada Evening News*, February 13, 1966.
———. *St. Andrews*. London: Batsford, 1954.
———. *Surly Sullen Bell*. New York: Fleet Publishing, 1962.
———. "The Unexpected Visitors." *Ada Evening News*, April 5, 1966.
———. *Watchers at the Strait Gate*. Sauk City, WI: Arkham House, 1984.
Peter Stanlis to Warren Fleischauer, September 23, 1965, in Stanlis Papers, Russell Kirk Center for Cultural Renewal, Mecosta, MI.
Rousseau, Jean-Jacques. *The Social Contract and Other Later Political Writings*. Edited by Victor Gourevitch. New York: Cambridge University Press, 1997.
Ryn, Claes G. *Will, Imagination, and Reason: Irving Babbitt and the Problem of Reality*. Washington, DC: Regnery Publishing, 1986.
———. Introduction to *Character and Culture: Essays on East and West*, by Irving Babbitt. New Brunswick, NJ: Transaction, 1995.

Seward Collins to PEM, 17 December 1930, in Box 24, Folder 3, PEM Papers (C0054), Princeton University.

Warren, Austin. "The 'New Humanism' Twenty Years After." *Modern Age* 3, no. 1 (Winter 1958–59): 81–87.

Warren Fleischauer to Peter Stanlis, September 18, 1965, in Stanlis Papers, Russell Kirk Center for Cultural Renewal, Mecosta, MI.

Wilson, Edmund. "Notes on Babbitt and More," in *The Critique of Humanism: A Symposium*. Edited by C. Hartley Grattan. New York: Brewer and Warren, 1930.

Wreszin, Michael. *The Superfluous Anarchist: Albert Jay Nock*. Providence, RI: Brown University Press, 1971.

CHAPTER FOUR

The Pillars of Hercules

Babbitt, Warren, and the Dangers of Scientific Naturalism

Justin D. Garrison

> There are two laws discrete,
> Not reconciled,—
> Law for man, and law for thing;
> The last builds town and fleet,
> But it runs wild,
> And doth the man unking.[1]
> —Ralph Waldo Emerson

On the 1620 title page to Francis Bacon's *New Organon*, one can see a ship sailing through the Strait of Gibraltar, the ancient Pillars of Hercules, into an undiscovered country. Below the ship is a Latin motto, taken from the Book of Daniel, which reads, "Multi pertransibunt et augebitur scientia" or "Many shall run to and fro, and knowledge shall increase." In its original context, these words are part of an admonition to Daniel to keep secret what has been revealed to him about the coming end of the world. Bacon takes these words as a divine invitation extended to him and all other human beings to commence just the type of revolutionary scientific mission he describes in *New Organon*. Developing a new method of natural science and a corresponding new way of seeing the world are the crucial steps humanity must take if it is to sail past the Pillars and experience unprecedented levels of happiness, peace, and progress in material well-being. The title page represents well Bacon's zeal for a new science. This image also captures the widespread disposition toward science and progress held by many Americans.

REPRESENTATIVE AMERICAN VIEWS OF SCIENCE

Michio Kaku is a professor of theoretical physics at City College of New York, but he is perhaps best known as a prominent public intellectual generating enthusiasm for science. An author of many best-selling books, he regularly delivers public lectures to audiences eager to hear about life-changing scientific advances just around the corner. In his 2011 *Physics of the Future*, Kaku predicts a wide range of developments that should take place in the next century. To mention just a few of these wonders, a space elevator and "outposts on Mars and perhaps the asteroid belt" are possible.[2] Genetic research might produce "designer children."[3] Robots and nanotechnology will revolutionize health care. Computers should provide affordable four-wall screens, turning an empty room into a place where families separated by thousands of miles can congregate in 3D.[4] Borrowing from the imagination of Gene Roddenberry, creator of *Star Trek*, Kaku explains universal translators and molecular replication systems—he calls the latter a "holy grail"—are likely on the horizon.[5] Scientific progress will also make breathtaking contributions to politics, economics, and the cause of peace among all people. He sees human beings moving harmoniously toward a world more or less united in a common language, technological framework, economic system, and culture. Reflecting on the implications for human life of some of his predictions, Kaku writes, "Some futurists have commented that the future might look like something out of a fairy tale. If we have the power of the gods, then the heaven we inhabit will look like a fantasy world."[6]

Kaku's book was published during Barack Obama's first presidential term. Obama regularly invited talented schoolchildren to a White House science fair. At these events, he praised the students, stating on one occasion, "You teach us about the power of reason and logic, and trying things and figuring out whether they work ... you remind us that, together, through science, we can tackle some of the biggest challenges that we face."[7] Obama often sought to place their achievements within broader historical and policy contexts. In one speech, he drew attention to the legacies of scientific interest and discovery left by Americans such as Benjamin Franklin and Thomas Jefferson. In another, he explained, "the United States has always been a place that loves science ... It's in our DNA."[8] For him, the future of American scientific discovery would surpass its past. Children in his audience and others like them around the country would be the ones to make breakthroughs in cancer research, environmental sustainability, and technologies capable of generating political transformations around the world. Securing this future demanded a substantial federal presence as well as public-private financial investment, especially in science and technology education. Concluding one speech, he said, "We are counting on all of you to help build a brighter future, and for you to use your talents to help your communities and your country and the world. We will be with you every step of the way."[9]

In their representative remarks, Kaku and Obama are dazzled by the scientific progress the world has experienced, especially in the last century. Life expectancy and standards of health are higher now than they have ever been. Transportation is easier, cheaper, and more accessible than in past centuries and decades. Technology has created unprecedented degrees of global connectedness. Neither Kaku nor Obama is merely interested in the products of scientific thought. They celebrate the *way* science is conducted, how it sees the world as a whole. Science is successful because it uses abstract logic and empirical observation to test hypotheses about and develop knowledge of the material world. Modern science does not start from antiquated philosophical or theological premises. Rather, it emerges historically as a response to the inadequacies of such ideas to explain the natural world. For both of these men, and for countless other political figures, academics, and ordinary Americans, the fruits of modern scientific research recommend the broad, perhaps exclusive, application of its method of inquiry to many areas of life, including the study of politics and the human person.

CONCERNS ABOUT SCIENCE CONSENSUS IN AMERICAN LITERATURE AND PHILOSOPHY

The ways in which scientific thought and imagery have come to capture the minds of many Americans has left some with reasons for concern. Two such people are Irving Babbitt and Robert Penn Warren. A turn-of-the-century professor of comparative literature and pioneer of the American New Humanism movement, Babbitt is best known for his works of literary criticism, especially *Rousseau & Romanticism*, as well as his thoughts on modern politics and culture such as those found in *Democracy and Leadership*. Like Kaku and Obama, the Americans of Babbitt's day celebrated scientific progress and its alleged potential to make the world a better, more ethical place. About such expressions of unqualified scientific optimism he writes, "Physical science is excellent in its own place, but when supreme moral issues are involved, it is, as has been rightly remarked, only a multiplying device." Here Babbitt is engaged in concrete observation and reflection, not abstract speculation. About the then recently concluded First World War, he explains, "A gross and palpable error of the era that is just closing has been its confusion of mechanical and material progress with moral progress."[10] For him, to extend science beyond its natural limits is to embrace what he calls scientific naturalism.

A Pulitzer Prize–winning poet and fiction author, Warren is perhaps best known for his 1946 novel *All the King's Men*. For those unfamiliar with the text, offering a brief sense of its main characters and their interactions will be helpful. Warren tells a story in which Willie Stark rises from poverty to become governor and almost absolute ruler over an unnamed state. Jack Burden, Willie's aid and the novel's narrator, plays an important role in Willie's political career. Jack does the research Willie needs to strong-arm those who stand between him and his political aspirations. Adam Stanton, Jack's childhood friend, is a highly successful medical doctor who abhors politics. Nevertheless, Willie is able to draw Adam into participating in his grand hospital building project. The relationship among these characters is tense and comes to a violent conclusion toward the end of novel. In an introduction to a later edition of the text, Warren reflects on his review of an early, dramatized version of his story, stating, "another theme had crept in—the theme of the relation of science (or pseudo-science) and political power, the theme of the relation of the science-society and the power-state, the problem of naturalistic determinism and responsibility, etc."[11] When read through this lens, it is striking how often Willie, Jack, and Adam defend their actions and express ideas about politics and human nature in scientific and pseudo-scientific arguments, analogies, and images. In the novel, Warren echoes Babbitt's concerns about the dangers as well as the benefits of modern science.

Both Babbitt and Warren distinguish between genuine modern science, on the one hand, and what, on the other hand, they variously call pseudo-science, scientific naturalism, and naturalistic determinism. In this chapter, the latter three terms will be used interchangeably. To analyze their support for authentic science and their critiques of pseudo-scientific thought, especially as applied to politics and understandings of the human person, a broader examination of Warren's novel and Babbitt's thought is needed. Since *All the King's Men* is a work of the imagination and not reason, the latent philosophical concepts within it must be drawn out with reference to appropriate thinkers. Selected ideas from Francis Bacon and Thomas Hobbes will be used to meet this need. Beyond illuminating the nature and dangers of scientific naturalism, this chapter will also provide some sense of how Babbitt and Warren think it possible to overcome the challenges pseudo-science presents to individuals and societies without attempting something as drastic and self-defeating as abandoning modern science. Their diagnoses of and remedies for scientific naturalism may be especially important to the contemporary United States.

WARREN, BABBITT, SCIENCE, AND PSEUDO-SCIENCE

Jack captures the essence of Adam's personality when he states, "[Adam] is a scientist, and everything is tidy for him, and one molecule of oxygen always behaves the same way when it gets around two molecules of hydrogen, and a thing is always what it is."[12] His devotion to scientific learning and the practice of medicine has admirable components. Adam is a highly skilled doctor. He regularly performs surgery and frequently undercharges his patients when they give him hints of financial hardship, no matter how vague. He also teaches at the state's most prestigious medical school, conducts impressive research, and speaks at conferences around the world. Despite the potential to turn his career into a means for acquiring wealth and increased social standing, Adam lives simply and alone.

Two scenes from the novel capture an interesting tension in the scientific outlook embodied by Adam. Toward the end of the novel, Willie's son Tom suffers a terrible spinal injury during a football game. Willie immediately turns to Adam for help. Adam devotes much time to Tom's case, calling in an expert for a second opinion, but the outlook is bleak. Tom is paralyzed. If the spinal cord is crushed, the paralysis will be permanent; if it is obstructed by a broken bone, relieving that pressure through surgery might return to Tom some or all of his mobility. Adam does not give Willie false hope. About the surgery itself, Adam explains, "I want you to know that it is radical. That it is the outside chance. It is a gambler's chance."[13] Willie bets it all on the surgery, and the results are staggering. The spinal cord is crushed, and Tom is permanently paralyzed. There are limits to what a person with Adam's scientific abilities can accomplish, and Adam knows this to be true. There is a sense of medical humility in this moment.

Nowhere in the novel is Adam's mastery of medicine on more vivid display than in a scene where he gives a patient a lobectomy, removing portions "of the frontal lobe of the brain." As he tells Jack, he decides on this surgery for a person suffering from "catatonic schizophrenia" in the hopes that the procedure will alleviate the patient's suffering. Adam explains, "after we are through with him he will be different. He will be relaxed and cheerful and friendly.... He will be perfectly happy." When Jack quips that everyone should undergo the procedure if perfect happiness is the result, Adam says, "there have been cases—not mine, thank God—where the patient didn't become cheerfully extroverted but became completely and cheerfully amoral."[14] Unlike the scene of Tom's back surgery, here Adam exhibits an intriguing mixture of humility and pride about the powers of medical science. This procedure still has risks, Adam admits, but the accent in his description is on the ways in which science can serve human beings by making them happy, a happiness brought about, in this case, by surgical means.

In a number of Adam's attitudes regarding the power and purpose of science, Warren has given imaginative expression to a number of ideas and concerns philosophically articulated by one of the most prominent figures in the emergence of a new scientific method and corresponding worldview, Francis Bacon. Bacon admired the dynamism of the "mechanical arts," and he was pleased to see the happiness and comfort produced by technologies such as gunpowder, the magnetic compass, and the printing press.[15] By comparison, he was deeply disappointed in the lack of impressive discoveries made by the natural sciences. The authority of investigative methods derived from Antiquity and the Middle Ages bred complacency and factional disputes. The anti-intellectual zeal of religious movements such as Puritanism discouraged as impious the type of inquiry Bacon desired to make. In his mind, there was no way to build from such foundations. In *New Organon*, he writes, "We declare that the inept models of the world ... which men's fancies have constructed in philosophies, have to be smashed."[16] For Bacon, a reliable and accurate method for investigating the natural world needed to be developed because it alone was capable of producing more impressive and more frequent technological and scientific progress. Only a clean and total break with the past would create the conditions for such a venture.

In many instances, Bacon celebrates the power to subjugate nature that is within the grasp of human beings if they endeavor to follow him and develop a new scientific method. He encourages others to join him as "true sons of the sciences ... so that we may pass the antechambers of nature which innumerable others have trod, and eventually open up access to the inner rooms."[17] At times, he is aware that his vision might be dangerous. He offers prayers that the new science he seeks will not permit "unbelief in the face of the mysteries of God" to "arise in our hearts."[18] Worried about how others, especially those in authority, might interpret his project, Bacon claims his desire to liberate the natural sciences from the past has only a superficial resemblance to the efforts of those who wish to liberate people from belief in God. He stresses that those who conduct true scientific research must do so only "for the uses and benefits of life, and to improve and conduct it in charity." "Charity knows no bound," Bacon argues, and the children of science are obligated to serve humanity by contributing to "human progress and empowerment."[19]

To bring into further theoretical clarity what Warren intuits in the novel, Babbitt's understanding of human nature and his analysis of the advent of modern natural science need to be explained. Babbitt refers often to Emerson's distinction between the "law for man" and "law for thing," because he thinks it captures poetically something that is universally true about the nature of human life. The latter is what Babbitt calls the "natural law."[20] For him this is the overarching concept that encompasses the research methods, experiments, discoveries, and inventions associated with fields such as physics, chemistry, and biology. The former is what he calls the "human law." The human law is the accumulated wisdom about human nature and the moral life discovered and expounded by figures including Confucius, the Buddha, Jesus of Nazareth, and Aristotle. Drawing from these and many other religious and humanistic sources, Babbitt believes the human law teaches the individual is a divided being. Moral and immoral impulses compete in the soul of each person to be translated into action. Every individual is obligated to act on his or her ethical knowledge and intuitions while restraining their opposites. To do this is to exercise what Babbitt calls in different places the "inner check," the "will to refrain," or "ethical will."

The character of the natural law is to expand human mastery over the natural world, and it is this law that makes significant contributions to a person's material satisfaction. In contrast, the human law is guided by principles such as concentration, selection, and decorum. When followed, this law gradually gives the individual ethical self-mastery and makes for peace in civil society. Fidelity to the human law is the key to happiness for individuals and nations. For Babbitt, like Emerson, these laws are complimentary but distinct. Being attuned to and working according to both laws is important. While it is true that understanding of the human law has been reached in different historical periods and geographical regions by means of what is often called revelation, Babbitt stresses that knowledge of both laws, natural and human, has been and can be experientially derived. In other words, the reality of the human law can be known with or without the intervention of the supernatural. With Babbitt's understanding of the two laws in mind, his evaluation of the modern scientific project will make more sense.

Babbitt writes at length in many of his works about the origins and influence of modern science on how human beings understand the natural world, politics, and themselves. Like Warren, Babbitt is no Luddite. He finds much to admire in various scientific fields, and he acknowledges a number of important scientific discoveries and technological inventions. He is sympathetic to the way modern science emerged as a response to a demand for a critical foundation for acquiring knowledge of the natural world—one that did not depend on credulous assent to mistaken ancient and medieval claims backed by a declining religious authority. Babbitt often refers to Bacon, seeing him as a central figure in the creation of modern natural science. Bacon made no scientific discoveries of his own, but his success in inspiring others to undertake his type of project has been tremendous. Calling Bacon a "prophet of the kingdom of man," Babbitt writes, "[Bacon] was, in short, one of those rare beings over whom brooded almost visibly the 'prophetic soul of the wide world dreaming on things to come.' "[21]

Babbitt has a number of concerns about Bacon and his followers. Although Bacon occasionally stresses the compatibility between traditional ideas and the new science, the imaginative wonder and concrete results of the new science he champions have left many to view its methods of investigation as the only means by which knowledge of any kind can be obtained. Even Bacon seems drawn to this possibility, admitting that his desire to put natural science on an entirely new and productive methodological foundation could extend to other fields of study including, "Logic, Ethics and Politics."[22] Such a comprehensive reorientation requires new meanings to be given to various images and concepts. Bacon and others often use the word progress, but by it they usually mean advances in technological invention and standards of material comfort. Scientists who provide this type of progress are described as performing acts of charity or service. The appropriate scale of charity is reimagined as global, focusing on developing systematic programs for uplifting the human race as a whole. In his words and deeds, Warren's Adam Stanton holds many if not all of these views. For all the benefits of modern science, Babbitt sees notions such as these reflecting "a weakening of the idea of a law for human nature as something distinct from the law for physical nature."[23] For Babbitt and Warren, this signifies the movement from science to pseudo-science.

WARREN, BABBITT, PSEUDO-SCIENCE, AND POLITICS

The seemingly modest problems of the entanglement of science and scientific naturalism already on display in Adam and Bacon are amplified when these notions are brought to bear more directly on political thought and practice. Like other doctors, Adam experiments, collaborates, and discovers objective truths about the body, applying his medical knowledge to the alleviation of human suffering. It should not be surprising that Adam's scientific relationship to the world would shape his understanding of politics. In a snide but accurate description of Adam's view of politics, Jack explains, "he has lived all his life in the idea that there was a time a long time back when everything was run by high-minded, handsome men ... who sat around a table and candidly debated the good of the public thing."[24] Jack attributes this attitude to Adam's romanticism, but there is also strong and overlooked connection between such a view and science. For Adam, politics should mirror the practice of medicine. Politics should be conducted by individuals inspired by a duty to serve the interests of all while dispassionately searching for the best way to accomplish this overarching goal in each circumstance. There is no room in politics for competing truths to find expression, prompt discussion, and possibly facilitate compromise. People who have interests other than service and discovering of the truth have no business in politics and should not be taken into consideration. For Adam, politics should be altruistic and tensionless.

Francis Bacon has a similar understanding of the influence a new scientific method should exert on politics. One of the problems he sees with politics as traditionally conceived is that it is a local affair. Whatever benefits a government may bestow are limited in scope and duration. There is also a high degree of variation in the forms and ends of politics. If the new science can produce systematic and rapid progress in its traditional areas of concern, the extension of that method to the study and practice of politics should yield similar results. Politics should combine with the new science because the latter holds the possibility of conferring permanent advantages on all human beings, including a template for the true form of government along with material progress, comfort, and happiness. This understanding of the needed synthesis of politics and science is given a potent expression in Bacon's *New Atlantis*.

In this posthumously published utopian tract, sailors happen upon the island of Bensalem. The people of the island are equal, moral, religious, chaste, and technologically advanced. The government of the island supports the research activities of Salomon's House, an institution of priestly scientists that operates much like an ideal (though not real) modern research university. Those belonging to Salomon's House are the ones who make the island's impressive and perpetual scientific progress; they wield the true power on Bensalem. Many examples of their scientific progress are given, and improvements in human health, especially in the areas of curing diseases and prolonging life, receive repeated attention. About their overarching goal, the Father of Salomon's House explains, "The end of our foundation is . . . the enlarging of the bounds of human empire, to the effecting of all things possible."[25] Increasing their dominion over nature is the purpose of this fictitious society. No one disagrees with the appropriateness of this end, and there is no conflict over who should pursue this objective and by what means. For Bacon, like Adam, scientific politics should be a collective humanitarian project.

Willie Stark is the character most interested in bringing politics into line with the commitments to service and rationality found in the ideas of Adam and Bacon. As a county treasurer, he wants to take the best bid for a school building project, even if that decision is unpopular. In his first run for state governor, he gives speeches filled with detailed accounts of the State's fiscal and administrative challenges while offering meticulous policy proposals for tax, regulatory, infrastructure, and bureaucratic reforms. These pursuits end in disaster and embarrassment. After a vile smear campaign, Willie is voted out as county treasurer and a bid from a shady contractor with deep political connections is accepted. Willie's campaign speeches are uninspiring. About his inability to connect with the voters he tells Jack, "They don't care. God damn 'em. They deserve to grabble in the dirt and get nothing for it but a dry gut-rumble. They won't listen."[26] His frustrations grow when learns he was recruited to run for governor by one faction in the state to split the vote of a competing faction. In the face of rank popular stupidity and establishment deception, Willie becomes increasingly bitter toward the people he wants to help.

Adam already believes real campaigns, elections, and legislative action are irredeemably corrupt, and he mostly avoids politics all together. Willie comes to agree with Adam about the dishonest nature of politics. Through rough experiences he has learned people will never trade diversion for progress presented in a social science lecture, even if it would be to their advantage. Rather than withdraw from political life, Willie continues to pursue power, eventually becoming governor of the state. He resorts to bribery, blackmail, and intimidation tactics to secure votes and to defuse political scandals that threaten his authority. He uses such means not only to maintain and grow his power, but also to promote a number of his older legislative desires along with new goals of a similar type. Willie defends his practices by invoking scientific and other deterministic imagery. Discussing his opponents' complaints about his corrupt practices, Willie acknowledges his use of immoral means to pursue his ends, stating, "sure, there's some graft, but there's just enough to make the wheels turn without squeaking. . . . There never was a machine rigged up by man didn't represent some loss of energy."[27] Dishonestly is explained away with an analogy to mechanical inefficiency, and most of his admirers seem content with his justification.

Willie shares the essence of his political success at different times with Jack and Adam. In a conversation with Jack, Willie explains that he used to think about politics and leadership in terms of the exemplary characters and accomplishments of past figures he learned about as part of his self-education. Willie's actual experience of politics has made him wiser. About the person who wrote one of his high-minded textbooks, he says, "He didn't know a thing. I bet things were just like they are now. A lot of folks wrassling round."[28] When Willie invites Adam to join his hospital project, Adam is reluctant to associate with such a morally compromised leader. To help Adam overcome his prudishness, and to justify his actions, Willie tells Adam, "When your great-great-grandpappy climbed down out of the tree, he didn't have any more notion of good or bad, or right and wrong, than the hoot owl that stayed up in the tree." Willie has learned societies are not organized by commitments to timeless truths. They live by values they improvise to give their desires a veneer of moral support. As society's needs change, so too does its values.[29] The secret of Willie's political success is his discovery that the only truth about the world is that there is no truth. In the character of Willie, a lingering interest in serving others is combined with misanthropy and a strong desire of power.

In rejecting as unreliable past views of politics and morality, in interpreting his personal experience of politics as universal and authoritative, and in reducing politics to the pursuit of the power to impose one's will while providing society with order and comfort, Willie has much in common with the scientific politics of Thomas Hobbes. Hobbes served briefly as a secretary to Francis Bacon, and he was deeply interested in the scientific developments of his time, especially in the field of mathematics. Like Bacon, Hobbes finds appealing the ability of the sciences to settle disputes and command assent on the basis of logical theories proven through abstract reasoning or the observation and interpretation of clear sensory evidence. Whereas Bacon holds past accomplishments in the natural sciences in contempt, Hobbes rejects them along with traditional ideas about human nature, morality, and politics. For Hobbes, past philosophers simply had no clue what they were doing. Specifically about the inability of philosophers to state clearly the meanings of their various terms, in *Leviathan* Hobbes writes, "For there is not one of them that begins his ratiocination from the definitions, or explications of the names they are to use; which is a method that hath been used only in geometry, whose conclusions have thereby been made indisputable."[30] Hobbes believes he can develop a science of politics as objectively accurate and compelling as Euclidean geometry.

Unlike Bacon, Hobbes's presentation of a new political science has no trace of utopian visions of progress. His observations of people as they are, not as how ancient and Christian theories imagine them to be, leads him to pessimistic conclusions about politics. For Hobbes, people are naturally driven by passions, not reason; reason is reduced to calculating the best means to achieve desires. In the state of nature, there are no objective meanings for words such as just and unjust, good and evil, because those and similar words merely signify objects and experiences of pleasure and pain. Since individual tastes in these areas vary, all values are subjective. It is the combination of total freedom, unrestrained desire for power, and moral relativism that makes the state of nature violent and warlike. He writes, "during the time men live without a common power to keep them all in awe, they are in that condition which is called war, and such a war as is of every man against every man." In such a state, there are no possibilities for acquiring and enjoying material objects. There are no opportunities for peace. Without an all-powerful sovereign, human life is "solitary, poor, nasty, brutish, and short."[31]

Hobbes describes the sovereign as the "great Leviathan ... that *Mortal God*."[32] The Leviathan is an artificial creation of human beings analogized to the mechanical unity of the human body. "Sovereignty" is an "artificial soul," advisors and other officials are "memory," "sedition" is "sickness," "civil war" is "death," and so on.[33] Construction of the sovereign is complete when a people consent to exit the state of nature and alienate all of their natural rights to a person or group of people. The sovereign uses this combined power to alleviate the suffering and terror found in the state of nature and to create conditions for the safe pursuit of material satisfaction and comfort. These goals are achieved by imposing an arbitrary moral and political order enforced through the exercise of absolute power. Stripped of utopian pretensions, Hobbes's approach still demands tensionless politics. If and when the contract dissolves, the sovereign's political and ethical conventions no longer apply. If a new sovereign emerges from a new contract, a new world is theirs to create.

There are some clear differences between Willie and Hobbes. As an elected official, Willie acts within a broad and intricate system of existing social and political patterns. He does not wield the same creative power possessed by Hobbes's sovereign, and he does not seem to have an inclination to remake the entire world in his image. In discussing the fluidity of social values, there is an evolutionary and democratic dimension to his account that has no counterpart in Hobbes's thought. These differences should not obscure awareness of their philosophical and political affinities. Like Hobbes, Willie rejects the idea that politics can serve some transcendent purpose. As governor, Willie pursues the Hobbesian goal of using power to provide a better life for citizens, but better is conceived solely in terms of comfort. Like Hobbes, Willie jettisons his belief that politics can be conducted in an honest, rational manner. The collaborative, disinterested methods of natural science are not applicable to the practice of politics. Order must be imposed with force, and Willie is deeply motivated by the desire for undiluted political power. Hobbes would understand and approve this drive. As Babbitt explains, "If we view life solely from the naturalistic level and concern ourselves solely with the world of action, we are justified in neglecting, like Hobbes, the other lusts and putting supreme emphasis on the lust for power."[34]

Hobbes and Willie amplify potential problems latent in Bacon's thought and Adam's character. In *Rousseau & Romanticism*, Babbitt states, "Scientific progress has inspired man with a new confidence in himself at the same time that the positive and critical method by which it has been achieved detached him from the past and its traditional standards of good and evil."[35] Adam holds together in a strange mixture his interest in natural science and his rigid commitment to traditional morals. Bacon seems to be aware of the ways in which his project could undermine the ethical norms of society, and he makes some efforts to discourage traveling down the road Babbitt describes. With Hobbes and Willie, these concerns are dropped. They invoke seemingly scientific ideas and metaphors to reject religious and humanistic experiences and accounts of the ethical check and the human law as "mere moonshine."[36] Specifically about Hobbes, Babbitt writes, "Though Hobbes is Machiavellian in his emphasis on the law of cunning and the law of force, he is, unlike Machiavelli, not merely systematic but metaphysical. He seeks to develop the postulates of naturalism into a logical and closed system."[37] With varying degrees of consistency and sophistication, all four figures construct visions of politics grounded almost exclusively in the natural law. For Warren and Babbitt, this is a troubling development.

In *The New Laokoon*, Babbitt argues, "Science, we should add, may become false either by holding its own law too dogmatically, or else by trying to set up this law as a substitute for the human law."[38] Bacon, Adam, Hobbes, and Willie each fail one or both of Babbitt's tests. Bacon sees his demand for a new natural science as the key to realizing his dreams of material progress. Without an orientation toward the human law, one wonders what the idea of progress means in the political sense. The invention of the airplane is a type of progress, but is the plane to be used for travel or "to scatter bombs on women and children?"[39] Baconian definitions of progress give no answer. Babbitt explains, "Progress according to the natural law must, if it is to make for civilization, be subordinated to some adequate end; and the natural law does not in itself supply this end."[40] Like Adam, Bacon believes politics should be conducted in a spirit of cooperation and selflessness. There should be no tension among individuals or groups; the right answer to any question should be discovered and implemented. For Babbitt, such notions are plausible only if the human law's teaching of the "civil war in the cave" of the human soul is dismissed as wrong and human natural goodness is assumed.[41]

Following the spirit of Bacon, Hobbes constructs a theory of politics with pretensions to scientific rigor and neutrality. Like Bacon, he desires a politics without conflict and with peace and comfort as its objectives. Unlike Bacon, Hobbes does not believe such an order can be established through rational interactions among people appealing to and pursuing a scientifically determined common good. Like Willie, Hobbes rejects the human law. Neither the literary character nor the philosopher can quite make up his mind about whether human beings are naturally amoral or wicked but they know people are not naturally good. Conflict is the natural human state. Political order is artificial, not natural, and, if it is to take hold, it must be imposed on a people. There is no progress in the Baconian sense. Willie loosely develops a number of these ideas through political practice, but Hobbes proclaims them in a state of philosophical reflection. This leads Babbitt to describe Hobbes as a proponent of a "violent materialism" that "opposes to the dogmas and metaphysical assumptions of the traditionalists other assumptions that are almost equally metaphysical."[42] To take such steps in the name of scientific thought is to sink into a dangerous state of "metaphysical illusion."[43]

To work either according to the natural or the human law takes tremendous effort. Willie is a gifted orator and tireless campaigner. Once Willie discards his childlike notions about human goodness and rational politics, he experiences repeated electoral and legislative victories. When considering these achievements, there is no gainsaying his intuitive genius. At the same time, the allegedly scientific emancipation from the human law championed by Hobbes and Willie generates a serious problem for politics. In *Rousseau & Romanticism*, Babbitt writes, "To work outwardly and in the utilitarian sense, without the inner working that can alone save from ethical anarchy is to stimulate rather than repress the most urgent of all lusts—the lust of power."[44] In the case of Willie Stark, Warren gives Babbitt's insight imaginative expression. Lurking underneath his public professions of humanitarian service to the people is an imperial personality thirsting to dominate others. One of the main reasons Willie describes society and morality as constituted by the random collisions of scientific and historical forces is to justify his unrestrained and unethical pursuit of power. In his thinking about and practice of politics, Willie has many characteristics of what Babbitt would call an "efficient megalomaniac."[45] In the hands of Hobbes and Willie, the utopias of Adam and Bacon descend into narrow absolutisms in which politics is conducted by appeals to the "principle of naked force."[46]

WARREN, BABBITT, PSEUDO-SCIENCE, AND THE INDIVIDUAL

Beyond the complications it presents to politics, Warren and Babbitt see a socially authoritative scientific naturalism as harmful to the well-being of individuals. Outside of the office and the cutting table, Adam does not seem to be happy or even a complete person. He seems to have undergone a metaphorical lobectomy without experiencing its proclaimed benefits. Jack describes his friend as a person who "snuggled up to Life, to keep warm perhaps, for he didn't have any life of his own—just the office, the knife, the monastic room." Anne worries that her brother's focus on work may be his way of trying to keep the world, with all of its imperfections, at a distance.[47] At some level, Adam seems aware of the lopsided nature of his life. On rare occasions, the levee that keeps Adam away from a full life breaks with a force that is impossible for anyone nearby to resist. In such moments, Adam takes to activities such as dancing with such vigor that, as Jack writes, "You would think of a great turbine or dynamo making a million revs a minute and boiling out the power and about to jump loose from its moorings." In the aftermath of one of these outbursts of life, Jack continues, "The cold would settle down and the lid would go on right quick."[48]

The perceived lack of character development Adam receives in the novel is often expressed as a point of criticism about the text. At least in terms of Adam's status as a man of science, Warren gives an artistic depiction of the larger costs of pursuing the scientific life celebrated by Bacon. In *New Organon*, Bacon envisions the new scientists as high priests of the natural world. He prays to God on this topic, writing, "that you may be pleased to bless the human family with new mercies, through our hands and the hands of those others to whom you will give the same mind."[49] If it is to succeed, the practice of the new science must be protected against corruption by the individuality of researchers. His new science should be leaderless and impersonal.[50] Though Bacon hopes for unimaginable progress from his proposed fresh start for scientific investigation, he is aware of the price his followers will likely have to pay. He explains, "For ourselves, swayed by the eternal love of truth, we have committed ourselves to uncertain, rough and solitary ways."[51] Bacon seems to have expected such sacrifice only as it applies to the experiments of science themselves. In the character of Adam, the isolation necessary for scientific discovery expands into an entire way of life. The consequences for him and others are terrifying.

Adam translates the demand for perfection appropriate to medicine into standards for evaluating human conduct as such. Without any hesitation or sense of remorse, he discards all who do not measure up to his ideals. When Adam learns that his deceased father, a venerable past governor of whom he was very fond, participated in a corruption scheme during his time in office, his response is to "damn his soul to hell!"[52] Upon discovering his sister Anne is engaged in an affair with Willie, he concludes that his sister exchanged sex for Adam's appointment by Willie to the hospital project. Enraged at his sister's perceived behavior, Adam pushes her to the ground saying, "he wouldn't be paid pimp to his sister's whore."[53] Acting with the same sense of objective righteousness, Adam shoots Willie under the rotunda of the state capitol. Willie dies of his wounds a few days later. Adam's inability to reconcile his devotion to the sterilized order of medicine with experience of the contaminated world outside of science leads him to greater and greater acts of violence.

Willie's difficulties with maintaining human relationships are more obvious, but no less disturbing. His conflicted feelings about the citizens he serves have already been addressed. Within Willie's administration, misanthropy takes a specifically pseudo-scientific form. Byram White, a minor figure in the Stark administration, gets caught participating in a corruption scheme established on his own initiative. Willie is furious with Byram, not because Byram acted illegally and immorally, but because Byram's actions created an impeachment crisis. Willie tells Byram he will fix the situation so he can make the distraction go away. When Hugh Miller, the Attorney General, reminds Willie that Byram is guilty of bribery, Willie replies with feigned incredulity, "My God, you talk like Byram was human! He's a thing! You don't prosecute an adding machine if a spring goes bust and makes a mistake. You fix it. Well, I fixed Byram."[54] In *Leviathan*, Hobbes gives Willie's description of Byram the status of a normative interpretation of the human person, writing, "life is but a motion of limbs ... what is the heart, but a spring; and nerves, but so many strings?"[55] The mechanical metaphor explains away not only Byram and Willie's moral responsibilities but also the very idea of human beings as bearers of free will.

Willie's personal life is not exempt from the effects of his seeing the world as an arbitrary and temporary assemblage of values and desires. With the possible exception of Jack, Willie has no friends or meaningful human relationships. When trying to implement Adam's type of tensionless politics, Willie never drinks alcohol and is faithful to his wife. After embracing a more Hobbesian vision, Willie becomes an alcoholic and serial philanderer. In the amoral world he imagines himself living in and governing, he cannot understand why Adam would try to kill him over something as meaningless as a sexual relationship with Anne. He asks Jack, "Why did he do it to me? ... I never did anything to him. ... He was all right. The Doc."[56] For Willie, there is an inverse relationship between his success in imposing an order on the state and his control over himself. Like Adam, the imbalance in Willie's life has disastrous consequences for himself and so many others.

Jack is much the same as Adam and Willie. He also works and lives according to Babbitt's natural law. Much of the information Willie uses against others comes from Jack. He is ideally suited to this type of work because he too has learned something about the world. After failing to discover the deeper truth about his doctoral research subject, the meaning of the life and death of a distant relative, Jack quits his dissertation, becomes a journalist, and eventually joins Willie's administration. Through experience, Jack comes to realize that facts do not reveal truth about the world because there is no such thing to uncover. Facts can be accumulated through dispassionate investigation, but they serve merely as means for exploiting others and increasing a person's power, in his case, Willie's power. While Willie expounds and acts on a theory of the nature of politics reminiscent of Hobbes, Jack puts a Baconian commitment to rigorous research into the service of Willie's Hobbesian political ambitions.

Like Adam and Willie, Jack has no friends. He often refers to himself as an inanimate object, such as a "piece of furniture," and to others, especially his many stepfathers, by nicknames.[57] In so doing, he makes the world less real—and less likely to hurt him. This approach takes on a specifically mechanical cast when Jack thinks about his first wife, Lois, whom he describes as a "well-dressed animal." About his relationship with her, Jack explains, "I had loved Lois the machine, the way you love the filet mignon or the Georgia peach, but I definitely was not in love with Lois the person."[58] The less Lois resembles a sex machine, the more Jack's interest in her diminishes. In his cynical imagination, Anne is always an exception. She symbolizes a possibility for existence different from the pseudo-scientific imagery that prevails in his mind. When he learns of her affair with Willie, the news plunges Jack into a profound depression during which he develops a vivid and terrifying scientific metaphor for existence and human action that seems to permeate his views as well as those of Adam and Willie. Jack conjures the Great Twitch.

In the aftermath of his discovery about Anne, Jack flees to California. There he claims to have learned his belief in a difference between Anne and Lois was illusory. People have no distinctiveness. Words themselves signify nothing objective. He explains, "for names meant nothing and all the words we speak meant nothing, and there was only the pulse in the blood and the twitch of the nerve, like a dead frog's leg in the experiment when the electrical current goes through."[59] The truth is that all people are the same; they are stimulated to act solely by invitation of irrational impulses. During the lobectomy scene with Adam, Jack goes so far as to baptize the patient about to be made happy through surgery "in the name of the Big Twitch, the Little Twitch, and the Holy Ghost. Who, no doubt, is a Twitch, too."[60] If the Great Twitch is true, then feelings of love and betrayal, shame and righteous indignation are foolish. Jack describes himself as now possessing strength through "secret knowledge" that enables him to survey reality "from the height of my Olympian wisdom."[61] He claims to have discovered "the dream of our age."[62]

Babbitt would not be surprised that someone like Jack would develop the Great Twitch as a metaphor for the very essence of human existence. As Jack and others in the novel know, there is something that seems liberating about

sloughing off the weight of the human law on the pretext of pseudo-scientific knowledge. Babbitt explains, "Why should a man struggle to acquire character if he is convinced that he is being moulded [sic] like putty by influences beyond his control—the influence of climate, for example?"[63] Indeed, Willie's theory of historical and moral relativism is the Great Twitch writ large. Its superficial appeal notwithstanding, Jack's pseudo-scientific vision is ultimately grounded in the thinking "of a spoiled child." The Great Twitch is an example of moral indolence and existential despair.[64] In different ways, Adam, Willie, and Jack live large portions of their lives in tune with this image. By avoiding work according to the human law, they create the conditions for the "sense of isolation, of remoteness from other men" they find so difficult to bear.[65] They dehumanize others and themselves.

In the novel, not only does avoidance of the human law increase despair and decrease the ability to form genuine human relationship, it makes the inevitable encounters between people much more likely to result in violence. Because he is not disciplined to the human law, Willie sees no harm in threatening to tear apart a corrupt contractor if any graft finds its way into the hospital project. He sees no danger in whipping up crowds with "nail 'em up" campaigns, demands for a "hammer" or a "meat ax," and prophecies of the spilled blood of opponents.[66] Because he is not disciplined to the human law, one of Jack's factual research projects culminates in him telling Judge Irwin he knows about the latter's participation in a bribery scheme in the distant past. The judge, who Jack later learns is his biological father, commits suicide as a result of Jack's impartial disclosure of the facts. Because he is not disciplined to the human law, Adam feels justified in murdering Willie. Thinking about the scientific humanitarians of his own time, those who believed scientific progress would achieve a lasting peace and then proceeded to set the world on fire in 1914 to pursue that dream, Babbitt argues, "Efficient megalomania, whether developed in individuals of the same group or in whole national groups in their relations with one another, must lead sooner or later to war."[67] On this tendency toward violence, the only difference between these examples from the novel and those Babbitt has in mind is the scale of the ferocity.

For Babbitt and Warren, scientific naturalism cannot provide happiness to a society or to individuals under its sway; it simply "unkings" its acolytes. The glittering prizes of the laboratory are no substitute for the individual happiness and social harmony that result only from attunement to the ethical center of human existence.

WARREN, BABBITT, AND RECOVERING FROM SCIENTIFIC NATURALISM

Even in the midst of violence, alienation, and depression, there is hope for Jack at the end of the novel. Judge Irwin's suicide has a profound effect on Jack, but it does not instantly and permanently transform him into an ethically mature individual. His moral recovery is tentative. Given his situation, it could hardly be otherwise. He does not have the right individual habits to guide him. In the corrupt state in which he lives, Jack has no suitable role models or traditional sources of belief on which he can draw to orient his mind and will toward action. Whatever might have held the state together in the past has deteriorated to the extent that it has no authority in Jack's present. Despite such limited means, Jack takes the steps he can to start working according to the human law. He tells Willie he is no longer going to do the kind of research assignments that led to the judge's death. After Willie's death, he refuses to tell Sugar Boy, Willie's most devoted bodyguard, who in Willie's administration set Adam in motion as Willie's assassin. Doing so would only lead to more death. When his mother asks him why the judge took his own life, Jack lies and says the judge's poor health led him to end his life. He spares his mother the increased suffering that would come with the truth.

In these moments, Jack acts on the discovery that the facts are never neutral and all disclosures have consequences for himself and countless others. Indirectly responding to Willie's historical and moral relativism, Jack approvingly quotes Willie's former attorney general as saying, "history is blind, but man is not."[68] Through painful concrete experience, Jack learns that the pseudo-science of the Great Twitch, along with its implications for understanding politics and the human person, is false. In his circumstances, trying to act on this insight is no small accomplishment. Indeed, working on the knowledge he has, however limited and incomplete it may be, seems a sign of growing wisdom. Babbitt affirms the truth of Warren's intuitive insight. Reflecting upon the ideas of the Buddha, Babbitt writes, "Life reveals its secret ... only to the man who acts; and of all forms of action the most difficult is inner action."[69]

Jack appears to be on a road to recovery, and that path seems more humanistic than traditionally religious. Babbitt would not be surprised by such a state of affairs. Babbitt argues that the humanist and the religious traditionalist agree that in efforts to make ethical rather than material progress "mere knowledge is insufficient: conversion is also necessary." The key difference between the humanist and the religious traditionalist is in how they understand the process of conversion to take place. Although Babbitt does not discount the possibility of total and instantaneous transformations of character, as a humanist he focuses his attention on more common types of conversions. He writes, "[the humanist] conceives of man's turning away from his ordinary sense—and here he is much nearer in temper to the man of science—as a gradual process."[70] Over time, Jack might be able to align his will with the demands of the moral life. If he is successful, and if his state is not too far gone down the road of decadence, it is possible that he and others could work toward the establishment of a new set of social and political conventions inspired by the human law. In situations as dire as the one Jack encounters, this is the one, true hope for civilizational renewal.

A FUTURE FOR SCIENCE AND HUMANISM IN AMERICA

In Canto XXVI of *Inferno*, Dante the pilgrim meets Ulysses and hears the story of his demise and condemnation. Unrestrained in his desire for knowledge, undeterred by his obligations to family and Ithaca, uninterested in the welfare of his crew, Ulysses embarked on a new journey. He tells Dante that he and his crew sailed past the Pillars of Hercules, glimpsing the seven-story mountain at the other end of the world before a wind capsized the ship and dragged them into the watery abyss. Dante the poet was knowledgeable of and comfortable with the scientific ideas of his day. He saw no inherent conflict between his faith and scientific reason. For him, the Pillars do not symbolize a barrier made by humans setting a capricious limit to their knowledge. In his imagination, the Pillars instruct and warn that all things on earth and in heaven must be kept in balance lest an immodest desire for knowledge or power be a person's ruin. Thinking about the consequences of unrestrained living in a way that applies equally to Ulysses and to Adam and Willie, Babbitt writes, "This inordinate reaching out beyond bounds is . . . an invitation to Nemesis."[71]

As was argued above, Bacon's understanding of the symbol of the Pillars captures with vivid imagery much of what many Americans find appealing about science. Modern natural science has accomplished a great deal in various areas of theoretical research and practical invention. In defending his speculation on future technological development, Kaku correctly identifies a number of seemingly wild past predictions of discoveries and inventions that eventually became real. President Obama is not wrong to promote science education or to encourage young American students to think and work in the modes of contemporary science. At times, awareness of the moral problems of scientific progress is even expressed by such figures. Kaku occasionally refers to science as a "double-edged sword; it creates as many problems as it solves."[72] He thus calls for the cultivation of wisdom to guide the proper use of science, but he sees this virtue as the spontaneous product of liberal-democratic institutions. Babbitt would agree that a type of wisdom is needed to allow science to contribute to ordered politics and human happiness, and he would agree that education plays a vital role in forming the character of citizens. Nevertheless, he would see a definition of wisdom like Kaku's, or a focus on science education like Obama's, as evidence of profound and enduring ignorance of the human law.

Kaku and Obama as well as Bacon, Hobbes, Adam, Willie, and, until the end of the novel, Jack, all miss something about education, politics, human life, and happiness that is so clear in the minds and imaginations of Dante, Warren, Emerson, and Babbitt. Thinking and, above all, acting according to the human law is what makes the difference between civilization and its opposite.[73] In situations of great disorder, times in which traditional norms are waning, no amount of moral evasion, technological sophistication, political reforms, or legislative pursuits can substitute for the efforts individuals must make to will the good for themselves as well as the broader society. In a society in which scientific naturalism has become predominant, most if not all people will have to undergo the type of conversion Babbitt describes if a civilizational collapse is to be avoided. Neither Babbitt nor Warren is oblivious to the resistance such efforts will encounter. The scientific personality deeply invested in pseudo-science may be the one most in need of such a reorientation to the human law.

Given the challenges presented by scientific naturalism, it is not difficult to understand the desires of some to recommit to traditional religious beliefs and ways of life. From the humanist perspective of Babbitt, there is no reason to discourage such efforts, and some might even bear some fruit. Nevertheless, in an age such as the present, one in which skepticism of dogmatic propositions and established religious institutions is only growing, these endeavors at best are likely to have a modest impact. A way forward that might have greater success is one that can appeal to and work with demands for evidence and argument generated out of the concrete experience of individuals. The similarities between such an approach and the best spirit of modern natural science are clear. Babbitt writes, "Now the man of science at his best is like the humanist at his best, at once highly imaginative and highly critical."[74] With a critical spirit, the scientific person may be the one most open to a humanistic transformation. With a critical spirit adjusted to the human law, the scientific person may be the one best prepared to work with likeminded people to create new, ethically oriented patterns for life capable of gaining broad social acceptance.

Babbitt and Warren have identified serious practical and moral problems with scientific naturalism. The United States seems intoxicated with the very pseudo-science these figures reject. Assuming this is correct, and assuming a descent into the abyss of naturalism is undesirable and avoidable, then a next step would be for morally sound Americans to build on the insights of Babbitt and Warren, as well as those of others who have confronted the challenges of pseudo-science, by working out a new set of civilizing conventions that give the right amount of focus to the natural and the human law. Such a suggestion will make uncomfortable those who believe naturalism is a minor problem, if it exists at all. To such people, this argument will have fallen on deaf ears. Others might agree with the diagnoses of Babbitt and Warren, but despair over the enormity of the task of renewal. If such an undertaking is realized as necessary but seems far-fetched, then a dose of humanistic rather than scientific optimism is in order. About the ability of individuals and nations to undergo just the type of conversion process needed, even in situations of widespread decadence, Babbitt writes, "Human nature, and this is its most encouraging trait, is sensitive to a right example."[75]

NOTES

1. Ralph Waldo Emerson, "Ode to Channing," in *Ralph Waldo Emerson: Essays & Poems* (New York: Library of America, 1996), 1113.
2. Michio Kaku, *Physics of the Future: How Science Will Shape Human Destiny and Our Daily Lives by the Year 2100* (New York: Anchor Books, 2011), 326.
3. Kaku, *Physics of the Future*, 159.
4. Kaku, *Physics of the Future*, 34–35.
5. Kaku, *Physics of the Future*, 231.
6. Kaku, *Physics of the Future*, 41.
7. Barack Obama, "Remarks by the President at the White House Science Fair, April 13, 2016," accessed June 4, 2017, https://obamawhitehouse.archives.gov/the-press-office/2016/04/13/remarks-president-white-house-science-fair.
8. Barack Obama, "Remarks by the President at the White House Science Fair, March 23, 2015," accessed June 4, 2017, https://obamawhitehouse.archives.gov/the-press-office/2015/03/23/remarks-president-white-house-science-fair.

9. Barack Obama, "White House Science Fair, April 13, 2016," accessed June 4, 2017.

10. Irving Babbitt, *Democracy and Leadership* (Indianapolis, IN: Liberty Fund, 1979), 159.

11. Robert Penn Warren, "Introduction to the Modern Library Edition of *All the King's Men*," in *Twentieth Century Interpretations of All the King's Men: A Collection of Critical Essays*, ed. Robert H. Chambers (Englewood Cliffs, NJ: Prentice Hall, 1977), 94.

12. Robert Penn Warren, *All the King's Men*, 2d Harvest ed. Repr. (New York: Harcourt, 1946/1996), 373.

13. Warren, *All the King's Men*, 571.

14. Warren, *All the King's Men*, 475, 476.

15. Francis Bacon, *The New Organon*, eds. Lisa Jardine and Michael Silverthorne (New York: Cambridge University Press, 2000), 7.

16. Bacon, *The New Organon*, 96.

17. Bacon, *The New Organon*, 30.

18. Bacon, *The New Organon*, 12.

19. Bacon, *The New Organon*, 13.

20. Especially for those familiar with Aquinas, Babbitt's use of "natural law" and "human law" to describe the physical and metaphysical aspects of human existence might be confusing. To help readers in the briefest manner possible, it is enough to state Babbitt is not drawing from Aquinas or the Thomistic natural law tradition when he uses these terms.

21. Irving Babbitt, *Literature and the American College: Essays in Defense of the Humanities* (Washington, DC: National Humanities Institute, 1986), 91.

22. Bacon, *The New Organon*, 98.

23. Irving Babbitt, *The New Laokoon: An Essay on the Confusion in the Arts* (New York: Houghton Mifflin, 1910), 200.

24. Warren, *All the King's Men*, 370.

25. Francis Bacon, "The New Atlantis," in *The Major Works*, ed. Brian Vickers (New York: Oxford University Press, 2008), 480.

26. Warren, *All the King's Men*, 117.

27. Warren, *All the King's Men*, 592.

28. Warren, *All the King's Men*, 100.

29. Warren, *All the King's Men*, 386–87.

30. Thomas Hobbes, *Leviathan*, ed. Edwin Curley (Indianapolis, IN: Hackett, 1994), 24.

31. Hobbes, *Leviathan*, 76.

32. Hobbes, *Leviathan*, 109.

33. Hobbes, *Leviathan*, 3.

34. Irving Babbitt, *Rousseau & Romanticism* (New Brunswick, NJ: Transaction, 2002), 192.

35. Babbitt, *Rousseau & Romanticism*, 217.

36. Irving Babbitt, "The Problem of Style in a Democracy," in *Character & Culture: Essays on East and West* (New Brunswick, NJ: Transaction, 1995), 179.

37. Babbitt, *Democracy and Leadership*, 64.

38. Babbitt, *The New Laokoon*, 213.

39. Babbitt, *Rousseau & Romanticism*, 343.

40. Babbitt, *Democracy and Leadership*, 25.

41. Babbitt, *Rousseau & Romanticism*, 138, 147.

42. Babbitt, *Democracy and Leadership*, 66, 64–65.

43. Babbitt, *Rousseau & Romanticism*, 170.

44. Babbitt, *Rousseau & Romanticism*, 331.

45. Babbitt, *Rousseau & Romanticism*, 346.

46. Babbitt, *Democracy and Leadership*, 51.

47. Warren, *All the King's Men*, 359, 369.

48. Warren, *All the King's Men*, 318.

49. Bacon, *The New Organon*, 24.

50. Benjamin Farrington, *The Philosophy of Francis Bacon: An Essay on Its Development from 1603 to 1609 with New Translations of Fundamental Texts* (Liverpool, UK: Liverpool University Press, 1964), 100.

51. Bacon, *The New Organon*, 11.

52. Warren, *All the King's Men*, 381.

53. Warren, *All the King's Men*, 586.

54. Warren, *All the King's Men*, 203.

55. Hobbes, *Leviathan*, 3.

56. Warren, *All the King's Men*, 602.

57. Warren, *All the King's Men*, 49.

58. Warren, *All the King's Men*, 457.

59. Warren, *All the King's Men*, 466.

60. Warren, *All the King's Men*, 480.

61. Warren, *All the King's Men*, 470, 480.

62. Warren, *All the King's Men*, 467.

63. Babbitt, *Rousseau & Romanticism*, 163.

64. Babbitt, "Style in a Democracy," 174; Babbitt, *Rousseau & Romanticism*, 343.

65. Babbitt, *Rousseau & Romanticism*, 317.
66. Warren, *All the King's Men*, 144, 220.
67. Babbitt, *Rousseau & Romanticism*, 366.
68. Warren, *All the King's Men*, 658.
69. Babbitt, *Democracy and Leadership*, 195.
70. Babbitt, *Rousseau & Romanticism*, 385.
71. Babbitt, *Rousseau & Romanticism*, 350.
72. Kaku, *Physics of the Future*, 19.
73. Babbitt, *Democracy and Leadership*, 254.
74. Babbitt, *Rousseau & Romanticism*, 363.
75. Babbitt, *Democracy and Leadership*, 334.

BIBLIOGRAPHY

Babbitt, Irving. *Character & Culture: Essays on East and West*. New Brunswick, NJ: Transaction, 1995.
———. *Democracy and Leadership*. Indianapolis, IN: Liberty Fund, 1979.
———. *Literature and the American College: Essays in Defense of the Humanities*. Washington, DC: National Humanities Institute, 1986.
———. *The New Laokoon: An Essay on the Confusion in the Arts*. New York: Houghton Mifflin, 1910.
———. *Rousseau & Romanticism*. New Brunswick, NJ: Transaction, 2002.
Bacon, Francis. *The Major Works*. Edited by Brian Vickers. New York: Oxford University Press, 2008.
———. *The New Organon*. Edited by Lisa Jardine and Michael Silverthorne. New York: Cambridge University Press, 2000.
Chambers, Robert H., ed. *Twentieth Century Interpretations of All the King's Men: A Collection of Critical Essays*. Englewood Cliffs, NJ: Prentice-Hall, 1977.
Emerson, Ralph Waldo. *Ralph Waldo Emerson: Essays & Poems*. New York: Library of America, 1996.
Farrington, Benjamin. *The Philosophy of Francis Bacon: An Essay on Its Development from 1603 to 1609 with New Translations of Fundamental Texts*. Liverpool, UK: Liverpool University Press, 1964.
Hobbes, Thomas. *Leviathan*. Edited by Edwin Curley. Indianapolis, IN: Hackett, 1994.
Kaku, Michio. *Physics of the Future: How Science Will Shape Human Destiny and Our Daily Lives by the Year 2100*. New York: Anchor Books, 2011.

Obama, Barack. "Remarks by the President at the White House Science Fair, April 13, 2016." Accessed June 4, 2017. https://obamawhitehouse.archives.gov/the-press-office/2016/04/13/remarks-president-white-house-science-fair.

———. "Remarks by the President at the White House Science Fair, March 23, 2015." Accessed June 4, 2017. https://obamawhitehouse.archives.gov/the-press-office/2015/03/23/remarks-president-white-house-science-fair.

Warren, Robert Penn. *All the King's Men*. 1946. 2d Harvest ed. Reprint, New York: Harcourt, 1996.

CHAPTER FIVE

Luminosity, Imagination, Truth
On Voegelin and Ryn

S. F. McGuire

There are many similarities between Eric Voegelin's and Claes G. Ryn's accounts of the human condition. Importantly, they both emphasize its historical character, insisting that human experience, knowledge, and action always remain tied to the concrete circumstances of life. As a result, human beings are incapable of gaining a purely transcendent or universal perspective on reality from which to develop an objective or complete account of it. This position does not lead either man to embrace relativism, however. Rather, each argues in his own way that we experience and attempt to live in accordance with transcendent truth, goodness, and beauty as they manifest themselves through our immanent, particular, concrete existence. Further, they also reject the idea that human beings could take a disinterested or neutral stance toward reality. We are wholly engaged as participants in reality, and find ourselves compelled to work out ethically, intellectually, aesthetically, and spiritually how we should live our lives. Thus, for both Voegelin and Ryn, the moral and spiritual imperative of existence takes priority over abstract intellectual activity.

Despite their common cause, Ryn has advanced a handful of important critiques of Voegelin's work. One of his chief criticisms is that Voegelin does not adequately account for the role of imagination in the human search for moral, political, and spiritual order. Ryn argues in his own work (in which he synthesizes and builds on the ideas of Irving Babbitt and Benedetto Croce) that imagination has the essential function of providing an intuitive, concrete vision of the nature of reality.[1] He adds that this imaginative vision is ethically charged, as it both reflects and orients the will in a mutually impacting relationship. Finally, prioritizing the good over the true (and thus character over knowledge), he claims that will and imagination are epistemologically significant because the morally infused imagination provides the comprehensive picture of reality that reason then systematically explicates. Thus, in Ryn's account, imagination plays a central role (one more fundamental than reason) in orienting a person toward both the good and the true.

Whereas imagination is central to Ryn's philosophy from the start, Voegelin only begins to give imagination a systematic place in his philosophy in his late work. Noting this in a recent essay, Ryn expresses surprise at Voegelin's general lack of attention to the imagination, suggesting that his philosophy of consciousness, which focuses on the human capacity to gain and articulate insight into the nature of reality through experience and symbolization, seems to call for an account of it: "One might have thought that Voegelin's interest in symbols and 'experience' would have made him deal in some depth with the imagination."[2] He goes on to suggest that the imagination might be inchoately or compactly contained in Voegelin's thought: "some of his key terms may be viewed as composites and as accommodating more than one aspect of consciousness. Voegelin's notion of nous, for example, was rather compact and can be interpreted as containing an element of what Babbitt, borrowing the phrase of Edmund Burke, calls 'the moral imagination.' "[3] Ryn's critique of Voegelin is not that he is hostile to the imagination—he always acknowledges that Voegelin at least implicitly recognizes that "for a person to be receptive to truth, his intuitive-volitive orientation must predispose him toward reality"[4]—but that he does not adequately differentiate it as a key component in the search for order. The question thus arises: how much room is there in Voegelin's philosophy for an account of the imagination similar to Ryn's?

The answer appears to be quite a bit. A survey of Voegelin's corpus reveals several instances in which he uses the term in a manner that appears to be compatible with Ryn's usage, and, as has already been noted he explicitly incorporates it into his philosophy of consciousness in his late work, including "The Beginning and the Beyond: A Meditation on Truth" and the fifth volume of *Order and History, In Search of Order*.[5] Before these texts, Voegelin most notably refers to the imagination in a negative sense when discussing ideological revolt against the order of being. But he also occasionally refers to the imagination when discussing classic experiences and symbolizations of order such as those found in the works of Plato and the Book of Genesis. And there are other reasons for suspecting that a positive account of the imagination is implicitly at work in Voegelin's thought throughout his career as well: his own attention to works of the imagination, including the mythical imagination, ancient poetry, and other works of art and literature throughout history. In addition, Voegelin often uses literary metaphors to describe the human condition. Finally, in his late work, he begins to incorporate the imagination into his philosophy of consciousness more systematically. All of this evidence confirms a positive and essential role for the imagination in his philosophy. In fact, Voegelin's account might even surpass Ryn's in a crucial respect—in identifying what Voegelin refers to as its "luminous" dimension—but he would certainly agree that imagination must be differentiated as a distinct structure of reality.

RYN ON THE IMAGINATION

Ryn defines imagination as a capacity for "pre-conceptual, intuitive, concrete vision"[6] and argues that it has an indispensable part to play in both ethics and epistemology. He adds that imagination is a creative capacity: it "institutes wholes which did not exist before,"[7] and it denotes a " 'perceiving' [that] is really a *con*ceiving."[8] It is integral to ethics because, in his view, "corresponding qualities of character and imagination tend to beget and reinforce each other."[9] Following Irving Babbitt, Ryn argues that the human will, which he defines as "the generic, categorical name for that infinity and variety of impulse that orients the individual to particular tasks,"[10] is "dualistic, forever torn between higher and lower potentialities."[11] In the course of working out the orientation of their wills, "men develop such imagination as is pleasing to their underlying orientations of character."[12] It follows from this that the quality of one's imagination is tied to the quality of one's will or character: "the most penetrating imagination can emanate only from a human soul attuned to the real ethical opportunities and dangers of existence."[13] Thus, great beauty is tied to morality: "truly great works of the imagination are such not by virtue of their intuitive coherence alone but by virtue of the moral quality of experience they convey."[14]

Will and imagination also take priority in Ryn's epistemology, setting the parameters within which a person's reason operates. Reason still plays a crucial role in the development of knowledge of reality, but it must take its bearings from the will and the imaginative insight into the nature of reality that comes with it. As Ryn writes, "knowledge of reality rests upon a certain orientation of the will and upon the corresponding quality of imagination (intuition) that the will begets. Reason is dependent for the truth and comprehensiveness of its concepts on the depth and scope of the material that it receives from the imagination."[15] In essence, will and imagination mutually influence one another to create an intuitive grasp of reality that is then systematically explicated by reason. Knowledge of reality thus depends most fundamentally on the quality of one's will and imagination. This means, then, that the imagination plays a more critical role than reason in knowledge of reality. As he writes, "The imagination in its higher form ... is man's most important source of humane *knowledge*, a knowledge, to be sure, which is non-intellectual in nature. Through the moral imagination man has an *intuitive* perception of the universal."[16] This claim is corroborated by faulty philosophical systems that are logically coherent but still untrue: "if philosophy or history relies on imagination and the latter can present illusory vision, the resulting ratiocination may lead deeper and deeper into error, no matter how splendidly the philosopher or historian writes or how keenly he argues emerging points of theory."[17]

The ethical and epistemological quality of an imaginative vision depends crucially on the degree to which it recognizes and remains within the historical character of human existence. Ryn admits a distinction between transcendence and immanence but stresses that "human experience does not know any transcendence that is not indistinguishably immanent in the world of particulars in which the will is moving."[18] Similarly, he writes, "We penetrate the universal through the particular."[19] Ryn's historicism is not relativist; he does not deny truth, but argues that we only know it as it manifests itself historically. There is no ahistorical perspective on reality; character and knowledge must both be worked out from within the concrete perspective in which we live. To posit otherwise would be an example of the "idyllic imagination," which, following Babbitt, he juxtaposes to the "moral imagination." The idyllic imagination seeks to escape the nature and limits of human existence, whereas the moral imagination remains firmly grounded in and expressive of historical reality. Cultivating a moral imagination is thus integral to the development of both character and wisdom.

VOEGELIN ON CONSCIOUSNESS AND HISTORY

Like Ryn, Voegelin attends to the historical character of human existence and knowledge. He argues that we do not and cannot occupy an "Archimedean point," from which we could know reality in its wholeness and completeness because we are participants within reality. Following Plato, he uses the symbol "metaxy" (which translates as "between") to characterize the human condition, arguing that we experience ourselves as existing in tension between "poles of existence," which are symbolized historically in a variety of ways: ignorance and knowledge, mortality and immortality, immanence and transcendence, and so forth. These poles are not things or objects, but experiences that frame or constitute human experience.

Voegelin stresses the "participatory" character of existence in the metaxy, by which he means that human existence is charged with moral and spiritual meaning and involves the whole of our being. In this context, he argues that human life is most fundamentally defined by the search for order. Human beings experience and symbolize insight into the nature of reality, including transcendent moral and spiritual order, and the course of history is defined most fundamentally by the ongoing struggle to achieve individual and social order as it is experienced and symbolized. Thus opens the first volume of *Order and History* with the observation that "the order of history emerges from the history of order."[20]

In his later work, Voegelin develops a more systematic account of his philosophy of consciousness. He argues that consciousness has a "paradoxical structure" because it can be predicated both to a particular person and to reality itself.[21] Corresponding to these two structures of consciousness, he distinguishes between intentionality and luminosity. In the first sense, consciousness refers to a concrete individual's (a subject's) experience of the world as something out there (an "object intended"). In the second sense, reality becomes the subject and consciousness is recognized as an occurrence within reality. From this second perspective, "reality is not an object of consciousness but the something in which consciousness occurs as an event of participation between partners in the community of being."[22] Luminosity thus refers to consciousness as an event within reality. Voegelin ties the distinction between the two structures of consciousness to the "metaxy," stating that "the luminosity of consciousness is located somewhere 'between' human consciousness in bodily existence and reality intended in its mode of thingness." As will be discussed below, Voegelin differentiates the imagination in this late account of his philosophy of consciousness, suggesting that it plays an essential role in the experience and symbolization of order. Throughout most of his work, however, the imagination does not rise to the level of a technical term.

IMAGINATION IN VOEGELIN

Although Voegelin's references to the imagination before *In Search of Order* are occasional and unsystematic, they nevertheless point to an important role for the imagination in his account of the historical struggle for order. Most often, he refers to imagination in a negative sense, using the term to discuss the phenomenon of ideological revolt against the order of being. A notable example is his essay, "The Eclipse of Reality," in which he refers to imagination frequently in his analysis of the "second realities" created by ideologues to justify themselves. He notes, for example, that a thinker with an imaginatively deformed consciousness, finding himself in conflict with common sense reality, "will put his imagination to further work and surround the imaginary self with an imaginary reality apt to confirm the self in its pretense of reality."[23] In this text, he consistently refers to the ideologue as the "imaginator,"[24] and he uses terms such as "projective imagination"[25] and "imaginative construction"[26] to describe the process of generating a second reality. He links this process to "madness in the sense in which the Greek tragedians and philosophers have used the term."[27] Thus, this text and others in which he discusses the various revolts against the order of being tend to suggest that imagination is a problem—that it is the process by which we deviate from reality.

Voegelin also sometimes places acts of the imagination in conflict with experience and reason (two key terms in his own philosophy of order), thus suggesting that those who live in truth operate according to experience and reason, whereas indulging the imagination deforms one's consciousness. Thus, in the text presently under consideration, he juxtaposes the imaginary nature of second reality with "common experience" and "reason." He distinguishes between "realities imagined and experienced" and comments that "a reality projected by imagination ... is not the reality of common experience." He also observes that "the philosopher's reason is man's tension toward the divine ground of his existence becoming luminous to itself, while the philodoxer's reason is an image designed to obscure the reality of existential tension."[28] In these passages, Voegelin recognizes a problem that Ryn and Babbitt associate with the idyllic imagination, but does he also recognize the possibility of a moral imagination? He seems to set up a dichotomy between imagination, on the one hand, and reason and experience, on the other. But is that really what he intends? Would such a position be consistent with his own philosophy?

Voegelin's usage of imagination in this essay and other works can certainly give the impression that the exercise of imagination is involved in the revolt against the order of being but not its experience and symbolization. But that is an unlikely and apparently inaccurate interpretation of what Voegelin's position must be, even if his own language is misleading at times. It would be odd if Voegelin held that the human mind includes a faculty that plays an entirely negative role in the search for order. A much more likely position would be that the imagination has a distinct role in the search for order that it can play well or poorly. And, in fact, even in "Eclipse of Reality," Voegelin uses language that suggests a positive role for the imagination. For instance, in a discussion of how experiences of order are symbolized, he mentions that "the knower refers to the known through the images and language symbols engendered by the event or process that we call experience."[29] Although Voegelin uses his preferred term, "engender," here, the reference to images suggests the possibility that one might equally say imagination. He also notes that a conflict arises "when we encounter persons who produce imagery at variance with the images supposed to be true. Imagination, it appears, can cut loose from reality and produce the sets of images that we call Second Reality because they pretend to refer to reality though in fact they do not."[30] This passage suggests that imagination can and should play a positive role in the articulation of symbolizations of the truth of existence: if it "*can* cut loose from reality," then is not the suggestion that it need not or ought not to? The distinction between the ideologue and the spiritually healthy soul, then, would be (at least in part) a question of the imagination—the distinction between one in tune with reality and one that is not. If so, this would suggest that Ryn is correct to see the possibility of something like an implicit "moral imagination" in Voegelin's account of various experiences and symbolizations of order such as the classical Greek reason (*nous*).

There are other instances in which Voegelin refers, although perhaps somewhat casually, to the imagination in accounting for the discernment and articulation or order. In *Anamnesis*, he states, "Plato had the creative imagination to develop a symbolic language adequate for the expression of new spiritual experiences."[31] Elsewhere, discussing Plato's *Republic*, he says, "here we can witness the origin of social science in the creative imagination of the philosopher who wishes to overcome disorder."[32] His use of this term goes back at least as far as *Israel and Revelation*, the first volume of *Order and History*, in which he writes: "The spiritual sensitiveness of the man who opened his soul to the word of Yahweh, the trust and fortitude required to make this word the order of existence in opposition to the world, and the creative imagination used in transforming the symbol of civilizational bondage into the symbol of divine liberation—that combination is one of the great and rare events in the history of mankind. And this event bears the name of Abram."[33] So, at the very least, Voegelin was not averse to appealing to the imagination in his earlier works dealing with what he saw as the major differentiations of order in the Western tradition.

Beyond the specific references to imagination and its cognates, it must be recognized that Voegelin often uses the language of works of the imagination to account for the nature of the human condition. He describes the human condition as a "story," "tale," "quest," and a "drama." In *Israel and Revelation*, he memorably describes the "perspective of participation"—the human experience of being a participant in, rather than a mere observer of, reality—using the metaphor of an actor: "man is not a self-contained spectator. He is an actor, playing a part in the drama of being and, through the brute fact of his existence, committed to play it without knowing what it is." He goes on to describe the engrossing nature of this experience.

> Participation in being, however, is not a partial involvement of man; he is engaged with the whole of his existence, for participation is existence itself. There is no vantage point outside existence from which its meaning can be viewed and a course of action charted according to a plan, nor is there a blessed island to which man can withdraw in order to recapture his self. The role of existence must be played in uncertainty of its meaning, as an adventure of decision on the edge of freedom and necessity.[34]

He maintains this language into his late work as well. In *In Search of Order*, for instance, he writes of the "comprehending story of the It,"[35] and argues that "the story is the symbolic form the questioner has to adopt necessarily when he gives an account of his quest as the event of wresting, by the response of his human search to a divine movement, the truth of reality from a reality pregnant with truth yet unrevealed."[36] Human existence has the form of a narrative.

The importance of imagination in Voegelin's thought is further implied by his extensive studies of ancient myth and poetry in *Order and History*, as well as his lifelong attention to art, music, literature, and hieroglyphics. Voegelin takes a participatory approach to these works of the imagination; he studies them as contributions to the human search for order.[37] As he writes in a letter to his friend, Robert Heilman, his "occupation with works of art, poetry, philosophy, mythical imagination, and so forth, makes sense only if it is conducted as an inquiry into the nature of man."[38] These sources document the variety of experiences and symbolizations of order in history, and thus reveal something about the nature of the human condition. Thus, Voegelin clearly sees works of art contributing to the human search for order. In this connection, it is worth noting that Voegelin also takes several key terms, including "second reality," from literary sources.

IMAGINATION IN VOEGELIN'S LATE WORK

Based on the evidence thus far presented, it is not surprising to find that Voegelin recognizes in his late work the need to develop a more technical and systematic account of the imagination and its role in the experience and symbolization of right order. Imagination begins to take a more prominent place in his thought at least as early as the 1977 essay, "The Beginning and the Beyond," and he fully differentiates imagination as a structure of consciousness in the final volume of his philosophy of consciousness, the unfinished and posthumously published *In Search of Order*.

In *In Search of Order*, he notes that imagination shares in the "paradoxical structure of consciousness and its relation to reality."[39] This means it has both intentional and luminous dimensions: "Imagination, as a structure in the process of a reality that moves toward its truth, belongs both to human consciousness in its bodily location and to the reality that comprehends bodily located man as a partner in the community of being."[40] Thus, Voegelin uses the term in one sense, that is, with reference to intentionality, to account for the human ability to symbolize experiences of truth and order. He claims that this process is "imaginative in the sense that man can find the way from his participatory experience of reality to its expression through symbols,"[41] and he uses the term "to denote this ability to find the way from the metaleptic experiences to the imagery of expressive symbols." At the same time, he stresses that imagination must also have a second, luminous sense, as it also designates the whole process of reality revealing itself through the human beings who attempt to represent their experiences of order. As Voegelin goes on to explain,

> There is no truth symbolized without man's imaginative power to find the symbols that will express his response to the appeal of reality; but there is no truth to be symbolized without the comprehending It-reality in which such structures as man with his participatory consciousness, experiences of appeal and response, language, and imagination occur. Through the imaginative power of man the It-reality moves imaginatively toward its truth.[42]

In short, imagination is a human faculty, but it is also an event within reality that remains somewhat obscure. This suggests that imagination is not a faculty over which the human being has complete control. Voegelin emphasizes this when he writes elsewhere of "the forces of imagination and language which emerge mysteriously in man's experiential response to the reality of which he is a part. From the experiential response arise, within reality, images of reality and language symbols to express the images."[43] As will be discussed below, this is perhaps one respect in which Voegelin's account of imagination differs from Ryn's, as Ryn does not seem to stress the mysterious nature of imagination. For Voegelin, imagination refers to both the human power to create the symbols that represent experiences of order and the entire process by which we experience and symbolize order.

Voegelin thus establishes what could only be suspected in his earlier work: that imagination plays a positive and irreducible role in the search for order as the creative process through which human beings experience and symbolize the order of reality. He notes the creative nature of imagination as he goes on to explain how it can also be a vehicle for rebellion against that order. "By virtue of his imaginative responsiveness man is a creative partner in the movement of reality toward its truth; and this creatively formative force is exposed to deformative perversion, if the creative partner imagines himself to be the sole creator of truth."[44] Interestingly, Voegelin now claims that imagination can facilitate such rebellion by aping its own proper function, as he connects "the resistance to truth to the ground it has in common with the resistance to untruth, to its ground in the assertive imagination of man as a force in reality."[45] As Voegelin explains, "Every thinker who is engaged in the quest for truth resists a received symbolism he considers insufficient to express truly the reality of his responsive experience. In order to aim at a truer truth he has to out-imagine the symbols hitherto imagined, and in the assertion of his imaginative power he can forget that he is out-imagining symbols of truth, but not the process of reality in which he moves as a partner."[46] Whereas the positive function of imagination was only implied before, now it is the standard from which the alternative is a deviation. Voegelin concludes with reference to Platonic anamnesis: "Imaginative remembrance of the process, the remembrance intended by Plato, implies the potential of imaginative oblivion."[47]

The imagination becomes so central to Voegelin's thought in this late account that Charles R. Embry has argued one can speak of a "cognitive-imaginative complex" in Voegelin's philosophy of consciousness.[48] In this complex, "participatory imagination" becomes one of the fundamental categories by which Voegelin explains the experience and symbolization of order, even taking precedence over *nous* or reason. This point is made especially clear in "The Beginning and the Beyond," where Voegelin circumscribes *nous* within imagination.

> "Imaginative vision," emerging from reality in response to the appeal of reality, is the comprehensive event of experience and symbolization. The philosopher's meditation can operate only within the comprehensive vision and make it self-reflectively luminous for man's existence in tension toward the Beyond. Hence, imaginative vision and noesis are not independent, rival, or alternative sources of knowledge and truth but interacting forces in the historical process of an imaginative vision that has noetic structure.[49]

He further explains with specific reference to Plato.

> The *opsis*, the vision, is Plato's technical term for the experiential process in which the order of reality is seen, becomes reflectively known, and finds its appropriate language symbols. The "vision" in this comprehensive sense, which includes the noetic vision, appears in the key-passages of *Timaeus* 47 as the *opsis* of the order in the cosmos, and in *Republic*, 507–509, as the *opsis* of the Agathon that creates the order in the soul of man. Moreover, Plato, is careful about precluding subjectivist misunderstandings. The "vision" is not somebody's fancy but the imaginative power of response to the reality seen; and the reality seen is the cause (*aition*) of this power (*dynamis*).[50]

Although Voegelin does not fully elaborate this position in *In Search of Order*, it seems to require that the imagination is prior to reason in the sense that experience and symbolization of nous is itself part of the imaginative process. Voegelin's study of the history of experience and symbolization of order—the various languages of myth, faith, and reason that constitute the order of history—confirms this point, as they are all examples of the participatory imagination at work. Thus, imagination refers to the comprehending power by which reality reveals itself through human participation.

The foregoing establishes that imagination can and does play an important part in Voegelin's philosophy. But would he entirely agree with Ryn's account of the imagination and its role in the human search for order? Would he be willing to use intuition as a synonym for imagination? Would he accept Ryn's account of the relationship between will, imagination, and reason? As suggested above, it is likely that Voegelin would argue that Ryn does not adequately account for the luminous dimension of imagination. Ryn moves in the direction of Voegelin's position when he notes that "will, imagination and reason are not 'things.' They are potentialities of life, forms of activity and consciousness,"[51] and they "are not phenomena in psychology, 'functions,' or data among others. They are distinct and yet closely related fundamental categories of our humanity, shaping the potentialities of our experience."[52] He even adds that "these powers realize some of the higher potentialities of reality" and, taking the will as an example, writes that it "reveals itself."[53] The language of these passages suggests the need to put the person in the passive or predicative position vis-à-vis reality, but Ryn does not fully develop or make central this need, as Voegelin does. While Ryn agrees with Voegelin on the need to offer a nonobjective account of reality, he continues to treat the individual as subject and the imagination as predicate. He thus misses out on the receptive nature of human imagination—that the intentional or creative imagination of the person operates within the luminous imagination that structure reality and moves the individual. This issue cannot be fully explored here because it is connected to another, as yet undiscussed, difference between Voegelin and Ryn, namely, Voegelin's stronger emphasis on mystery and revelation, faith and grace as essential components of philosophy since its inception. But it is worth noting that Ryn seemingly endorses Babbitt's separation of philosophy and religion and embraces his humanism,[54] which forecloses the possibility of agreeing with Voegelin that philosophy is itself a kind of revelation. This, in turn, means that Ryn's philosophical account of imagination focuses much more on its intentional rather than luminous character.

These important issues aside, the foregoing indicates there is room for some agreement between Voegelin and Ryn. This is certainly the case in the treatment of ideology. As another student of Ryn's has observed, Voegelin, like Ryn, believes that "the modern crisis is ultimately a problem of will and imagination, not intellect."[55] Voegelin makes this point in his essay, "On Debate and Existence," in which he discusses the impossibility of rational debate with interlocutors who refuse to acknowledge common experiences as the basis for any such debate. As he says in "The Eclipse of Reality," "rational discussion presupposes a community of existence in truth."[56] The ideologue's problem runs deeper than logic: "imaginative perversion is not a mistake in a syllogism or a system, to be thrown out for good once it is discovered, but a potential in the paradoxic play of forces in reality as it moves toward its truth."[57] Voegelin thus agrees that imagination orients a person toward or away from reality in a fundamental way. Beyond the diagnosis of ideology, he also seems to agree that imagination is a creative faculty through which human beings participate in the unfolding of reality and that it precedes reason in the sense that reason operates within the vision generated by the imagination. In sum, while Ryn is correct to suggest that Voegelin should have devoted more attention to the imagination, it is evident that there is a significant place for imagination in Voegelin's account of human consciousness—one that Voegelin himself eventually recognized.

NOTES

1. The most comprehensive statement is Claes G. Ryn, *Will, Imagination, and Reason: Babbitt, Croce, and the Problem of Reality* (New Brunswick, NJ: Transaction Publishers, 1997).

2. Claes G. Ryn, "Eric Voegelin and Irving Babbitt," *VoegelinView*, November 7, 2014, https://voegelinview.com/eric-voegelin-irving-babbitt/.

3. Ibid.

4. Ryn, *Will, Imagination, and Reason*, 158.

5. Eric Voegelin, "The Beginning and the Beyond: A Meditation on Truth," in Eric Voegelin, *The Collected Works of Eric Voegelin*, vol. 28, *What Is History? And Other Late Unpublished Writings*, ed. Thomas A. Hollweck and Paul Caringella (University of Missouri Press, 1990) and *The Collected Works of Eric Voegelin*, vol. 18, *Order and History*, vol. V, *In Search of Order*, ed. Ellis Sandoz (Columbia: University of Missouri Press, 2000).

6. Claes G. Ryn, "Imaginative Origins of Modernity: Life as Daydream and Nightmare," Humanitas X.2 1997. http://www.nhinet.org/ryn10-2.htm.

7. Ryn, *Will, Imagination, and Reason*, 62.

8. Ibid.

9. Ibid., 149.

10. Ibid., 147.

11. Ibid., 148.

12. Ibid.

13. Ibid., 152.

14. Ibid., 9.

15. Ibid., 16.

16. Ibid., 154.

17. Ibid., 157.

18. Ibid., xi.

19. Ibid., 185.

20. Eric Voegelin, *The Collected Works of Eric Voegelin*, vol. 14, *Order and History: Israel and Revelation*, ed. Maurice Hogan (University of Missouri Press, 2001), 19.

21. Voegelin, *In Search of Order*, 29.

22. Ibid.

23. Eric Voegelin, "The Eclipse of Reality," in Eric Voegelin, *The Collected Works of Eric Voegelin*, vol. 28, *What Is History? And Other Late Unpublished Writings*, ed. Thomas A. Hollweck and Paul Caringella (Columbia: University of Missouri Press, 1990), 112.

24. Ibid., 112, 134.

25. Ibid., 116.

26. Ibid., 153.

27. Ibid., 132.

28. Ibid., 136.

29. Ibid., 113.

30. Ibid., 114.

31. Eric Voegelin, *The Collected Works of Eric Voegelin*, vol. 6, *Anamnesis: On the Theory of History and Politics*, trans. M. J. Hanak and Gerhart Niemeyer, ed. David Walsh, (Columbia: University of Missouri Press, 2002), 82.

32. Voegelin, *The Collected Works of Eric Voegelin*, vol. 27, *The Nature of the Law and Related Legal Writings*, ed. Robert Anthony Pascal, James Lee Babin, and John William Corrington (Columbia: University of Missouri Press, 1991), 108.

33. Voegelin, *Israel and Revelation*, 241.

34. Ibid., 40.

35. Voegelin, *In Search of Order*, 38.

36. Ibid., 38.

37. This point is stressed by Charles R. Embry, *The Philosopher and the Storyteller: Eric Voegelin and Twentieth-Century Literature* (Columbia: University of Missouri Press, 2008), 57–58.

38. Voegelin, "Letter to Robert Heilman, August 22, 1956," in Charles R. Embry, ed. *Robert B. Heilman and Eric Voegelin: A Friendship in Letters 1944–1984*, foreword by Champlin B. Heilman (Columbia: University of Missouri Press, 2004), 157.

39. Voegelin, *In Search of Order*, 29.

40. Ibid., 52.

41. Ibid.

42. Ibid.

43. Eric Voegelin, *The Collected Works of Eric Voegelin*, vol. 12, *Published Essays, 1966–1985*, ed. Ellis Sandoz (Columbia: University of Missouri Press, 1990), 372.
44. Voegelin, *In Search of Order*, 53.
45. Ibid., 54.
46. Ibid., 53–54.
47. Ibid., 55.
48. Embry, *The Philosopher and the Storyteller*, 46.
49. Voegelin, "The Beginning and the Beyond," 227.
50. Ibid., 229.
51. Ryn, *Will, Imagination and Reason*, xxi.
52. Ibid., xxii.
53. Ibid., xxi
54. Ibid., 38.
55. Michael P. Federici, *Eric Voegelin: The Restoration of Order* (Wilmington, DE: ISI Books, 2002), 185.
56. Voegelin, "The Eclipse of Reality," 133.
57. Voegelin, *In Search of Order*, 53.

BIBLIOGRAPHY

Embry, Charles R. *The Philosopher and the Storyteller: Eric Voegelin and Twentieth-Century Literature*. Columbia: University of Missouri Press, 2008.

Federici, Michael P. *Eric Voegelin: The Restoration of Order*. Wilmington, DE: ISI Books, 2002.

Ryn, Claes G. "Eric Voegelin and Irving Babbitt," *VoegelinView*, November 7, 2014.

———. "Imaginative Origins of Modernity: Life as Daydream and Nightmare." *Humanitas* 10, no. 2 (1997): 41–60.

———. *Will, Imagination, and Reason: Babbitt, Croce, and the Problem of Reality*. New Brunswick, NJ: Transaction Publishers, 1997.

Voegelin, Eric. "The Beginning and the Beyond: A Meditation on Truth." In *The Collected Works of Eric Voegelin*. Vol. 28, *What Is History? And Other Late Unpublished Writings*. Edited by Thomas A. Hollweck and Paul Caringella. University of Missouri Press, 1990.

———. *The Collected Works of Eric Voegelin*. Vol. 6, *Anamnesis: On the Theory of History and Politics*. Translated by M. J. Hanak and Gerhart Niemeyer, Edited by David Walsh. Columbia: University of Missouri Press, 2002.

———. *The Collected Works of Eric Voegelin.* Vol. 12, *Published Essays, 1966–1985.* Edited by Ellis Sandoz. Columbia: University of Missouri Press, 1990.

———. *The Collected Works of Eric Voegelin.* Vol. 14, *Order and History (Vol. I): Israel and Revelation.* Edited by Maurice Hogan. Columbia: University of Missouri Press, 2001.

———. *The Collected Works of Eric Voegelin.* Vol. 18, *Order and History (Vol. V): In Search of Order.* Edited by Ellis Sandoz. Columbia: University of Missouri Press, 2000.

———. *The Collected Works of Eric Voegelin.* Vol. 27, *The Nature of the Law and Related Legal Writings.* Edited by Robert Anthony Pascal, James Lee Babin, and John William Corrington. Columbia: University of Missouri Press, 1991.

———. "The Eclipse of Reality." In *The Collected Works of Eric Voegelin.* Vol. 28, *What Is History? And Other Late Unpublished Writings.* Edited by Thomas A. Hollweck and Paul Caringella. Columbia: University of Missouri Press, 1990.

———. "Letter to Robert Heilman, August 22, 1956." In *Robert B. Heilman and Eric Voegelin: A Friendship in Letters 1944–1984.* Edited by Charles R. Embry, Foreword by Champlin B. Heilman. Columbia: University of Missouri Press, 2004.

Part III
Ethics and Character

For the humanist of a Babbittian stripe, the aesthetic dimension of human life is no mere independent realm of activity, capable of being entered into from time to time, but constitutes the broad cultural milieu in which a person's character is formed. Individual experience always combines with this broader cultural framework to shape the imaginations of ethical actors, for better or worse. While the will is the ultimate arbiter of ethical choices, not all options are created equal for the historically formed personality—the deck is loaded, so to speak, in advance of the moment of decision by the type of imagination that has been cultivated in the individual. For both Babbitt and Ryn, the "moral imagination" is the disposition of character that is oriented toward life's higher potentialities, inclining the individual from the outset toward those choices that realize the good life for self and community. Echoing his great intellectual forebear, Aristotle, Babbitt believes the cultivation of such persons of good character, over and above any individual decision, to be the ultimate standard or reference point toward which we must look in all ethical questions. The authors of these chapters share this fundamental orientation and discuss several areas in which this moral-imaginative conception of character plays out: in the shared underpinnings of moral discourse, in the practical wisdom of particular situations, and in the sound interpretation of religious doctrine.

In "Politics, Moral Judgment, and the Enlightenment Project," William F. Byrne examines the question of social strife and the recent malaise that has emerged in response to pluralism and the lack of a common ground of ethical orientation supporting political discourse. Appropriating Ryn's phenomenology of moral understanding as the interplay between will, imagination, and reason, Byrne attributes much of this recent angst to the Enlightenment project's attack on tradition in the name of abstract, universal reason. Without a historically rooted, common ground of understanding, the individuals in large democratic societies are set adrift, both insofar as they lose a shared set of meanings for moral and political dialogue as well the sober check on impulse that helps make dialogue civil. Furthermore, the presumption of a universal reason and identification of the latter with each person's self-evidently "true" perspective breeds acrimony, according to Byrne, since individuals reflexively dismiss or attack those who disagree with them as being "irrational." Building on insights from Tocqueville, Byrne concludes by suggesting that prospects for the renewal of moral imagination nonetheless remain if we seek to kindle local sources of cohesion and humility.

In "Natural Law, the Moral Imagination, and Prudent Exceptions," Robert C. Koons is in fundamental agreement with Ryn, Babbitt, and Burke on moral imagination as a necessary precondition for sound ethical judgment. At the same time, his chapter seeks to push back against these traditionalists insofar as their criticisms of moral rationalism target natural law philosophy. Koons thus argues that these humanists unfairly group natural law thinking together with Enlightenment rationalism and its more extreme exponents, such as Rene Descartes, who turn moral reasoning into mere mathematical deduction. While it is true that sensitivity to circumstance and contextual judgment are essential to sober decision-making, Koons argues that such charges of omission vis-à-vis the natural law tradition are misplaced. Drawing in particular on the thinking of St. Thomas Aquinas, Koons thus reaffirms natural law theory's connections with Aristotelianism and the interdependence of imagination and reason that is fully appreciated by Thomas. To the extent that natural law theory seeks to apply universal principles to questions of morality, Koons shows that these requirements are minimal, and that charges of intellectualism amount to a straw man argument. For Koons, the need for historically-informed judgment famously championed by Burke in the *Reflections* is capable of reconciliation with Thomism.

Finally, in "Irving Babbitt and Christianity: A Response to T. S. Eliot," Ryan R. Holston aims to correct the common misunderstanding of Babbitt among Christians connected to the criticisms made by Babbitt's most famous student, T. S. Eliot. In this chapter, Holston argues not only that humanism is compatible with Christianity, as Babbitt long contended, but that its insights into the importance of moral-imaginative character can help to avoid what Babbitt calls "sham spirituality." In other words, ideological calls to renew the faith that emphasize strictness of doctrine are not only potentially hollow, becoming a mere pretext for moralistic posturing, but can even be dangerous, insofar as the individual set adrift from tradition might become a zealous partisan of anything in the name of "Christianity." For Holston, the insight into the moral-imaginative dimension of human character offered by Babbitt is thus a support for the life of and fidelity to genuine Christianity. Consequently, a Babbittian or historically informed understanding of the interplay between will and imagination points to the fact that any renewal of spiritual life must begin not simply with a commitment to a strict set of rules but with the building up of concrete ways of living and the individual striving to overcome selfish inclination or temptation that those institutions exist to support.

CHAPTER SIX

Politics, Moral Judgment, and the Enlightenment Project

William F. Byrne

While for decades commentators have noted growing political and social conflict and strife in the US and elsewhere, this has lately reached alarmingly high levels. This strife is accompanied by a general malaise and dissatisfaction, and a sense that existing social and political structures and institutions are not working. While such problems are hardly new, and particular manifestations inevitably wax and wane over time due to varying local circumstances, it is argued here that they are also traceable to a serious long-term dynamic. This is the playing out of what various thinkers have called "the Enlightenment Project," described by Alasdair MacIntyre as an effort to "discover rational foundations for an objective morality."[1] While characterizations of the French Enlightenment vary, it undeniably incorporated a popular emphasis on "reason," typically understood in opposition to tradition and religion. This essay examines some of the contemporary social and political implications of the Enlightenment project with special reference to the thought of Claes Ryn, who has explored moral and epistemological questions with emphasis on the roles of the imagination and will. One of the first thinkers to confront the Enlightenment Project, Edmund Burke, is also utilized as a resource in understanding and addressing today's challenges.

Much contemporary strife can ultimately be rooted in moral-epistemological problems involving individuals' inclinations and judgment. These in turn are partly rooted in particular, simplistic views of "reason" that have become predominant in the West since the Enlightenment. Our concern here is not with sophisticated philosophical thought of the Enlightenment but with what has emerged as often-unspoken popular impressions—including those among many self-styled intellectuals. In this framework, "reason" is typically contrasted with tradition, orthodox religion, long-established beliefs and practices, and other customary ways of thinking and doing. It is treated as an alternative, independent source of knowledge, ignoring the need for content upon which instrumental reason can act, or the potentially problematic nature of that content. "Reason" becomes a synonym for right-thinking, and this is simply identified with the particular views of the person employing the term.

The consideration of one's own particular views as self-evident to anyone employing "reason" enhances political and social acrimony. If one's perspective is the very definition of rationality, the differing perspectives of others are per se irrational. The others are therefore cognitively impaired, or simply stupid or ignorant, since anyone who is not stupid or ignorant would hold to the "correct" view. Or, if the others cannot plausibly be described as stupid or ignorant, they must be evil. They are out to cause trouble, in pursuit of their own selfish ends. They must be aware that their goals are harmful, since basic rationality demands such knowledge.

The tendency of many thinkers to understand "reason" in opposition to traditional practices and beliefs exacerbates this problematic line of thought. At one time, the departure of one's viewpoint or understanding from more customary and long-held ones might have been considered a reason for extra caution or tentativeness. This followed from the basic idea—articulated by thinkers like Burke but long held intuitively by most people—that established ways, having demonstrated at least some functionality, reflected at least some wisdom. Departure from them meant movement into a dangerous unknown, in which our reason may be unable to grasp and respond effectively to all of the variables in play. Consequently, one way to undermine support for a public policy proposal in Burke's day was to tag it as an "innovation."[2] When "reason" is understood in opposition to tradition, however, the relationship can be flipped. The greater the departure of a view from what is taken to be the traditional one, the more "rational" that view may be taken to be; innovation becomes a badge of authority and source of legitimacy. One with countertraditional beliefs may therefore conclude that those beliefs must be the rational ones by virtue of their novelty.

This points to other, related dimensions of the contemporary moral-epistemological problem: the high level of social and political divergence within the US and other Western democracies, the prevalence of debased views of the world, and the contribution of these to the resulting strife, dissatisfaction, and malaise. While diversity of thought is valuable and promotes intellectual growth, liberal democracy—indeed, any sound polity—requires a significant degree of consensus. Widespread variation in fundamental understandings of reality presents an acute, perhaps insurmountable problem. Approaching this problem effectively requires a better understanding of human judgment and understanding, one that moves away from popular understandings since the Enlightenment and instead emphasizes the historical dimension of morality and knowledge.

THE PROBLEM OF KNOWING

The problems of judgment, morality, and knowledge, are for Claes Ryn intimately tied to "the problem of reality," or what Irving Babbitt calls "the epistemological problem."[3] The problem of right action hinges in part on the problem of understanding, or of one's perception of the world. And for Ryn, our understanding, put simply, is a function not just of "reason" but of three elements: reason, imagination, and will. One's grasp of the world depends on all three elements. It is the imagination that creates a coherent reality within which one may function; hence, the shape of one's imagination powerfully influences the results of one's "reason." Ryn has stated that "philosophic reason gives conceptual self-awareness to the categorical structure of experience, experience having been constituted into a pre-cognitive whole by the imagination."[4] Likewise, perception involves willing, and the orientation of one's will powerfully influences one's perception of the world and the conclusions to which one "reasons."

Although Edmund Burke engaged in explicit philosophical speculation only at a young age, he appears to have had a similar sense of the workings of human understanding. When discussing artistic taste, he identified it as a form of judgment, and found its contributors to be the senses, and imagination, and "the reasoning faculty." It is on the imagination that Burke places his emphasis. Like others, Burke identified the imagination as a power that finds resemblances among things; it creates wholes from which the reasoning faculty can make distinctions. For Burke, differences in taste proceed largely from differences in imagination, not from differences in reason. Burke never has an occasion to treat judgment broadly, but from the fact that he identifies taste as a form of judgment and the fact that he discusses the imagination in broad terms, it is reasonable to assume that he sees any form of judgment as a function of both the imagination and the reasoning faculty.[5]

Burke never discusses the will conceptually, but in various ways he demonstrates at least an intuitive sense of its linkage to one's perception of reality. For example, he offers this portrait of a revolutionary ideologue.

> Nothing can be conceived more hard than the heart of a thorough-bred metaphysician.... They are ready to declare that they do not think two thousand years too long a period for the good that they pursue. It is remarkable, that they never see any way to their projected good but by the road of some evil. Their imagination is not fatigued, with the contemplation of human suffering thro' the wild waste of centuries added to centuries of misery and desolation. Their humanity is at their horizon,—and, like the horizon, it always flies before them. The geometricians and the chemists bring, the one from the dry bones of their diagrams, and the other from the soot of their furnaces, dispositions that make them worse than indifferent about those feelings and habitudes which are the supports of the moral world. Ambition is come upon them suddenly; they are intoxicated with it, and it has rendered them fearless of the danger which may from thence arise to others or to themselves. These philosophers, consider men in their experiments, no more than they do mice in an air pump, or in a recipient of mephitick gas.[6]

In a parallel to Burke's observation, Ryn quotes Babbitt observing that "the penalty that science pays for [the] quantitative method is a heavy one. The farther it gets away from the warm immediacy of perception the less real it becomes; for that only is real to a man that he immediately perceives."[7] Burke's monster "metaphysician" is consumed with ambition and driven by an idealistic imagination. He suffers from a deformed will, lacking all sense of restraint. The lack of restraint follows from a kind of disconnection from reality. Although he pursues an idealistic dream, he lacks moral grounding. He does not have the sense of a greater order that inspires humility and provides a check on one's aspirations. His dreams are real to him, while the mundane considerations involved in getting there, including the suffering of others, are not. As Burke notes, the "metaphysician" (a common eighteenth-century political term for a revolutionary, ideological thinker) has turned against traditional sources of moral guidance. A kind of circularity exists between the metaphysician's understanding of the moral world and his will; his contempt for tradition frees his will, while his willfulness feeds his contempt for tradition. Ryn has noticed a similar circularity; one can get on a sort of "track" that leads increasingly to right or wrong action, as the will and imagination mutually feed each other.

Contemporary discussions of phenomena like "confirmation bias" repeat long-standing observations about human understanding and about how our perceptions can become deformed. A teenage Burke wrote to a friend, "How fond are we of our own opinions, purely because they are ours.... How often do we invent false reasonings and Arguments to uphold 'em, and who to deceive but ourselves."[8] Burke recognized even then a willful dimension to belief, and its relationship to one's broader worldview. He knew that sheer intellectual power was not the only—and, in many cases, not the primary—factor behind one's grasp of the world. Ryn has likewise noted that "an important source of faulty philosophical reasoning is misleading intuition which misdirects the attention of reason."[9] "Misleading intuition"—that is, an unsound imagination—is behind a great deal of faulty reasoning and the political and social difficulties that flow from it.

Indeed, while proponents of theories of "deliberative democracy" like to speak of conflicts of "values" and "interests," one can readily observe that a great deal of political conflict today—perhaps the vast bulk of political conflict today—includes disagreements over facts. Various aspects of existing conditions are often in dispute, as are understandings of cause and effect, whether those understandings are clearly articulated or are unspoken assumptions. Of course, the differences in perceived facts tend to flow from different values and different preferred courses of action, every bit as much as different values and different preferred courses of action flow from different perceptions of facts. We seek coherence in our worldviews and tend to believe what we need to believe to maintain that coherence. Part of what makes political and social disagreement so intractable and acrimonious today is the dramatic diversity in worldviews among members of a particular society or political order.

ABSTRACT RATIONALISM VERSUS TRADITIONAL KNOWLEDGE

The Enlightenment project's emphasis on "reason" incorporated an emphasis on conceptual language in place of much that was formerly implicit. There is much gained from this broader application of conceptual, categorizing thought, but there are drawbacks as well. When characterizing one of Babbitt's observations, Ryn explains: "Common to systems of signs and humanistic symbols is that their truth is never final and complete.... What man catches in his net of concepts or 'laws' is not necessarily unreal; by them he tries to lay hold on life's element of unity and permanence. But an integral part of reality is its inexhaustible manifoldness-concreteness-individuality-change, which leaves knowledge provisional.... Reality baffles our attempts to imprison it in concepts once and for all."[10] We are always grasping at reality but that grasp is never perfect or complete. Our conceptual language is a symbolic representation of deep and complex truths; this language is useful, but becomes problematic when it is mistaken for reality itself. Much popular debate and discussion of rights, for instance, seems to presume that rights are things, with an independent existence, instead of shorthand ways of expressing what are actually very complex beliefs about human beings and about how we think they should be treated. Even when we are more cognizant of the limitations of our conceptual language, this language can shed more heat than light on public discussions, creating a false precision that can heighten the acrimony of debates. While much is gained through Enlightenment rationalism, there is a loss also. Ryn has noted that "Man is not afforded an uninhibited spectator view of an independently existing reality, but perceives structural reality *through* a more or less limited historical perspective."[11] This fact tends to be forgotten in popular discourse and in much intellectual discourse as well.

We do not possess a God's-eye view of the world, perfectly comprehending everything from a position outside of historical reality. Our perspective is always limited. Yet much of the popular Enlightenment language surrounding "reason" suggests that we can in fact achieve such a perspective. We can be "objective." Of course, we can, in fact, be more or less "objective" in our understanding of the world; if we are more educated, if we have a broader range of life experiences, if we strive for detachment, we might be able to get a better handle on some things. All views are certainly not equally valid. But our knowledge and understanding are always imperfect. And, in fact, in some cases those who most associate their own thought with "reason" and "objectivity" may be most likely to be in serious error, due to a lack of humility and self-criticism. In areas of political, social, or moral judgment in particular, the benefits of formal education may be limited and mixed. A recent newspaper column discussing the present crisis of Western elites observes the following:

... America's unfortunate record over the past couple of decades, whether in economics, in politics, or in foreign policy, doesn't suggest that the "meritocracy" is overflowing with, you know, actual merit.

In the United States, the result has been Trump. In Britain, the result was Brexit. In both cases, the allegedly elite—who are supposed to be cool, considered, and above the vulgar passions of the masses—went more or less crazy. From conspiracy theories (it was the Russians!) to bizarre escape fantasies (A Brexit vote redo! A military coup to oust Trump!) the cognitive elite suddenly didn't seem especially elite, or for that matter particularly cognitive.[12]

No matter how sophisticated a thinker pretends to be, that person's judgment, and perception of the world contributing to that judgment, is profoundly shaped by his or her imagination and will. "Reason" does not propel one to a higher plane, above the flux. Especially in matters of potentially profound practical importance, one's personal psychological investment powerfully shapes one's intuitions, and these intuitions shape the workings of "reason."

Burke showed how a monster "metaphysician," presumably well-educated in some ways, could lose touch with reality, including moral reality. In the wrong sort of person an emphasis on "abstract" conceptual language actually seems to facilitate this disconnect, since it helps one live in an idealized world, ignoring the messy inconveniences of historical reality. It also contributes to false precision and false certainty, as one mistakes one's world of symbols for the whole of reality. Burke famously noted that "the legislators who framed the ancient republics knew that their business was too arduous to be accomplished with no better apparatus than the metaphysics of an undergraduate, and the mathematics and arithmetic of an exciseman."[13] This sort of simplistic ahistorical reasoning is characteristic of much political debate today.

Various thinkers have noted the existence of distinctly different forms of knowledge. For example, Michael Oakeshott has framed a distinction between "technical" and "practical" knowledge. "Technical" knowledge is the sort that is overtly taught and is typically expressed in the form of rules or doctrines; "practical" knowledge is largely inarticulate, is demonstrated and learned in practice, and can also be referred to as "traditional knowledge."[14] Oakeshott's problem with an "ideological style of politics" is that "it suggests that a knowledge of the chosen political ideology can take the place of understanding a tradition of political behaviour."[15] It cannot; doctrinal-type knowledge, Oakeshott observes, as might be found in the instructions in a cookbook, presumes a base of "practical" knowledge, which comes down largely in the form of traditions. Indeed, as Oakeshott notes, "technical" knowledge is derived from the experience of "practical" knowledge. For example, Burke wryly noted that the critics of the British constitution ignored the fact that the theories by which they criticized the British constitution were themselves derived from their experience with the British constitution.[16]

An emphasis on ahistorical, conceptual language that downplays "practical" or traditional knowledge tends to leave people unanchored. This is one of the fundamental issues of modernity. In a 2013 article Ryn noted that "special attention needs to be paid to the explicitly stated desire for liberation from earlier beliefs and ways of life that is most commonly called modernity. Two seemingly disparate but intimately connected currents have given that part of modernity its distinctive flavor and dynamic: One is a belief in rational enlightenment. The other is entertaining 'idealistic' dreams of human existence transformed. Both currents assume the coming of a new, superior world, an era of liberty, harmony, and general well-being."[17] For Ryn, as for Babbitt, a prime exemplar of this tendency is Rousseau, who would, as Burke noted, be celebrated by the French Revolutionaries. Ryn finds that "Rousseau himself did not much care for Enlightenment rationalism, but idealistic imagination formed in the West an antitraditional alliance with rationalism. What the two currents had in common was that they rejected the old stress on moral character as the key to a satisfying life. All over the Western world this informal alliance exhibited a "head" that was narrowly technocratic and instrumentalist and a "heart" that was full of dreamy sensibility. The quintessentially modern Westerner has sophisticated technical ideas and equipment and a sentimental imagination. His goals are idealistic, his method for enacting them is social engineering."[18] Modernity yields a moral-imaginative dynamic that leads to a peculiar sort of politics.

Burke's monster metaphysician is again evident. In that case, the methods of enacting the idealistic goals are, Burke indicates, downright evil. Many of the horrors of the twentieth century stand in testament to the accuracy of Burke's observation. But most manifestations of the "anti-traditional alliance" of rationalism and idealism are more subtle. A great deal of contemporary politics is dominated by it, and it is especially pervasive among the elites of today's so-called meritocracy. Ryn notes that "the criteria for entering the better universities and hence the elites of society became in time strongly biased in favor of a capacity for abstract, ahistorical reasoning, as measured by the SAT, LSAT,

GRE and similar tests."[19] Previous generations of elites, though far from perfect, tended to be grounded in the traditions and values of their civilization, and in fact served as representatives of a sort of these traditions and values. Today they are more likely to stand in opposition to them. Ryn argues: "Consider the power that lies in being able to define what intelligence is. It is the power to decide which kind of rationality is to be respected and favored, first of all in the universities. It is to that extent the power to select society's gatekeepers. By enthroning abstract, instrumental rationality, and discrediting a more historical, experientially based form of reason, it became possible to cut people in the West off intellectually from the sources of their civilization. Their civilization could be defined out of existence—a process that is today far advanced."[20]

In throwing off one's civilization, one throws off moral constraints and the grounding of a sound morality. A repeated point of Ryn's is that traditional civilization, including the religion associated with it, emphasized the presence of higher and lower potentialities in humankind. Constant vigilance—with regard to society as a whole and with regard to one's own self—is demanded to foster the higher potentialities and discourage the lower ones. This function of civilization has, however, been undermined. Ryn finds that "a central task of civilization is to tame, direct and refine the desire for power, to make power serve admirable motives. But the rise of rationalism coincided, not incongruously, with a desire to throw off the moral-religious and cultural restraints and tastes of traditional Western society. It became, among other things, the instrument for an increasingly unchecked desire for power and wealth. People rebelling against the old hierarchy of values and the corresponding social pecking order found in rationalism a potent weapon."[21]

Burke famously finds all that is good in European civilization to rest on "the spirit of a gentleman and the spirit of religion."[22] Religion provides a basic moral grounding and, especially, a sense of humility in the face of a great, mysterious order. The spirit of a gentleman exists, to a degree, in tension with the spirit of religion, since it fosters a kind of pride and superiority. Yet it is pride and superiority bound up with the social group of which one is a member, and that is humbled by recognition of all that one owes to one's social group, to the broader society, and to one's civilization for the position that one is in. It fosters a sense of responsibility and obligation. Both the spirit of religion and the spirit of a gentleman encourage one to strive to be better and do better, but, critically, both do so while also fostering a spirit of self-criticism and a sense of restraint. Indeed, one can say that for Burke the primary goal of the sound political order is fostering restraint and discouraging the "caprice" that leads both to disorder and to tyranny. In throwing off the traditional order, caprice is given free rein.

MODERN SOCIETY'S DESTRUCTIVE POWER

In a 2009 essay Ryn has emphasized the role of modern commercialism and associated "oligarchy" in the throwing off of tradition and embrace of an ahistorical rationalism.[23] While many on the political left tend to think of big business as a force of "conservatism," Karl Marx himself knew better, finding that "the bourgeoisie, whenever it has got the upper hand, has put an end to all feudal, patriarchal, idyllic relations. It has pitilessly torn asunder the motley feudal ties that bound man to his 'natural superiors,' and has left remaining no other nexus between man and man than naked self-interest, than callous 'cash payment.' It has drowned the most heavenly ecstasies of religious fervor, of chivalrous enthusiasm, of philistine sentimentalism, in the icy water of egotistical calculation."[24] Sounding almost like Burke, Marx goes on to find that "All fixed, fast-frozen relations, with their train of ancient and venerable prejudices and opinions, are swept away, all new-formed ones become antiquated before they can ossify. All that is solid melts into air, all that is holy is profaned...."[25] At one time, the revolutionary tendencies of commercially driven society were well recognized.

It is important, however, to remember that while modern commercialism and the oligarchic tendencies arising from it have helped promote a rationalistic disconnect from tradition, they are not the root cause, and are in fact but symptoms of a greater phenomenon. Recall that Burke found that the monster metaphysicians were "worse than indifferent about those feelings and habitudes which are the supports of the moral world."[26] The new elites—of almost any sort—are in some ways highly competent, but in other ways are ill-equipped for moral and effective action in the real world. Ryn finds that "People who had let abstract rationality and a general bias against old traditions and elites separate them from humane values in the concrete found it increasingly difficult to distinguish between morality and immorality, honesty and crime."[27] In Oakeshott's language, they may be strong on "technical knowledge" of particular types but weak in "practical knowledge," especially "practical knowledge" related to fundamental questions of human relations and the good life. The traditions and old narratives that they eschew provided a depth of wisdom and guidance that rules and doctrines cannot, including those expressed through popular contemporary catchphrases. Importantly, the traditions taught humility; moreover, respect for tradition is itself a lesson in humility, as one grasps one's indebtedness to those who have come before. With proper humility one continually checks oneself, and is likely to perceive the world more soundly than it is typically perceived by one with a rationalistic-idyllic imagination. The recent observations in newspaper columns of the repeated failures in judgment of various elites, and of their emotional irrationality when confronted by realities that contradict their prior perceptions, highlight just some of the inadequacies of contemporary approaches.

While elites are especially important because they set the tone for society and shape so much that goes on, the phenomena noted here are not confined to elites but are pervasive. Liberal society famously purports to offer a "thin" order that is "neutral" regarding ends. Of course, in practice liberalism is neither as neutral nor as thin as it purports to be. But there certainly is a thinness of a sort in its overt rejection of many elements of traditional order. For Burke, such elements furnished the "wardrobe of a moral imagination."[28] As in the case of some of the French Enlightenment's self-styled *philosophes*, people today furnish their imaginations not with traditional wisdom but with an ad hoc collection of popular ideas, trendy concepts, and so on. A largely unrecognized, underlying body of traditionalism nevertheless remains, and it is largely because of this remnant that society continues to function. The more this deteriorates, the more reliance on less sound alternatives increases. One's imaginative grasp of the world becomes less effective, and with this the imaginative frameworks of different people also become more disparate. Without a strong traditional basis for understanding, concepts come to lack precise, practical common meanings. Unbound by the idea of an existing order or the humility that goes with it, individuals insist that their own particular, idealistic visions for society predominate, and are uncomprehending and outraged when others' views clash with theirs.

THE WAY FORWARD

The problem of political and social strife and malaise is but one component of a much broader set of problems confronting the late-modern world. Addressing these problems is extraordinarily challenging because of their interrelationships and circularity. While the attitudes and worldviews that have arisen as late effects of Enlightenment rationalism have done much to shape the contemporary world, conditions of the contemporary world in turn enhance those effects and make them especially difficult to combat. This is not the sort of problem that lends itself to a political quick fix. Our problems are at root largely problems of imagination, and, secondarily, of will. That is, they are ultimately problems of character. Reshaping character requires cultural change. While government and politics impact culture and character and therefore cannot be ignored, their role is limited and unpredictable; the changes needed in society are not the sort that are readily ordered-up through government action.

Over the years, Ryn has repeatedly called for "fresh, penetrating artistic vision ... that can inspire a reorientation of the imagination and spark new, perhaps daring action."[29] Artistic works can play a powerful role in shaping the imagination and thereby bringing change; Burke noted that "the theatre is a better school of moral sentiments than churches...."[30] But how does such artistic vision appear and flourish in a civilization that is so decayed? At present a great deal of creative energy—as well as a great deal of money—goes into works that further degrade the culture. In his book *Coming Apart*, political scientist Charles Murray faults American elites for, among other things, failure to foster the right sort of culture. Though a self-identified libertarian, Murray recognizes relationships between various traditional values or behaviors and positive outcomes. Although Murray fails to develop his critique philosophically, parallels exist between his criticisms of contemporary elites and Ryn's discussion of their transformation in today's "meritocracy." Notably, however, Murray observes that, although very few of today's elites are traditionalists, most live lives that are in some ways quite in line with traditional patterns, at least superficially. Unlike lower-class Americans, elites rarely have children outside of marriage, and they generally frown on this within their own circles. They tend to get married and stay married. They place great value on gainful employment and on productive contributions to society, and frown on those who seek to avoid work. They even attend church at a higher rate than lower-class Americans. Yet, Murray notes, these elites, responsible for so much of our popular culture, rarely use their works to uphold the values, or at least the behaviors, that they implicitly recognize as good.[31] In fact, a great deal of the material that they put out communicates the opposite message, ridiculing or dismissing those values and behaviors. Given the state of our elites, their dominance of the media, and their failure to promote even their own desirable behaviors, the challenges to new positive artistic visions are indeed great. Still, these are a necessary part of cultural change, and space still exists for individual efforts to create and to patronize such works.

Like the arts and media, formal education has a powerful effect on culture and character. It also represents a huge challenge, in part due to the condition of the current education establishment and the monopolization of education by that establishment and, with it, the state. Nevertheless, space exists for initiatives in the improvement of education and for the exercise of preferences by students and parents. As in the case of artistic expression, however, the problem exists of bringing about the right sort of change within a culture that is differently attuned.

To the extent that the US still remains decentralized, opportunities for cultural reinvigoration are enhanced. As Ryn and many others have noted, Alexis de Tocqueville emphasized America's decentralization and local engagement as a key factor in its maintenance of healthy democracy.[32] Although Tocqueville was, generally speaking, favorably impressed with the Americans and their democratic order, he was concerned about their future. He saw in liberal democracy the sort of individualism that could readily lead either to social and political disintegration or to highly centralized, hegemonic, possibly tyrannical government. For Tocqueville, the nation's decentralization, along with Americans' religiosity, had so far protected the US from such a fate. Christianity provided a moral grounding and sense of commonality that tempered the individualism of liberal democracy, while local affiliations and face-to-face citizen cooperation fostered the kind of tempered republicanism necessary for a sound democratic state.[33] Today both the decline in religiosity and the expansion of centralized government threaten these imaginative underpinnings of a sound order, although remnants of the older American outlook remain.

Over the years countless thinkers have noted the importance to character development of sustained face-to-face interaction and permanent relationships. There is a big difference between working with, helping, and loving, individuals directly, and loving humankind in the lump, or advocating government action to assist others. The growing complexity of society, coupled with the massive expansion of government services and centralization, has severely altered interpersonal dynamics and, in the process, compromised the imaginative frameworks of citizens. Moreover, Ryn has noted that "the effect of idealism in America as elsewhere has been to trivialize and weaken love of neighbor and thus to undermine the support for traditional decentralized political and social structures. At the same time it has helped inspire a vast accumulation and centralization of state power."[34] As in other cases, there is a circular dynamic present; the movement away from traditional orientations toward an idealistic imagination prompts citizens to advocate changes in societal conditions and the state; these changes, in turn, act to undermine character and cause citizens to advocate further harmful changes. Circularity, however, may also work in a positive direction. Numerous thinkers, including some from the mid-twentieth century such as Robert Nisbet and Wilhelm Roepke, have noted with concern the harmful effects of an increasingly centralized society—a centralization encompassing the political, social, and economic spheres.[35] With better understanding of the moral-epistemological implications of the issues facing us, perhaps more progress can be made in addressing our problems by creating conditions that foster greater depth of character and moral restraint.

It may be that the dynamics unleashed by the Enlightenment Project will fully play out to a bleak conclusion. But this is not necessarily the case. It may be that heightened problems of social and political acrimony and malaise will help to trigger appropriate responses, including greater soul-searching by elites and ordinary people alike, as well as greater curiosity about the nature of our situation and the prospects for improvement. Efforts to increase understanding of the challenges we face may yet, in fact, contribute to recovery and renewal of culture, and with it the rebuilding of imaginations conducive to human flourishing in a healthy republic.

NOTES

1. Alasdair MacIntyre, *After Virtue: A Study in Moral Theory*, 3d 3e. (Notre Dame, IN: University of Notre Dame Press, 2007), 6.

2. Francis P. Canavan, *The Political Reason of Edmund Burke* (Durham, NC: Duke University Press, 1960), 168.

3. For an extensive discussion of this subject, see: Claes G. Ryn, *Will, Imagination, and Reason: Babbitt, Croce, and the Problem of Reality* (New Brunswick, NJ: Transaction Publishers, 1997).

4. Ibid., 144.

5. Burke treats this subject in his preface on taste to: Edmund Burke, *A Philosophical Enquiry into the Origin of Our Ideas of the Sublime and Beautiful* in Paul Langford, general editor, *The Writings and Speeches of Edmund Burke*, vol. I (Oxford: Clarendon Press, 1989). The present writer discusses this dimension of Burke's thought in some detail in William F. Byrne, *Edmund Burke for Our Time: Moral Imagination, Meaning, and Politics* (DeKalb, IL: Northern Illinois University Press, 2011).

6. *A Letter from the Right Honorable Edmund Burke to a Noble Lord, on the Attacks Made upon Him and His Pension*, in *The Writings and Speeches of Edmund Burke*, vol. IX, 176–77.

7. Ryn, *Will, Imagination, and Reason*, 67 quoting Irving Babbitt, *Rousseau and Romanticism* (New Brunswick, NJ: Transaction Publishers, 1991), 138–39.

8. Burke, Letter to Richard Shackleton, 1745, in *The Correspondence of Edmund Burke*, vol. I (Chicago, IL: University of Chicago Press, 1958), 50.

9. Ryn, *Will, Imagination, and Reason*, 17.

10. Ibid., 75–76.

11. Ibid., 126.

12. Glenn Harlan Reynolds, "Trump and the Crisis of Meritocracy," *USA Today*, 20 February 2017.

13. Edmund Burke, *Reflections on the Revolution in France* (Indianapolis, IN: Hackett Publishing Company, 1987), 162.

14. Michael Oakeshott, *Rationalism in Politics and Other Essays* (Indianapolis, IN: Liberty Press, 1991), 12.

15. Ibid., 55.

16. Edmund Burke, *Speech on Reform of Representation*, in: *The Works of the Right Honorable Edmund Burke* (Boston, MA: Little, Brown & Company, 1865–67), vol. VII, 97.

17. Claes G. Ryn, "Power Without Limits: The Allure of Political Idealism and the Crumbling of American Constitutionalism," *Humanitas* XXVI, nos. 1–2 (2013): 13.

18. Ibid, 18.

19. Claes G. Ryn, "From Civilization to Manipulation: The Discrediting and Replacement of the Western Elite," *Humanitas* XXII, nos. 1–2 (2009), 15.

20. Ibid., 15.

21. Ibid., 16.

22. Burke, *Reflections*, 69.

23. Ryn, "From Civilization to Manipulation."

24. Karl Marx and Friedrich Engels, *Manifesto of the Communist Party*, in: Robert C. Tucker, ed., *The Marx-Engels Reader*, 2d ed. (New York: W. W. Norton & Company, 1978), 475.

25. Ibid., 476.

26. *A Letter from the Right Honorable Edmund Burke to a Noble Lord*, in *The Writings and Speeches of Edmund Burke*, vol. IX, 177.

27. Ryn, "From Civilization to Manipulation," 18.

28. Burke, *Reflections*, 67.
29. Ryn, "From Civilization to Manipulation," 22.
30. Burke, *Reflections*, 71.
31. Charles Murray, *Coming Apart: The State of White America 1960–2010* (New York: Crown Forum, 2010).
32. Ryn, "Power without Limits."
33. Alexis de Tocqueville, *Democracy in America*. Ryn mentions Tocqueville's observations in: Ryn, "Power without Limits."
34. Ryn, "Power without Limits," 25.
35. See Robert Nisbet, *The Quest for Community* (Wilmington, DE: ISI Books, 2010). Among various works by Roepke see Wilhelm Roepke, *A Humane Economy* (Wilmington, DE: ISI Books, 1998).

BIBLIOGRAPHY

Babbitt, Irving. *Rousseau and Romanticism*. New Brunswick, NJ: Transaction Publishers, 1991.

Burke, Edmund. "Letter to Richard Shackleton, 1745." In *The Correspondence of Edmund Burke*. Vol. 1. Chicago, IL: University of Chicago Press, 1958.

———. "A Letter from the Right Honorable Edmund Burke to a Noble Lord, on the Attacks Made upon Him and His Pension." In *The Writings and Speeches of Edmund Burke*. Vol. 9, *The Revolutionary War, 1794–1797, and Ireland*. Edited by Paul Langford. Oxford: Clarendon Press, 1989.

———. *A Philosophical Enquiry into the Origin of Our Ideas of the Sublime and Beautiful*. In *The Writings and Speeches of Edmund Burke*. Vol. 1, *The Early Writings*. Edited by Paul Langford. Oxford: Clarendon Press, 1989.

———. *Reflections on the Revolution in France*. Edited by J. G. A. Pocock. Indianapolis, IN: Hackett Publishing Company, 1987.

———. "Speech on Reform of Representation." In *The Works of the Right Honorable Edmund Burke*. Vol. 7. Boston, MA: Little, Brown & Company, 1865–67.

Byrne, William F. *Edmund Burke for Our Time: Moral Imagination, Meaning, and Politics*. DeKalb, IL: Northern Illinois University Press, 2011.

Canavan, Francis P. *The Political Reason of Edmund Burke*. Durham, NC: Duke University Press, 1960.

MacIntyre, Alasdair. *After Virtue: A Study in Moral Theory*. 3d ed. Notre Dame, IN: University of Notre Dame Press, 2007.

Marx, Karl, and Friedrich Engels. *Manifesto of the Communist Party*. In *The Marx-Engels Reader*, 2d ed. Edited by Robert C. Tucker. New York: W. W. Norton & Company, 1978).

Murray, Charles. *Coming Apart: The State of White America 1960–2010*. New York: Crown Forum, 2010.

Nisbet, Robert. *The Quest for* Community. Wilmington, DE: ISI Books, 2010.

Oakeshott, Michael. *Rationalism in Politics and Other Essays*. Indianapolis, IN: Liberty Press, 1991.

Reynolds, Glenn Harlan. "Trump and the Crisis of Meritocracy." *USA Today*, February 20, 2017.

Röpke, Wilhelm. *A Humane Economy*. Wilmington, DE: ISI Books, 1998.

Ryn, Claes G. "From Civilization to Manipulation: The Discrediting and Replacement of the Western Elite." *Humanitas* 22, nos. 1–2 (2009): 5–22.

———. "Power without Limits: The Allure of Political Idealism and the Crumbling of American Constitutionalism," *Humanitas* 26, nos. 1–2 (2013): 5–27.

———. *Will, Imagination, and Reason: Babbitt, Croce, and the Problem of Reality*. New Brunswick, NJ: Transaction Publishers, 1997.

de Tocqueville, Alexis. *Democracy in America*. Edited by Stephen D. Grant. Indianapolis, IN: Hackett Publishing Company, 2000.

CHAPTER SEVEN

Natural Law, the Moral Imagination, and Prudent Exceptions

Robert C. Koons

The terms *natural law theory* or *natural law ethics* pick out a central tradition in the history of ethics, political theory, and jurisprudence in the West—a tradition that begins with the works of Aristotle, penetrates the consciousness of the Latin world in the works of Cicero, and reaches a paradigmatic expression in the work of Thomas Aquinas. This way of thinking about the moral world and our place in it forms the common foundation for thinking about constitutional issues in the early modern period, from the judicious Richard Hooker and Hugo Grotius to Thomas Hobbes, John Locke, Samuel von Pufendorf, and the American Founders. This tradition emphasizes human reason (as a manifestation of divine reason) and the formulation of general rules and principles that can be applied logically (through the "practical syllogism") to particular cases at all times and in all places. In both its rationality and its pursuit of generality and universality, the classical natural law tradition resembles the ethical rationalism of such modern thinkers as Locke, Kant, Mill, and Rawls.

Claes Ryn, drawing on the work of Edmund Burke and Irving Babbitt, has trenchantly criticized ethical rationalism and generalism, on behalf of an approach that prefers the use of historical memory and the moral imagination over pure reason and that respects the uniqueness of the moral demands of the particular situation over reliance on general rules. Ryn includes both ancient and modern versions of generalizing rationalism within the scope of his critique. He has been especially critical of the Thomistic and scholastic version of natural law theory.

I will argue that the natural law tradition, including Thomas Aquinas, is more balanced and more complex in its epistemology and methodology than Ryn's critique would imply. The tradition does make room for the indispensable role of both experience and imagination in right moral judgment: it does not reduce moral judgment to a mechanical, algorithmic application of general rules to particular situations. Instead, the virtue of prudence (practical wisdom) plays an indispensable role, one that cannot be fully codified in general rules. Although it does include the postulation of exceptionless general prohibitions (always negative in nature), it does not entail that we can completely satisfy the demands of morality by simply following those negative rules, and it includes the recognition that even in the application of exceptionless rules to particular cases, judgment and the use of the imagination are unavoidable.

In the first section, I will sketch an outline of natural law ethics as found in the works of Aristotle, Cicero, and Thomas Aquinas, and I will summarize Ryn's critique of that tradition. In the second section, I will sort out the three issues that Ryn's critique raises: extreme versus moderate generalism, exceptionless versus defeasible generalizations, and the role of pure reason versus experience and the moral imagination. I take up each of these issues in turn in the three succeeding sections, proposing an irenic reconciliation of Ryn's Burkean particularism with the natural law tradition in the concluding section.

1. NATURAL LAW THEORY AND ITS CONSERVATIVE CRITICS

I will focus on the works of three seminal figures: Aristotle, Cicero, and Thomas Aquinas. From Aristotle I will draw primarily from *The Nicomachean Ethics*, but also from his *Politics*. The relevant works of Cicero's are *On Obligations* (*De Officiis*) and *On the Laws* (*De Legibus*), and I will take into account Part Two of Thomas Aquinas's *Summa Theologiae*, both the general discussion of happiness, virtues, and the law in the First part of the Second Part, and the discussion of particular virtues in the Second part of the Second Part.

This tradition unfolds in three stages. First, it examines the nature of the universal human end: happiness, *eudaemonia*, or *felicitas*. Second, it describes a set of moral and intellectual virtues (excellences of mind and character) that are essential to the actualization of human happiness. Finally, it looks to the institution of the law, both positive and natural, as the social framework needed for the nurturing of virtue. The resulting theory is sometimes described as eudaemonism or teleological perfectionism, sometimes as virtue theory, and sometimes as natural law theory. All three labels are appropriate, since each of the three dimensions is essential. In all three seminal figures (Aristotle, Cicero, and Aquinas), it is the discussion of the virtues that predominates (in terms of the volume of material), and the discussion of happiness invariably takes first place in the order of development. Law in general and the moral and natural law in particular take up an important but clearly subordinate and ancillary position in the theory.

In all three thinkers, the very possibility of morality depends on human rationality. It is our capacity to think in universal terms that enables us to conceive of an overarching human end. In addition, since rationality is the specific difference that ultimately defines our human essence, the universal human end is to be identified with a life of rationally ordered activity. The virtues that enable us to live this good life are ultimately excellences associated with human reason: either the capacity to make rational judgments about what to think and to do, or the docility and malleability of our subrational drives and instincts in relation to the supervising guidance of rational intelligence. Our capacity for reason endows us with the will, which Aquinas defines as the "rational appetite" and which is the fundamental mainspring of all human action.[1]

At the same time, the Aristotelian conception of human reason is not purely a priori, logical, or formalistic. In contrast to Platonism, the Aristotelians suppose that human reason derives its understanding of the world entirely from the data of sensory experience.[2] We grasp universals, but we always do so by abstracting them from particular exemplars encountered in sensory experience and in memory. Aristotelian reason is inductive and abductive as well as deductive (*Posterior Analytics* and the *Topics*). It is a capacity for finding the universal element within the sensible world, not through purely formal or introspective cognizing, and not through mystical states of awareness.

For Aristotle and his successors, the highest form of human thought, science, consists in the acquisition and contemplation of universal definitions—which are definitions of things and their essences, and not merely of words or other conventional signs (see Aristotle's *Metaphysics*).[3] Nonetheless, Aristotle,[4] Cicero,[5] and Thomas Aquinas[6] all recognize that science (theoretical wisdom) and understanding do not suffice for right moral action. In addition, practical wisdom (*phronesis* or *prudentia*) is required, and the acquisition and exercise of prudence requires breadth of experience, since it involves the understanding of both universals and particulars.

Aristotelian and Thomistic epistemology has a much richer internal structure than most of its modern counterparts. Unlike, say, the logical empiricism of Hume, Russell, or the Vienna Circle, Aristotelians recognized more fundamental sources of knowledge than just formal logic and sense data. For example, there are a number of cognitive capacities that involve the coordination of information from the senses and from memory. Aristotle and Thomas Aquinas attribute to all of the higher animals a *common sense*, which combines and coordinates information from the various senses and constructs a model of a moving three-dimensional world, and an *estimative sense*, which enables animals to learn from past experience. In human beings, the estimative sense is combined with reason in a *cogitative sense*, which enables us to recognize patterns and which provides the foundation for successful induction to sound scientific theory.[7] The common and cogitative senses play a role similar to that attributed by Kant and Coleridge to the *imagination*. In relation to moral notions, the cogitative sense is a kind of *moral imagination*, to use Edmund Burke's language.

We can find general principles or maxims of a practical nature at four distinct places within the Aristotelian tradition. First, there is that most general maxim that directs us to our ultimate end. Thomas Aquinas identifies this with the "first principle" of the natural law:[8] seek what is good, and avoid what is evil. Second, there are those maxims that prescribe the forms of excellent thought and action that constitute the various virtues: be wise, temperate, courageous, and just. Third, we find rules that exclude certain forms of action as intrinsically evil and contrary to reason: do not intentionally kill the innocent or commit adultery, for example. And, finally, there are all of the derivative principles of the natural law, including principles of commutative and distributive justice, the necessity of respect for parents and for public authorities, the protection of property and respect for contracts, and so on. However, the philosophers in this tradition do not claim that mere acceptance of these maxims is sufficient for the moral life. They provide the indispensable universal dimension to our moral understanding, but moral action also requires good judgment about particular cases, and this good judgment does not consist in merely deducing particular cases from universal generalizations.

However, Ryn has criticized this tradition as failing to understand the central and ubiquitous function of the imagination.

> Good philosophy in the last two centuries has established the primacy of the
> imagination in constituting our grasp of the world. Today only thinkers who are

ignorant of this advance or wearing ideological blinders contemplate a return to the kind of classical-medieval intellectualism that attributes to the imagination a passive and preliminary role in the search for reality.[9]

On the role of our historical knowledge of particulars, Ryn recognizes that it would be "anachronistic to attribute to Plato and (especially) Aristotle a purely ahistorical rationality,"[10] but he does not extend a similar courtesy to medieval thinkers, like Aquinas. He argues that the concept of a universal good (which figures prominently in Aquinas's ethics) that "invests human existence with a higher and enduring significance" is a "highly questionable and potentially pernicious abstraction."[11] Ryn also calls into question the very possibility of ethics and politics as a completed science: "A claim to having captured universality once and for all is in effect a denial of the historical nature of human existence."[12] Ryn also argues that the moral imagination gives us a "non-conceptual awareness of the universal."[13]

Furthermore, Ryn is highly skeptical about the role of general maxims in moral life and the possibility of exceptionless moral rules. Ryn points out, "The individuals who are most qualified to discriminate tend to be the same who incline against categorical, unqualified statements regarding the specific ways in which goodness, truth, and beauty can be manifested."[14] Ryn makes a similar claim about "abstract principles": "Abstract principles can be more or less expressive of universality, but by themselves they are, precisely because of their lack of concreteness, actually without real normative authority."[15]

Finally, Ryn argues that "philosophical reason" does not promulgate "principles," "specific rules," or "goals of conduct."[16] He even suggests that human activities are "dialectical" in such a way that "makes formalistic logic—the alternative of 'is' or 'is not'—inapplicable to them."[17]

We find in Edmund Burke's *Reflections on the Revolution in France* a similar, apparent rejection of the universality of ethical truths as grounded in the metaphysical structure of human nature. Burke writes, "These metaphysic rights entering into common life, like rays of light which pierce into a dense medium, are, by the laws of nature, refracted from their straight line.... It becomes absurd to talk of them as if they continued in the simplicity of their original direction."[18] Burke seems to suggest here a fairly radical modification (by "refraction") of the universal truths or maxims of the natural law by the details of the particular situation, as found in the flux of history.

2. SORTING OUT THE ISSUES

There are three points of apparent conflict between Ryn's Burkeanism and the natural law tradition. First, can moral goodness be reduced to the following of general rules and maxims? Second, are there moral rules or principles that hold in all possible circumstances, without exception? Third, is moral knowledge entirely a matter of pure reason, or are the faculties of sense perception and the imagination (in particular, a moral imagination) also necessary?

a. Extreme versus Moderate Generalism

It is clear that Ryn and the Burkean tradition that Ryn follows (Burke, Babbitt, and Kirk) reject the idea that moral knowledge consists in deriving (by deductive logic alone) particular conclusions from a fixed and finite set of universal principles. However, as we shall see in section 3, the natural law tradition is equally emphatic in its opposition to such a reduction. Let's call the thesis of the reducibility of moral judgment to logical deductions from general principles "extreme generalism." Both Burkeans and the natural law tradition reject extreme generalism. There is a weaker form of generalism, which we could call "moderate generalism." According to moderate generalism, every moral judgment does involve some reference to at least one general moral principle. However, the moderate generalist does not insist that the relation between general principle and particular judgment be simply one of logical deduction. Instead, the moderate generalist is open to the need for an uncodifiable faculty of judgment (including the use of the moral imagination) in applications of principles to concrete cases. Moderate generalism is a component of the natural law tradition, but it is fully consistent with Burkean particularism.

b. Exceptionless versus Defeasible Generalizations

Thomas Aquinas clearly believes in the validity of absolutely universal, exceptionless moral rules, such as the prohibition of the intentional killing of innocent human beings, and Ryn is clearly skeptical, on Burkean grounds, about any such claims to absolute universality. If all the rules and principles of morality were exceptionless in this way, Aquinas's theory would imply the kind of extreme generalism discussed above, since exceptionless general rules can be applied to particular cases by logic alone.

However, Thomas Aquinas taught that these exceptionless generalizations are themselves exceptional. The exceptionless rules are all negative in nature: that is, absolute prohibitions. There are certain things (like murder and adultery) that are, by virtue of their immediate object, their end, or their circumstances intrinsically evil and so can never be commanded by a right use of reason.[19]

Aristotle also recognized the existence of such morally forbidden actions.

> But not every action nor every passion admits of a mean; for some have names that already imply badness, e.g. spite, shamelessness, envy, and in the case of actions adultery, theft, and murder; for all of these and suchlike things imply by their names that they are themselves bad, and not the excesses or deficiencies of them. It is not possible, then, ever to be right with regard to them; one must always be wrong. Nor does goodness or badness with regard to such things depend on committing adultery with the right woman, at the right time, and in the right way, but simply to do any of them is to go wrong.[20]

However, the satisfaction of such absolute prohibitions is (according to the natural law tradition) only one part of morality. It is admittedly an important part: one cannot attain to moral excellence while continuing to resort to intrinsically evil actions. However, mere avoidance of evil in this way does not suffice for virtue. There are many positive duties of morality—including respect for parents or love for God and neighbor—that cannot be reduced to a set of negative prohibitions. Any rule or principle that can be derived from such positive duties—such as "obey your father!" or "pay your debts!"—admit of many possible exceptions. They are defeasible rather than exceptionless principles, and it is a matter of rational judgment, and not just formal logic, to know whether a defeasible rule really applies in any given situation.

c. Role of Experience and the
Imagination versus "Pure" Reason

The natural law tradition insists that morality and the law are fully rational. Cicero, in particular, was quite explicit in identifying the law with reason:

> Law is the highest reason, inherent in nature ... when that reason is fully formed and completed in the human mind, it, too, is law ... [The law] is right reason commanding and forbidding.... There is one single justice. It binds together human society and has been established by one, single, law. That law is right

reason in commanding and forbidding. A man who does not acknowledge this law is unjust, whether it has been written down anywhere or not.... That original and final law is the intelligence of God, who ordains or forbids everything by reason.[21]

Thomas Aquinas reaffirms Cicero's identification of law with reason. The natural law is nothing more than our participation in divine reason, as Aquinas explains in Question 91 of the *Pars Prima Secundae*: "The rational creature has a share of the Eternal Reason, whereby it has a natural inclination to its proper act and end: and this participation of the eternal law in the rational creature is called the natural law."[22] Aquinas elaborates further in Question 94, Article 3 of that same Part: "Wherefore, since the rational soul is the proper form of man, there is in every man a natural inclination to act according to reason: and this is to act according to virtue. Consequently, considered thus, all acts of virtue are prescribed by the natural law: since each one's reason naturally dictates to him to act virtuously."[23]

However, the natural law tradition conceives of reason in this context as encompassing human intelligence in all of its capacities. We must not identify reason with logic or with the intuitive grasp of formal principles. For Aristotelians, human reason is a fully embodied capacity, one anchored in sensory experience and imagination. For Aristotle, to act virtuously is a matter of obtaining the correct mean between two or more extremes: "Virtue, then, is a state of character concerned with choice, lying in a mean, i.e. the mean relative to us, this being determined by a rational principle, and by that principle by which the man of practical wisdom would determine it."[24] So, for example, courage is a matter of accepting the right degree of personal risk in action, neither too little (cowardice) nor too much (foolhardiness).

Every virtuous action is a particular action in particular circumstances, and the discovery of the right mean for each action requires an exercise of "perception": "For in everything it is no easy task to find the middle.... But up to what point and to what extent a man must deviate before he becomes blameworthy is not easy to determine by reasoning, and more than anything else that is perceived by the senses; such things depend on particular facts, and the decision rests with perception."[25]

The kind of *perception* involved is not a matter of the use of the exterior senses of sight, hearing, smell, taste, and touch but rather of the interior senses: the common sense and the cogitative sense.[26] These interior senses correspond closely to the notion of the constructive imagination as it is found in Kant,[27]

Coleridge,[28] and Burke.[29] The interior senses enable us to recognize and to classify the objects both of sense perception and memory in terms of evaluative concepts like *wholesome, dangerous, appropriate,* or *excessive.*[30]

The interior senses of human beings have much in common with the corresponding senses of some of the higher animals (i.e., those capable of learning by experience), but at the same time these senses are transformed by the presence of human rationality. Thus, Aquinas uses the word "estimative" for the interior sense of recognition as found in animals and "cogitative" for the corresponding sense in human beings. For Aristotelians, there is in human beings no such thing as pure reason or pure sensuality. Human rationality is inseparable from our sensual natures, and our sensuality is profoundly transformed by the presence of rationality.

3. IN DEFENSE OF MODERATE GENERALISM

The natural law tradition includes a commitment to moderate generalism, in the sense that every moral judgment and every virtuous choice must involve the apprehension of a universal principle. Why is this element of universality necessary?

The answer is primarily one of philosophical anthropology. The essence of a human being is *rational animality*. An action is human only insofar as it is rational, and it is rational only insofar as the human agent apprehends the action as good. But no action is simply good: goodness is always grounded in and supervenes on other qualities and properties of the action. Each particular good action is good for some concrete reason: because it advances knowledge or aids one's friend or meets a human need, or for some similar consideration. These considerations correspond to moral rules or generalizations: any action whatsoever, insofar as it advances knowledge or aids one's friend, and so forth, is good for that same reason. Hence, to choose an action as good is to apprehend a corresponding moral generalization under which the action falls.

However, these generalizations do not have to be exceptionless. In fact, very few of them are. For the most part, moral generalizations hold in most cases—the normal cases—but can fail when the circumstances are abnormal. There are two cases of exceptionless moral rules: those very high-level principles that simply tell us to "do what is good" and to "avoid evil," and those negative prohibitions that forbid certain forms of intrinsic evil (murder, adultery, etc.). All positive rules that involve specific descriptions are derivative rules that admit of exceptions, as Thomas Aquinas explains,

> It is therefore evident that, as regards the general principles whether of speculative or of practical reason, truth or rectitude is the same for all, and is equally known by all.... But as to the proper conclusions of the practical reason, neither is the truth or rectitude the same for all, nor, where it is the same, is it equally known by all. Thus it is right and true for all to act according to reason: and from this principle it follows as a proper conclusion, that goods entrusted to another should be restored to their owner. Now this is true for the majority of cases: but it may happen in a particular case that it would be injurious, and therefore unreasonable, to restore goods held in trust; for instance, if they are claimed for the purpose of fighting against one's country. And this principle will be found to fail the more, according as we descend further into detail, e.g. if one were to say that goods held in trust should be restored with such and such a guarantee, or in such and such a way; because the greater the number of conditions added, the greater the number of ways in which the principle may fail, so that it be not right to restore or not to restore.[31]

Aristotle also recognized this lack of perfect generality in the law. In Book V of the *Nicomachean Ethics*, he uses this fact to explain the necessary role of equity in applying the law to particular cases. Although he is speaking here about the positive law, what he says must apply equally to the natural or moral law, since it implies the impossibility of an exceptionless generalization.

> ... all law is universal but about some things it is not possible to make a universal statement which shall be correct. In those cases, then, in which it is necessary to speak universally but not possible to do so correctly, the law takes the usual case, though it is not ignorant of the possibility of error.... In fact this is the reason why all things are not determined by law, viz. that about some things it is impossible to lay down a law, so that a decree is needed. For when the thing is indefinite the rule also is indefinite, like the leaden rule used in making the Lesbian moulding; the rule adapts itself to the shape of the stone and is not rigid, and so too the decree is adapted to the facts.[32]

Notice that Aristotle does not suppose that we can do without rules altogether. Rather, we need flexible rules, like the malleable lead of the Lesbian moulding. Just as the lead moulding adjusts itself to the irregular edges of the things being joined, so a rule must adjust itself to irregular circumstances. The rule must be universal in content, so that it can be rational, and yet it must not be universal in actual application, since we must exercise judgment, based on experience, in order to perceive the existence of exceptions.

4. ROLE OF EXCEPTIONLESS PROHIBITIONS

As we've seen, the natural law tradition, beginning with Aristotle, has recognized the existence of absolute prohibitions: certain types of actions that cannot be performed by any virtuous person, no matter what the circumstances or comparative consequences of the act. These prohibitions have typically included idolatry, blasphemy, the intentional killing of innocent human beings, intentional adultery, and lying. The aim of every human being is to act well, and to act well (given our rationality) is to act in accordance with reason. Certain types of action are in their very essence contrary to reason. Therefore, no morally well-educated and competent human agent will so much as consider choosing such actions.

What makes an act contrary to reason? Take blasphemy, for example. If I believe that God exists, then I must recognize that I owe respect to God above all other considerations, but blasphemy would involve treating the dignity of God as something secondary and optional.

What about lying? Clearly, the essence of speech is the attempted articulation of truth, for the good of oneself and one's audience. So, to articulate falsehood with the intention of harming others is to act contrary to the very nature of speech itself, and so to act irrationally. However, it is obvious that not every intentional expression of a falsehood is a case of lying. One can intentionally express what is false in telling a joke, in creating a fiction, in making a metaphor, or in expressing oneself sarcastically or ironically without thereby lying. At the very least, lying includes an intention to deceive another human being. Suppose that one's hearer is incapable of believing the truth: in such a context, expressing a falsehood, even intentionally, cannot be a lie, since one who is invincibly ignorant of a fact cannot be said to be *deceived* about it. But what does it mean to *believe the truth*? Believing the truth cannot be reduced to merely assigning the right truth-value to this or that sentence, as in a multiple-choice of true-false exam. Rather, it must involve the apprehension in pragmatically relevant ways.

Take the classic problematic example: May one lie about the whereabouts of an intended victim to someone intent on doing murder? In the relevant sense, such a would-be murderer is incapable of believing the truth, since he cannot apprehend, while intending to kill, that a fellow human being, who is undeserving of death, is located in such and such a place. In such a context, expressing a falsehood to the would-be murderer about the potential victim's location is therefore not a case of lying and so does not fall within the scope of the absolute prohibition against lying. To discern whether a particular case of intentionally false assertion is a case of lying may involve an element of judgment or perception, an element that is not codifiable in an exceptionless formula.

Consider also the case of the absolute prohibition of the intentional taking of innocent human life. Much turns on the meaning of *innocent*. Thomas Aquinas (along with Cicero and Augustine) admits the possibility of just war, and in the context of just war, enemy combatants are not *innocent*, however reasonable (even admirable) may be their motivations as patriotic members of their countries.

Jonathan Dancy, who rejects the existence of exceptionless moral rules, is nonetheless open to the possibility of what he calls "absolute" prohibitions, including the prohibition of killing the innocent.

> Now the choice of innocence here is interesting. It seems to me to encapsulate the thought that only an act of one's own can justify one's being killed. If one has done nothing wrong, one is innocent and there is a complete reason against one's being killed. There are of course (or may be) various ways in which one can undermine one's own immunity against being killed. But to say straight out that one is innocent is to say in advance that none of those ways has been operated in this case. So to kill someone who is innocent is to kill someone of whom we know already that there is no justification for their being killed. It is not surprising that an action of this sort is always wrong; but its wrongness is, as it were, a structural feature, built into the description.... Innocence is merely the absence of a justification for the killing.[33]

Thus, even in the case of absolute prohibitions, the natural law tradition does not reduce morality to the mechanical application of logical formulas to particular cases. An exercise of moral judgment, grounded in experience and imagination (the inner sense) can be required in assessing the applicability of absolute prohibitions in individual cases. This does not make such prohibitions mere tautologies. In order for human beings to lose their innocence, they must actively *do* something that justifies killing them. The justification cannot come from the victim's origin, family, status, or the actions of others. But what exactly must be done for innocence to be lost is not reducible to a rigid formula.

5. INTERDEPENDENCY OF REASON AND THE IMAGINATION

A reasonable person acts with practical wisdom (*phronesis, prudentia*). Practical wisdom does not consist merely in understanding a set of universal truths: there is also an irreducible element of particular knowledge, derived from experience.

This is why young people cannot be prudent, no matter how much abstract instruction they have received:

> A young man of practical wisdom cannot be found. The cause is that such wisdom is concerned not only with universals but with particulars, which become familiar from experience, but a young man has no experience, for it is length of time that gives experience.... Practical wisdom is concerned with the ultimate particular, which is the object not of scientific knowledge but of perception.[34]

Thomas Aquinas explains that prudence involves the understanding of both universal truths and particular circumstances.

> ... [T]he reasoning of prudence must proceed from a twofold understanding.... The right estimate about a particular end is called both "understanding," in so far as its object is a principle, and "sense," in so far as its object is a particular. This is what the Philosopher means when he says (Ethic. v, 11): "Of such things we need to have the sense, and this is understanding." But this is to be understood as referring, not to the particular sense whereby we know proper sensibles [i.e., sight, hearing, smell, etc.], but to the *interior* sense, whereby we *judge* of a particular.[35]

In Question 51, Article 4 of the same Part, Aquinas discusses the virtue of "gnome," which denotes "a certain discrimination in judgment" needed to discern those cases that are not covered by the "common rules of actions."[36] *Gnome* consists of the capacity to know how one must judge according to a more "general law" (like "do the just thing") in a case in which the common but particular (like "return what you've borrowed") does not apply.

This interior perception is that capacity by which we shape the impressions of the five senses into a coherent, three-dimensional world consisting of things that are (in Heidegger's expression) "ready to hand."[37] The gnomic aspect of that capacity enables us to discern when we are confronting an exceptional case to which the ordinary or common rules of morality do not apply. It lights up those aspects of the concrete situation that are morally relevant and enables us to synthesize those aspects in a single moral judgment. These capacities are developed and honed over time: they are acquired skills, and they do not consist in the mere memorization of formulas. Nonetheless, they count as fully rational, in the sense that they enable us to relate particular situations to universal values, something nonrational animals are incapable of.

6. CONCLUSION: A RECONCILIATION

When discussing Edmund Burke's account of moral reasoning, Russell Kirk makes a crucial distinction between *principle* and *abstraction*: "Principle is right reason expressed in permanent form; abstraction is its corruption. Expedience is wise application of general knowledge in particular circumstances; opportunism is its degradation."[38]

Among these principles are the natural rights of man: "The rights of men are in a sort of *middle*, incapable of definition, but not impossible to be discerned."[39] By *discernment*, Burke refers to that capacity that Aquinas had labeled "gnomic": a rational capacity for judgment that is grounded in experience and that applies directly to a concrete situation as experienced. Burke's rejection of *abstraction* is highly qualified: "I do not put abstract ideas wholly out of any question, because I well know that under that name I should dismiss principles; and that without principles, all reasonings in politics, as in everything else, would be only a confused jumble of particular facts and details, without the means of drawing out any sort of theoretical or practical conclusion."[40]

We can, therefore, reconcile ancient and scholastic intellectualism with Burke's rejection of excessive abstraction and with the indispensability of experience-based judgment. Universal principles are essential to human life, and they retain their validity at all times and places, even though they may not apply to all situations. The discernment of the exceptional case, even if uncodifiable, is nevertheless an expression of essential human rationality.

In *Will, Imagination, and Reason*,[41] Ryn sees one aspect of Aristotle's epistemology that both accords with his own understanding of the primacy of the imagination and that has been overlooked by later interpreters of Aristotle: poetry as a source of knowledge. In fact, in chapter 22 of the *Poetics*,[42] Aristotle suggests that the right use of metaphor is a "sign of genius," which involves the "intuitive perception of similarity in dissimilars." This poetical source of knowledge is in fact recognized by Thomas Aquinas in the context both of ethics[43] and of theology.[44] This recognition is simply Aquinas's celebrated theory of *analogy*. It is through the intuitive grasp of analogy that we reason from our concrete experience of one form of value to another. As long as reason is understood as an organ of analogy and not simply of calculation, we can assign due weight to the imaginative and concrete aspects of ethics. Thus, the origins of the sort of modern abstractionism against which Burke, Croce, Babbitt, and Ryn warn us must be found in later philosophy, including Duns Scotus's insistence on the univocity of reason (*Ordinatio* 1.3.1.1–2) and Descartes's clear and distinct ideas in the Second and Third Meditation.[45] As Gilson observed,[46] it was Descartes who made mathematical reason the paradigm of rationality, in sharp contrast to the Aristotelian and scholastic traditions, which recognized the inherently rough and precise nature of ethical reality.[47]

NOTES

1. Thomas Aquinas, *Summa Theologiae*, I Q40, A2, September 12, 2017, http://dhspriory.org/thomas/summa/index.html.

2. Aristotle, *On the Soul, Parva Naturalia, On Breath*, trans. W. S. Hett (Cambridge, MA: Harvard University Press, 1957), Book 3, chapter 4; Thomas Aquinas, *Summa Theologiae*, Part I, Q85.

3. Aristotle, *Metaphysics*, Book VII, chapter 11.

4. Aristotle, *The Nicomachean Ethics*, trans David Ross (Oxford: Oxford University Press, 1925), Book 6.

5. Cicero, *On Obligations*, trans. P. G. Walsh (Oxford: Oxford University Press), Book I, paragraphs 152–60.

6. Aquinas, *Summa Theologiae*, II-II, Q47.

7. Aristotle, *On the Soul*, Book III, 425a27–425b4, and Aquinas, *Summa Theologiae*, I, Q78, A4.

8. Aquinas, *Summa Theologiae* I-II, Q94, A2

9. Claes G. Ryn, "Philosophical Reason: Historical, Systematic, and Humble," *Humanitas* VI, no. 2 (1993):86.

10. Claes G. Ryn, "Universality and History: The Concrete as Normative," *Humanitas* VI, no. 1 (1992):15.

11. Ryn, "Universality and History," 12.

12. Ryn, "Universality and History," 26.

13. Claes G. Ryn, *Will, Imagination, and Reason: Babbitt, Croce, and the Problem of Reality* 2d ed. (New Brunswick, NJ: Transaction), 187.

14. Ryn, "Universality and History," 37.

15. Ryn, "Universality and History," 38.

16. Ryn, "Philosophical Reason," 83, 85.

17. Ryn, *Will, Imagination, and Reason*, 186.

18. Edmund Burke, *Reflections on the Revolution in France*, vol. 2, *Works* (London: George Bell & Sons, 1886), 334–35.

19. Aquinas, *Summa Theologiae*, I-II, Q18.

20. Aristotle, *The Nicomachean Ethics*, trans. David Ross (Oxford: Oxford University Press, 1925), 39 (1109a1–5).

21. Cicero, *The Republic and The Laws*, trans. Niall Rudd (Oxford: Oxford University Press, 1998), 103, 105, 112, 124.

22. Aquinas, *Summa Theologiae*, I-II Q91, A2.

23. Aquinas, *Summa Theologiae*, I-II, Q94, A3.

24. Aristotle, *Nicomachean Ethics*, 39 (1106b36–40).

25. Aristotle, *Nicomachean Ethics*, 46, 47 (1109b15–22).

26. Aristotle, *On the Soul*, Book III, 425a27–b4, and Aquinas, *Summa Theologiae* I, Q78, A4.

27. Immanuel Kant, *Critique of Pure Reason*, trans. Norman Kemp Smith (New York: St. Martin's Press, 1929), 129–75, 180–87, 191–94.

28. Samuel Coleridge, *Biographia Literaria*, 161–67 (Chapter XII).

29. Burke, *Reflections*, 349.

30. Aristotle, *On the Soul*, 161–63, 177–79 (428b10–429a2, 431 b2–9); Thomas Aquinas, *Commentary on De Anima*, trans. K. Foster and S. Humphries (Notre Dame, IN.: Dumb Ox Books, 1994), 95–98, 120–23 (Book II, Lectures VI and XII).

31. Aquinas, *Summa Theologiae*, I-II, Q94, A4

32. Aristotle, *Nicomachean Ethics*, 133 (1137b12–32).

33. Jonathan Dancy, *Moral Reasons* (Oxford: Blackwell, 1993), 229–30.

34. Aristotle, *Nicomachean Ethics*, 148 (1142a15–20, a27).

35. Aquinas, *Summa Theologiae*, II-II, Q49, A2. Emphasis mine.

36. Aquinas, *Summa Theologiae*, II-II, Q51, A4.

37. Martin Heidegger, *Being and Time*, trans. John Macquarrie and Edward Robinson (Oxford: Blackwell, 1962), 95–107.

38. Russell Kirk, *The Conservative Mind from Burke to Eliot* (Washington, DC: Regnery Publishing), 40.

39. Burke, *Reflections*, 335.

40. Edmund Burke, "Speech on the Petition of the Unitarians," vol. 6 in *Works* (London: George Bell & Sons, 1886), 113–14.

41. Ryn, *Will, Imagination, and Reason*, 154.

42. Aristotle, *The Rhetoric and Poetics of Aristotle*, trans. Rhys Roberts and Ingram Bywater (New York: Random House, 1954), 255 (1459a6).

43. Thomas Aquinas, *Commentary on Aristotle's Ethics*, trans C. J. Litzinger (Notre Dame, IN: Dumb Ox Books, 1993), 31–32 (Book I, Lesson 7).

44. Aquinas, *Summa Theologiae* I, Q13, A5

45. René Descartes, *Meditations on First Philosophy*, trans. Laurence J. Lafleur (Indianapolis: Bobbs-Merrill, 1960), 32, 24.

46. Etienne Gilson, *Methodical Realism*, trans. Philip Trower (Ft. Royal, VA: Christendom Press, 1990), 84–86.

47. Aristotle, *Nicomachean Ethics*, 2–4.

BIBLIOGRAPHY

Aquinas, Thomas. *Commentary on De Anima*. Translated by K. Foster and S. Humphries. Notre Dame: Dumb Ox Books, 1994.
———. *Commentary on Aristotle's Ethics*. Translated by C. J. Litzinger. Notre Dame, IN: Dumb Ox Books, 1993.
———. *Summa Theologiae*. Translated by Fathers of the English Dominican Province. New York: Benziger Brothers, 1947.
Aristotle, *Metaphysics*. Translated by W.D. Ross. Oxford: Clarendon Press, 1958.
———. *The Nicomachean Ethics*. Translated by David Ross. Oxford: Oxford University Press, 1925.
———. *The Rhetoric and Poetics of Aristotle*. Translated by Rhys Roberts and Ingram Bywater New York: Random House, 1954.
———. *On the Soul, Parva Naturalia, On Breath*. Translated by W. S. Hett. Cambridge, MA: Harvard University Press, 1957.
Burke, Edmund. *Reflections on the Revolution in France*. In *Works*. Vol. 2. London: George Bell & Sons, 1886.
———. "Speech on the Petition of the Unitarians." In *Works*. Vol. 6. London: George Bell & Sons, 1886.
Cicero, Marcus Tullius. *On Obligations*. Translated by P. G. Walsh. Oxford: Oxford University Press, 2008.
———. *The Republic and The Laws*. Translated by Niall Rudd. Oxford: Oxford University Press, 1998.
Coleridge, Samuel Taylor. *Biographia Literaria*. Oxford: The Clarendon Press, 1962.
Dancy, Jonathan. *Moral Reasons*. Oxford: Blackwell, 1993.
Descartes, René. *Meditations on First Philosophy*. Translated Laurence J. Lafleur. Indianapolis, IN: Bobbs-Merrill, 1960.
Gilson, Etienne. *Methodical Realism*. Translated by Philip Trower. Front Royal, VA: Christendom Press, 1990.
Heidegger, Martin. *Being and Time*. Translated by John Macquarrie and Edward Robinson. Oxford: Blackwell, 1962.
Kant, Immanuel. *Critique of Pure Reason*. Translated by Norman Kemp Smith. New York: St Martin's Press, 1929.

Kirk, Russell. *The Conservative Mind from Burke to Eliot*. Washington, DC: Regnery Publishing, 2016.

Ryn, Claes. "Philosophical Reason: Historical, Systematic, and Humble." *Humanitas* 6, no. 2 (1993): 81–90.

———. "Universality and History: The Concrete as Normative," *Humanitas* VI, no. 1 (1992): 10–39.

———. *Will, Imagination, and Reason: Babbitt, Croce, and the Problem of Reality*. 2d ed. New Brunswick, NJ: Transaction, 1997.

CHAPTER EIGHT

Irving Babbitt and Christianity

A Response to T. S. Eliot

Ryan R. Holston

> Either make the tree good, and its fruit good; or make the tree corrupt, and its fruit corrupt: for the tree is known by its fruit.
> —Matthew 12:33

Notwithstanding the work of a small number of acolytes, the reception of Irving Babbitt's humanism among Christians has been rather chilly, to say the least.[1] Part of the reason for this is undoubtedly the criticism leveled against Babbitt's ideas by his most prominent student, the great poet and literary critic T. S. Eliot, who nonetheless remained under Babbitt's intellectual influence throughout his lifetime.[2] Eliot's criticisms were significant, not only because of his prominence and intellectual kinship with Babbitt, but because they offered an explicitly Christian interpretation that saw his New Humanism as problematically trying to supplant the religious foundations of Western civilization with a secular alternative. It is interesting that even among contemporary Christian writers who extol the idea of a "Christian Humanism," there has likewise been a reluctance to see the thinking of Babbitt as compatible with or supportive of Christianity.[3] The present essay seeks to remedy what is seen as a misinterpretation of Babbitt from the Christian perspective, which has its origins in these criticisms of Eliot. In order to do so, it will reframe this early discussion, arguing that Babbitt's humanism is not only compatible with Christianity but that his early phenomenological account of moral decision-making actually bolsters Christian ethics. In the end, the essay will argue that Babbitt's relationship to Christianity should be understood as comparable to that of Aristotle, insofar as Babbitt may be seen to anticipate and inform the contemporary philosophical approach known as virtue ethics, which has much to offer Christian thinking about the ethical life.

BABBITT AS HERETIC?

Eliot's criticisms of Babbitt's thinking are various, but they may be distilled into a few central claims. First, Eliot accuses Babbitt of developing an ethical system that resembles an extreme form of liberal Protestantism or that makes "a Catholic platform out of Protestant planks."[4] The thrust of Eliot's charge here is that the idea central to Babbitt's humanism, the exercise of an "inner check" or "higher will" that restrains the appetite, resembles the Christian attempt to control man's sinful nature, but without the institutional support of the church, thus elevating the moral autonomy of the individual.[5] However, Eliot believes this has caused Babbitt to overestimate private judgment, naively and optimistically assuming that human beings on their own can exercise the same control of the will that the church, with its magisterium and its doctrine, has long supported. Second, Eliot believes that without Christian doctrine, the outer goal or purpose toward which one aims in ethical conduct is lost and that Babbitt's is essentially an ethical system of empty form. He famously complains: "What is the higher will to *will*, if there is nothing either 'anterior, exterior, or superior' to the individual? If this will is to have anything on which to operate, it must be in relation to external objects and to objective values."[6] Finally, there is the charge that Babbitt's philosophy engages in an "attempt to build a purely human world without reliance upon grace."[7] Thus, Eliot suspects that Babbitt, himself an unbeliever, was aspiring to an entirely secular, empirical philosophy "at the expense of God."[8] Described by Eliot in the terms of a modern heretic, Babbitt's disbelief thus becomes central to his critique,[9] along with the idea that Babbitt was motivated by a personal concern to make his humanism in no way dependent on faith or divine revelation, of which he, himself, was incapable.

Although less overt as a criticism of Babbitt, there is another issue—connected with the last of these—that is worth mentioning. An additional feature of Babbitt's thinking and writing that appears unsettling to Eliot is Babbitt's relationship to Buddhism, which Babbitt sees as a source of ethical wisdom in the Eastern world that echoes important insights that Christianity has likewise contributed to Western civilization. This relationship is central to Babbitt's lengthy introduction to the ancient Buddhist text, *The Dhammapada*, for which he also provided a translation.[10] The affinity Babbitt feels for this particular religious tradition is, in fact, rooted in the same sensibility—an aversion to dogmatic theological commitments—which Eliot interprets as a wholesale rejection of divine revelation.[11] The more accurate understanding of Babbitt's outlook is that he sees genuine religiosity as grounded in concrete, spiritual effort rather than professions of commitment to dogma, a priority expressed in particular within early Buddhism. Moreover, the achievement of self-control and the successful avoidance of selfish indulgence that Babbitt admires in Buddhism is something he actually sees as a priority in the best of Christianity as well.[12] However, Eliot interprets Babbitt's relationship to Buddhism and other religious traditions rather differently. On his reading, Babbitt has so deeply immersed himself in a wide variety of world religions that he actually becomes incapable of belief in any of them.[13] Consequently, it is worth noting that in the background of Eliot's claim regarding Babbitt's diminishment of divine authority is his view that Babbitt, himself, is incapable of any belief in the transcendent beyond this world. On Eliot's view, Babbitt's affinity for the practical teachings of the Buddha, whom he sees as a sort of "religious empiricist,"[14] is essentially all the faith that Babbitt can muster.

BABBITT AS CHRISTIAN?

While critics such as Eliot may be correct in pointing to the fact that Babbitt was not a believer in Christian revelation in the strict sense, it is often neglected that he did more than merely accommodate Christian belief within his philosophical outlook, allowing for its compatibility or coexistence with a belief in humanism. More accurately, it must be admitted that Babbitt was much more of a partisan of Christianity, not merely in the sense of appreciating its salutary social consequences, but in actively recognizing the universal truths contained within the Christian message. For example, much as his humanism finds great wisdom and inspiration among the ancient Greeks for their conception of the well-ordered soul, Babbitt points to the superior ethical insight of Christianity, insofar as it emphasizes the primacy of the will over the intellect as this abiding source of moral order in human affairs.[15] On other occasions, as Babbitt identifies particular ethical truths from a humanistic perspective, he notes the corresponding articulation and corroboration of the idea as it has been put forth within Christianity. Thus, with respect to the humanistic observation regarding the natural proclivity toward moral indolence, Babbitt refers to the counterpart of this notion in the Christian tradition, which he identifies as the doctrine of Original Sin.[16] Elsewhere, Babbitt says that the higher will, which represents the humanist's conception of morally inspired behavior, may justly be compared to the Christian understanding of Grace, which makes ethical conduct possible.[17]

But Babbitt actually goes much further than recognizing Christianity's possession of universal truths that correspond to those he believes are known to humanism. In his definitive statement of his humanist philosophy, which was written partly in response to the criticisms raised by Eliot, Babbitt makes clear the relationship that he sees between humanism and religion, and he is explicit that the former is *not* a substitute or alternative to the latter, rendering it unnecessary or irrelevant. On the contrary, Babbitt states unequivocally in this essay that, "It is an error to hold that humanism can take the place of religion," and he even goes so far as to emphasize the superior autonomy of religious belief when he adds, "Religion indeed may more readily dispense with humanism than humanism with religion."[18] Further still, Babbitt openly admits that with respect to moral insight, theological doctrines may contain truths that go beyond what is accessible to the experiential wisdom of humanism.[19]

However, in spite of this space that Babbitt carves out for the privileged insights of religion over humanism, it ought be made clear that such a relationship is not, in fact, the main thrust of this essay. Rather, the principal theme is that there is ultimately no great tension, threat, or antagonism between humanism and the great religious traditions of East and West, because the relationship between them is, in the end, one of complementarity, rather than competition.[20] Babbitt is clear, therefore, that "[humanism] gains immensely in effectiveness when it has a background of religious insight."[21] And he writes approvingly, in particular, of the Catholic Church's "discipline and the definite standards that could protect society against the individual,"[22] while also lamenting the decline of traditional religion.[23] At the same time, Babbitt believes that humanism, by focusing on experiential wisdom and avoiding doctrinal disagreements, has the potential to forge peaceful cooperation within and among religious groups, providing the social and political environment in which the pious may continue "further down the path" in the ordering of the soul.[24]

Important as this mutually supportive relationship between humanism and religion is for Babbitt, his intentions in setting aside questions of religious doctrine in public life and drawing on shared experiential wisdom among religions is not ultimately grounded in pragmatism. Rather, the importance of humanistic discipline as the basis of such cooperation lies in the fundamentally ethical nature of Babbitt's concerns. Specifically, it is out of a priority of upholding the standards of civilization in this world that humanism focuses exclusively on the concrete human conduct in which any true religion or philosophy of life issues. It is interesting to note that although Babbitt does indeed claim that the sights of humanism are set considerably lower than those of the seeker of eternal salvation,[25] his concern for upholding these standards of the ethical life, for both individual and society, do not yield in the face of religious beliefs that fall short of them. The result is that using concrete experience as a standard—specifically the practice of ethical restraint—Babbitt believes we may distinguish pseudoreligiosity, or what he refers to as "sham spirituality,"[26] from genuine religiosity. This is because Babbitt believes that the moral universal, insofar as it penetrates into this world, is ultimately something that must be lived and willed rather than merely held as a set of beliefs in the human consciousness.[27] Our ability to discriminate "between the spiritual athlete and the cosmic loafer, between a St. Paul, let us say, and a Walt Whitman,"[28] is precisely that which allows us to "discriminate] practically and concretely between true and false religion."[29] It is in this context that Babbitt's thinking can first be seen as bolstering or supporting Christianity, insofar as its emphasis on the experiential evidence or "fruits"—by which he means the peace, harmony, or well-being (*eudaimonia*) it promotes both within and among individuals—will allow Christians to differentiate the pious avowal of dogma that often characterizes modern religiosity from the concrete willing of the Word of God that results in real self-transformation.

If humanism is used to discriminate between true and false religion and thus to support the identification of genuine Christianity in the manner suggested, must we not, then, consider the objection that humanism makes a standard external to Christianity a reference point for judging it? While this is admittedly an important question to consider, it is one that ultimately must be answered in the negative. In the first place, "Christianity" is not a monolith but has various contending strains within it. And it is important to be clear that Babbitt's wariness is of the historically "Neo-Platonic side" of Christianity, with its otherworldliness, as well as the modern utilitarian-sentimental permutations of Christianity, with their humanitarian impulses.[30] These various forms of "[s]piritual romanticism"[31] pose dangers, Babbitt believes, by virtue of their idealistic reverie, which includes a general unwillingness to deal with the hard realities of human nature and life in this world.[32] By urging Christianity in a more "experiential" direction, however, Babbitt is not engaging in an external critique, but is actually evoking resources already within it, which he believes have been obscured or insufficiently represented, particularly within modernity. Indeed, it is in order to compensate for previous alterations and distortions, which have effected changes in Christian ethics, that Babbitt sees this critical task as paramount.

Consequently, instead of seeing Babbitt's appeal to the concrete experience of the ethical life in order to expose "sham spirituality," as judging Christianity with standards external to it, this is more appropriately understood as a realignment with Christianity's true message, motivated by a concern for the ethical ramifications of previous historical alterations. In his famous work on St. Thomas Aquinas, G. K. Chesterton similarly recognizes such a role with respect to Thomas' appropriation of Aristotle against the abstractions of Augustinianism. It is possible, Chesterton argues, for an "outside" influence such as this to help restore and renew the truth in the original or essential message of the faith.[33] Chesterton thus says that by bringing the pagan, Aristotle, into Christianity, there was in fact nothing heathen or heretical introduced, such that he bluntly remarks, "St. Thomas was making Christendom more Christian by making it more Aristotelian."[34] And later, Chesterton echoes and further clarifies this observation, when he adds that despite drawing on Aristotle, "St. Thomas was becoming more of a Christian, and not merely more of an Aristotelian, when he insisted that God and the image of God had come in contact through matter with the material world."[35] Similar to Chesterton's critique of Augustinianism, Babbitt sees a "spiritual Romanticism," particularly in the last two centuries, as having altered the substance of Christianity, which otherwise is—and indeed must be—consonant with experiential wisdom.[36] As a result, Babbitt does not see the corroboration of genuine religiosity by such concrete evidence as an external critique or syncretic intrusion but a return to and a renovation of the essential spirit of the faith.

In support of this interpretation, it is worth considering that other observers have noted how Babbitt's humanistic scrutiny of modern Christianity in fact echoes an impulse that has historically been internal to the faith itself. Arguably, Babbitt's disagreement with Eliot can thus be understood through the lens of the famous argument within Christianity regarding the nature of justification before God and whether this may principally be said to take place through "faith" or "works."[37] When viewed in this light, it is possible to conceive of Babbitt's critique of "spiritual Romanticism" within Christianity as akin to the justification by works argument, checking the excessive value that is sometimes placed on theological creeds or dogmas, which can become formalistic and thus detached from the concrete, living reality that has given life to them.[38]

To be sure, Babbitt's position might be seen as a more extreme variety of this family of arguments, insofar as the priority of "works" has been elevated to such significant status that it entirely eclipses faith, rendering the latter irrelevant. However, such criticisms would be misplaced, since Babbitt never claims to be offering up a complete theology.[39] Focused on the ethical conduct attendant to Christianity (and other religious traditions), he offers only a reminder of a single dimension of what can help differentiate true from false religion. Eliot's critique of Babbitt, by contrast, is to a large extent based on the idea that the works of the will are inconceivable without the right creed or doctrine at which to aim. Without spiritual beliefs to guide the will, right conduct seems aimless, for Eliot. It is this perspective—not any such aspiration on Babbitt's part—that ultimately leads to Eliot's conclusion that Babbitt seeks to "replace" Christianity. The problem, therefore, is Eliot's own premise that the only impetus for ethical conduct is spiritual goals, understood as ideational or otherworldly phenomena, and it is this that causes him to impute such purposes to Babbitt.

Babbitt's emphasis on the centrality of the ethical will, knowing the soundness of one's religiosity through the "fruits" it produces, along with his emphasis on the achievement of habits of ethical character, are more appropriately seen as echoing the Christian argument for justification by "works." Indeed, this is a standard internal to Christianity that helps differentiate true religion from sham spirituality—to argue otherwise would be to deny this historical impulse within Christianity. Alternatively, Babbitt's humanism may be seen as helping to reconnect Christians with the concrete experiences that once gave rise to the traditional understanding of the Gospel (as opposed to its modern, interpretive distortions). In doing so, Babbitt negatively calls into question the Romantic temperament whose professions of strict adherence to religious norms are little more than empty posturing—moralistic cover for the indolent dreamer who, while making pious proclamations of universal love, secretly avoids the struggle of resisting selfish temptation.[40] Thus, while Babbitt's interests are fundamentally ethical, not theological, his humanism similarly helps to expose these sorts of spiritual romanticism that transform Christianity from its essential message into something other than itself.

BABBITT AS ARISTOTELIAN

The argument thus far has been that while Babbitt cannot accurately be viewed as a heretic, as Eliot portrays him, neither is he a Christian, in the strict sense of that term, for which belief in Biblical revelation would be necessary. There is, however, a middle position between these that is thought to better capture Babbitt's relationship to Christianity. This middle position that Babbitt occupies resembles that of Aristotle's practical science of ethics, which itself has historically been closely joined with Christian thinking—most famously in that of St. Thomas Aquinas and the Scholastics—and thought to support the latter through its reflection on lived experience, asking what it is that we are doing when we behave ethically. Babbitt's writings are not only littered with various references to Aristotle's thinking,[41] but in its essentials, his humanism adopts a number of key features associated with Aristotelian ethics, on which Babbitt may be said to build. Thus, in the first instance, it is worth noting that Babbitt, like Aristotle, brings an "experiential," or what he sometimes terms "positive" or "experimental," approach to the study of ethics, because he believes, like his ancient mentor, that moral universality is sufficiently infused and imbedded within the concrete, material world in which human beings live that its reality is observable as empirical facts, as undeniable as those of the natural scientist. Like Aristotle, as well as many other thinkers who follow in his footsteps, such as Edmund Burke, Babbitt also has a strong aversion to abstract theorizing and speculation,[42] and he believes this "immediate data of consciousness" to be more reliable than any "mystical-transcendental mist."[43] Additionally, Babbitt understands the ultimate goal or purpose at the heart of his ethical science, like Aristotle, to be the fulfillment of our universal human nature, which brings with it our happiness or flourishing (*eudaimonia*)—the inner peace and harmony that accompanies a life well-lived.

The principal manner in which the last of these is to be achieved, for Babbitt as for Aristotle, is by living one's life in accordance with the law of measure. Therefore, the operation of Babbitt's inner check or higher will is not aimed at the renunciation of all feeling and desire, as if the goal were the complete negation of or withdrawal from the life of the senses, but as with Aristotle's doctrine of the mean, achieving proportion and the avoidance of extremes with respect to these.[44] Additionally, Babbitt shares with Aristotle the recognition that the achievement of such proportion will require an awareness of the variability of events and the changing circumstances in which they take place. Echoing Aristotle's argument for the preeminent role of the virtue of practical wisdom (*phronesis*), Babbitt avers, "Whoever has succeeded in bridging the gap between the general precept and some particular emergency has to that extent achieved the fitting and the decorous. Decorum is simply the law of measure in its more concrete aspects."[45] At the same time, Babbitt is sober regarding the capacities of individual decision-makers and the preconditions of such judgment. Thus, once more, he follows Aristotle's emphasis on the development of sound habits (*hexeis*) and the need for habituation in the acquisition and exercise of ethical judgment.[46] Consequently, Babbitt is hardly an "optimist"[47] when it comes to the individual's capacity for ethical decision-making and in fact laments the decline of institutions, such as traditional religion, which once stood in support of such habituation and development of sound character.[48]

What is more, Babbitt is most explicit that the priority of the law of measure is more than simply a matter of prudential calculation, such that it might be dismissed as an effective means of pragmatically satisfying one's long-term, selfish interests. Rather, Babbitt describes the proportion at which one aims in terms that are clearly intended to echo the natural law tradition and the writings of its ancient precursors: "The law of measure on which [humanism] depends becomes meaningless unless it can be shown to be one of the 'laws unwritten in the heavens' of which Antigone had the immediate perception, laws that are 'not of today or yesterday,' that transcend in short the temporal process."[49] Although informed by both intuition and convention, he says, such laws actually have their "deep root in the nature of things."[50] Moreover, Babbitt is clearly self-conscious of how the natural law doctrine of Aquinas made use of Aristotle in a similar fashion, in order to recognize the powers of universal moral discernment that are accessible to human beings outside of Christian revelation.[51] Babbitt thus recognizes that the ecumenicism in his thinking, in this regard, actually has roots in Christianity itself.[52]

Further, although Babbitt points not only to humanistic wisdom, but to that of other religions, such as Buddhism, to demonstrate the recognition of the moral law across cultures, it ought to be acknowledged that preeminent Christian writers such as C. S. Lewis have been no less reluctant to point to religious traditions outside of Christianity for their illustrations of the universal moral order.[53] Explicitly identifying the natural law as pointing to the same universal truths as those which are recognized in the Chinese religious-philosophical tradition, Lewis actually prefers to refer to moral universality throughout the entirety of *The Abolition of Man* as "the *Tao*."[54] Moreover, Lewis elsewhere expresses an overt rejection of the provincially Christian view, when he says, "It is often asserted that the world must return to Christian ethics in order to preserve civilization. Though I am myself a Christian, and even a dogmatic Christian untinged with Modernist reservations and committed to supernaturalism in its full rigour, I find myself quite unable to take my place beside the upholders of [this] view. It is far from my intention to deny that we find in Christian ethics a deepening, an internalization, a few changes of emphasis in the moral code. But only serious ignorance of Jewish and Pagan culture would lead anyone to the conclusion that it is a radically new thing."[55] Echoing such ecumenicism within the natural law tradition, Babbitt can thus be seen as making use of Buddhism and Confucianism in his writings in a similar manner, ultimately demonstrating the universal discernibility of the same moral law that is recognized by Christianity.

If Aristotle is the paragon of humanism for Babbitt for the reasons identified above, it should be acknowledged that even in spite of his various criticisms of abstract thinking, Babbitt is a Platonist in at least one important sense. Like Plato, Babbitt sees the harmony that is achieved in the well-ordered soul simultaneously running parallel to and supporting the harmony of the political community. In other words, Babbitt believes that insofar as the individual is successful at checking his selfish desires and living according to the law of measure, not only does he bring his individual soul into a state of harmony and achieve individual happiness (*eudaimonia*) but this negation of selfishness at the same time acts as a will to civilization: "[T]he individual who is practising humanistic control is really subordinating to the part of himself which he possesses in common with other men, that part of himself which is driving him apart from them. If several individuals submit to the same or a similar humanistic discipline, they will become psychically less separate, will, in short, move towards a communion."[56]

Babbitt's understanding of the "will to civilization," which is so derided by Eliot, is thus not an elite intellectual's substitute for religion, nor is it simply a pragmatic consensus under the conditions of pluralism, rather it is what the great religions of the world have independently intuited as the harmonious existence and coexistence of individual and community, respectively: "[Babbitt's] ambition is to articulate what the great religious and ethical systems have in common. They have all emerged, he argues, in response to one and the same intuition of transcendent purpose."[57] Neither secular, in that it often draws on religious practice, nor theological, in that it is concrete action rather than the revealed word itself, the "will to civilization" is the ethical core—the "living reality of practice and intuition"—on which the great religions of East and West have converged.[58] It is the truth of religion, as it were, that is discovered through their "vast body of historical experience."[59] Thus, far from establishing an empty, formalistic goal, which renders religion superfluous, Babbitt's "will to civilization" actually points to the corroboration of Christianity's universal truth in the similar experiential knowledge of other religious traditions.

BABBITT AS VIRTUE ETHICIST

Given what has been said thus far, it may be tempting to conclude that the problem with Babbitt, from the Christian perspective, is not so much that his humanism is unconventional or unorthodox but that, on the contrary, his humanism appears so highly conventional in its proximity to classical thinking that there is little to offer that can be considered new or insightful. Indeed, much of what has been said in the previous section, which primarily relates the thinking of Babbitt to that of Aristotle, goes a good deal of the way toward establishing Babbitt as a precursor to the modern philosophical approach known as "virtue ethics,"[60] which itself has drawn heavily on classical thinking in recent decades. Indeed, of the three principal focuses of virtue ethics, two have already been mentioned above as being shared by Babbitt with Aristotle—the focus on the fulfillment of our universal human nature, which brings about happiness or flourishing (*eudaimonia*), and the focus on prudence or practical wisdom (*phronesis*) as the form of knowing that is necessary to achieving that, given life's circumstantial variety and contingency. Together with its third focus, which is on the development of excellence with respect to particular virtues, this more traditional method of ethical inquiry has challenged the basic presuppositions of contemporary deontological and consequentialist philosophy, seeking to replace the driving question of "What ought I to do?" with that of "Who (or what sort of person) ought I to become?" And, although Babbitt is less specific in his identification of particular virtues, he may be said to echo this third concern as well, insofar as his emphasis on the law of measure and avoiding extremes evokes Aristotle's doctrine of the mean, which suggests that virtue is the midpoint of any feeling or action.

Writing several decades before even the earliest work in contemporary virtue ethics had been published, Babbitt was clearly cognizant of the need for the sort of paradigm shift or questioning of fundamental premises with respect to questions of morality that those in more recent decades have sought. The ultimate standard to which all ethical questions must finally refer, Babbitt concludes, is not a theory of right conduct, but the "man of character," which he calls "the ultimate human reality."[61] Therefore, Babbitt explicitly eschews action-guiding rules in the manner of contemporary virtue ethics and instead sees good character as the ultimate aim of the ethical life. For Babbitt, becoming the right sort of person is not merely the means of bringing about ethical conduct, it *is* the fundamental purpose of the ethical life, since the ethical will, which he emphasizes so heavily, is not only what acts in the world, but a central feature of the human personality. On his view, what guides us in ethical conduct is thus not the external reference point—rules, principles, or doctrines—sought by Eliot and others, particularly in the tradition of philosophical rationalism. Rather, it is the person we have already become through past conduct. One hears strong echoes here of Aristotle's emphasis on habits (*hexeis*), which are the predispositions of ethical conduct brought about through the proper training and exercise of the virtues. However, where Babbitt truly distinguishes himself both from Aristotle as well as modern virtue ethicists is his account of the interaction between the will and the imagination, the faculty we use to make sense of the world and which likewise constitutes a central part of our character.

What Babbitt means by the imagination, or intuition, is the faculty one uses to make sense of or understand reality, that which creates order and coherence out of the empirical flux.[62] One *con*ceives, as opposed to *per*ceiving, the world in which we find ourselves, bringing together diverse pieces of information, which, in actuality, are never really separate, but always part of the whole that constitutes our lens of understanding. The prejudices of our own individual experience and collective experience (or tradition) thus shape our imaginations, such that our understanding is never neutral or objective but always colored in various ways by diverse priorities and associations. As such, the imagination is not only the vision of what life is but assembles for us as well the possibilities of what life can be—it presents us with possibilities for acting in the world from which the will ultimately chooses. In this sense, the imagination precedes the will with respect to our action in the world, framing the ways in which it is possible for us to act long before we choose and engage in willful conduct.

However, in another very important sense, Babbitt identifies the manner in which the will shapes the imagination and is determinative of our conceptual vision of reality. The creative assemblage of reality that takes place in the person habituated to exercising ethical restraint and the check on appetite looks very different from that in whom desires are routinely indulged and the inner check is indolent. The imagination, in other words, has different moral qualities that correspond to those of the will, which define our action in the world. What Babbitt terms the moral or ethical imagination is that vision of life's possibilities, the background for the choices we make every day, that he believes sees more deeply and truly life as it really is. The moral imagination "knows," not in the sense of the reason or intellect, but as intuition, the misery that accompanies selfish indulgence, and it tends to conceive reality in a way that sees possibilities for action—those conducive to moderation, cooperation, and order—that are commensurate with this knowledge. Conversely, Babbitt calls the idyllic imagination that which distorts reality because it is part of a personality that is accustomed to the indulgent pursuit of short-term pleasure. The idyllic imagination creates a corresponding vision of self-serving action and hedonistic desire-satisfaction through pleasing illusions and self-deceptions about the nature of reality and one's ultimate purposes. In each case, our predispositions of conduct established by the will essentially shape the way we see the world, creating choices for action that are conducive to those actions toward which we are already inclined. Our imaginations do this, in the first case, through a willingness to admit realities that are often uncomfortable and in the most literal sense, realistic, while in the second case, they do so by selectively admitting information that will perpetuate pleasing illusions that condone our pursuit of pleasure. The apprehension of reality through the imagination, for Babbitt, is ultimately bound up with the concrete choices we are already making. The imagination, in its dynamic interaction with the will, constitutes a central—perhaps *the* central—component of our character.

Christian ethics stands to benefit from Babbitt's insights regarding the voluntative-imaginative constitution of our character for the very reason that Eliot had thought humanism to be inadequate from a Christian perspective. Insofar as the will and the imagination are involved in the sort of dialectical relationship that Babbitt sees, it would appear evident that the symbols of the Christian imagination are in need of continual nourishment from the exercise of Christian works. As Babbitt shows, will and imagination are so intimately implicated in one another's activity, it is indeed difficult to tell where the operation of one faculty ends and the other begins. Therefore, it turns out that the very "external objects" and "objective values" on which Eliot had placed so much importance—the doctrinal and revelatory commitments that he saw lacking in humanism and that he thought were essential to the faith—do not actually exist independently of the concrete practice of Christianity in any meaningful sense.

To be perfectly clear, this is not simply to reiterate the old point that "faith" is nothing without "works"—although this is certainly true and related, Babbitt's phenomenology actually takes Christian thinking further. The point, instead, is that there *are* ultimately no doctrines or creeds that are "there," waiting to be believed in without a willful interpreter. Our understanding of these symbols is not only informed with the help of the imagination, but as Babbitt shows us, the latter will always, itself, possess a concrete history. To put a finer point on it, it is not simply that creedal formulations and symbols matter less than or tend to follow good works. It is that the very meaning of such symbols is dependent on the existence of a Christian imagination in believers. Without the latter, the meaning of scripture is set wildly adrift, and it becomes no surprise to discover that even great moral calamities have been committed in the name of "Christianity."[63] In contemporary Western society, radically diverse interpretations of scripture may, indeed, be traced to the proper attunement (or lack thereof) of the imagination by the will. Or, to put the point still more dramatically, one may say that there is, for all intents and purposes, no Gospel in any meaningful sense without persons of Christian character to interpret it. And, consequently, calls to recommit Western society to "the faith" are ultimately hollow without cultivating the types of imaginations that are prepared to believe.

This brings us back to the will, which for Babbitt, was fundamental. To be sure, as has already been admitted, the imagination itself has a role in providing the images from which individuals must choose to live. And, as many observers have noted, there is indeed a case to be made here for reforming the cultural-aesthetical images within which the individual imagination must operate. However, from a Babbittian perspective, all of the Christian symbols and imagery in the world would be impotent—if not potentially harmful—without the ethical personality to interpret it. The renewal of Christian ethics, and even the preservation of the faith that Eliot saw as vital to Western civilization,[64] must begin with concrete behavior.[65] It is in the life of the family, the church, the neighborhood, and the community—those institutional supports for resisting temptation, whose decline Babbitt once lamented, that such work must therefore begin. Still, the renewal of such institutions is merely support, not panacea, since what they assist is the operation of the ethical will in individuals whose imaginations must, in the end, be engaged. No romantic dreams of a return to an age of tighter-knit communities, therefore, will suffice—only the conditions that will make such work conceivable. For, the development of ethical character, though reliant on God's grace, can only be undertaken when there is a willful acceptance of it by the individual.

NOTES

1. Among Babbitt's contemporaries, the foremost Christian writer who saw his humanism as supportive of Christianity was Paul Elmer More. Others include Louis J. A. Mercier, Lynn Harold Hough, and Leo Ward. See Claes G. Ryn,

"Introduction," Irving Babbitt, *Character and Culture: Essays on East and West* (New Brunswick, NJ: Transaction Publishers, 1995), xxxvi.

2. For these criticisms, see T. S. Eliot, "The Humanism of Irving Babbitt," in *Selected Essays* (New York: Harcourt, Brace & World, 1964); "Introduction," in *Revelation*, eds. John Baillie and Hugh Martin (New York: The Macmillan Company, 1937), 1–39; *After Strange Gods: A Primer of Modern Heresy* (London: Faber & Faber, 1934). Similar criticisms are put forth in Eliot, "Second Thoughts about Humanism" in *Selected Essays*, however his target in that essay is principally Norman Foerster, a disciple of Babbitt's. With respect to Babbitt's continued influence on Eliot's thinking, see Eliot's tribute in *Irving Babbitt: Man and Teacher*, Frederick Manchester and Odell Shepard, eds. (New York: Greenwood Press, 1969), 104.

3. One notable exception is Bradley J. Birzer. See, for example, Birzer, *Russell Kirk: American Conservative* (Lexington, KY: The University Press of Kentucky, 2015), 139.

4. Eliot, "The Humanism of Irving Babbitt," 424.

5. It is for this reason that Eliot repeatedly refers to Babbitt as an "individualist" and claims that Babbitt has an "instinctive dread of organized religion, a dread that it should cramp and deform the free operations of his own mind," Ibid.

6. Ibid., 425. Emphasis in the original.

7. George A. Panichas quoting Eliot, "Babbitt and Religion," *Modern Age* 28, nos. 2–3 (1984), 178.

8. Ryn, "The Humanism of Irving Babbitt Revisited," 257.

9. See, in particular, Eliot, *After Strange Gods*. Such criticisms are often *ad hominem*, as when Eliot speculates that secularists such as Babbitt and D. H. Lawrence are "suffering from a condition of repression painful for those in whom it is repressed, who yearn for the fulfillment of belief, although too ashamed of that yearning to allow it to come to the consciousness." Eliot, "Introduction," in *Revelation*, 37.

10. See Irving Babbitt, "Buddha and the Occident" in *The Dhammapada: Buddhist Philosophy*, trans. Irving Babbitt (New York: Oxford University Press, 1965 [1936]).

11. Eliot accuses Babbitt of a "downright rejection of revelation." Eliot, "Introduction," in *Revelation*, 21. However, this is a clear misreading of Babbitt. The passage of Babbitt's on which Eliot relies reads as follows: "It would seem desirable, then, that those who object on either humanistic or religious grounds to the overreaching attitude of scientific naturalists should not burden themselves

with any unnecessary metaphysical or theological baggage, and that their appeal should be to experience rather than to some counter dogma." Babbitt quoted in ibid. Certainly, Babbitt is not interested in religious believers abandoning their theological commitments, which is how Eliot interprets the phrase "not burden themselves with any unnecessary... theological baggage." Rather, the context of opposing scientific naturalists here indicates a specific situational need to set aside such grounds of appeal. In sum, Babbitt is suggesting a deliberative or argumentative strategy vis-à-vis those for whom revelation would have no persuasive power based on his sense that the concrete experience on which humanism relies is likely to be found more compelling.

12. While both religious traditions exhibit an emphasis on spiritual work, knowable by the "fruits" that it produces, Babbitt believes Christianity has been marred at times by a fanaticism that focuses on commitment to doctrines or creeds. See Babbitt, *On Being Creative*, xxxiii–xxxiv.

13. In the concluding paragraph of his principal statement on Babbitt's humanism, Eliot says, "Professor Babbitt knows too much; and by that I do not mean merely erudition or information or scholarship. I mean that he knows too many religions and philosophies, has assimilated their spirit too thoroughly (there is probably no one in England or America who understands early Buddhism better than he) to be able to give himself to any. The result is humanism." Eliot, "The Humanism of Irving Babbitt," 427–28. This remark in itself betrays a rather odd, almost relativistic premise on Eliot's part regarding religious and other beliefs— that they are the function of little more than particularistic cultural assimilation. One gets a similar impression from Eliot's reason for his own abandonment of the study of Sanskrit and Indian philosophy—that he feared the thorough assimilation required for understanding its "ultimate mysteries" would require losing the fundamental outlook of a European or American. Eliot, *After Strange Gods*, 40–41. Combined with the quotation above, the implication appears to be that exclusive assimilation to a particular cultural framework is the sine qua non for maintaining the perspective of a believer. This is what Eliot saw Babbitt as having lost in his thorough assimilation of foreign religions, what he thought would be necessary in order to understand the ultimate mysteries of Indian philosophy, and what he feared would be compromised in his own extant worldview if he undertook the latter.

14. See Babbitt, *On Literature, Culture, & Religion*, ed. George Panichas (New Brunswick, NJ: Transaction Publishers, 2006), 240.

15. See Ryn, "Introduction to the Transaction Edition," *Rousseau and Romanticism* (New Brunswick, NJ: Transaction Publishers, 2004), xxvi.

16. Babbitt, *Rousseau and Romanticism*, 153. See also Milton Hindus, *Irving Babbitt, Literature, and the Democratic Culture* (New Brunswick, NJ: Transaction Publishers, 1994), 50.

17. See Babbitt, *On Literature, Culture, & Religion*, 10. Ryn also notes Babbitt's comparison of the higher will to the Christian concept of the Holy Spirit. See Ryn, "The Humanism of Irving Babbitt Revisited," 257. What is interesting is that even in spite of his various criticisms, Eliot, himself, realizes Babbitt's proximity to orthodox Christianity, particularly what he calls Babbitt's "doctrine of Grace in *Democracy and Leadership*, [which] is singularly near to Christianity." See Eliot's letter to Roger Chitty on April 29, 1927 cited in "The Return of Foxy Grandpa," in *The Complete Prose of T. S. Eliot: The Critical Edition, Literature, Politics, Belief, 1927–1929*, vol. 3, Frances Dickey, Jennifer Formichelli, and Ronald Schuchard, eds. (Baltimore: Johns Hopkins University Press, 2015), 265, n11. At the conclusion of his review of two books on religion by Alfred North Whitehead, Eliot writes, "for anyone who is seriously concerned, not with 'religion,' that gelded abstraction, but with Christianity, there is far more to be learned from Irving Babbitt's *Democracy and Leadership* than from Professor Whitehead's soporific elixirs." Ibid., 264.

18. Babbitt, "Humanism: An Essay at Definition," 43–44. He reiterates the first of these assertions when he remarks on another occasion that, "I am not setting up humanism as a substitute for religion." Babbitt, *On Being Creative*, xviii. Babbitt makes clear in the context of this remark that his purpose in restricting his arguments exclusively to experience is, once again, to refute naturalism on its own terms, not because of any skepticism or hostility toward religion. Ibid. Lest there be any doubt about these purposes, on yet another occasion, he is explicit that in the debate between the naturalists and supernaturalists, "I range myself *unhesitatingly* on the side of the supernaturalists." Babbitt, "Humanism: An Essay at Definition," 39. Emphasis added.

19. Ryn, "Introduction," *Rousseau and Romanticism*, xl.

20. See Babbitt, "Humanism: An Essay at Definition," 43.

21. Ibid., 39.

22. Babbitt, *The Masters of Modern French Criticism* (New York: Houghton Mifflin Company, 1912), 330. Babbitt's admiration here for the Church's support of the higher will would appear highly problematic for Eliot's charge above that Babbitt is a thoroughgoing "individualist" who rejects all such external authority.

23. Panichas, "Babbitt and Religion," 180. Babbitt even indicates his sympathy with the would-be religious traditionalist who maintains that "Dogmatic and revealed religion ... was *alone* capable of rescuing the ancient world from a deca-

dent naturalism. It *alone* affords an avenue of escape from the analogous situation that confronts the world today." Babbitt, "Humanism: An Essay at Definition," 36–37. Emphasis added. Similarly, Ryn notes Babbitt's belief that the American constitutional order cannot survive the decline of the Christian sense of man's sinfulness. Ryn, "Introduction," *Rousseau and Romanticism*, xxv.

24. Babbitt, "Humanism: An Essay at Definition," 46. For a fuller development of this Babbittian notion of the relationship between humanistic and religious knowledge and their distinct roles in the well-ordered society, see Ryn, "The Things of Caesar: Notes Toward the Delimitation of Politics," *Thought* 55, no. 219 (December 1980): 439–60.

25. Babbitt claims that "the world would have been a better place if more persons had made sure they were human before setting out to be superhuman." Babbitt, "Humanism: An Essay at Definition," 28–29.

26. Babbitt, *Character and Culture*, 240; Babbitt, *Rousseau and Romanticism*, 287, 364.

27. Babbitt, *On Being Creative* (Boston: Houghton Mifflin Company, 1932), xxxvi.

28. Babbitt, *Rousseau and Romanticism*, 349.

29. Panichas, "Babbitt and Religion," 180.

30. Ibid., 176, 179. As one prominent illustration, Babbitt points to the Protestant churches, who (during the Social Gospel movement) instead of teaching about overcoming sin and resisting temptation preached the "doctrine of social service," thus distracting human beings from the hard reality of inner moral struggle with idealistic dreams of social reform. Alternatively, Panichas points to the utopianism of liberation theology as an illustration of strains of Christianity to which Babbitt would later have objected, insofar as its goals of liberation refuse to recognize limitations with regard to human nature and political reality. Ibid., 174, 179.

31. Ibid., 179.

32. Panichas, "Introduction to the Transaction Edition," *On Literature, Culture, & Religion*, xi.

33. G. K. Chesterton, *St. Thomas Aquinas: The Dumb Ox* (New York: Doubleday, 1956 [1933]), 10.

34. Ibid., 16.

35. Ibid., 20.

36. Panichas, "Babbitt and Religion," 176. Although Babbitt believes experiential wisdom capable of exposing "sham spirituality," and thus helping to differentiate true from false religion, he is also careful to note that not all religious

beliefs may be susceptible to such verification. Still, where there is dissonance between articles of faith and concrete, ethical reality, we are given reason to doubt the veracity of such religious claims.

37. See Ryn, *Will, Imagination and Reason*, 39 and Panichas, "Babbitt and Religion," 175.

38. See Ryn, *Will, Imagination and Reason*, 39. Ryn argues that in pointing to this potential for doctrine to lose contact with their "originating experiences," Babbitt anticipates the later work of Eric Voegelin, who expresses concern over such reification and deformation of theological symbols within Christianity. Voegelin, *The Ecumenic Age* (Baton Rouge: Louisiana State University Press, 1974), 266; 58 cited in ibid.

39. Panichas warns of what amounts to a category error: "We must not judge Babbitt according to a systematic or dogmatic theology; his concern was not a concern with what Paul Tillich designates as the theology that 'is the methodological explanation of the contents of the Christian faith.'" Panichas, "Babbitt and Religion," 179. In the end, Babbitt was concerned with the practice of ethical conduct, and thus, while the purpose of this essay is to argue for humanism's potential to bolster Christian ethics, it ought to be kept in mind that Babbitt is not a theologian. The comparison of humanism to the argument for justification by "works" is thus only of limited value, since Babbitt is not aiming to establish "justification" *in another world*. The importance of "works" in relation to religion, for Babbitt, is to show which religious outlooks are (or are not) of a piece with concrete, ethical conduct *in this world*.

40. Ibid, 39–40.

41. Babbitt refers to Aristotle as "unsurpassed in his humanism." Babbitt, *Character and Culture*, 82.

42. Babbitt's substantial affinity for the thinking of Burke, which he finds to be a welcome antidote to the metaphysical abstractions of Rousseau, is demonstrated most clearly in *Democracy and Leadership* (Indianapolis: Liberty Fund, 1979 [1924]), ch. 3. In his aversion to metaphysical speculation, it is also possible to hear echoes of David Hume and his critique of "false philosophy." See Donald Livingston, *Philosophical Melancholy and Delirium: Hume's Pathology of Philosophy* (Chicago, IL: University of Chicago Press, 1998), esp. chapters 2, 12.

43. Babbitt quoted in Panichas, "Babbitt and Religion," 169.

44. Babbitt, "Humanism: An Essay at Definition," 26. See also Ryn, "Introduction," *Character and Culture*, xxxv.

45. Babbitt, "Humanism: An Essay at Definition," 26.

46. Ryn, "The Humanism of Irving Babbitt Revisited," 254.

47. For a refutation of one such misinterpretation of Babbitt, see Ryn, "Irving Babbitt and the Christians," *Modern Age* 32, no. 4 (Fall 1989): 346–49.

48. Panichas, "Babbitt and Religion," 180.

49. Babbitt, "Humanism: an Essay at Definition," 27.

50. Ibid.

51. Ibid., 44.

52. Ibid. Ryn notes this affinity as well. Although, in spite of the strong emphasis within Christianity on the ethical will, he notes that the natural law tradition nonetheless places greater emphasis than humanism on the faculty of reason. Ryn, "Introduction," *Rousseau and Romanticism*, xxxiv.

53. See C. S. Lewis, *The Abolition of Man* (New York: Macmillan Company, 1947). In particular, Lewis's appendix, titled "Illustrations of the Tao," is remarkably ecumenical in its detailed identification of particular precepts of the natural law across various religious and philosophical traditions. They include: Ancient Egyptians, Ancient Jewish, Old Norse, Babylonian, Hindu, Ancient Chinese, Roman, Christian, Anglo-Saxon, Greek, American Indian, Australian Aborigines, etc.). See Lewis, *The Abolition of Man*, 51–61.

54. Lewis is explicit at several points about this choice: "This conception in all its forms, Platonic, Aristotelian, Stoic, Christian, and Oriental alike, I shall henceforth refer to for brevity simply as 'the *Tao*.' ... [W]hat is common to them all is something we cannot neglect. It is the doctrine of objective value, the belief that certain attitudes are really true, and others really false, to the kind of thing the universe is and the kind of things we are." And later he says, "This thing which I have called for convenience the *Tao*, and which others may call Natural Law or Traditional Morality or the First Principles of Practical Reason or the First Platitudes, is not one among a series of possible systems of value. It is the sole source of all value judgements. If it is rejected, all value is rejected. If any value is retained, it is retained." Ibid., 12, 28.

55. Lewis quoted by David J. Theroux in "C. S. Lewis on Mere Liberty and the Evils of Statism," in *Culture and Civilization* (New Brunswick, NJ: Transaction Publishers, 2011), 197. Like Babbitt, Lewis's focus here is ethical, not theological, focusing on truths that are essential to "preserve civilization." In this spirit, he also writes, "I may add that though I myself am a Theist, and indeed a Christian, I am not here attempting any indirect argument for Theism. I am simply arguing that if we are to have values at all we must accept the ultimate platitudes of Practical Reason as having absolute validity ... Whether this position implies a supernatural origin for the *Tao* is a question I am not here concerned with." Lewis, *The Abolition of Man*, 32.

56. Babbitt, "Humanism: an Essay at Definition," 49. It is for this reason that Babbitt also acknowledges that as Christians continue further down the path of

self-mastery, there may indeed be truer or more perfect forms of community that emerge among them. Ibid.

57. Ryn, "The Humanism of Irving Babbitt Revisited," 259.

58. Ryn, *Will, Imagination, and Reason*, 38.

59. Ibid.

60. The literature in virtue ethics is voluminous. Some of the most well-known statements include: G. E. M. Anscombe, "Modern Moral Philosophy," *Philosophy*, 33 (1958): 1–19; Philippa Foot, *Virtues and Vices* (Oxford: Blackwell, 1978); Alasdair MacIntyre, *After Virtue*, 3d ed. (Notre Dame, IN: University of Notre Dame Press, 2007[1981]); Bernard Williams, *Ethics and the Limits of Philosophy* (Cambridge, MA: Harvard University Press, 1985).

61. Babbitt, *Democracy and Leadership*, 197; Babbitt, *On Literature, Cultures, & Religion*, 182.

62. See the account of this relationship between will and imagination in Babbitt's thinking in Ryn, *Will, Imagination, & Reason*, ch. 9.

63. Richard Gamble thus documents the use of Christian doctrine for the justification of the First World War in *The War for Righteousness: Progressive Christianity, the Great War, and the Rise of the Messianic Nation* (Wilmington, DC: ISI Books, 2003). Stanley Hauerwas has also noted that many Roman Catholics and Lutherans pointed to Romans 13 to justify their obedience to Hitler. See Stanley Hauerwas, "A Pacifist's Look at Memorial Day: Duke University Divinity Professor Stanley Hauerwas on Nonviolence, Iraq, and Killing Hitler," interview, accessed December 31, 2018, https://www.beliefnet.com/news/2004/06/a-pacifists-look-at-memorial-day.aspx?

64. See Eliot, *The Idea of a Christian Society* (Boston, MA: Houghton Mifflin Harcourt, 2014 [1939]).

65. I have called attention to this oversight in Eliot's thinking via a comparison of his hermeneutics to that of the twentieth-century philosopher, Hans-Georg Gadamer. See Holston, "Historical Truth in the Hermeneutics of T. S. Eliot," *Harvard Theological Review* 111, no. 2 (April 2018): 264–88.

BIBLIOGRAPHY

Anscombe, G. E. M. "Modern Moral Philosophy." *Philosophy* 33 (1958): 1–19.

Babbitt, Irving. "Buddha and the Occident." In *The Dhammapada: Buddhist Philosophy*. Translated by Irving Babbitt. New York: Oxford University Press, 1965. Reprint, 1936.

———. *On Being Creative*. Boston: Houghton Mifflin Company, 1932.

———. *Character and Culture: Essays on East and West*. New Brunswick, NJ: Transaction Publishers, 1995. Reprint, Cambridge, MA: The Riverside Press, 1940.

———. *Democracy and Leadership*. Indianapolis: Liberty Fund, 1979. Reprint, London: Constable and Company, 1924.

———. "Humanism: An Essay at Definition." *Humanism and America: Essays on the Outlook of Modern Civilisation*. Ed. Norman Foerster. New York: Farrar and Rinehart, 1930.

———. *On Literature, Culture, & Religion*. Edited by George Panichas. New Brunswick, NJ: Transaction Publishers, 2006.

———. *The Masters of Modern French Criticism*. New York: Houghton Mifflin Company, 1912.

———. *Rousseau and Romanticism*. New Brunswick, NJ: Transaction Publishers, 2004. Reprinted, Boston: Houghton Mifflin Company, 1919.

Birzer, Bradley J. *Russell Kirk: American Conservative*. Lexington, KY: The University Press of Kentucky, 2015.

Chesterton, G. K. *St. Thomas Aquinas: The Dumb Ox*. New York: Doubleday, 1956. Reprinted, New York: Sheed & Ward, 1933.

Eliot, T. S. *After Strange Gods: A Primer of Modern Heresy*. London: Faber & Faber, 1934.

———. "The Humanism of Irving Babbitt," in *Selected Essays*. New York: Harcourt, Brace & World, 1964. Reprinted, New York: Harcourt, Brace and Company, 1932.

———. *The Idea of a Christian Society*. Boston, MA: Houghton Mifflin Harcourt, 2014. Reprinted, London: Faber and Faber, 1939.

———. "Introduction." In *Revelation*, Edited by John Baillie and Hugh Martin. New York: Macmillan Company, 1937.

———. *Irving Babbitt: Man and Teacher*. Edited by Frederick Manchester and Odell Shepard. New York: Greenwood Press, 1969.

———. "The Return of Foxy Grandpa." In *The Complete Prose of T. S. Eliot: The Critical Edition, Literature, Politics, Belief, 1927–1929*. Volume 3, *Literature, Politics, Belief, 1927–1929*. Edited by Frances Dickey, Jennifer Formichelli, and Ronald Schuchard. Baltimore: Johns Hopkins University Press, 2015.

Foot, Philippa. *Virtues and Vices*. Oxford: Blackwell, 1978.

Hindus, Milton. *Irving Babbitt, Literature, and the Democratic Culture*. New Brunswick, NJ: Transaction Publishers, 1994.

Lewis, C. S. *The Abolition of Man*. New York: The Macmillan Company, 1947.

Livingston, Donald. *Philosophical Melancholy and Delirium: Hume's Pathology of Philosophy*. Chicago: University of Chicago Press, 1998.

MacIntyre, Alasdair. *After Virtue*, 3d ed. Notre Dame, IN: University of Notre Dame Press, 2007.

Panichas, George A. "Babbitt and Religion." *Modern Age* 28, nos. 2–3 (Spring/Summer 1984): 169–80.

———. "Introduction to the Transaction Edition." *On Literature, Culture, & Religion*, Edited by George Panichas. New Brunswick, NJ: Transaction Publishers, 2006.

Ryn, Claes G. "The Humanism of Irving Babbitt Revisited." *Modern Age* 21, no. 3 (Summer 1977): 251–62.

———. "Introduction." In *Character and Culture: Essays on East and West* by Irving Babbitt. New Brunswick, NJ: Transaction Publishers, 1995.

———. "Introduction to the Transaction Edition." In *Rousseau and Romanticism* by Irving Babbitt. New Brunswick, NJ: Transaction Publishers, 2004.

———. "Irving Babbitt and the Christians." *Modern Age* 32, no. 4 (Fall 1989): 346–49.

———. "The Things of Caesar: Notes Toward the Delimitation of Politics." *Thought* 55, no. 219 (December 1980): 439–60.

———. *Will, Imagination, and Reason: Irving Babbitt and the Problem of Reality*. Washington, DC: Regnery Publishing, 1986.

Theroux, David J. "C. S. Lewis on Mere Liberty and the Evils of Statism." In *Culture and Civilization*. New Brunswick, NJ: Transaction Publishers, 2011.

Voegelin, Eric. *The Ecumenic Age*. Baton Rouge: Louisiana State University Press, 1974.

Williams, Bernard. *Ethics and the Limits of Philosophy*. Cambridge, MA: Harvard University Press, 1985.

Part IV
America and Constitutional Spirit

In the context of law and government, the nature of constitutions is to preserve certain types of social order. The challenge of any theory of constitutionalism is how this can be done amid changing historical circumstances. Fundamental assumptions about human nature and what it is that can be hoped for in political life will ultimately inform one's view of this question. On the humanistic account, the framers of the U.S. Constitution, following the classical and Christian tradition, held human nature to be dualistic—individuals were deemed capable of virtue, but more often prone to egotism and power seeking. Consequently, they created institutions that, while providing conditions for the ascent of prudent leaders, nonetheless curbed their appetitive behavior through a variety of checks and balances. In government, assemblies were made small to encourage deliberation and reflection. On the whole, governing was to be slow and arduous. Based on the view that the passions are fickle, institutional hurdles were designed to require the sustained efforts of legislators, a process that fleeting impulses could not survive. What emerged was "the cool and deliberate sense of the community."

Babbitt and Ryn have argued that beginning in the Progressive Era, a new philosophical anthropology and quality of imagination took hold in America and, consequently, a dramatically different orientation toward constitutional government was adopted. In contrast to the older view, the progressive outlook sees human nature as fundamentally good. The evils that plague society are not tied to human fallibility but to historically rooted institutions that restrict liberty and equality. Government should therefore seek to liberate human beings from the past, whose institutions reflect the ignorance and superstition of previous times, at best, or were designed to exclude and oppress particular groups of people, at worst. Given this perspective, the constitutional structure inherited from the framers is seen as needing constant revision and improvement, as the barriers to freedom and equality are continually removed. The dispersing of power through devices such as a bicameral legislature, the electoral college, advice and consent, and so on merely frustrates such reforms, which can either be made by the people themselves or in the name of the people, thus bringing about a more free and equal society.

The two authors of this section share in the humanistic account of American constitutionalism, and both are grappling with the fallout of progressivism's displacement of the traditional view of human nature, political power, and a more chastened view of what is possible in political life. In "Can Constitutions Preserve the Engendering Experiences of Order?," Michael P. Federici connects the rise of progressive constitutionalism to the embrace of a fundamentally Rousseauistic outlook. In *On the Social Contract*, Rousseau famously vacillates between an understanding of the general will as an objective "true will of the people" and a unanimous agreement by the people on what is in the common good. Federici argues that in the emergence of progressive constitutionalism, the former view has prevailed, allowing elites, particularly judges, to choose which legislation to uphold or nullify based on their understanding of such an allegedly objective will. Drawing on Babbitt and Voegelin, Federici traces this approach to a distorted conception of reality, according to which human depravity is curable through institutional transformation that achieves the will of the people, or what has come to be known as "social justice." This "second reality" can only come about through changes in the imagination, according to Federici. Thus, a deep disconnect has developed with the experience of order in the soul, which has resulted in a related disconnect in our grasp of reality. When the imagination is cut loose in this manner, politics is no longer bound by the possible but becomes highly utopian in its aspirations to instantiate an idyllic and dubious conception of a free and equal society. It is only by restoring and maintaining fidelity to historical experiences of order that the limits of political reality may be recovered and that such utopian politics can be averted. The current crisis of post-constitutionalism in America, Federici concludes, is less a political problem than it is a moral and spiritual one.

Bruce P. Frohnen's essay, "On the Moral Necessity of Constitutionalism: Claes Ryn and Ethical Democracy," operates within this same humanistic framework according to which progressive constitutionalism has largely displaced the view of the framers. He begins by echoing Ryn's important distinction between constitutional and plebiscitary democracy, explaining the classical nature of Ryn's understanding of the relationship between ethics and politics. Frohnen agrees with Ryn's fundamentally Aristotelian account, according to which there is an obvious correspondence between the character of the souls of a people and the regimes that they comprise. Just as the ethical individuals exercise an inner check on their appetitive nature, Ryn says that a constitutional democracy will ensure the same sorts of checks on its impulsive volitions. Like Frohnen's own concept of "constitutional morality," Ryn believes that the good regime ultimately requires good citizens, an admission that liberalism and progressivism do not allow in the strict division they establish between public and private. However, in light of developments in the administration of law and policy since ancient Greece, Frohnen questions too close an identification of citizen and regime. Although sympathetic with humanism's more traditional constitutionalism, Frohnen cautions that local government and associations must be the agencies of public morality in such large, complex societies. One must, therefore, temper expectations about what constitutions can do besides limiting the powers of administrators and preserving the authority of those local associations, which are closer to the historically evolved customs of the people.

CHAPTER NINE

Can Constitutions Preserve the Engendering Experiences of Order?

Michael P. Federici

> Amnesia with regard to past achievement is one of the most important social phenomena.
> —Eric Voegelin, *Israel and Revelation*

> The life of the law has not been logic: it has been experience.... The law embodies the story of a nation's development through many centuries, and it cannot be dealt with as if it contained only the axioms and corollaries of a book of mathematics. In order to know what it is, we must know what it has been, and what it tends to become. We must alternately consult history and existing theories of legislation.
> —Oliver Wendell Holmes, *The Common Law*

The Anglo-American tradition of constitutionalism has ancient origins. It has developed over the course of thousands of years, and it is the consequence of efforts to tame political power and the *libido dominandi*. Exercised in the hands of human beings, power is not naturally or instinctively used in accordance with higher aspirations like happiness, justice, and the good. To minimize the arbitrary use of political power, constitutions provide ways to check and restrain political rulers as well as the people. In short, political power must be limited by law, process, and virtue in order to prevent its abuse. James Madison's statement in Federalist No. 51 about the connections between government and human nature is a classic American understanding of why power has a corrupting influence on human beings. Likewise, Alexander Hamilton noted that a "fondness for power is implanted in most men, and it is natural to abuse it when acquired."[1] Such statements are typical of the American Constitution's framers who, on balance, were steeped in a tradition that was sober about human nature and the limits of politics. The American Constitution cannot be understood apart from this underlying view of human nature.

The American framers' understanding of power stems from a tradition of political theory that encompasses much more than power and politics. It is easily forgotten that American constitutionalism and the Anglo-American political tradition from which it derives include an underlying philosophical anthropology that assumes a view of human nature and human society as well as our relationship to transcendent reality. Constitutionalism is, in other words, the outgrowth of philosophical, artistic, literary, and religious insights about the human condition and the meaning of human existence. Specific constitutional characteristics like checks and balances, the separation of powers, federalism, and judicial review presuppose a view of human existence that justifies entangling human beings in a web of procedures and restraints that helps to safeguard political power. The particular institutional and legal characteristics of constitutional societies may vary according to their respective cultural and historical heritage, but they can share a common philosophical anthropology that serves as the spiritual lifeblood of the political culture. If the philosophical anthropology is called into question or replaced by a rival conception of meaning and existence, the political institutions that were derived from the original conception of human nature and society are subject to decay and deformation.

Of particular interest to the analysis provided here is the connection between human nature and political constitutions. The American Constitution, for example, reflects underlying philosophical and historical insights about what it means to be human, and it assumes that political order is dependent on attunement to a transcendent source of order. When Americans lose consciousness of this insight and the engendering experiences of order become separated from the language of constitutionalism, the Constitution evolves in a way that undermines its core principles and leads to a radically new constitutional order. The American framers were well aware that documents alone are incapable of creating and preserving a just constitutional order. Written constitutions are composed of language symbols that can evoke historical experience, but they are not the experience itself. Over time constitutions are prone to derailment and deformation that evoke not engendering experiences of order but what Eric Voegelin and others have called second reality, a distorted conception of reality that is typically a fragment of reality purporting to be its whole.

The political theory of Irving Babbitt and Eric Voegelin can be used to analyze the problem of constitutional preservation in a climate of ideological deformation. In his early work, Voegelin found that political science was losing touch with the full range of human experience, especially given the increasing influence of positivism, a concern shared by Babbitt.[2] Legal positivists, for example, studied law and constitutions without reference to the moral and spiritual aspects of human existence. As Voegelin would later state, "Questions of social order can be discussed rationally only if the whole concept of the order of human existence, of which the social order forms a part, is viewed in its entirety and right back to its transcendental origin."[3] Likewise, Babbitt focused his analysis of human nature and politics on what he terms the higher will that is "ultimately divine."[4] Babbitt and Voegelin opposed both positivism and ideology because they truncated the horizon of reality with which scholars worked. It became clear to both thinkers that the restoration of consciousness of transcendent reality was paramount to the ability of scholars to penetrate to the core of the human condition. In characterizing the Western crisis, Voegelin asserted that the "true dividing line . . . does not run between liberals and totalitarians, but between the religious and philosophical transcendentalists on the one side and the liberal and totalitarian immanentist sectarians on the other side."[5] In Voegelin's view, political science must account for transcendent reality as an essential part of what constitutes political life.

Babbitt identifies "naturalistic philosophy" and its erosion of traditional standards as the source of American constitutional decline. The movement toward scientific and romantic naturalism meant the loss of an older classical and Christian view of morality and politics that placed the source of evil in the human heart and was suspicious of power when placed in the hands of morally dualistic human beings. Liberty, then, depended on a higher will that checked passions and inclinations that were inconsistent with justice and the common good. In Babbitt's view, this central reality of the ethical life is reflected in the institutions of American constitutionalism. The elaborate system of checks and balances and separated powers including federalism, staggered elections, the electoral college, executive veto, and judicial review are justified by the rich tradition of moral dualism that was sufficiently present in eighteenth-century American culture to shape American political institutions. The efficacy of these institutions is dependent on the prevalence of the underlying political theory and its engendering historical experiences that gave them life.

How can a constitutional system be maintained when the experiences of order that engendered it have faded from memory and been replaced by second realities that represent a radically different and incompatible understanding of human existence, including human nature? What happens to a constitutional order when the historical and philosophical substance of its political principles and constitution are faded from memory and replaced by an alternative ethos? The writings of such thinkers as Herbert Croly (1869–1930) and Edward Bellamy (1850–1898) can be used to characterize progressive constitutionalism, an outgrowth of naturalism, and contrasted to the constitutionalism of the American framers. In drawing this distinction between competing types of constitutionalism, it will be evident that the American Constitution cannot be preserved unless its antecedent experiences of order are a living force in political life. Originalism has failed to preserve these experiences of order because it amounts to the dogmatization of experience that has lost contact with the engendering experiences. Revival of the constitutional order requires nothing less than a restoration of the experiences of order to consciousness, the shared objective of Voegelin's and Babbitt's scholarship.

CONSTITUTIONAL MEANING AND THE RISE OF PROGRESSIVE CONSTITUTIONALISM

Over the course of more than a century, debates have raged about the proper role of judges and other public officials in interpreting the American Constitution. Much of the debate has centered on the degree to which judges have the discretion to reshape the meaning of the Constitution given the needs and desires of a particular age. A common way to determine contemporary need is to assume that the popular will, at any given time, provides the general direction of efficacious change. This sentiment is indicative of a romantic and populist view of democracy identified by Babbitt as a strain of naturalism rooted in the philosophy of Rousseau and at odds with the Constitution's underlying political theory. While not designed by the American framers as a branch of government that reads the momentary will of the people into the clauses of the Constitution, the judiciary has been in some ways democratized in this regard. The contemporary desires of the people, once identified, serve to validate readings of the Constitution that embrace the democratic will and contrast with the older original meaning of the Constitution. In an inversion of a central principle of American constitutionalism, democratic will is superior to constitutional will. Yet, this inversion does not preclude the opposite possibility that judicial interpretation of the Constitution will subvert the democratic will. What drives the living constitutionalism of the progressive is not the desire to align constitutional meaning to popular will as an end in itself, but a progressive ideology emanating from a view of equality that has as its objective the expansion of rights to an increasingly wider range of individuals. If the expansion of rights is supported by democratic impulse—whether it be national or international, as in *Atkins v. Virginia*—then activist judges cloak their opinions in the language of democracy and egalitarianism. If the advancement of rights, however, requires subverting the popular will, as was the case in *Romer v. Evans*, then the Court resorts to its role as check on democratic will, but it does so in the name of the same egalitarian objectives. These egalitarian objectives are consistent with Rousseauistic naturalism that in one instance insists that the general will be followed because the people are naturally good, and in the next instance suggests that the state needs to force individuals to be free who refuse to comply with the general will. As it turns out, democratic will is more apt to be defined by rulers who insist that their will embodies the democratic will than by an expression of popular will.

While progressive ideology aims to expand rights, it also tends to expand centralized government power. Stemming from the arguments of progressive thinkers like Croly and Bellamy, progressives desire greater liberty for individuals in the domain of law dealing with civil liberties, but they want greater government power in areas of law and governing that relate to economic inequality, consumer protection, labor rights, environmental protection, and economic regulation. In the first instance, government needs to have less power to regulate human life; in the second case, government needs to be empowered so that it can protect the weak from the strong. In cases like *Kelo v. City of New London*, the progressive impulse to help the less fortunate meant helping a large corporation at the expense of a powerless homeowner in order to generate higher tax revenues that could be used for urban renewal projects that would benefit the larger community. That the Constitution limits government takings of private property for "public use" was easily transgressed by reading into the takings clause of the Fifth Amendment the substitute language "public purpose." The point is that progressive ideology has as its paramount principle not constitutional fidelity, or more or less government, or remaining faithful to judicial precedents, or abiding by the people's will, but social justice, a derivative of naturalism and the overriding concern of most progressives.

"Social justice" can be distinguished from an older conception of justice found in the works of classical thinkers like Plato, Aristotle, and Cicero, as well as Christian thinkers like St. Augustine and Thomas Aquinas. In the older view, justice has social implications, but it is largely thought of as the outcome of virtue, the right ordering of the soul. Virtue requires the careful scrutiny of competing passions and inclinations in accordance with an ethical standard like Babbitt's higher will. Aquinas remarks that "Justice, properly speaking, concerns what one human being owes to another. . . ."[6] Justice requires the ordering and checking of appetites and passions in accordance with a transcendent standard of good. Without attunement to divine will, justice is impossible. For Cicero and the Christians, justice emanates from following natural law. The purpose of law is to lead individuals to virtue gradually. Social justice has much less to do with virtue and more to do with the distribution of wealth and power in a more egalitarian manner.[7] It tends to measure injustice by social statistics that identify wide discrepancies between classes of people that have either more or less than they deserve or need. The causes of such inequalities are considered to be institutional and systemic, requiring changes to laws and public policies that rectify inequality.[8] The hard data is combined with a soft humanitarian sentiment for the less fortunate. Unlike the older conception of justice, social justice is not dependent on classical or Christian virtue or what Buddha calls *appamāda*, a spiritual strenuousness that is characterized by self-control. Social justice requires control of political power and reform of institutions and public policies.

Benjamin Cardoza, who served on the Supreme Court (1932–1938), is explicit about the primacy of social justice in *The Nature of the Judicial Process*.[9] Adapting the Constitution to the needs of the day requires reading the text in a way that restricts or permits government depending on what promotes the progressive vision of social justice. Progressive constitutionalism is fundamentally at odds with the political philosophy of the eighteenth-century framers, because it operates from a fundamentally different set of philosophical assumptions. It rejects "negative constitutionalism" in favor of "positive constitutionalism."[10] The former emphasizes the dark side of human nature and the tendency of human beings and governments to abuse power. Constitutions exist, in this view, to limit and restrain government. The latter is based on a more optimistic view of human nature. Consequently, it views constitutions as instruments that empower government to do social good.[11] Felix Frankfurter expresses the progressive prejudice for empowering government when he claims, "that which is reasonably defensible on economic or social grounds . . . cannot be offensive on constitutional grounds."[12]

As living constitutionalism has ascended in American politics, its rival theory of judicial review, originalism, has become more prominent. As advocated by Justice Antonin Scalia and Robert Bork, originalism considers the meaning of the Constitution to be fixed and the role of judges to be limited to interpreting not making law. Judicial restraint means that judges should refrain from using their personal or ideological views to decide cases and be hesitant to overturn laws that are the product of the democratic process. First and foremost, the Constitution means what it says. To interpret law otherwise is to subvert the democratic process. The Constitution and the laws made in accordance with it express the sovereign will of the people. If judges substitute their will for the people's constitutional will, then popular sovereignty has been violated.[13]

There is an extent to which originalists, like Bork and Scalia, are constitutional fundamentalists. They treat the words of the document as reified truth and consider deviation from its original meaning as a violation of constitutional fidelity. What they fail to realize is that the framers of the Constitution have lost their authoritative place in American politics. The efficacy of originalism depends largely on widespread acceptance of the framers' constitutionalism including its underlying philosophical anthropology. Separated from their engendering experiences of order, constitutional clauses and principles are vulnerable to deformation and unlikely to be accepted as representative of justice. In fact, Supreme Court Justices like Thurgood Marshall and William Brennan were openly hostile to originalism because it privileged the ideas and values of a noninclusive class of white men who supported slavery and other injustices. Operating from the starting point of most progressives, the sober view of politics presented in *The Federalist* and embodied in the original Constitution stands little chance of support in an age dominated by romantic and idealistic conceptions of politics.

Judges are drawn from a culture that reflects the *zeitgeist*. Justice Cardozo explains that judges are no different than other human beings in that they possess an "underlying philosophy" that "gives coherence and direction to thought and action." Judges use their underlying philosophy, especially when cases involve laws that are unclear. In these cases, the "judge as the interpreter for the community of its sense of law and order must supply omissions, correct uncertainties, and harmonize results with justice through a method of free decision." Using the method of free decision is justified by "the great generalities of the constitution" that "have a content and a significance that vary from age to age."[14] Judges develop patterns of meaning over time as precedents in a given area of law develop. But, as Cardoza makes clear, there is something experimental about judicial decision making. If applying the standard precedents results in an unjust outcome, then judges are free to reformulate precedent or create a new foundation for a new thread of precedents.

Cardoza's view is not in itself inconsistent with the framers' constitutionalism, especially in the context of the common law where judges must exercise discretion to find justice in circumstances that are never exactly the same. Yet there is a difference between the common law and constitutional law. The former is far more flexible than the latter. Why, then, has Cardoza's view of the common law been applied by progressive judges to constitutional law? The transformation is part of the progressive deformation of American constitutionalism. Progressives reject the philosophical anthropology of the Constitution's framers. They tend to disparage the parts of the Constitution and constitutional principles that stem from it. Croly and Bellamy are representative examples. Both thinkers suggest that political rulers who are sufficiently enlightened and committed to social justice can be elevated above the rule of law and constitutional checks and restraints.[15] The liberation of political rulers as well as government itself is a central tenet of progressive constitutionalism.

Progressivism is part of political liberalism. Both were developed as a reaction to traditional authority, like the church, and its sober view of the human condition. While progressivism recognizes imperfection in man and society, it does not consider the depravity of man to be incurable. Beginning with the publication of Rousseau's *Discourse on the Origins of Inequality*, many liberals and progressives have tended to believe in the natural goodness of human beings. According to this view, evil and imperfection are the consequence of institutional organization and characteristics. Once emancipated from traditional authority and institutions, it is possible for the innate goodness of human beings to blossom and inspire a creative transformation of the world in a way that eliminates, in some cases permanently, evil. As representative of the dominant ideology of the twentieth century, progressive political leaders in America have expressed the ability to end war, fear, poverty, drug use, terrorism, economic hardship, and a host of other social ills. For progressives, centralized government is the primary instrument by which reform can be created and implemented.

Consequently, the older, darker view of human nature and government professed by *Publius* in *The Federalist* is rejected in favor of a far more glowing view of human nature and the possibilities of politics.[16] Early-twentieth-century progressives like Theodore Roosevelt, Woodrow Wilson, and Croly pronounced a new democratic age in which the people would be trusted with power, as would their leaders. The framers' concern with majority tyranny was therefore replaced by suspicion of powerful minorities that represented moneyed interests and big business. In his 1912 speech, "The Right of the People to Rule," Roosevelt identified what he considered to be the primary obstacle to progress.

> [W]e are today suffering from the tyranny of minorities. It is a small minority that is grabbing our coal deposits, our water powers, and our harbor fronts. A small minority is battening on the sale of adulterated foods and drugs. It is a small minority that lies behind monopolies and trusts. It is a small minority that stands behind present law of master and servant, the sweat-shops, and the whole calendar of social and industrial injustice. . . . The only tyrannies from which men, women, and children are suffering in real life are tyrannies of minorities."[17]

Roosevelt's political prescription for the tyranny of minorities was direct democracy reforms and a strong executive. Like Wilson, he believed that the people's will was best promoted by executive power that was relatively unencumbered by legislative and judicial checks and balances. By contrast, Babbitt argued that popular will was no substitute for ethical standards. It could only be consistent with liberty if it was sufficiently refined and enlarged, to use Madison's words, by constitutional deliberation. For progressive reforms to have any chance of success, government would have to become more powerful and more efficient than was possible in the eighteenth-century framers' system of constitutionalism.[18] Yet, as progressives divorced rulers from ethical and constitutional restraints, Babbitt argued, they became less, not more inclined, to use power in accordance with the good.

Central to the progressive imagination is the idea that human nature itself is capable of reform, if not perfection. For example, Croly was convinced that "the aim of democracy is a better quality of human nature effected by a higher type of human association."[19] He went so far as to argue that "Democracy must stand or fall on a platform of possible human perfectibility. If human nature cannot be improved by institutions, democracy is at best a more than usually safe form of political organization; and the only interesting inquiry about its future would be: How long will it continue to work? But if it is to work better as well as merely longer, it must have some leavening effect on human nature; and the sincere democrat is obliged to assume the power of the leaven."[20]

Operating from their respective views of human nature, Croly and the framers approach politics in vastly different ways. The framers tend to focus on the need to check and restrain individuals who are prone to engage in selfishness and injustices against others. Government itself must be checked and restrained to prevent tyranny. Progressives, however, tend to follow Croly and believe that politics should look outward in order to reform institutions to expand liberty and equality.[21] As long as government is in the hands of the enlightened, more government power means an increased capacity to progress. The concerns of the framers that power will have a corrupting effect on political leaders and that the greater the power the more likely the corruption are outside the progressive way of thinking about politics and human existence. That accumulated power might one day fall in the hands of a demagogue or tyrant, a primary concern of the framers, is of no or little concern to the reformer who is fixated on the progressive march toward social justice.

As Cardoza indicates, Supreme Court justices bring to each case they review a preexisting worldview enforced by the work of their imagination. In some instances, their imagination matters more than their technical knowledge of the law. Why, for example, have arguments to base court decisions on original intent fallen largely on deaf ears? Why did Justices Brennan and Thurgood Marshall react so violently against originalism? In short, originalism does not comport with their imaginative conception of constitutional politics. As liberals, they favored progressive change and reform, things that are difficult to justify using the philosophical anthropology of the framers. Living constitutionalism, however, coincides with their desire to make American society more equal and more tolerant of personal differences. It also builds into the process of deciding cases and interpreting the Constitution the discretion to update the document to the needs of the day without concern for what the framers may think. The darkness of original sin and human depravity does not fit their imaginative conception of reality.

Croly expressed progressive attitudes regarding American constitutional politics. He was more attentive than Thurgood Marshall to the need for wider cultural reform as the prelude to political change, but he was equally abstract in failing to account for the moral realities of human nature. To reform American society, it is necessary to give government "larger powers" and "a better faith in human excellence" that are justified by "the natural goodness of human nature."[22] The federal courts should play a central role in the new American republic. Federal judges should not be tied to the "immutability of the Constitution"[23] and, in fact, "the government should no longer be subject to the Law."[24] What matters is not the substance of the law but the discretion of the judges who interpret and apply it in ways that fit the circumstances before them. The commerce clause is an example of a part of the Constitution sufficiently vague to allow judges to stretch its meaning in accord with the needs of progress.

As has already been suggested, the incompatibility of progressive constitutionalism and the framers' constitutionalism does not mean that originalism is necessarily a sound and realistic approach to constitutional politics. Both theories are deficient in their conception of the possibilities of politics and thus abstractionist. While progressive constitutionalism, like romanticism lacks an ethical center, insofar as it believes that no ethical work is required for progress, originalism, like neoclassical theory and judicial formalism, tends to be romantic in its belief that eighteenth-century views necessarily translate to twenty-first-century circumstances. There is also a degree to which originalism lacks creativity and rests the hope for politics on imitation of older political forms rather than creative renewal. From a Voegelinian perspective, originalism is insufficiently attentive to the problem of symbols and experience separating, which then leads to the reification and devitalization of the symbols.

The progressive drift as demonstrated in the opinions of various Supreme Court justices and Edward Bellamy's *Looking Backward* has been inspired by an imaginative vision that is characterized by several related components. A faith in the moral evolution of humanity and a parallel political movement is present in many progressive ideas. Progress requires an escape from the past that is identified as the source of imperfection and evil. Principles such as equality and liberty, abstractly conceived, provide the progressive imagination with a seemingly concrete objective. The movement is engendered by an existential if not gnostic impatience with historical life and a desire to escape from all that it implies, that is, economic hardship, injustice, crime, disease, boredom, uncertainty, war, disappointment, and death. Especially remarkable is the absence of ethical work or effort. The transformation of society flows naturally from the reformation of institutions and the placement of power in the hands of enlightened leaders who are liberated in the new constitutionalism from traditional checks and balances. Croly captures humanity's emancipation from law when he states that, "the Law is to be subordinated to the government instead of the government to the Law."[25] Were the new progressive human being subjected to and restrained by inner checks and moral constraints, emancipation from the outer law might be justified. Yet, as is typically the case with progressive ideology, human emancipation occurs as an end in itself; to some progressives, it is the very meaning of history. This view of man and society is what Voegelin would call a gnostic deformation because it fails to account for the reality of historical and moral life and the insights of civilization over the course of centuries. Babbitt, like Edmund Burke, would question the wisdom of emancipating human beings from constraints that serve to civilize them.

Missing from most of the debates over the meaning of the Constitution is a fundamental question about the nature of constitutions in general. To what extent do constitutions preserve historical experience that gave political life to a particular society? Are constitutions capable of preserving historical experience while creating the flexibility to adapt to changing circumstances? These questions point to what is the seeming paradox of constitutional politics. Constitutional societies must strike a balance between preservation and change. If change moves the society too distant from its engendering heritage, it has undergone something akin to a revolution. Its older identity and purpose are replaced by new and perhaps radically different ways of self-understanding and purpose.

Yet, even when change moves society in a new direction, Americans tend to keep their grip on the past. Rarely are the American founders or constitutional principles openly disparaged. Most reformers pay homage to the founders and talk about building on their achievement rather than tearing it down. Such homage can obviously be a pretense, a disguise that masks what are truly revolutionary changes. Rarely, however, do American leaders advocate a radical break from the nation's cultural and political heritage.

GNOSTIC ESTRANGEMENT IN EDWARD BELLAMY'S *LOOKING BACKWARD*

In Voegelin's analysis of Nazi Germany, he identifies a problem of order that is indicative of societies that have become closed to the divine ground of existence. He uses the term *estrangement* to describe the spiritual disorientation of German society in the Nazi era. Voegelin, following Shelling, refers to the spiritual disease as pneumopathology.[26] Voegelin also draws on Greek thinkers (Heraclitus, Aeschylus, Plato, and Thucydides) who analyzed the fall of Greek civilization and Cicero's experience with the decline of Rome. These thinkers identify a pneumopathology described by Voegelin as "a disturbance in the spiritual and intellectual order of the dreamer's existence."[27] They create a language of disorder, including Cicero's *morbus animi*, a disease of the mind that is a rejection of reason (*aspernatio rationis*). This spiritual sickness leads to the creation of what Robert Musil and Heimito von Doderer term *second reality*, a false conception of reality that validates an ideologue's dream world.[28] The ideologue recognizes first reality, not as a limit or constraint to the possibilities of political action, but as something to be transfigured. The very *metaxic* structure of reality is to be replaced by a new order of being that has eliminated the parts of first reality that cause the ideologue such great existential anxiety and inspire gnostic revolt against what Voegelin considers the permanent structure of reality. The gnostic ideologue attempts to change the unchangeable by using "trick action" or magic.[29]

Magical politics has as one of its primary characteristics metastatic faith, which is the belief that the limits of the *metaxy* can be transgressed and that the tension of the *metaxy* between good and evil can be abolished. Voegelin makes clear that metastatic faith is "one of the great sources of disorder, if not the principal one, in the contemporary world." Opposing it is a matter of "life and death" because it will destroy us if we don't find remedies against it. "Ideology is existence in rebellion against God and man.... it is the *nosos*, the disease of the spirit, if we want to use the language of Aeschylus and Plato."[30] For Voegelin, political and social disorder, like totalitarian tyranny, are the consequence of existential disorder.

Bellamy's *Looking Backward* provides an example of a progressive second reality that brings to life in imagination a post-*metaxic* world that has been realized through magical politics. There are a few key characteristics of Bellamy's progressive imagination, which is to say that he makes post-*metaxic* assumptions about human nature, society, and the possibilities of politics. In *Looking Backward*, Bellamy creates a utopian American society that is the consequence of a century of reform. Julian West, who has slept from 1887 to 2000, awakens to find the city of Boston, the United States, and the world radically transformed. Dr. Leete spends great time and care explaining to West how the transformation occurred and why it is superior to what it replaced. The new society has among its features universal and free education and national service that is fulfilled as part of a national industrial army. Individuals serve for three years, during which they are trained and given the opportunity to see what occupation is desirable. There is a separate industrial army for women; they keep working if they get married, but leave to bear children. At forty-five years of age everyone but a select few retire. There is no money, no unemployment, no war or international conflict, and no real crime.

How can it be that nearly all crime has been eliminated? Dr. Leete explains to West:

> In your day fully nineteen-twentieths of the crime, using the word broadly to include all sorts of misdemeanors, resulted from the inequality in the possessions of individuals; want tempted the poor, lust of greater gains, or the desire to preserve former gains, tempted the well-to-do. Directly or indirectly, the desire for money, which then meant every good thing, was the motive of all this crime, the taproot of a vast poison growth, which the machinery of law, courts, and police could barely prevent from choking your civilization outright.[31]

To reach a more egalitarian distribution of wealth and thus eliminate the source of crime, products are distributed by the nation directly to consumers, that is, there are no retailers. There is no commercialization of goods, no marketing, no economic competition. Each person receives a yearly debit card that gives them adequate purchasing power for both necessities and luxuries. All institutions are designed to foster egalitarianism.[32]

What accounts for these dramatic changes? Mr. Barton explains the transformation of society metaphorically in a sermon that illustrates the common progressive disparagement of the past and previous generations. He compares humanity to a rosebush that was planted in soil and a climate unconducive to its health. The powerful elites insisted that the bush remain in its original environment and its gardeners treated the symptoms but failed to realize the cause of the problem, the environment. Once it was recognized that the plant might flourish in different conditions, it was moved to an environment in which it could thrive.

The lesson of the sermon is that great progress was made once the old ways of life were replaced by enlightened policies and attitudes. Liberating humanity from the tyranny of tradition leads to progress in all aspects of life. Barton explains that " 'The betterment of mankind from generation to generation, physically, mentally, morally, is recognized as the one great object supremely worthy of effort and of sacrifice. We believe the race for the first time to have entered on the realization of God's ideal of it, and each generation must now be a step upward.' "[33] The historical reality of degeneration has been broken. Civilization can only improve and move toward its fulfillment and perfection. Mr. Barton expresses the eschatological flavor of the new world.

> Do you ask what we look for when unnumbered generations shall have passed away? I answer, the way stretches far before us, but the end is lost in light. For twofold is the return of man to God 'who is our home,' the return of the individual by the way of death, and the return of the race by the fulfillment of the

evolution, when the divine secret hidden in the germ shall be perfectly unfolded. With a tear for the dark past, turn we then to the dazzling future, and, veiling our eyes, press forward. The long and weary winter of the race is ended. Its summer has begun. Humanity has burst the chrysalis. The heavens are before it.[34]

The new age of light contrasts sharply with the old order: " 'It is a strain on our imaginations to conceive the social arrangements of our immediate ancestors. We find them grotesque.' "[35]

It is typical of progressives to view the past as an age of darkness, when primitive conventions and ideas kept human beings from achieving their potential. Once liberated from this past, every social, economic, and moral problem becomes solvable. The chains of despotism and ignorance can finally be removed and the true goodness of humanity can blossom. The contrast between the past and the present is stark. The pride that Mr. Barton exhibits in the new world is effusive.

> For the first time since the Creation every man stood up straight before God. The fear of want and the lust of gain became extinct motives when abundance was assured to all and immoderate possessions made impossible of attainment. There were no more beggars nor almoners. Equity left charity without an occupation. The ten commandments [sic] became well nigh obsolete in a world where there was no temptation to theft, no occasion to lie either for fear or favor, no room for envy where all were equal, and little provocation to violence where men were disarmed of power to injure one another. Humanity's ancient dream of liberty, equality, fraternity, mocked by so many ages, at last was realized.[36]

These principles, born from the French Revolution, illustrate Bellamy's progressive commitment to ahistorical abstraction and the magical politics that emanates from metastatic faith. Progress results when the historical past, with all its flaws and injustices, is rejected in favor of an imagined future in which these imperfections have been eradicated.

There is something odd about Bellamy's story. Writing in the late nineteenth century he is attached, to some degree, to an older Christian and Victorian worldview. God's desires for humanity matter to Bellamy. And yet it is difficult to believe how Adam and Eve, who wanted for nothing in the Garden of Eden and yet sinned, could beget descendants, who in the twentieth century want for nothing, but do not sin. Likewise, why would economic equality as exists in Bellamy's utopia rid the world of moral problems like marital infidelity, crimes of passion, and mere greed and lust? Does it make sense that sexual lust for others would be eliminated by a regular monthly income? The Original Sin was a sin of pride not of want. Here is found a profound difference between the progressive imagination and that of the Christian imagination as represented, in particular, by St. Augustine.

Bellamy's portrayal of the human condition is truncated and incomplete. It shares, in this regard, much with Butterfield's Whig historian, insofar as it subordinates "the past to the present." It tells the story of the past in a way that validates an ideological predisposition and ignores or misinterprets historical and philosophical evidence that is contrary to the sanitized version of history.[37] In doing so, it neglects to account for dimensions of human life that are central parts of Augustine's view of man and society. Bellamy suggests that elimination of economic want destroys the very desire to steal. Augustine, however, has a deeper and a more complete understanding of sin and theft. Humans steal, at times, or in part, because of want, but they also do so for the pleasure of sin itself. As Augustine explains in the *Confessions*, "I willed to commit theft, and I did so, not because I was driven to it by any need, unless it were by poverty of justice, and dislike of it, and by a glut of evil-doing. For I stole a thing of which I had plenty of my own and of much better quality. Nor did I wish to enjoy that thing which I desired to gain by theft, but rather to enjoy the actual theft and the sin of theft."[38] He recounts an episode when in his youth he and a band of "bad youngsters" stole pears and threw them to pigs. "We did this," he confesses, "to do what pleased us for the reason that it was forbidden.... I sought nothing from the shameful deed but shame itself!"[39] There is a perversion of good in sin for which Bellamy does not account. Economics and material want cannot explain the disparate complexity of sin.

Bellamy fails to account for the desire to sin for the pleasure of sin. He also fails to consider the need for conversion (*metanoia/perigoge*) inspired by grace. Augustine is well aware that turning away from sin is a painful and trying process that requires introspection and attention to the inner life. Social and political order is dependent on the order of the soul. Bellamy's utopia develops without any transformation of the inner life. Since the cause of evil lies outside the soul, the remedy for social ills is politics and public policy, not spiritual work (*appamāda*). In short, Bellamy substitutes public policy and institutional reform for spiritual work. His futuristic society is born in revolt from the past. It transforms human life not from the experience of ancestors or the virtue of individuals. Rather, evil is eliminated when society embraces abstract egalitarian principles and uses them to formulate policies and shape institutions. The point here is not that Bellamy explicitly rejects the older American constitutionalism as Croly does. The movement away from the older American constitutionalism in Bellamy's case is more subtle. Rather, he contributes to the creation of an alternative ideology that rejects the fundamental part of the older philosophical anthropology that considers human beings to be of a morally mixed nature and dependent on divine inspiration to achieve justice and the good.

THE RESTORATION OF ORDER IN AMERICAN CONSTITUTIONALISM

The framers believed that morally mixed humans needed to be checked and restrained and that government needed to be limited. Bellamy's utopia, however, is the product of political reform that assumes, like Croly, that human nature can be transformed by political action. Once this view gains influence, it is only a matter of time before constitutional structures like the separation of powers and checks and balances are viewed as obstacles to progress. Supreme Court justices following the progressive zeitgeist are then likely to chip away at those constitutional structures and principles as they free political rulers from their constitutional shackles. The gnostic impulse to remake the world and eliminate evil cannot be reconciled with the sober moral realism of the American Framers. Daniel Lazare expresses the logical outcome of the progressive imagination when he states, "Government in America doesn't work because it's not supposed to work. In their wisdom, the founders created a deliberately unresponsive system in order to narrow the governmental options and force us to seek alternative routes. Politics were dangerous; therefore, politics had to be limited and constrained. But America cannot expect to survive much longer with a government that is inefficient and none too democratic by design. It is impossible to forge ahead in the late twentieth century using governmental machinery dating from the late eighteenth."[40] Lazare thus explicitly rejects the separation of powers and limited government, because they inhibit the democratic will that is the standard for measuring progress.[41]

In Voegelin's analysis, the proper response to gnostic ideology inspired by pneumopathology is not doctrines that appeal to the authority of a past that has ceased to be a living force. It does little good to argue with an ideologue about the specific substantive details of a given ideology. When human beings replace God as the ground of being, rational appeals to the correctness of an older transcendent-based truth will not penetrate the gnostic closure and pry it open. The problem is one of a more fundamental dimension that reaches to the very essence of human existence and requires the evocative reconstitution of engendering experiences of order. What these experiences of order convey is the *metaxic* structure of reality that cannot be changed by gnostic second reality, metastatic faith, or the politics of magic.

In the Supreme Court's majority opinion in *Planned Parenthood v. Casey*, Justice O'Connor states that "At the heart of liberty is the right to define one's own concept of existence, of meaning, of the universe, and of the mystery of human life."[42] If this statement means that human beings are free to create their own structure of reality, including what constitutes a human life, then the line that separates first and second reality has been crossed. The prevalence in American politics of metastatic faith means that originalism is powerless to address what is a disorder of the soul. In one sense, the crisis is less about politics and more about spiritual and religious life.

Constitutional societies face the persistent challenge of preserving the engendering experiences of constitutional order through time. The American Constitution was not made in a philosopher's closet. It was the product of a convention that brought together representatives who shared a cultural heritage that reached back to the ancient world of Greece and Rome. The experiences of order that gave the Constitution life emanated from a philosophical focal point that understood human beings as morally dualistic, imperfect and imperfectable, and thus in need of the rule of law. In the language of the Judeo-Christian tradition, humans are fallen, or in the words of Alexander Hamilton in Federalist No. 6 "men are ambitious, vindictive, and rapacious."[43] This underlying view of human nature justifies the particular aspects of the Constitution that include the separation of powers, checks and balances, the rule of law, judicial review, the electoral college, federalism, and limited government. Preserving a constitutional order requires historical memory and an acute sense of the experiences of order that brought specific constitutional principles and provisions to life, not only in the United States but in Western civilization generally. Voegelin's and Babbitt's works are useful to sorting out the challenges of constitutional preservation because they emphasized the primacy of experience and understood that the crisis of the West emanated from a loss of historical memory and contact with engendering experiences of order that was due, in part, from the rise of dogmatic propositions that obscured experiences of order. Voegelin identifies a sequence that illustrates how engendering experiences are originally articulated and then reified into dogmatic propositions leading to skepticism about the engendering truth. The sequence reveals the incremental loss of consciousness of historical experiences of order that convey truth that "is the source of right order in human existence."[44]

The problem of doctrinalization, ensuing skepticism, and rise of gnostic alternatives can be seen in the unfolding of the American constitutional crisis. The historical sources of order that were part of the development of Western and American constitutionalism became reified into political or constitutional doctrines over time. As they lost their cultural vitality, rival understandings of order, some gnostic, appeared and reduced the traditional American understanding of constitutionalism to one among several competing ideologies. Chief among these is progressivism, an ideology fundamentally at odds with traditional American constitutionalism.

Voegelin was also acutely aware of the older Western view of human nature and the rise of gnostic ideologies that aimed to replace it with pneumopathologically derived, immanentizing conceptions of humans and society. Consider, for example, his study of order and history. Voegelin asserts the fundamental reality of the "primordial community of being" that includes "God and man, world and society."[45] Moreover, not only is human existence historical, but human societies are organized "for partnership in the order of being that has its origin in world-transcendent divine Being." Humans' historical existence is an effort to discover the meaning of human nature, a nature that Voegelin claims is "constant" and "existence in truth under God." Social order, of which politics is a part, "is an attunement of man with the order of being."[46] Existential, social, and political order are dependent on attunement to the transcendent source of order. Historical experiences of order are represented symbolically in language that becomes embodied in laws, institutions, traditions, literature, and myth.

The American Constitution is an example of a document that embodies historical experience in both its specific principles and institutional structures, but also its underlying philosophical anthropology. The American understanding of human nature unfolds in its constitutional founding, as well as in other historical experiences. The Constitution is, among other things, an effort to preserve engendering experiences of order. What can be said about this effort of preservation is that it was deeply enriched by the older Western tradition of ethical dualism. The point is not that the specifically American way of politically constituting the truth of the order of being is universal in its particular institutional form. There is something universal about the American experience because human beings of all cultures share a common nature and a common quest of attunement and self-understanding, but the truth of existence can be manifest in any number of ways given the characteristics of a given society.

We learn from Voegelin that there are two fundamental challenges to the preservation of engendering experience. The first is the problem of amnesia. Human beings have imperfect memory and as time passes, memory tends to fade. Amnesia is exacerbated by a second problem, which is gnosticism. Once embedded in institutions and traditions, a society's understanding of the truth of existence is subject to gnostic deformation and derailment. Amnesia, which is never a sudden and instant occurrence, happens gradually over time in increments that can make the loss of memory difficult to recognize. Gnosticism can take the form of imposter ideologies that resemble the older truth, but are at odds with it in fundamental ways. Gnosticism, like communism, can also form as overt challenges to the traditional order that intend to overthrow it and replace it with a radically new ideology.

In the case of the American Constitution, it should be remembered that there is not a fixed meaning of the Constitution that one can easily reference in a book or the text itself. Original meaning, as it is sometimes called, is open to dispute even among originalists. In addition, constitutions must adapt to changing circumstances. The changes that occur in the process of adaptation may or may not be consistent with the engendering insights that gave the Constitution life. Voegelin was no legal fundamentalist. He appreciated that the symbols that articulated the engendering experiences of order were an approximation of the truth derived from historical experience. It was possible to improve on the articulation of engendering experience or to lose contact with it. The Western crisis was considered by Voegelin to be caused by the increasing opaqueness of the symbols that articulated the engendering experiences of order. Restoration was necessary to recall to memory these experiences and to make them a living force in the contemporary world. Anamnetic exploration was a central part of Voegelin's efforts at restoration.

As time has passed, the American memory has been increasingly incapable of recalling the engendering experiences of order, while gnostic ideologies have undermined efforts to restore the meaning of the Constitution. The increasing influence of ahistorical conceptions of rights and their underlying political theory undermine the older foundations of American constitutionalism.

These are the specific historical experiences that gave life and meaning to the Constitution. For the words/language symbols of the Constitution to maintain a connection to these engendering experiences, they must remain a living force in the imaginations and hearts of the political leaders and the people. The task of restoring and maintaining fidelity to these experiences faces the challenge of rival understandings of the human condition that lead to alternative ways of interpreting the Constitution. They can take the form of second realities that contain partial truths, but ultimately represent a derailment from the engendering experience. Moreover, fidelity to a constitution presents the additional problem of doctrinalization—the reification of experience into dogmas that have become divorced from engendering experience. How can constitutions adapt to changing circumstances and remain connected to engendering experience? The historical experiences must be preserved in order to avoid the movement toward second realities.

CONCLUSION

A few points of clarification are necessary at the conclusion of this analysis. The notion that constitutions are based on historical experience does not mean that every constitution is rightly constructed and that any deviation from it indicates derailment and second reality. Constitutions vary in the degree to which they represent the order of being and are attuned to transcendent reality. It is entirely possible that a constitution can be based on abstract ahistorical principles or rights that are tangentially, if at all, connected to historical reality. The problem of constitutional preservation discussed here assumes that the constitution is relatively sound in its representation of the human condition and that it creates institutions, processes, and a rule of law that comport with the realities of the order of being. This assumption does not preclude the possibility that improvements can be made to a sound constitution as insights are gained. The American Constitution was to some degree the consequence of a new science of politics that Hamilton addresses in Federalist No. 9. The American framers did not abandon the British constitutional tradition as much as they reconstituted it for their unique circumstances. Reconstitution is, however, different than derailment. Derailment and second reality indicate that a society is losing its grip on a realistic understanding of the human condition as historically constituted. Voegelin's term *metastatic faith* expresses the idea that politics takes on a highly idealist or utopian quality that places far too much faith in the ability of politics to transform human nature and society.

The challenge of maintaining a constitutional order is not as simple as abiding by principles and rules. However true to the reality of the human condition the principles and rules may be, they can become detached from the historical experience that gave them life and take on a life of their own.

Consequently, constitutional order requires a balance between preservation and change. What serves as a guiding standard in marking such a point of balance is that in preserving both old principles and rules, as well as reform, one remains attuned to the historical experiences of order. Edmund Burke captures this tension between preservation and change in his concept of the spirit of philosophic analogy. With this concept in mind, Burke suggests that "in what we improve we are never wholly new; in what we retain we are never wholly obsolete."[47] Thus, Burke advocated change that maintained continuity with a society's cultural and historical heritage. Change was necessary to preserve the wisdom of the past by meeting the challenges of new circumstances in a way that reconstitutes tradition.

Voegelin's work on *Order and History* makes it clear that civilizations search for the transcendent/divine source of order. Because they believe that political and social order are dependent on existential and cosmological order, attunement to the divine ground of being is necessary for human beings to realize the ends of human existence, justice, happiness, and the good. To relate Voegelin's philosophy of history to an analysis of American constitutionalism and the question of constitutional preservation requires a few points of clarification.

(1) The order of Western civilization from which the American order emanates presumes attunement and a philosophical orientation that embraces divine reality and its ordering power on human beings and human society.

(2) Constitutions are, then, derivative of the larger historical and transcendent order.

(3) To preserve a constitution/constitutional order requires the preservation of the larger philosophical anthropology articulated by Voegelin.

(4) As the civilization's understanding of order as attunement to transcendence and dependence on virtue depreciate, the institutions and principles developed from such an understanding of order likewise disintegrate. The underlying moral realism that serves as the foundation for the constitutional order is gradually replaced by a rival, largely secular ideology that undermines the legitimacy of the older political philosophy. Central to this political and historical movement is the declining influence and transformation of Christianity and its antecedent Hebrew, Greek, and Roman heritage.

(5) In short, a constitutional system contingent on the traditional Western philosophical anthropology cannot survive without an underlying political

theory that provides an understanding of moral realism that justifies specific constitutional characteristics and principles like checks and balances, the separation of powers, federalism, and limited government itself. Constitutions can only preserve the engendering experiences of order when the historical experiences of order that gave the constitution life remain a living force in the culture of a constitutional society. Once that connect is lost, it is only a matter of time before rival ideologies, some masquerading as the engendering tradition, destroy the cultural substance that sustains the constitution. Restoration of the philosophical heritage is possible, but extremely difficult.

(6) Progressivism is one ideology that serves to undermine American constitutionalism. Bellamy, for example, undermines the notion that justice requires virtue. Croly posits that politics can transform human nature. If Croly and Bellamy are correct, it is difficult to justify American constitutional principles like the separation of powers, checks and balances, the rule of law, and limited government itself.

(7) What few in the West seemed to realize about the totalitarian era is that it marked a great crisis in Western civilization, not simply because security and democracy were at stake, but because Nazism and communism were symptoms of a larger Western crisis, a spiritual estrangement that indicated that the engendering heritage of Western civilization was coming apart. What communism, Nazism, and progressivism share in common is a rejection of the moral realism that inspired and justified the development of limited government and the Western political, social, and economic institutions that were derived from it. The defeat of totalitarianism was, in some respects, an incomplete victory that masked the deeper spiritual crisis of the West. It has been in the posttotalitarian era that the disintegration of traditional Western culture has accelerated. The American Constitution cannot preserve the engendering experiences of order because its underlying moral realism has ceased to be a living force in American culture. What defines American politics as much as anything since the early twentieth century is the extraordinary proliferation of the centralized state, a phenomenon difficult to reconcile with the American framers' decentralized republic.

NOTES

1. *The Papers of Alexander Hamilton*, ed. Harold C. Syrett et al. 27 vols. (New York: Columbia University Press, 1961–1987), I: 126 (hereafter *PAH*).

2. For Voegelin's early writings on law, constitutions, and their relation to spiritual dimensions of human existence see *The Collected Works of Eric Voegelin*, vol. 32, *The Theory of Governance and Other Miscellaneous Papers (1921–1938)*, ed. William Petropulos and Gilbert Weiss (Columbia and London: University of Missouri Press, 2003); vol. 7, *Published Essays (1922–1928)*, ed. Thomas W. Heilke and John von Heyking (Columbia and London: University of Missouri Press, 2003); vol. 8 *Published Essays (1929–1933)*, ed. Thomas W. Heilke and John von Heyking (Columbia and London: University of Missouri Press, 2003) (hereafter *CWEV*).

3. Voegelin, "On Readiness to Rational Discussion," in *Freedom and Serfdom: An Anthology of Western Thought*, ed. Albert Hunold (Dordrecht, Holland: D. Reidel, 1961), 278.

4. Irving Babbitt, *Democracy and Leadership* (Indianapolis, IN: Liberty Fund, 1979), 28.

5. Voegelin, "The Origins of Totalitarianism," in *The Collected Works of Eric Voegelin*, vol. 11 (Columbia and London: University of Missouri Press, 2000), 22.

6. Thomas Aquinas, *Treatise on Law*, trans. with an introduction by Richard J. Regan (Indianapolis. IN and Cambridge, MA: Hackett, 2000), 73.

7. Voegelin identifies a trend that begins at the time of the French Revolution that rejects the older justifications for governing in favor of "the doctrine of freedom and equality." From the late eighteenth century, "political theory has developed as part of the political struggle against traditional forms of governance, indeed against any form of governance, and it has therefore neglected to survey the full range of the problems involved" (*CWEV*, 32: 345).

8. For a detailed analysis of the difference between a classical and Christian conception of justice and social justice see Thomas Patrick Burke, *The Concept of Justice: Is Social Justice Just?* (London and New York: Bloomsbury Publishing, 2011).

9. Benjamin N. Cardozo, *The Nature of the Judicial Process* (e-book) (Mineola, NY: Dover Publications, 2005), loc. 949.

10. See Sotirios A. Barber and James E. Fleming, *Constitutional Interpretation: The Basic Questions* (New York: Oxford University Press, 2007). I disagree with Barber and Fleming that *The Federalist* comports with positive constitutionalism. Publius's concern with preventing tyranny and the abuse of power is central to the arguments made throughout the eighty-five essays. For Hamilton's constitutionalism see Michael P. Federici, *The Political Philosophy of Alexander Hamilton* (Baltimore: Johns Hopkins University Press, 2012).

11. For progressive arguments lamenting the inefficiency of the American Constitution see James MacGregor Burns, *The Deadlock of Democracy: Four-Party*

Politics in America (Englewood Cliffs, NJ: Prentice Hall, 1963) and Daniel Lazare, *The Frozen Republic: How the Constitution is Paralyzing Democracy* (New York: Harcourt Brace & Company, 1996).

12. Felix Frankfurter, *Law and Politics: Occasional Papers of Felix Frankfurter 1913–1938*, ed. By Archibald MacLeish and E. F. Prichard, Jr. (Gloucester, MA: Peter Smith, 1971), 8.

13. For an argument opposing the antidemocratic tendencies of activists courts see J. Harvie Wilkinson III, *Cosmic Constitutional Theory: Why Americans Are Losing Their Inalienable Right to Self-Governance* (New York: Oxford University Press, 2012). Bork contributed to a symposium in *First Things* in 1996 that was titled: "The End of Democracy? The Judicial Usurpation of Politics." Both sides in the debate are thus intent on claiming to be the champions of democracy.

14. Benjamin N. Cardozo, *The Nature of the Judicial Process* (e-book) (Mineola, NY: Dover Publications, 2005), locations 35, 71, 82.

15. See Croly, *Progressive Democracy* (New Brunswick, NJ and London: Transaction Publishers, 1998), 122; Edward Bellamy, *Looking Backward: 2000–1887* (New York: Signet Classics, 2009). In Bellamy's case, his futuristic society puts almost every aspect of society in the control of government, but provides no checks or restraints on the rulers. He simply ignores such concerns in the novel.

16. Alexander Hamilton exhibits this darker view of human nature when he writes to Richard Harrison in 1793, "The triumphs of Vice are no new things under the sun. And I fear, 'till the Millenium comes, in spight of all our boasted light and purification—hypochrisy and Treachery will continue to be the most successful commodities in the political Market" (*PAH*, 13: 470).

17. Theodore Roosevelt, "The Right of the People to Rule," in *American Progressivism*, ed. by Ronald J. Pestritto and William J. Atto (Lanham, MD: Lexington Books, 2008), 252. Consistent with progressivism's faith in human nature, Roosevelt states in this speech that "the American people are, as a whole, capable of self-control" (251).

18. For an analysis of the rise of progressive ideology in American thinking see Frank Tariello Jr. *The Reconstruction of American Political Ideology (1865* Frank Tariello Jr. *1917)* (Charlottesville: University Press of Virginia, 1982).

19. Herbert Croly, *The Promise of American Life* (Boston, MA: Northeastern University Press, 1989), 166.

20. Ibid., 400.

21. For Croly's influence on Supreme Court Justice Felix Frankfurter see *Law and Politics: Occasional Papers of Felix Frankfurter 1913–1938*, ed. by Archibald MacLeish and E. F. Prichard, Jr. (Gloucester, MA: Peter Smith, 1971), 305–13.

22. Croly, *The Promise of American Life*, 170, 12.

23. Ibid., 200.

24. Croly, *Progressive Democracy* (New Brunswick, NJ and London: Transaction Publishers, 1998), 122.

25. Croly, *Progressive Democracy*, 126.

26. Voegelin, *Science, Politics and Gnosticism* (Chicago, IL: Regnery Gateway, 1968), 101.

27. Eric Voegelin, "Wisdom and the Magic of the Extreme," in *The Collected Works of Eric Voegelin*, vol. 12 (Baton Rouge and London: Louisiana State University Press, 1990), 322.

28. Voegelin, *Hitler and the Germans*, in *The Collected Works of Eric Voegelin*, vol. 31 (Columbia and London: University of Missouri Press, 1999), 108.

29. Voegelin, "Wisdom and the Magic of the Extreme," 322–25.

30. Voegelin, *Israel and Revelation*, 23–24.

31. Edward Bellamy, *Looking Backward: 2000–1887* (New York: Signet Classics, 2009), 131.

32. Bellamy, 56–57.

33. Ibid., 190.

34. Ibid., 190–91.

35. Ibid., 189.

36. Ibid., 186–87.

37. Herbert Butterfield, *The Whig Interpretation of History* (New York: W. W. Norton & Company, 1965), 16.

38. Augustine, *Confessions* (Garden City, NY: Image Books, 1960), 69–70.

39. Ibid., 70.

40. Daniel Lazare, *The Frozen Republic: How the Constitution is Paralyzing Democracy* (New York: Harcourt Brace & Company, 1996), 5.

41. Ibid., 9.

42. See Planned Parenthood of Southeastern Pa. v. Casey, 505 U.S. 833 (1992).

43. Hamilton, *The Federalist*, ed. With an introduction by George W. Carey and James McClellan (Indianapolis, IN: Liberty Fund, 2001), 21.

44. Eric Voegelin, "Immortality: Experience and Symbol," in *The Collected Works of Eric Voegelin*, vol. 12 (Baton Rouge and London: Louisiana State University Press, 1990), 53.

45. Voegelin, *Israel and Revelation*, ed. Maurice P. Hogan, in *The Collected Works of Eric Voegelin*, vol. 14 (Columbia and London: University of Missouri Press, 2001), 39.

46. Voegelin, *The World of the Polis* (Louisiana State University Press, 1980), 2, 6, 2.

47. Edmund Burke, *Reflections on the Revolution in France*, ed. J. G. A. Pocock (Indianapolis, IN and Cambridge, MA: Hackett, 1987), 30.

BIBLIOGRAPHY

Aquinas, Thomas. *Treatise on Law*. Translated by Richard J. Regan. Indianapolis, IN: Hackett, 2000.
Augustine. *Confessions*. Garden City, NY: Image Books, 1960.
Babbitt, Irving. *Democracy and Leadership*. Indianapolis, IN: Liberty Fund, 1979.
Barber, Sotirios A., and James E. Fleming. *Constitutional Interpretation: The Basic Questions*. New York: Oxford University Press, 2007.
Bellamy, Edward. *Looking Backward: 2000–1887*. New York: Signet Classics, 2009.
Bork, Robert H., Russell Hittinger, Hadley Arkes, Charles W. Colson, and Robert P. George. "The End of Democracy? The Judicial Usurpation of Politics." *First Things*. November 1996. https://www.firstthings.com/article/1996/11/the-end-of-democracy-the-judicial-usurpation-of-politics.
Burke, Edmund. *Reflections on the Revolution in France*. Edited by J. G. A. Pocock. Indianapolis, IN: Hackett, 1987.
Burke, Thomas Patrick. *The Concept of Justice: Is Social Justice Just?* New York: Bloomsbury Publishing.
Burns, James MacGregor. *The Deadlock of Democracy: Four-Party Politics in America*. Englewood Cliffs, NJ: Prentice Hall, 1963.
Cardozo, Benjamin N. *The Nature of the Judicial Process*. Mineola, NY: Dover Publications, 2005.
Croly, Herbert. *Progressive Democracy*. New Brunswick, NJ: Transaction Publishers, 1998.
———. *The Promise of American Life*. Boston, MA: Northeastern University Press, 1989.
Federici, Michael P. *The Political Philosophy of Alexander Hamilton*. Baltimore: Johns Hopkins University Press, 2012.
Frankfurter, Felix. *Law and Politics: Occasional Papers of Felix Frankfurter 1913–1938*. Edited by Archibald MacLeish and E. F. Prichard Jr. Gloucester, MA: Peter Smith, 1971.
Hamilton, Alexander. *The Federalist*. Edited by George W. Carey and James McClellan Indianapolis, IN: Liberty Fund, 2001.
———. *The Papers of Alexander Hamilton*. Edited by Harold C. Syrett and Patricia Syrett. New York: Columbia University Press, 1987.
Lazare, Daniel. *The Frozen Republic: How the Constitution is Paralyzing Democracy*. New York: Harcourt Brace & Company, 1996.

Roosevelt, Theodore. "The Right of the People to Rule." In *American Progressivism*. Edited by Ronald J. Pestritto and William J. Atto. Lanham, MD: Lexington Books, 2008.

Tariello, Frank, Jr. *The Reconstruction of American Political Ideology (1865–1917)*. Charlottesville, VA: University Press of Virginia, 1982.

Voegelin, Eric. *The Collected Works of Eric Voegelin*. Vol. 7, *Published Essays (1922–1928)*. Edited by Thomas W. Heilke and John von Heyking. Columbia, MO: University of Missouri Press, 2003.

———. *The Collected Works of Eric Voegelin*. Vol. 8, *Published Essays (1929–1933)*. Edited by Thomas W. Heilke and John von Heyking. Columbia, MO: University of Missouri Press, 2003.

———. *The Collected Works of Eric Voegelin*. Vol. 14, *Order and History (Vol. I): Israel and Revelation*. Edited by Maurice P. Hogan. Columbia, MO: University of Missouri Press, 2001.

———. *The Collected Works of Eric Voegelin*. Vol. 31, *Hitler and the Germans*. Columbia, MO: University of Missouri Press, 1999.

———. *The Collected Works of Eric Voegelin*. Vol. 32, *The Theory of Governance and Other Miscellaneous Papers (1921–1938)*. Edited by William Petropulos and Gilbert Weiss Columbia and London: University of Missouri Press, 2003.

———. "Immortality: Experience and Symbol." In *The Collected Works of Eric Voegelin*. Vol. 12, *Public Essays (1966–1985)*. Edited by Ellis Sandoz. Baton Rouge and London: Louisiana State University Press, 1990.

———. "The Origins of Totalitarianism." In *The Collected Works of Eric Voegelin*. Vol. 11, *Published Essays (1953–1965)*. Edited by Ellis Sandoz. Columbia, MO: University of Missouri Press, 2000.

———. "On Readiness to Rational Discussion." In *Freedom and Serfdom: An Anthology of Western Thought*. Edited by Albert Hunold. Dordrecht, Holland: D. Reidel, 1961.

———. *Science, Politics and Gnosticism*. Chicago, IL: Regnery Gateway, 1968.

———. "Wisdom and the Magic of the Extreme." In *The Collected Works of Eric Voegelin*. Vol. 12, *Public Essays (1966–1985)*. Edited by Ellis Sandoz. Baton Rouge and London: Louisiana State University Press, 1990.

———. *The World of the Polis*. Louisiana State University Press, 1980.

Wilkinson, J. Harvie, III. *Cosmic Constitutional Theory: Why Americans Are Losing Their Inalienable Right to Self-Governance*. New York: Oxford University Press, 2012.

CHAPTER TEN

On the Moral Necessity of Constitutionalism
Claes Ryn and Ethical Democracy

Bruce P. Frohnen

For decades, politics in the West has been dominated by calls for social justice. Some goals of the social justice movement might be described as morally laudable. Attempts to address problems of lasting poverty and to extend due process of law to all citizens, for example, would seem in keeping with norms deeply embedded in Western culture. But the general tendency of such movements has been deeply troubling, in no small measure because the ideology on which they are based has undermined our constitutional and legal order. And that order is needed by all—especially the worst off—to provide predictability in dealings with social and political forces and, hence, to provide the possibility of a decent life. Under the name of social justice, this ideology treats both politics and law as tools designed to help us get what we want out of society and its people. Such tools are to be shaped, reshaped, and even discarded when they do not serve our purpose of the moment. This instrumental view of society's ordering norms is justified as "democratic" in that it would put into action the putative will of the majority, which allegedly shares its social justice goals. However, such revolutionary democracy actually fosters tyranny by isolating individuals from one another and removing counterweights and internal restraints on centralized power.

From his earliest to his most recent work, Claes Ryn has analyzed the misunderstanding at the heart of the claims of revolutionary (what he terms "plebiscitary") democracy.[1] That misunderstanding is the view that democracy, or any political system, can rightly be seen as a mere tool for decision making. Politics, Ryn has demonstrated, is not merely a means by which certain groups get what they want. It is rather a fundamentally moral undertaking, requiring systemic concern to promote the common good, lest society devolve into potentially violent, debilitating struggles over power.

Most fully in *Democracy and the Ethical Life* and most pointedly in *America the Virtuous*, Ryn has shown the roots of today's plebiscitary democracy in the abstract, counterfactual ideology of Jean-Jacques Rousseau. That ideology was put into murderous form by the French Revolutionary Jacobins; it fosters political violence in the name of "the people" to this day. As important, Ryn has shown the ethical necessity of constitutionalism—the systemic opposite of plebiscitary democracy—as the restrained political context within which the people must rule if the good life is to be possible.

My purpose, here, is to outline Ryn's view of the relationship between constitutionalism and the ethical life and to address the problem I believe Ryn's rather Aristotelian conception of politics raises in modern nation-states. That problem concerns how to maintain constitutionalism and the rule of law when social complexity has so differentiated law from custom and government from society that instrumentalism appears inevitable. I do not deem this problem necessarily fatal to good government (that is, government recognized as a limited means by which a people pursue the good life in common). That said, it is a problem I believe is perpetual and not liable to any final solution because it embodies a tension inherent in our nature as social beings living in large, complex societies.

The problem of administrative complexity can be ameliorated by minimizing the need for and scope of instrumentalism. To begin with, the gaps between law and custom, on the one hand, and government and society, on the other, must be kept as narrow as practicable. In part this means keeping the number of distant and abstract laws low so that the need for detailed statutes is lessened, and the need to forego detailed statutes in favor of broad discretion is minimized. As important, it is necessary for any free society to take care to foster among its citizens a constitutional morality appropriate to limited, decentralized government in which broader, more general goods are pursued as capstones to, rather than transformers of, more local, particular associational goods.[2] The need is for a constitution that mediates conflict among more fundamental groups without descending into the modern liberal trap of instrumentalism and compartmentalization of social, political, and cultural modes of conduct.

PLEBISCITARY DEMOCRACY AND POLITICAL INSTRUMENTALISM

Ryn defines plebiscitary democracy as "a form of popular rule... which gives maximum freedom and power to the momentary majority of the people by placing no strongly resistant legal obstacles in the way of emerging popular wishes."[3] Modern social scientists, always keen to reduce concepts to their "cash value," interpret and praise plebiscitary democracy in instrumental terms, separating it from any cultural context or ultimate goal. Thus, democracy is seen merely as a set of procedures for determining governmental action on the basis of majority will.[4]

On this view, the results of democratic processes by nature are correct, or at any rate in no need of justification. Yet we all know that some governmental actions would be morally repugnant whatever the means of their determination. Mass slaughter of innocents undertaken after a vote would remain, ethically speaking, a great wrong. How do democratic ideologues avoid facing such a contradiction? Rousseau himself showed that he recognized this kind of problem, for example, by opposing unchecked executive power. "To protect against such abuse, Rousseau prescribes 'fixed and periodic assemblies which nothing can abolish or prorogue.'" Yet, despite presenting these institutional provisions as fundamental, Rousseau nowhere provides for their constitutional protection.[5]

How, then, is tyranny or other immoral public action to be avoided in plebiscitary democracy? This is done by changing the nature of the people. Rousseau famously asserted that spontaneous acts of the will are moral because human nature is naturally good. But this nature has, according to Rousseau, been corrupted by society, making it necessary to reform it. And such reform is the job of the state, acting through the means of public education and, where necessary, coercion. In Rousseau's words, "It is good to know how to deal with men as they are, it is much better to make them what there is need that they should be. The most absolute authority is that which penetrates into a man's inmost being, and concerns itself no less with his will than with his actions. It is certain that all peoples become in the long run what the government makes them.... Make men, therefore, if you would commend men."[6]

Plebiscitary democracy is not, then, a mere means of translating the spontaneous desires of the majority into political action. It is a means of transforming the people themselves through political action. Perhaps ironically, this transformation requires convincing the people of their right to exercise unmediated power over society through the mechanism of a centralized state. As Ryn points out, Rousseau's plan for democracy was the same administrative and political centralization Alexis de Tocqueville feared would replace associational life in the United States.[7] By treating "the people" as an undifferentiated mass, whose will is to be measured as a unit rather than in family, church, and local association, Rousseau would make a new human being, who is dependent on the state for self-identity. He would separate people from one another, chaining them only to the state so that he might maximize the unity and strength of that state.

The idea of politics as plebiscite was imported into the United States, in particular through the thought of Thomas Jefferson.[8] Ryn points to James MacGregor Burns as one crucial importer of Jeffersonian ideals who sought to further concentrate power in Washington (and its executive branch) in the post–New Deal era. Already by this time, Progressive reformers had institutionalized Rousseauean ideology in national programs of political, economic, and social transformation. In place of limited, constitutional government, they had constructed a centralized mechanism for achieving a "public good," defined as the provision of governmental benefits through a direct link between individuals, the mass public, and the central state.[9] Ryn argues that this program has corrupted the American constitutional order and the American people, causing them to lose their understanding of the limits of human virtue and the importance of self-restraint.[10]

CONSTITUTIONALISM AND POLITICAL ENDS

Ryn is not the first to point out the totalitarian tendencies of Rousseau's plebiscitary democracy.[11] Nor is he the first to distinguish plebiscitary democracy from constitutional democracy, which he defines as "a form of popular rule designed to promote, not the instant and complete public implementation of the most recent will of the people, but the articulation of the 'deliberate sense' of the community."[12] What Ryn adds is an Aristotelian understanding of the nature and intrinsic goal of politics. Properly understood, Ryn points out, democracy is not merely a form of government, for all governments constitute, not just mechanisms of decision making, but ways of life.[13] And "the ultimate end of politics" is a good life. Ryn defines this good life as "community," by which he means "a special type of association, a civilized living together in which the intellectual, aesthetic, and economic life of society serves the moral destiny shared by all."[14]

How do we achieve a good life, lived in common with our fellows? The key, as Ryn points out, is recognizing and acting on the intrinsically moral nature and purpose of politics. Plebiscitary democracy uses power to grant the people what they desire and, more fundamentally, to transform the people in ways desired by their leaders. What is missing in this equation is ethical conscience, or "the awareness . . . that there is a sacred purpose to human life which transcends the transitory biases of individuals and peoples, and which can be violated only at the price of a loss of meaning and worth. Ethical conscience is that in man which wills, not the private advantage of individuals or groups as an end in itself, but the realization of the universal good for man."[15]

Because the intrinsic purpose of politics is to bring about a good life, and because this can only be done through the application of ethical conscience in politics, democracy itself "is ethically defensible only if it conceives of popular self-rule as designed in such a way as to *promote* the application of ethical conscience to political issues . . . The people has to impose some moral discipline on itself."[16] Not merely restraint in the name of practical or utilitarian efficiency, but real restraint aimed at promoting pursuit of the common good is essential to democracy as an ethical form. Lacking such restraint, democracy becomes mere rhetorical cover for potentially vicious interest group politics.

Following Irving Babbitt, among others, Ryn sees ethics in terms of conflict between persons' higher and lower selves. In Ryn's political theory, this means that a people has "two selves, one which always wills . . . the promotion of community in given circumstances, and one with an always varying content tending to divert the political order to merely partisan objectives." The essential political question, then, is "what self is to rule? The only morally defensible answer is that it must be the *higher* self of the people, or, if that phrase has too much of a metaphysical ring, the will to community in the individual citizens."[17]

Constitutional restraints such as separation of powers, legislative procedures and the like, do not aim merely to promote calm calculations of self-interest. They are intended to broaden persons' viewpoints. To achieve their political goals within a constitutional order, "competing groups, whether in the majority or the minority, are induced from the very start to adopt a politically inclusive perspective. To further their own cause, that same cause must be defined with a view to making it acceptable to other groups that might otherwise veto it."[18] The need to achieve consensus fosters in the people the virtue of genuine public concern to the benefit of each and all.

Individual and popular virtue are intertwined in Ryn's understanding. The fulfillment of his democracy is embodied in the person

> who acts under self-imposed moral restraints. To that kind of citizen corresponds a popular government under constitutional limitations designed to promote a certain quality of popular will. Only this type of democracy ... allows an opportunity to temper the forces of political self-seeking by considerations of the common good. It can be joined to and sustained by man's sense of higher purpose. Constitutional democracy at its best, we may conclude, would be popular self-rule in the cause of community.[19]

CONSTITUTIONALISM AND CULTURE

Laws and constitutional mechanisms may encourage virtuous practices. But they cannot produce good culture—though a noninstrumental understanding of law entails recognition that constitutions and culture are not widely separated to begin with. Ryn points out, for example, that

> The [American] Constitution and related documents all imply an entire view of human nature and society. The particular text assumes and forms an inextricable part of a more comprehensive and unwritten constitution, which includes the moral ethos of the Framers. The institutions and procedures prescribed by the written document imply a particular kind of civilization and a particular kind of human being. Without a certain personality type setting the tone in society, the government could not function as intended. The Constitution presupposes character traits in tune with its prescriptions, and those prescriptions are expected to foster that personality.[20]

Constitutionalism is not merely a political structure; it is a way of life, rooted in a particular conception of human nature, virtue, and the good life. For example, the American tradition was one of self-reliance and local action adhering to the Golden Rule.[21] The American Framers "assume the preponderance of a particular type of moral responsibility with deep roots in classical and Christian civilization." Unfortunately, while this "older kind of virtue manifests itself in individual, personal responsibility and tends to foster private and local community and a decentralized society, the more recent kind of virtue manifests itself in abstract ideas and sentiments and tends to foster a collectivistic and centralized society."[22]

The American Constitution assumes "the most significant meaning of 'the people' to be the citizens organized in groups of various kinds."[23] Living in these groups, coming to appreciate and desire to live up to their standards, people learn to be decent, ethical persons. Centralization, particularly of the plebiscitary variety, undermines the cultural groundings of self-restraint. By displacing the associations in which virtue forms, it destroys the character necessary for constitutional self-government.[24] Plebiscitary government establishes goals and commands social outcomes through mechanisms and masses. The resulting society is characterized by separate, atomized individuals ruled from the center. These individuals can assert control over the structures of their lives only through specifically political action. As Bertrand de Jouvenel noted, public life in such a regime becomes a competition to control the levers of a power that may lack efficacy, but is in principle absolute.

CONSTITUTIONAL MORALITY

There is a long tradition of analyzing, in Tocqueville's phrase, "democracy in America." The term makes sense as an indicator of America's relatively egalitarian, participatory society. America's lack of any formal aristocracy, combined with its relatively low levels of deference accorded various elites and long tradition of popular participation in various associations certainly looks "democratic" when compared with older European models' political forms, and even with contemporary European managerial elitism. That said, it is important to keep in mind that American politics at the federal and state levels in particular are not democratic in any formal sense; they are republican.

The phrase "constitutional democracy," strictly speaking, would apply properly only to a regime in which the constitution established and maintained a system in which the people as a whole governed directly through voting and through direct participation in political administration. Even were this form of government possible on a national scale, it currently does not exist. As important, the kinds of habits to which Ryn points as necessary for ethical democracy are not fully "democratic." While it is true that Montesquieu referred to republican "virtue" as love of the republic (and its laws), this is both undemocratic in its valuation of forms and structures above the will of the many (the sine qua non of democracy) and specifically political rather than more broadly social or cultural. Tocqueville, of course, saw virtue as rooted in aristocratic mores, hence, in persistent danger in America.

The point of harmonization between these two positions, and with Ryn's seeming intention, if not necessarily his vocabulary, lies in recognition of the multiplicity of virtues within a full, functioning culture. The virtues of a given person are many (as are his potential vices) according to his roles as political figure, father, soldier, worker, and so on. When these virtues in effect are consumed by the single, political virtue of love of the state, we no longer are in a republic, or what Ryn terms a constitutional democracy. With such concentration of affection and effort we enter a kingdom of totalitarian plebiscitary democracy.

The movement away from constitutional democracy toward its plebiscitary opposite is a transformation of structures, ideas, and most of all norms of behavior. Key to understanding such changes is the concept of constitutional morality. This specific form of republican virtue is not total—it does not relate to all of life, but only to political conduct. But it is crucial for constitutionalism of any kind. In order to survive, any constitutional system must rely on a people possessing an appropriate constitutional morality. That is, the people, and especially those who wield power, must recognize that it is their moral duty to follow the rules of that system. Constitutional morality requires that those holding office under a particular constitutional structure act with a requisite virtue, or set of virtues. The goal is not some abstract best person, but rather, a good member of Congress, good Supreme Court justice, good President, or good administrator. Persons in these positions properly share an appropriate subservience to constitutional requirements, especially the separation of powers, such that it makes sense to talk about the virtue of a political official at the national level and a general constitutional morality. Crucially, the people must share this morality and virtue; they must demand respect for the Constitution among officeholders if those officeholders are to be held accountable and their own constitutional norms are to be maintained.

Plebiscitary democracy undermines constitutional morality. When the unwritten constitution with its demand for forms and procedures gives way to plebiscitary ideology, constitutional provisions like the separation of powers come to be ignored. More generally, law comes to be used as a weapon in wars over interest and ideology (e.g., issues of "institutionalized racism and sexism") and so comes to lose that "special dignity" once attached to it "as an impartial norm serving the common good."[25]

Ryn refers to something at least very close to the concept of constitutional morality when he writes of "the spirit of constitutionalism," which requires that the people be committed to changing policies and structures of which they disapprove only through constitutionally prescribed methods.[26] But Ryn seems to tie the law and the spirit more closely together than even constitutional morality would demand. He states that "political institutions are indistinguishable from the cultural ethos of a people."[27] He extends this Aristotelian understanding of politics and society by asserting that "the words *government* and *constitution* are not names for something existing apart from the individual citizens. Those who participate in politics under the rules of a constitution accept it as a guide for their personal behavior, so that strictly speaking the constitution as a practical force is identical with the political activity of the individuals who assent to its provisions and supply or withhold the spirit of constitutionalism."[28]

Ryn is correct to point out the interrelationships between law (or constitutionalism) and culture. That said, we should not overstate how closely the two are intertwined. In part, Ryn is essentially pointing out the artificial and false nature of modern liberalism's public/private dichotomy.

> The "private" habits by which the individual tries to lift himself out of the ever-present inclination to yield to morally unexamined impulse cannot be sharply distinguished from those of his habits which he tries to follow for the same purpose in his "public" or "political" life. They are, in fact, only two aspects of one and the same attempt to achieve the moral end. Since the end itself is social but its attainment dependent on individual effort, the prerequisites are both "private" and "public."[29]

Here again Ryn reminds one of Aristotle's political thought. And it certainly is true that in Aristotle's Greece there was no real distinction between public and private. Indeed, Aristotle referred to the regime (*politeia*, often mistranslated as "constitution") as "a certain arrangement of those who inhabit the city." As Giovanni Sartori pointed out, the Greek "city states" are misnamed, for they were not states in any meaningful sense; they were city communities.

The extremely small, tribal societies of the Greek cities did not have states in any meaningful sense. They lacked political structures with a legitimacy and ethic separate from that of the community as a whole. The "political" principles of the given regime, be they democratic, aristocratic, or tyrannical, determined the nature of particular groupings of persons (e.g., who voted on what type of actions) and even such fundamental norms as whether the people would eat at common messes and whether working classes would be held as slaves.[30] Ancient Greek regimes are not equivalent, or even of the same type, as constitutions in the modern sense because they did not merely lay out governing procedures, instead literally constituting the entire community, in its political, social, religious, and even "private" (familial) aspects.[31]

Ancient Greek communities not only lacked states, they also lacked the rule of law. The laws did not reliably bind the rulers, so the ruled lived in rational fear of arbitrary actions by those rulers. There was little or no institutionalization of structures outside the communities themselves such that they held their own authority and legitimacy, setting down rules to be followed on their own authority. Attempts at such institutionalization were made through various "constitutions" as the laws of Solon. But these bodies of laws seldom lasted long in Greece because there was no ingrained habit of following them. Political powers were too broad and political stakes were too high to be confined by legal mechanisms.

In part, the extreme unity of the Greek regimes was a matter of scale—largely tribal populations measured in the thousands will be more tightly bound than populations measured in the millions. Simple fear of death in a never-ending struggle for survival among warring regimes that slaughtered their opponents was another reason for Greek communities to retain tight control over their people. In a climate of persistent potential annihilation, one had to defend oneself in the public square at all times for fear of being banished (or worse) by one's ever-fearful fellow citizens. The result was the very instability cited by Publius in rejecting ancient democratic models for the American Constitution.[32]

None of this is to say that Greek conceptions of political life are irrelevant today, or that "democracy" in the limited sense of rule by consent is inimical always and everywhere to ethical politics. But the Greeks, at least, did not achieve constitutional democracy because they did not have the rule of law. It was the Romans who first established a lasting commitment to binding rulers through force of law. They achieved much by establishing the custom-rooted Twelve Tables as a kind of holy writ and more by developing a rudimentary unwritten constitution that placed adherence to law above expediency and the will to power. Much more than their Greek predecessors, Romans of the republican period succeeded, through traditions of judging and rulemaking, in placing law above the desires of rulers, including assemblies.[33] These developments were beneficial to citizens because over time they subordinated the people to laws rather than to the whims of rulers. The results, beginning with the Roman republic, were increasingly predictable rules and an understanding of justice as the reasonable expectations of parties to a dispute, both of which provided people with the ability to plan their lives and with that "tranquility of mind" Montesquieu identified as the ground of liberty.[34]

During the medieval era, the rise of more complex social structures and institutions in Europe combined with respect for custom to aid the development of constitutionalism. As late as the thirteenth century, customary rules trumped arbitrary action, even where that action was labeled "law." The French king could make new law only during or in preparation for war, and then only with reasonable cause, for the benefit of the commonweal, and in accordance with the accepted law of God or morals.[35] The king was ethically, politically, and increasingly constitutionally bound to respect the "constitution" of the realm, defined as the body of different rights held by different individuals and groups in different things.[36] In feudal terms the king was only first among equals; even his "royal prerogative" was only a set of rights "necessary to the fulfillment of his office" that were limited and did not entitle him to "alter the status of his subjects."[37] Custom, in its way, was king. And while this was not always and everywhere conducive to human flourishing, it did constitute a law binding rulers—in other words, constitutionalism.

Constitutionalism also developed in medieval Europe through competition and low-level conflict among multiple authorities and legal jurisdictions. Kings, bishops, princes, and municipal councils were only the most prominent authority figures competing for power and self-governance. In addition, the church's canon law, the law merchant, and royal, common law were only the most prominent forms of law, enforced in separate courts with overlapping powers and jurisdictions that competed for power and fees from litigants by expanding and developing legal procedures and rights.[38] Constitutional documents like Magna Carta and various local charters[39] spelled out the lines of royal, church, and baronial jurisdiction, while canon law delineated the institutional rights of popes, cardinals, and cathedral chapters.[40] And cities' charters not only defined their rights in relation to kings but also spelled out the rights and duties of mayors, councils, and other officers.[41]

The lines of jurisdiction were less formal than would be the case with a fully codified constitution. The result was a loose system of competing jurisdictions, fostering competition and conflict. Critically, this competition took place within an overarching, natural law-based consensus that each competitor had a duty to abide by norms of legal process and pursuit of the common good.

While there was much debate and even conflict over principle and policy, all parties recognized (if imperfectly) their interest in cooperation and compromise. And this, combined with competition for the loyalty and patronage of various groups, helped produce significant protections for the rights of individuals and groups.[42]

The multiplicity of competing authorities that characterized medieval constitutionalism has been portrayed as detrimental to the rule of law and good government. But medieval constitutionalism's fracturing of power provided protections against large-scale tyranny. Like the so-called deadlock of democracy Progressives so abhor, the medieval constitution protected existing expectations more than the desires of would-be saviors, consensus more than power, the common good fostered in self-governing associations rather than centralizing ideological programs.

THE STATE VERSUS CONSTITUTIONALISM

Development of the state did not end with the loose sets of overlapping associations that characterized medieval constitutionalism. The thirst for power and the requirements of war encouraged centralization. Recent scholarship has confirmed the observations of Tocqueville and Jouvenel, among others, that late medieval demands for funds to produce arms and new powers to build mass armies brought administrative centralization, resistance, and a feedback cycle of political violence that damaged constitutionalism during the late medieval and early modern eras.[43] Centralizing monarchs like Henry VIII in England and Louis XIV in France sought to eliminate associations and power centers in competition with themselves.[44] A number of monarchs were able to centralize power through standing armies and tax structures, stripping rights from their former rivals in the balanced constitutions of the Middle Ages; in so doing, these monarchs, now claiming a divine right to absolute power, were enabled to form and rule territorial nation-states.[45]

It was this model of absolute power that the Jacobins adapted to their own ends during the French Revolution. It also was this model that Progressives built upon in undermining the (in important ways pre-modern) American constitution by establishing the administrative state. Woodrow Wilson in particular helped institutionalize the view that "administration" is about "doing the people's business" in the sense of delivering what is demanded by the majority. Here it is worth emphasizing Wilson's determination that administrators utilize top-down procedures to translate the political will into public action as efficiently as possible. The argument was that law is a mere tool, serving the majority, such that it should be kept separate from any cultural preconceptions. The result, over time, has been a weakening of constitutional morality and institutionalization of plebiscitary democracy.

CONSTITUTIONALISM AND THE TAMING OF THE MODERN STATE

By treating laws as mere tools rather than norms of conduct, progressivism severed the ties between law and traditional culture. As we have seen, however, the result is not efficient government. It is a centralized state that undermines the ethical dimension of democracy, replacing the common good with the good of the state as determined by those who wield power.

Still, self-conscious Progressives or Jacobins are not the only ones to support the separation of law from ethical conscience—and culture—that spawned modern plebiscitary democracy. Many "classical liberals" and libertarians praise the modern separation of law from culture as the root of our public/private dichotomy, along with the individualism seen as its product. Modern individualists share an instrumentalist view of government and constitutionalism, differing from Progressives only in that they believe it essential to keep the extent of state action to a minimum. But that "minimum" is defined in terms of the protection of individual rights—rights so open to interpretation and manipulation as to give carte blanche to the state with respect to their enforcement.

Individual rights may be defined against the central state. Then again, they generally have been defined as protections against nongovernmental actors as well. Indeed, much of today's plebiscitary state is justified as "defending" individuals against various forms of "private" social or economic oppression supposedly instigated by associations against individuals. Indeed, there seems to be no limit to the number or kinds of oppressor and oppressions the central state can seek to transform in the name of individualism. Most constitutional lawyers today demand guarantees of "positive" rights to political participation, financial security, and government services as necessary for individual empowerment.

Individualists and social justice warriors no doubt see themselves as at odds with one another's vision of what constitutional government should provide, entail, and demand. But they share a common element, which constitutes the single, defining, and destructive feature of plebiscitary democracy.

That element is the belief that laws and especially constitutions *command* the societies in which they exist—that they by their nature are political programs intended to shape the conduct of individuals, groups, and political actors to produce a society that has a specific character, whether it be deemed free, fair, or even oppressive.

A different conception of constitutionalism is rooted in historical practice and embodied in the United States Constitution as originally drafted and understood. According to that conception, a constitution properly does not command, but rather mediates among more primary associations. Drafters of a mediating constitution would not see it as a fundamental guiding force according to whose elements society will be shaped. Instead they would see it as a suit of clothes made to fit a society that is already there, the integrity of which must be respected. A mediating constitution seeks not to shape society from a grand original position, but to maintain peace, stability, and the rule of law so that the people and associations making up its way of life may flourish.

As Ryn points out, there is no escaping purpose in politics, because purpose is intrinsic to human life. But this does not mean that the central state must or even should define for all people, as individuals, the shape, context, and purposes of their lives. The state need not take direct responsibility, as it does in plebiscitary democracy, for the well-being of its citizens. Indeed, a true, ethical constitutional democracy in Ryn's terms would be one that leaves provision of the various elements making up a good life to the local associations in which a healthy people actually live.

The difference between mediating and commanding structures is not directly a matter of political program. The distinction rests, rather, on what role one believes a constitution can or should play in shaping a society. All peoples seek to pursue and protect some combination of public goods. These goods normally include things like defense, roads, trade, and education. They must be pursued through some combination of acts and institutions. A central question concerns which goods will be pursued through conscious activity backed by the coercive power of the central state. Roads, for example, may be built directly by the state through forced labor or the extraction of money from the citizens to pay laborers. Alternatively, the job of pursuing and protecting common goods may be left to some combination of individual, associational, and local political administration.

Vincent Ostrom portrayed this choice as one over whether administration—the organized pursuit of common goods—should be constructed along monarchical or democratic lines.[46] Of particular importance, according to

Ostrom, was the American Constitution's original, "democratic" system of federalism and separation of powers. This structure produced a set of overlapping jurisdictions with overlapping constituencies and terms of office. And this multiplicity of authorities allowed all citizens, by nature belonging to a variety of communities that administer public goods, to have their voices heard as more distant administrators checked and balanced one another to prevent arbitrary power. Moreover, *The Federalist*'s system relied on what Ostrom called "positive constitutional law," by which he meant the effective, law-like nature of constitutional provisions limiting the power and scope of action of administrators and politicians. According to his idea of "democratic" administration, fragmentation of authority is essential and must be maintained through "legally enforceable constitutional law."[47]

Ostrom ascribes the other, "monarchical" form of administration to Woodrow Wilson and the progressive ideology he promoted. It is a plebiscitary logic that concentrates power and authority in the central state. This power is wielded in the name of the people, taken as a numerical majority, but over time produces the kind of centralized bureaucracy properly associated with plebiscitary democracy.

Ostrom's "democratic" administration maintains the separate authority and power of associations, while limiting the state to its proper role of allowing the people, within and through their natural and customary associations, to pursue the good life in common with their fellows. This makes it important that the people have political power, but not directly as an unmediated mass. As Ryn points out, a constitutional democracy such as that embodied in the American Constitution does not seek to empower numerical majorities.

> One might even say that through its system of checks and balances it tends to thwart the will of the momentary national majority. In fact, the people, viewed as an undifferentiated mass, is not even given constitutional recognition. There is no institutional channel through which a mere numerical majority can work its will. The "people" of the constitution is made up of a number of overlapping, subdivided electorates. Not even the president is chosen by a national majority. He is selected by a majority of the Electoral College, a body chosen by pluralities in the various sates and according to a formula which further ignores the national majority by giving over-representation, by numerical standards, to the smaller states.[48]

In Ryn's understanding, not even the legislative branches—Senate and House of Representatives—provide means of establishing a "unified political will" to the "undifferentiated mass of the people." And the split between state and national governments places further impediments in the way of any putative General Will.[49] The result is (or was until recent decades) a system in which the people govern themselves in and through their natural, local associations and the central government plays a limited role, mediating among these institutions by, for example, preventing violence and prohibiting internal tariffs among them, and defending the whole from external threats.

To maintain this character and with it the ethical nature of constitutional democracy, administration must remain decentralized. That is, the constitution and constitutional morality must do their job of preventing capture of the state by forces of self-interest and/or ideology. Checks, balances, and other auxiliary precautions must prevent factional dominance. In addition, though, a healthy culture and constitutional morality must prevent adoption of grand Progressive schemes of social welfare, thereby wresting control of policy administration from local associations.

Whether in the name of safety, fairness, or the general will, programs of national transformation substitute detailed statutes for less formal, local norms to pursue the common good. They tie people to administrative mechanisms and formal rules, dissolving their ties to one another. Worse, because such formal rules cannot address all relevant circumstances, they quickly give way to massive transfers of discretionary power to administrators. The rule of law disintegrates along with public trust and the people become mere individuals to be shaped into an undifferentiated mass by the state. Only by eschewing grand projects and maintaining the authority of natural associations can the mechanisms of the modern state serve constitutionalism and the ethical life.

The problem facing Americans in the contemporary era is how to undo Progressivism's institutionalization of grand plans. Once a system of grand planning—a commanding constitution—has been established, how is one to reestablish the previous system of a limited, mediating constitution? The problem is acute because a commanding system is made possible by what it furthers, namely cultural decay or, in Ryn's terms, the ascendance of a people's base will. Ryn has no answer to this problem; indeed there is no easy, self-executing answer and so to offer one would be dishonest. We must, then, reorient ourselves (our wills in the Babbitt-influenced vocabulary) to the common good so as to make cultural renewal possible, and from it a return to the kind of republic or constitutional democracy Ryn values.

NOTES

1. See for example, Claes Ryn, "The Things of Caesar: Notes toward the Delimitation of Politics," *Thought* 55, no. 219 (December 1980): 439–60 for one early formulation of the problem. Later formulations are reviewed in this essay.

2. The term *constitutional morality* may not be familiar to most readers. It appeared in Clinton Rossiter, *The American Presidency* (New York: Harcourt, Brace and World, 1956) and was further developed by WIllmoore Kendall and George Carey in *The Basic Symbols of the American Political Tradition* (Baton Rouge: Louisiana State University Press, 1970). It is a central theme of Frohnen and Carey, *Constitutional Morality and the Rise of Quasi-Law* (Cambridge, MA: Harvard University Press, 2016).

3. Claes G. Ryn, *Democracy and the Ethical Life* (Washington, DC: Catholic University of America Press, 1990), 93.

4. Ibid., 5.

5. Ibid., 130–31.

6. Ibid., 119.

7. Ibid., 216.

8. Ibid., 186.

9. Ibid., 190–91.

10. Claes G. Ryn, *America the Virtuous* (New Brunswick, NJ: Transaction Publishers, 2009), 4–5.

11. See for example Robert Nisbet, "Rousseau and Totalitarianism," *Journal of Politics* 5, no. 2 (May 1943): 106.

12. Ryn, *Democracy and the Ethical Life*, 197.

13. Ibid., 197.

14. Ibid., 162.

15. Ibid., 8–9.

16. Ibid., 164. Emphasis in original. Ryn's use of the word "democratic" may be seen as problematic. Most theorists of democracy reject as illegitimate any substantive checks on the popular will. More important, the men who drafted perhaps the single most important constitution of the modern era (the American), with which Ryn clearly is in sympathy, openly rejected democracy as a failed and dangerous form of government. Ryn is using the term *democratic* in his own, specific sense only, here. I take up this issue below.

17. Ibid., 163. Emphasis in original.

18. Ibid., 169.

19. Ibid., 193.

20. Claes G. Ryn, "Political Philosophy and the Unwritten Constitution," *Modern Age* 34, no. 4 (Summer 1992): 303.

21. Ryn, *Democracy*, 216–17.

22. Ryn, "Political Philosophy and the Constitution," 304, 305.

23. Ryn, *Democracy*, 190.

24. Ryn, *America the Virtuous*, 55.

25. Ryn, *Democracy*, 235.

26. Ibid., 174.

27. Ibid., 197.

28. Ibid., 172.

29. Ibid., 172.

30. See the discussion of Aristotle in Frohnen and Carey, *Constitutional Morality*, 64–65 and references therein.

31. Giovanni Sartori, *The Theory of Democracy Revisited* (Chatham, NJ: Chatham House Publishers, 1987), I:279.

32. Alexander Hamilton, James Madison, and John Jay, *The Federalist*, ed., George W. Carey and James McClellan (Indianapolis, Liberty Fund, 2001), no. 9, 37–38.

33. On the Greeks and Romans see Frohnen and Carey, *Constitutional Morality*, especially 56–57.

34. Ibid., 23.

35. Kenneth Pennington, *The Prince and the Law, 1200–1600: Sovereignty and Rights in the Western Legal Tradition* (Berkeley: University of California Press, 1993), 92.

36. Ibid.

37. Ibid., 225.

38. Ibid., 151.

39. Filippo Sabetti, "Local Roots of Constitutionalism," *Perspectives on Political Science* 33, no. 2 (2004): 70. Sabetti provides an overview of a plethora of local charters establishing constitutional government in places like Sicily and binding monarchs in a manner similar to that of Magna Carta well before that charter's promulgation.

40. Bruce P. Frohnen and Kenneth L. Grasso, eds., *Rethinking Rights: Historical, Political, and Philosophical Perspectives* (Columbia: University of Missouri Press, 2009), 111.

41. Harold J. Berman, *Law and Revolution: The Formation of the Western Legal Tradition* (Cambridge, MA: Harvard University Press, 1983), 313.

42. Ibid. Berman goes so far as to argue that the result was appreciably "modern" rights. However, it is important to note the communal nature of many of these rights, as well as their reliance, not just on political and judicial forces for their protection, but also on social convention and institutions of civil society.

43. See generally Bruce D. Porter, *War and the Rise of the State* (New York: Free Press, 2008).

44. Alexis de Tocqueville, *The Old Regime and the Revolution*, trans. Alan S. Kahan, vol. 1 (Chicago, IL: University of Chicago Press, 2004).

45. Porter, *War and the Rise of the State*, 12.

46. Vincent Ostrom, *The Intellectual Crisis in American Public Administration* (Montgomery: University of Alabama Press, 1973).

47. Ibid., 88–89.

48. Ryn, *Democracy,* 155–56.

49. Ibid., 157.

BIBLIOGRAPHY

Berman, Harold J. *Law and Revolution: The Formation of the Western Legal Tradition.* Cambridge, MA: Harvard University Press, 1983.

Frohnen, Bruce and George W. Carey, *Constitutional Morality and the Rise of Quasi-Law.* Cambridge, MA: Harvard University Press, 2016.

Hamilton, Alexander, James Madison, and John Jay. *The Federalist.* Edited by George W. Carey and James McClellan. Indianapolis, IN: Liberty Fund, 2001.

Kendall, Willmoore and George W. Carey. *The Basic Symbols of the American Political Tradition.* Baton Rouge: Louisiana State University Press, 1970.

Nisbet, Robert. "Rousseau and Totalitarianism." *Journal of Politics* 5, no. 2 (May 1943): 93–114.

Ostrom, Vincent. *The Intellectual Crisis in American Public Administration.* Montgomery: University of Alabama Press, 1973.

Pennington, Kenneth. *The Prince and the Law, 1200–1600: Sovereignty and Rights in the Western Legal Tradition.* Berkeley: University of California Press, 1993.

Rethinking Rights: Historical, Political, and Philosophical Perspectives. Edited by Bruce P. Frohnen and Kenneth L. Grasso. Columbia: University of Missouri Press, 2009.

Ryn, Claes G. *America the Virtuous.* New Brunswick, NJ: Transaction Publishers, 2009.

———. *Democracy and the Ethical Life*. Washington, DC: Catholic University of America Press, 1990.

———. "Political Philosophy and the Unwritten Constitution." *Modern Age* 34, no. 4 (Summer 1992): 5–27.

———. "The Things of Caesar: Notes toward the Delimitation of Politics." *Thought* 55, no. 219 (December 1980): 439–60.

Rossiter, Clinton. *The American Presidency*. New York: Harcourt, Brace and World, 1956.

Sabetti, Filippo. "Local Roots of Constitutionalism." *Perspectives on Political Science* 33, no. 2 (2004): 70–78.

Sartori, Giovanni. *The Theory of Democracy Revisited*. Chatham, NJ: Chatham House Publishers, 1987.

Porter, Bruce D. *War and the Rise of the State*. New York: Free Press, 2008.

de Tocqueville, Alexis. *The Old Regime and the Revolution*. Translated by Alan S. Kahan. Edited by François Furet and Françoise Mélonio. Chicago, IL: University of Chicago Press, 2004.

Part V
America, Humanism, and the World

Humanistic concerns about culture, imagination, and ethical character are at the heart of how Babbitt, Ryn, and other scholars interpret different traditions of the American relationship with the world. Focusing on such levels of analysis, there seem to be two general periods of US international engagement. From the earliest days of the republic up to around the turn of the twentieth century, an American foreign policy tradition prevailed that has been variously described as "exemplary exceptionalism," "modest republicanism," and "moral realism." This tradition emphasized peaceful engagement with many nations but practiced rigorous moral and constitutional restraint when it came to questions of foreign policy, especially those related to war. Since the early 1900s, a different tradition has taken hold. This newer way of understanding the American relationship with the world emphasizes intervention in the affairs of other nations to promote ostensibly idealistic and universally acceptable goals such as the establishment of liberal democracy, individual rights, and economic free markets. Its champions in government and other elite echelons of the American establishment have celebrated this vision as the definitive expression of American virtue. Concrete examples of foreign policy failures resulting from efforts to achieve such ends are brushed off as evidence only of tactical or strategic errors of implementation. The ideas themselves are never questioned. Babbitt and Ryn understand the nature of the many failures of American foreign policy since the early twentieth century more clearly because they have seen the ideas that have inspired such undertakings for what they are—the impulses of empire pretending to be manifestations of morality.

If a humanistic renewal in America's post-constitutional age is to begin in earnest, then a substantial, critical engagement with the ahistorical and often unthinking American attachment to democratic imperialism needs to be offered. Historically informed and imaginatively vibrant alternatives to this dangerous dimension of US politics and culture need to be developed. The chapters in this section provide both types of insights.

In "' Let Things Be Called by Their Right Names': Difference as Constraint in American Exceptionalism," Richard M. Gamble offers an illustration of historical reasoning that exemplifies the spirit of Babbitt's humanistic commitment to the right defining of ideas. Gamble critiques both the "exemplary" and "missionary" strains of American exceptionalism, which are often associated with figures such as John Winthrop, Daniel Webster, and Woodrow Wilson. He challenges the widespread sense that exceptionalist ideas are both obviously true and representative of the long experience of Americans. In drawing the reader's attention to the contested nature of these ideas during the colonial and early republican periods of America, Gamble invites the reader to appreciate and explore the historical complexity and richness of the American tradition of thinking about the relationship between the US and the world. Gamble argues that exceptionalist thinkers have also committed significant and dangerous category errors, confusing the sacred and the secular, the things of God and the things of Caesar. For these reasons, he believes both versions of exceptionalism need to be abandoned and replaced by what he describes as "difference as constraint." Developing this alternative understanding of American distinctiveness will require renewed commitment to historical wisdom, ethical restraint, and moral imagination, Gamble suggests. In thinking of rehabilitating the American foreign policy tradition along such lines, he exhibits a humanistic approach that has much in common with Ryn and Babbitt.

Whereas Gamble focuses primarily on the conceptual level, in "A Little Place and a Big Idea: The Temptation to Imperialism and the Loss of Republicanism," Justin B. Litke argues that any serious reform of American foreign policy must be combined with a reconfiguration of the scale of American life. The question of scale is rarely discussed by Babbitt or Ryn, but Litke's engagement with this important topic is entirely at home with humanistic concerns about ethical restraint and imagination. Litke draws attention to Abraham Lincoln's Gettysburg Address and its recasting of the United States as a "propositional nation," that is, a nation defined by its commitment to ahistorical ideas (e.g., equality), rather than its concrete patterns of life and presence in the world. Litke also explains how the embrace of such an abstract notion of nationality inevitably encourages political and economic centralization in ways that transform American life, putting it on a colossal scale. In other words, American democratic imperialism not only fosters historical amnesia and hubris, as Gamble indicates, but it also creates a physical and imaginative landscape at home defined increasingly by rootlessness and despair. Invoking both the Anti-Federalists as well as the American novelist and essayist Wendell Berry, Litke identifies the kinds of questions and possible solutions needed to make the communities in which Americans live little places rather than indistinguishable motels of big ideas.

Finally, in "Resistance and Renewal: Irving Babbitt and China," Zhang Yuan and Justin D. Garrison describe the influence Babbitt's writings exerted over Chinese intellectuals interested in maintaining the best elements of Chinese culture while adapting creatively to the disorienting and often violent post-Qing environment of the early twentieth century. Such humanistic aspirations put Babbitt's followers at odds with the peculiar constellation of intellectual movements in China at the time, ranging from radical traditionalism, to Marxism, to a type of progressivism inspired by John Dewey. Babbitt ultimately has much to teach America and China, and that topic is addressed in the chapter itself. Here it is worth stating something obvious—on the international stage, China and the United States cannot avoid each other. A humanistic orientation toward diplomacy, one that includes but is not limited to the possibilities raised by Gamble, Litke, Zhang, and Garrison, would be a fruitful way of transcending the recurring impasses in relations between these two countries. For too long, each has engaged in relations guided by narrowly conceived strategic and economic considerations. While such concerns are important, discussing them, as Ryn and Babbitt know, is ultimately downstream from establishing deeper bonds, cultivated over time, which are inspired by sober thinking, ethical restraint, and the development of historical and imaginative points of common ground.

CHAPTER ELEVEN

"Let Things Be Called by Their Right Names"
Difference as Constraint in American Exceptionalism

Richard M. Gamble

Daniel Webster's role in the Compromise of 1850 may have earned him the epithet "Ichabod" for his troubles, but for many sons of New England the glory had not departed from the venerable statesman's brow. For them, Webster was the savior of the Union and still the greatest orator of the age. The New England Society of New York invited Webster to address the organization's annual dinner in 1850, marking the *Mayflower*'s landing at Plymouth.[1] Other dignitaries and speakers included a number of prominent clergy, heads of benevolent societies, the president of Columbia College, and Sir Henry Lytton Bulwar, British minister to the US and the Anglo half of the Anglo-American treaty the Senate had just ratified in May, smoothing the way for any future canal across the isthmus between North and South America.

Webster knew his audience and the occasion. The Bay State's senior senator praised the Pilgrim spirit that had purportedly animated the American people as a whole since 1620, carrying them across a continent, and now beckoning them to look beyond the nation's shores. The Pilgrims had launched the intrepid Americans on their national mission, and the Union had to be preserved for the sake of that high calling. That the Massachusetts senator should extol the Union at such a critical moment was no surprise; he had made his political career promoting American "nationality," though his desperate pleas for unity never sufficed to place him in the White House.[2] The year just ending had pushed the sectional crisis to the verge of the breakup of the federal republic. The Compromise, praised alike by the Democratic and Whig establishments but denounced by abolitionists and leading Southern statesmen, had sealed the deal on California's admission to the Union.

Webster acknowledged the Pilgrims had been a rigid lot, intolerant, sectarian, and austere. Thankfully, America had progressed to the higher ground of "milder virtues" and "a more enlarged and comprehensive Christian philanthropy." Indeed, America's benevolent mission, assigned to it by Providence, summoned the nation to show the world the wisdom of extending tolerance to all those who acknowledged Him and the authority of his Word. What better proof of America's generous spirit than the fact that a Catholic (Roger Taney) served as chief justice of the Supreme Court? The Whig senator then read the entire Mayflower Compact, spinning it somehow into a charter of the right of private judgment, a rereading of the sectarian past common at the time. He rejoiced that the Pilgrim spirit lived on; it had spread down the east coast, headed across North America, and now extended its reach to the Pacific. When he predicted that the following year a Pilgrim Society of California would celebrate the *Mayflower*'s landing, an audience member exclaimed, "Today; they celebrate to-day." That may indeed have been the case since the New England Society of San Francisco had convened in October to mark California's statehood.[3] The next destination of this irrepressible march westward was Asia, Webster predicted. The audience laughed and cheered as he vowed, "it shall yet go hard, if the three hundred millions of people of China—if they are intelligent enough to understand any thing—shall not one day hear and know something of the rock of Plymouth too!"[4]

These quotable lines from the quotable Daniel Webster prove tempting for any historian looking for evidence of an unconstrained Manifest Destiny, for the nation's habit of mixing the religious and the political, and for its self-understanding as history's "dangerous nation," putting tyrants and backward peoples everywhere on notice that the US stands ready to do more than vindicate its own liberty and progress.[5] Webster's speech did indeed embody all of these things, even to the point of winding up with a startlingly raw ideological imperialism. But how representative of America as a whole was Webster's speech and others in the same vein? How typical was Webster of the American imagination at mid-century? Does Webster's exuberance provide just one more marching band in the endless parade of America's righteous self-consciousness?

Three obstacles stand in the way of reaching a verdict on what or whom Webster spoke for in 1850. The first is the assumption that the Puritans who settled the rocky coast of New England were the true progenitors of whatever is truly and distinctively "American" about the nation's culture, religion, and political institutions. The second is the assumption that America lacked the theological and cultural resources in the nineteenth century to maintain the distinction between the secular and sacred. The third is that there has been a stable consensus among Americans that they have been called by history or by God to globalize their vision and values. Together, these related phenomena obscure all the complicated quarrels that lie at the heart of American intellectual and cultural history and really at the heart of the American identity.

Modern America's obsession with Winthrop's "city on a hill" provides almost daily reminders of how powerful this determination to trace the real America to the Puritans remains. Forgotten in all this is the fact that the Puritans themselves debated the significance of the Massachusetts Bay Colony at its founding. Ten years after Governor John Winthrop drafted his "Model of Christian Charity," he found himself on the receiving end of a stinging rebuke from another Puritan leader. William Fiennes (1582–1662), Lord Saye and Sele, an opponent of the Stuarts and a wealthy backer of the Puritan colonization of the New World, hotly disputed Winthrop's conception of the Puritan mission. Lord Saye had solid credentials. In 1630, the same year as the Puritan settlement of Massachusetts Bay, he had helped found the Providence Island company in the Caribbean, about 120 miles east of Nicaragua. The Spanish destroyed the fledgling colony in 1641, but its existence until then meant the Puritan colony in New England had some serious competition from a warmer climate. Only Lord Saye's reply to Winthrop survives in their exchange of letters in 1640, but his answer is detailed enough to reconstruct the main points of their dispute.[6]

The controversy between Winthrop and Lord Saye shows unmistakably that there was nothing self-evident, inevitable, or uncontested about New England's existence, let alone its contribution to American "exceptionalism." Governor Winthrop, fearful for the survival of his colony, rebuked Lord Saye in terms that cast his opponent in the role of the cowardly Israelites who spied out the land, brought back a bad report, and discouraged God's covenant people from entering the Promised Land. For good measure, Winthrop also compared Lord Saye to Sanballat and Tobiah, from the Book of Nehemiah, who mocked the Jews laboring to rebuild the walls of Jerusalem after their exile in Babylon.

Not intimidated in the least, Lord Saye gave as good as he got. "Whereas you speak in your letter of taking the name of God in vain, I pray consider seriously, and let our friends there be judges between us, whether this be not taking God's name in vain, to misapply Scripture in this manner ... by assuming ... that there is the like call from God for your going to that part of America and fixing there, that there was for the Israelites going to the Land of promise and fixing there"—or the same mandate from God that Nehemiah had, he continued. This letter contains much more of interest, including a thoughtful attempt to lower the stakes of colonization and confine the project to the realm of ordinary human prudence. Christians in these circumstances had the liberty and responsibility to exercise reason and weigh "possibilities" and "probabilities."[7]

This letter's implications are telling for the story of American exceptionalism: an esteemed Puritan leader and backer of colonization stated explicitly to John Winthrop (1) that his colony was *not* God's New Israel; (2) that he had misused the Bible in so claiming; and (3) that the question of colonizing the New World is *not* a matter of special revelation or even a matter of faith, but rather a matter of "means and probabilities" subject to human reason and judgment. It was as if Saye had told Winthrop that if the colonists under your care would rather live in the Caribbean than in Massachusetts, then God bless them. They have the liberty of conscience to do so. Don't bind them by telling them they are God's New Israel, blessed with a unique calling revealed and confirmed to them by special providences. Lord Saye, speaking from within the mainstream of English Calvinist orthodoxy, attempted to impose theological containment on the headstrong Winthrop. Puritanism, rather than dooming America to an exceptionalism of the most aggressive kind, actually had at its disposal means to strangle it in its cradle—even if those means were rejected.

Two hundred years later, Massachusetts had left its days as a fledgling Bible commonwealth far behind and was a populous and influential state within a diverse federal republic. It was proud of its heritage, and rightly so. But the custodians of the state's fame and glory did more than root for the home team. After the debacle of the Hartford Convention in 1815, with its embarrassing talk of secession in response to President Madison's war with Britain, Massachusetts historians and politicians set out to salvage their state's reputation. And they did so by rewriting history. They took up the task of telling the American story in such a way that Plymouth Rock and the Bay Colony (generally conflated) became the special place where it all began. They were ardent nationalists, but on their own terms; they imposed their sectional identity on the nation as a whole, in a project historian Harlow Sheidley aptly calls "sectional nationalism." There must be only one cultural agenda for a modern nation, and that agenda was going to dominate the continent.[8]

Even the otherwise judicious Alexis de Tocqueville fell under the spell of the new narrative he picked up from disgruntled New England Federalists and Unitarians in the 1830s.[9] He repeated what has persisted as textbook orthodoxy ever since.

> The New England principles spread first of all to neighboring states; subsequently, they reached successively the more distant, ending up, if I may put it this way, by *permeating* the entire confederation. Now they exert their influence beyond its limits to the whole American world. The civilization of New England has been like a beacon lit upon mountain tops which, after warming all in its vicinity, casts a glow over the distant horizon.[10]

The degree to which such claims became popularized is evident in the less capable hands of the Congregationalist minister who in 1852 celebrated the Pilgrim spirit in the most expansive terms. He told the New England Society of San Francisco (Webster's dream come true) that, while Virginia deserved chronological priority in the story of American settlement, the "noble and great" southern state "owes much of her glory to influences that went down to her from the north and east." It seemed obvious to him that "republicanism was born in the cabin of the Mayflower" in the form of the Mayflower Compact. And so the reinvented Pilgrims marched on. The task ahead for the hearty pioneers on the West Coast after statehood was nothing less than "to make California the Massachusetts of the Pacific."[11]

Sectional nationalism often relied on a civil religion that appropriated the Bible and Christian doctrine for the purposes of the nation. This tendency appeared among some Southerners as well, and of course religion had been called to the aid of America's wars and domestic nation-building for a long time. But even New Englanders themselves became wary of the emerging civil religion and put up resistance. They worried about the cost a "sacred" America would impose on the truly sacred cause of Christianity. As with Lord Saye two centuries before, they saw the problem, warned against it, and tried to sort out the muddled thinking. One of the best examples of the reaction against the effort to make America sacred came in response to the eulogies for Thomas Jefferson and John Adams in 1826. The two patriots died on July 4 of that year, the fiftieth anniversary of the Declaration of Independence. Anyone eager to spot what the old Puritans called "speaking providences" thought for sure they heard God's benediction loud and clear in this strange coincidence. Eulogists extolled this heavenly wonder as proof of the Almighty's special relationship with the United States, and their audiences seemed to welcome the flattery implicit in their words.

Nineteen eulogies from up and down the eastern seaboard, delivered between July and October 1826, were collected and published in a single volume. The anthologized speakers included Virginian John Tyler, Massachusetts state legislator Caleb Cushing, the venerable Daniel Webster, and Attorney General William Wirt.[12] When an editor at the *Christian Spectator* got hold of a review copy, he was not happy with what he found between the covers. As a matter of style, he objected to the eulogies' rhetorical excess but more urgently to their confusion of the sacred and secular. He wrote in terms that sound strangely modern, as if he had witnessed where all this civil religion was heading over the next two centuries. But then again, his objections echoed Lord Saye's from two centuries earlier. The theological critique of American political theology used similar tools for similar problems.

The *Christian Spectator*, founded in 1819 and later renamed the *Quarterly Christian Spectator*, published essays and reviews by Congregationalist and Presbyterian adherents of the so-called New Haven theology of Nathaniel W. Taylor. "Taylorism," as it was familiarly known, combined radically revised tenets of Calvinism with the earnest revivalism of the Second Great Awakening. Taylor founded what later became the Yale Divinity School, and he and his movement did battle with both the old Calvinist orthodoxy and the emergent Unitarians. New School Presbyterians found much to agree with in Taylor; Princeton's Old School did not, smelling the strong odor of Arminianism and Pelagian heresy in his theology. The *Christian Spectator* opposed slavery (though it favored colonization and dealt sympathetically with slaveholders) and helped promote Congregational and Presbyterian mission works in the expanding West.[13]

Given mainstream evangelicalism's enthusiasm then and now for bringing the Bible to bear on every aspect of public and private life, the autopsy the *Christian Spectator* performed on these pious and patriotic eulogies is all the more striking. Whatever the anonymous author's own convictions about Christian America's calling and destiny, he winced over category errors, exposed example after example of the confusion, and asked clergy and politicians to take more care with how they talked about the nation and its heroes. To be sure, eulogies are no time for balanced judgments of the dearly departed, but the reviewer found this "flood of glory" unnecessary and distracting. The overheated orators had caught the "contagion of hyperbolic woe."[14]

The critic reserved his harshest criticism for how several of the eulogists mishandled the Bible and abused theology. Virginia Governor John Tyler had hailed Jefferson "as the benefactor of the redeemed" and the Revolution as a "holy cause." Massachusetts legislator Caleb Cushing had assured the nation that the twin "apostles of liberty have fulfilled their mission, and leaving the scene of their generous toils below, are gone above to receive their reward." The anonymous reviewer objected first to the fact that the orators applied sacred language where it did not belong. They thereby "secularized" (his word) "sacred things." The reviewer highlighted the prevalence of such words as "redeemed," "holy cause," "Apostles of liberty," "mission," "Holy Patriarchs," and "apotheosis." The term *holy*, to take one instance from this list, "belongs exclusively to the department of theology," he warned. By moving words from one category or "department" to another, the orators did something irresponsible and unnecessary. They could have simply left the words *redeemed* and *holy* where they were and chosen language better suited to the kind of men Adams and Jefferson were and the kind of service they had rendered to the United States. They could have maintained the "sacred distinction" but instead chose to launch "invasions of sacred ground."

As with Lord Saye two centuries earlier, this reviewer in 1826 noticed, objected to, and resisted the abuse. And he did so not as a theological skeptic, or radical secularist, or proto-deconstructionist, but as a defender of the Bible, Christian doctrine, and the distinction between the sacred and secular and also between God's special providence, general providence, and the ordinary realm of human reason. In the nineteenth century as in the seventeenth, alert Christians had the tools they needed to urge self-restraint on their fellow citizens. There was nothing inevitable, therefore, about America coming to believe itself to be a nation superior to all others, endowed with a mission, and free from the constraints of history.[15] It was a choice. Or more accurately a series of choices that together became a fixed habit for countless Americans—whether politicians, preachers, journalist, or academics—a habit difficult for even the most cautious to avoid. Lord Saye and the writer for the *Christian Spectator* show that there was another path, not just available hypothetically, but a path actually followed by two men troubled by a way of thinking about God and America that was full of mischief for both church and state. Their religious convictions, far from predisposing them to infuse America with redemptive significance, exaggerate what was at stake in its success or failure, or "weaponize" the Bible for earthly warfare, actually imposed constraints on their imaginations. Christianity offered clarity and modesty, not confusion and vanity.

These dissenting voices are unknown to most students of American history and silenced in standard accounts of American identity and civil religion. The problem of their absence is compounded by another bit of amnesia: the loss of a kind of exceptionalism that had little or nothing to do with either "exemplary" or "missionary" impulses in American foreign policy. Exemplary and missionary exceptionalism can both be expressions of an imperial temperament, the one moral and the other militant. They both thirst for a kind of empire. They both want to remake the world. But another variety of exceptionalism, though it did not use that name, emphasized America's differences from Europe as reasons to practice what Walter McDougall calls "self-containment."[16]

William Graham Sumner, paired against Woodrow Wilson whose policies he did not live to see enacted during the First World War, staked out an impressive case for self-containment. In 1896, Sumner published "The Fallacy of Territorial Extension." This prescient piece, written two years before the US's war with Spain, has been overshadowed by the Yale sociologist's much longer and more famous lecture on "The Conquest of the United States by Spain." Sumner was part of a large and important group of American social scientists who became preoccupied in the 1890s with the problem of American exceptionalism, though they did not use that word. Dorothy Ross may overstate the dominance of the "exceptionalism" question in academia at the turn of the century, but her evidence for its significance in the debates of the time is overwhelming.[17]

Whatever his faults as a moral philosopher, Sumner articulated and defended a largely lost strain of American exceptionalism, one rooted in institutions rather than abstractions and grounded in experience. He also had the bad manners to point out that the *least* exceptional thing about America in the 1890s was its claim to have a divine mission. Every great power said the same thing of itself and resented any other great power with the temerity to question its appointed or anointed role in history.

Here is part of one paragraph from Sumner in 1896.

> This confederated state of ours was never planned for indefinite expansion or for an imperial policy. We boast of it a great deal, but we must know that its advantages are won at the cost of limitations, as is the case with most things in this world. The fathers of the Republic planned a confederation of free and peaceful industrial commonwealths, shielded by their geographical position from the jealousies, rivalries, and traditional policies of the Old World and bringing all the resources of civilization to bear for the domestic happiness of the population only.... It is the limitation [imposed by] this scheme of the state that the state created under it must forego a great number of the grand functions of European

states; especially that it contains no methods and apparatus of conquest, extension, domination, and imperialism.[18]

Most arresting in this excerpt is Sumner's defense of an American exceptionalism that imposed limitations on the nation's conduct in the world. Differences brought constraints; constraints maintained cherished differences. The nation's contrast with Europe, far from making it superhuman, a holy crusader, and transhistorical, checked its ambitions. Difference as constraint seems to be a concept alien to the reasoning of modern politicians of whatever party who argue that difference means America must take action, typically of a particularly aggressive and costly kind. Sumner in contrast argued that differences—historical, rooted, institutional, chosen differences—often mean that America must *not* act, or at least not act a certain way, not act contrary to the United States' first principles and not act like European empires in Africa and Asia in the 1890s. In Sumner's words, the advantages of liberty come at the cost of limitations, limitations a federated republic ought to value far above the vanity of empire.

Woodrow Wilson, in contrast, fully embraced what we might call "difference as empowerment," that is, exceptionalism as an outward-directed mission statement, divine marching orders for the benevolent empire. Once we start looking for difference as constraint (or difference defined in such a way as to remove constraint), evidence for Wilson's habit of mind appears in any number of his wartime speeches. In his War Message of April 2, 1917, he insisted that America was what amounted to an "un-nation." In his mind, the United States did not then and never had fought for the motives that have driven other nations. Here and elsewhere, Wilson said America fought as the dispassionate champion of other peoples. It was not motivated by any of the classic explanations for international rivalry going all the way back to Thucydides. A detailed list of negations followed immediately after his famous vow to "make the world safe for democracy."

> We have no selfish ends to serve. We desire no conquest, no dominion. We seek no indemnities for ourselves, no material compensation for the sacrifices we shall freely make. We are but one of the champions of the rights of mankind. We shall be satisfied when those rights have been made as secure as the faith and the freedom of nations can make them. Just because we fight without rancour and without selfish object, seeking nothing for ourselves but what we shall wish to share with all free peoples, we shall, I feel confident, conduct our operations

as belligerents without passion and ourselves observe with proud punctilio the principles of right and of fair play we profess to be fighting for.[19]

Wilson's "America the exceptional" (close in many ways to the consciousness Claes Ryn has called "America the Virtuous"[20]) supposedly does not act in fear, does not fight for material advantage, does not fight in anger, or in passion. It is the un-nation. It rises above the sordid world of fear, rivalry, and necessity and floats into a rarified world that escapes history. In other speeches Wilson insisted that his vision was fully consistent with America's founding principles. This was the moment of fulfillment. What America intended in 1918, he said in a speech at Mount Vernon in front of Washington's tomb, it had intended back in 1787.[21] In his July 1919 speech presenting the Treaty of Versailles to the Senate, Wilson said that the nation's crusader role in the world and its joining in common cause with the rest of humanity was what "we dreamed at our birth."[22] Some among the founding generation, such as Tom Paine and Joel Barlow, did indeed dream of a global transformation, but such ambitions had never been allowed to define US foreign policy. Wilson became the arch heretic from an older civil religion of constraint, as Walter McDougall persuasively shows.

Sumner spoke for an "old school" exceptionalism while Wilson was "new school" through and through. If old school exceptionalism has any appeal, it has a future only under certain conditions. The word *exceptionalism* is not remotely what is at stake here. It has become a substitute for sound thinking. America got along fine without the word for over a hundred years. It is now worn out, and has been made into a test of patriotism. What matters more than the word is the reconstitution, under whatever label, of a sober, earthbound way for America to think and talk about itself. Such a reconstitution requires Americans to retrace their steps, figure out where they took a wrong turn, and reintroduce themselves to alternatives that were once very much a part of the national conversation. Knowledge of America's past in all its rich complexity would restore a lost vocabulary and a lost way of reasoning.

In America's past lies not just a series of creedal affirmations to which all right-thinking people must subscribe, but a quarrel going all the way back to the earliest colonies of British North America. What many historians have depicted as the normative America was in fact just one version of a highly contested America, merely the one of several alternative Americas that won the argument through a complicated set of contingent historical circumstances and not necessarily by being right or wise or prudent. Robert Kagan, for instance, says a lot of true things about some Americans' desire to have the United States be history's "dangerous nation." But do these true things about America add up to the truth about America? He clearly wants America's normative identity to be the "dangerous nation," and he reaches all the way back to John Winthrop to try to prove it. Kagan and his readers might even think of his way of reading history as a "realist" position. But it is really just a variation on Woodrow Wilson's claim that this crusading is what "we dreamed at our birth." In Kagan's hands, American history becomes a flattering story of fulfillment.

If Winthrop and his purpose-driven colony were made normative only retrospectively and quite deliberately for ends that really had nothing to do with the Puritan colonists, then Americans have the liberty to stop talking about the "city on a hill" and to stop dragging the misappropriated words into every domestic and foreign policy debate from environmentalism to immigration. Lord Saye's rebuke of the governor makes it possible for us to imagine an alternative New England, still as deeply religiously founded, that did not think of itself as God's New Israel, that did not apply prophecy and Scripture proofs so directly to itself, and that did not transpose so many events out of the realm of human reason and prudential judgment and into the realm of God's special providence. This alternative could have happened. There was nothing inevitable about America, or even New England or even Boston, thinking about itself in such terms. None of this had to become, by the operation of some historical necessity, part of America's DNA.

Likewise, the reaction to the eulogies for Jefferson and Adams in 1826 shows something equally important: Some Americans had the ability to fight to maintain the distinction between the secular and the sacred, knew the difference between patriotism and religion, worried about the abuse of language and how we name and misname things in the world, and issued warnings against the presumption that man can read God's providence in the life of a nation as a special mark of his divine favor. Patriotism ought indeed to be cultivated, the anonymous editor wrote, "But let every memorial and every celebration, be characterized by republican simplicity and Christian moderation. Let things be called by their right names; and let not principles and actions be confounded, which are widely different, both in their nature and tendencies." In many ways, the story of American exceptionalism, indeed the story of American civil religion, is the story of the loss of simplicity and moderation, a growing inability to call things by their right names, and a deepening confusion of "principles and actions" that differ widely in their "nature and tendencies."

In his recent book on American civil religion and the derailment of US foreign policy, Walter McDougall uses the phrase "self-containment" early on to describe a lost virtue of American foreign policy. We think of "containment" as an objective of US foreign policy in the Cold War as articulated by the diplomat and historian George Kennan, though he came to hate the word. *Containment* in this sense labeled a broad range of often conflicting policies and ideologies deployed against Soviet and Chinese communism. McDougall means to be provocative by turning the much-abused word back on America itself as a call to recover a lost character trait. Americans had once cultivated the ethic of self-restraint for the survival of their union and to stay out of trouble in a dangerous world. Rather than striving to be the "dangerous nation" Robert Kagan sees as the nation's most authentic self, American statesmen at one time abided by an older cultural and political orthodoxy that limited their conduct in the world for the sake of narrowly defined interests. McDougall's principles—if I am not stretching them beyond what he envisions—are reinforced by the work of ethical theorists such as Irving Babbitt and Claes Ryn, both of whom emphasize self-control as the indispensable prerequisite to constitutionalism and limited government and as the best safeguard against mass democracy and imperialism.

What does all this have to do with Puritan colonists and overblown eulogies? Simply that the lost ethic of "self-containment" needs to be reinstituted not just by statesmen for the sake of America's wellbeing in the world but for the sake of Christianity's (and other religions') wellbeing in the world. One way for Christians to maintain their identity and the integrity of the institutional church is to practice "self-containment," even if the state does not return the favor. It is no stretch to argue that Lord Saye pleaded with John Winthrop to impose self-containment on his thoughts, words, and deeds. Winthrop's way of exegeting Scripture and applying holy writ to his own ambitions in the world led him to misconstrue what God required of his saints and the degree to which the Church was called to remake man and society. Likewise, when the anonymous editorial writer in 1827 remonstrated with politicians to observe the boundary between the work of redemption and the work of nation-building, he enjoined the same kind of self-containment. And if churches were powerless to control what politicians said, which they likely were, then ministers of the gospel could contain their own thoughts and words and refuse to confuse the City of Man with the City of God.

Whether at the time of the settlement of British North America, the Revolution, the War of 1812, the rise of romantic nationalism, the Civil War or right down to the present day, the ethic of self-containment has always been available to Americans concerned about their nation and their faith. Historians and political theorists would find their time well spent if they worked back through American history to piece together the quarrels over the American identity, to understand that everything could have been different, and, if they happen to have an eye toward public service, to recover the lost language and logic of resistance to fight the co-optation of the things of God for the things of Caesar. Now as always in America's past, the ethic of self-containment requires sound education, sound political theory, sound theology and ecclesiology, and a stubborn determination to "let things be called by their right names." In 1850, nothing in Christian theology or American political thought required Daniel Webster to take hold of the Pilgrims and send them hurtling across a continent and out across the Pacific. He secularized them, nationalized them, abstracted them, and turned them into a justification for the imperial imagination at the heart of American exceptionalism.

NOTES

1. *Dinner of the New England Society: With the Speeches of Messrs. Grinnell, Bellows . . .* (New York: 1851).

2. Robert F. Dalzell Jr., *Daniel Webster and the Trial of American Nationalism, 1843–1852* (Boston, MA: Houghton Mifflin, 1972).

3. *The Baltimore Sun*, December 11, 1850, p. 1. The Society petitioned the governor to call for a day of thanksgiving. Two years later, on December 22, 1852, the New England Society of San Francisco gathered to hear an address by the Rev. T. Dwight Hunt, pastor of the New England Church. *Address Delivered before the New England Society of San Francisco* (San Francisco, CA: Cooke, Kenny, & Co., 1853).

4. Ibid., 16–18, 21.

5. The phrase "dangerous nation" comes from Robert Kagan, *Dangerous Nation: America's Place in the World from Its Earliest Days to the Dawn of the Twentieth Century* (New York: Knopf Doubleday, 2009).

6. Reprinted in Robert C. Winthrop, *Life and Letters of John Winthrop*, vol. 2 (Boston: Ticknor & Fields, 1867), 422–27. Spelling and punctuation modernized.

7. "Letter of Lord Say and Sele to John Winthrop," in Robert C. Winthrop, *John Winthrop: From His Embarkation for New England in 1630, With the Charter and Company of the Massachusetts Bay, to His Death in 1649* (Boston: Ticknor & Fields, 1867), 422–27. Quotation at 423. (Spelling modernized.)

8. Harlow W. Sheidley, *Sectional Nationalism: Massachusetts Conservative Leaders and the Transformation of America, 1815–1836* (Boston, MA: Northeastern University Press, 1998).

9. See George Wilson Pierson, *Tocqueville in America* (Baltimore, MD: Johns Hopkins University Press, 1996), 399–401. The influence of Jared Sparks in particular on the quotation that follows seems obvious. Sparks was a prominent Unitarian minister, editor of the papers of George Washington, and president of Harvard from 1849 to 1853, and was among those New England intellectuals eager to advance his section as the true source of American civilization.

10. Alexis de Tocqueville, *Democracy in America and Two Essays on America*, translated by Gerald E. Bevan with an Introduction and Notes by Isaac Kramnick (New York: Penguin, 2003), 42.

11. T. Dwight Hunt, *Address Delivered before the New England Society on San Francisco* (San Francisco, CA: Cooke, Kenny & Co., 1853), 6, 13, 20. Hunt (1821–1895) pastored the First Congregational (known also as the New England Church) in the city.

12. *A Selection of Eulogies, Pronounced in the Several States, In Honor of Those Illustrious Patriots and Statesmen, John Adams and Thomas Jefferson* (Hartford, CT: D. F. Robinson and Norton & Russell, 1826).

13. Frank Luther Mott, *A History of American Magazines, 1741–1850* (Cambridge, MA: Harvard University Press, 1938), 310.

14. "Eulogies on Adams and Jefferson," *Christian Spectator*, new series 1, no. 4 (April 1827): 210–20 and *Christian Spectator*, new series 1, no. 5 (May 1827): 259–68. Most quotations here come from pp. 217–19.

15. Hilde Eliassen Restad, *American Exceptionalism: An Idea that Made a Nation and Remade the World* (New York: Routledge, 2015).

16. Walter A. McDougall, *The Tragedy of U.S. Foreign Policy: How America's Civil Religion Betrayed the National Interest* (New Haven: Yale University Press, 2016).

17. Dorothy Ross, *The Origins of American Social Science* (Cambridge, UK: Cambridge University Press, 1991).

18. William Graham Sumner, "The Fallacy of Territorial Extension," in Robert C. Bannister, ed., *On Liberty, Society, and Politics: The Essential Essays of William Graham Sumner* (Indianapolis, IN: Liberty Fund, 1992), 269.

19. Woodrow Wilson, "An Address to a Joint Session of Congress (April 2, 1917)," *The Papers of Woodrow Wilson*, edited by Arthur Link, et al. (Princeton: Princeton University Press, 1966–1994), 41: 525.

20. Claes G. Ryn, *America the Virtuous: The Crisis of Democracy and the Quest for Empire* (New Brunswick, NJ: Transaction, 2003).

21. Woodrow Wilson, "An Address at Mount Vernon (July 4, 1918)," *Papers of Woodrow Wilson*, 48: 517.

22. Woodrow Wilson, "An Address to the Senate (July 19, 1919)," *Papers of Woodrow Wilson*, 61: 436.

BIBLIOGRAPHY

A Selection of Eulogies, Pronounced in the Several States, In Honor of Those Illustrious Patriots and Statesmen, John Adams and Thomas Jefferson. Hartford, CT: D. F. Robinson and Norton & Russell, 1826.

Bannister, Robert C., ed. *On Liberty, Society, and Politics: The Essential Essays of William Graham Sumner*. Indianapolis, IN: Liberty Fund, 1992.

Dalzell, Jr., Robert F. *Daniel Webster and the Trial of American Nationalism, 1843–1852*. Boston: Houghton Mifflin, 1972.

"Eulogies on Adams and Jefferson." *Christian Spectator*, New Series 1.4 (April 1827): 210–20.

"Eulogies on Adams and Jefferson." *Christian Spectator*, New Series 1.5 (May 1827): 259–68.

Hunt, T. Dwight. *Address Delivered before the New England Society on San Francisco*. San Francisco, CA: Cooke, Kenny & Co., 1853.

Kagan, Robert. *Dangerous Nation: America's Place in the World from Its Earliest Days to the Dawn of the Twentieth Century*. New York: Knopf Doubleday, 2009.

McDougall, Walter A. *The Tragedy of U.S. Foreign Policy: How America's Civil Religion Betrayed the National Interest*. New Haven, CT: Yale University Press, 2016.

Mott, Frank Luther. *A History of American Magazines, 1741–1850*. Cambridge, MA: Harvard University Press, 1938.

Pierson, George Wilson. *Tocqueville in America*. Baltimore, MD: Johns Hopkins University Press, 1996.

Restad, Hilde Eliassen. *American Exceptionalism: An Idea that Made a Nation and Remade the World*. New York: Routledge, 2015.

Ross, Dorothy. *The Origins of American Social Science*. Cambridge, UK: Cambridge University Press, 1991.

Ryn, Claes G. *America the Virtuous: The Crisis of Democracy and the Quest for Empire* (New Brunswick, NJ: Transaction, 2003.

Sheidley, Harlow. *Sectional Nationalism: Massachusetts Conservative Leaders and the Transformation of America*. Boston: Northeastern University Press, 1998.

de Tocqueville, Alexis. *Democracy in America and Two Essays on America.* Translated by Gerald E. Bevan. New York: Penguin, 2003.

Wilson, Woodrow. *The Papers of Woodrow Wilson.* Vols. 4, 48, and 61. Edited by Arthur Link. Princeton, NJ: Princeton University Press, 1966–1994.

Winthrop, Robert C. *John Winthrop: From His Embarkation for New England in 1630, With the Charter and Company of the Massachusetts Bay, to His Death in 1649.* Boston, MA: Ticknor & Fields, 1867.

———. *Life and Letters of John Winthrop.* Vol. 2. Boston, MA: Ticknor & Fields, 1867.

CHAPTER TWELVE

A Little Place and a Big Idea

The Temptation to Imperialism and the Loss of Republicanism

Justin B. Litke

In Wendell Berry's finest novel, *Jayber Crow*, the title character thoughtfully reflects on the Second World War and what it did to his hometown, Port William.

> Anyhow, what I couldn't bring together or reconcile in my mind was the thought of Port William and the thought of the war. Port William, I thought, had not caused the war. Port William makes quarrels, and now and again a fight; it does not make war. It takes power, leadership, great talent, perhaps genius, and much money to make war. In war, as maybe even in politics, Port William has to suffer what it didn't make. I have pondered for years and I still can't connect Port William and war except by death and suffering. No more can I think of Port William and the United States in the same thought. A nation is an idea, and Port William is not. Maybe there is no live connection between a little place and a big idea. I think there is not.[1]

War is not possible without what Crow calls the "big idea." Because of its scale, to fight a war requires arguing that vast resources and numerous lives may justly be spent in pursuit of victory. This is what Crow cannot connect to Port William, where the real value of the lives of families is painfully obvious and the value of war is not. Crow's thinking seems to suggest a thoroughgoing pacifism, a position Berry himself has publically adopted in reference to the

Vietnam War and numerous conflicts since. Americans need not necessarily adopt the same view. Yet, in a time when the bigness of our politics is taken for granted, it may benefit all citizens to consider whether some political problems seem to be raised by the very scale on which our politics is practiced.

It is an old, but neglected theme in American political writing to note the relationship between grand scale, a concentration of political authority, and the temptation to abuse power. Anti-Federalists writers, seldom known for their eloquence, nevertheless perceived that the new Constitution might well lead to unintended consequences and an erosion of republicanism. In this, Anti-Federalists might be seen as rehearsing some of the well-worn arguments of the American Revolution, when the colonists' own understanding of English constitutionalism led them to argue that in order to tax and rule legitimately, a legislature had to be both responsible and responsive—and that this required close proximity to its constituents. Without this, there is no real representation or legitimate legislation. The same theme crops up again in the face of the annexation of Hawaii, Cuba, and the Philippines around the turn of the twentieth century. The US Senate was the main arena for that fight; opponents argued that the cost of these acts would exceed mere manpower and firepower—it would swallow the very principles of the government they served.

Only if the scale of politics is sufficiently local, the tradition holds, can a people rule itself deliberately. Only if power is dispersed among stakeholders of a political whole can that rule be informed by intimate knowledge of local circumstances. Only if institutions operate sufficiently close to their constituents can they be held to account. But if the nature of the institutions changes, so, too, may the means to attaining their end: the pursuit of empire entails a loss of republicanism. Jayber Crow does not know all of this. But as he reflects on the effect of the World War II on Port William, he echoes a major theme in the American political tradition from its earliest days.

By the late colonial period, the self-image of the English colonies' role in the world and vis-à-vis the Crown had matured into a constitutional argument. For much of their history, the colonies were given significant leeway in domestic policy and were satisfied to leave foreign and trade policy to London. With the close of the Seven Years' War in 1763, however, England began an effort to discharge its considerable war debt. The Stamp Act was intended to aid this effort, in part.[2] The colonists looked at the tax, however, as a usurpation of the traditional balance of political authority. Early on, Samuel Adams noted that

> By the Royal Charter granted to our Ancestors, the Power of making Laws for our internal Government, & of levying Taxes, is vested in the General Assembly: And by the same Charter the Inhabitants of this Province are entitled to all the Rights & Privileges of natural free born Subjects of Great Britain: The most essential Rights of the British Subjects are those of being represented in the same Body which exercises the Power of levying Taxes upon them, & of having their Property tryed by Jurys: These are the very Pillars of the British Constitution founded in the common Rights of Mankind.[3]

A colonies-wide meeting on the issue was called. The result of that meeting, "The Declarations of the Stamp Act Congress," reiterates Adams's argument and goes beyond it. After indicating both that the American colonists owe "allegiance" to the Crown and "all due subordination to that august body the Parliament of Great Britain," the delegates move to the constitutional crux of the matter in three successive resolutions.

> That it is inseparably essential to the freedom of a people, and the undoubted right of Englishmen, that no taxes be imposed on them, but with their own consent, given personally, or by their representatives.
>
> That the people of these colonies are not, and from their local circumstances cannot be, represented in the House of Commons in Great-Britain.
>
> That the only representatives of the people of these colonies, are persons chosen therein by themselves, and that no taxes ever have been, or can be constitutionally imposed on them, but by their respective legislatures.[4]

This meeting and others like it galvanized opposition to the Stamp Act and fomented a general boycott of British goods, leading to its repeal the next year. Simultaneous with that repeal, Parliament passed the Declaratory Act, indicating for the record that the king and Parliament

> had, hath, and of right ought to have, full power and authority to make laws and statutes of sufficient force and validity to bind the colonies and people of *America*, subjects of the crown of *Great Britain*, in all cases whatever.[5]

Clearly Britain would not back down from a fight with its own colonies. Over the next few years, other measures were variously passed and repealed by Parliament, culminating in the famed Boston Tea Party and Britain's response, the "Coercive Acts." The same laws were called the "Intolerable Acts" in the colonies and led the First Continental Congress to call for a colonies-wide embargo of Great Britain in 1774.⁶ Parliament did not budge and tensions ran high, erupting in violence at Lexington and Concord in April of 1775. Faced with overt British violence, the colonies assembled in Philadelphia once again to consider the question of collective American action. Without a true continental identity, nevertheless delegates came together to deliberate on and coordinate a common response.

In July 1775, the Second Continental Congress produced a document aptly named the "Declaration of the Causes and Necessity of Taking Up Arms." More than the 1774 embargo, this 1775 declaration argued that the colonies' immediate armed engagement with England was justified. Fighting commenced and the next July saw the passage of the more famous 1776 Declaration of Independence. But these two declarations tell two different stories. The 1776 Declaration severed ties with England. The 1775 declaration disclaimed even the desire to separate. A change in American self-image was clearly taking place: the First Continental Congress used, probably for the first time, the phrase "American rights" in 1774, suggesting something of a collective identity. Near the end of the 1775 document, however, the Second Continental Congress wrote: "Lest this declaration should disquiet the minds of our friends and fellow-subjects in any part of the empire, we assure them that we mean not to dissolve that union which has so long and so happily subsisted between us, and which we *sincerely wish to see restored*."⁷ It may seem remarkable to Americans today that their forebears *were decidedly not* itching to throw off the yoke of British rule. Yet, in a moment of deliberate action, the colonies expressed a clear desire to rejoin the empire after the Crown and Parliament relented from their unconstitutional actions. They were satisfied to stay—so long as their local self-rule was restored. The Second Continental Congress was convinced in 1775 of the practicability, desirability, and propriety of local, colonial control of most policy. When the Americans argued against Parliamentary control, they did not simultaneously argue for a new national government. This did not change with the 1776 Declaration of Independence. That more famous document did not inaugurate a wholly new state of affairs—that would come with the Articles of Confederation— but rather severed a connection that by this time had become perfunctory and unnecessary for the colonies' functioning.⁸ The Declaration of Independence cut ties with England's crown; but it did not empower the Second Continental Congress to act as a new, de jure national legislature and government— though that is how it served, de facto, for several more years. When there finally was a new government under the Articles of Confederation, the new states were said to be sovereign in all but a few cases and were practically sovereign in all.[9]

The Constitution changed this relationship formally, but did not alter the way the Americans saw themselves, namely, primarily as citizens of their respective states. This relationship—between the states and the new national government—stood at the center of the debates over the proposed Constitution. And the positions taken by the Anti-Federalist critics of ratification laid bare the deep connection between the concentration of power and the imperial impulse that is often at work in politics.

One of the most celebrated Anti-Federalists, Brutus, was convinced that the sort of government erected by the proposed Constitution would necessitate a great concentration of power at the center. "In a republic," he says, "the manners, sentiments, and interests of the people should be similar. If this be not the case, there will be a constant clashing of opinions; and the representatives of one part will be continually striving against those of the other," which will "retard the operations of government, and prevent such conclusions as will promote the public good."[10] Likewise, Agrippa noted,

> We find that the very great empires have always been despotic ... It is impossible for one code of laws to suit Georgia and Massachusetts ... new system is, therefore, a consolidation of all the States into one larger mass, however diverse the parts may be of which it is composed. The idea of an uncompounded republic, on an average, one thousand miles in length, and eight hundred in breadth, and containing six million white inhabitants all reduced to the same standard of morals or habits, and of laws, is in itself an absurdity and contrary to the whole experience of mankind. The attempt made by Great Britain to introduce such a system struck us with horror, and when it was proposed by some theorist that we should be represented in Parliament, we uniformly declared that one legislature could not represent so many different interests for the purposes of legislation and taxation. This was the leading principle of the revolution.[11]

Brutus writes similarly that, because of the cultural and economic diversity under the new national umbrella, "the magistrates in every government must be supported in the execution of the laws, either by an armed force ... or by the people turning out to aid the magistrate upon his command." The latter is unlikely and would result in the necessity (just as with Britain in the late colonial period) of keeping up a standing army in the midst of the citizenry, to "execute the commands of the prince or the magistrate ... when occasion requires." On the other hand, "A free republic will never keep a standing army to execute its laws. It must depend upon the support of its citizens." It requires the "confidence" of the people, which arises from the people knowing their magistrates personally, from "their being responsible" to the people for their conduct, and from the power that the people have of "displacing them when they misbehave." Without this power, the government will not have the requisite "confidence of the people" and must rule by "establishing an armed force to execute the laws at the point of the bayonet—a government of all others the most to be dreaded." Worse yet, the powers that would be required to govern adequately this vast territory would necessarily be so great as to afford a great temptation to "designing men."[12] This, the Anti-Federalists suggest, is the great danger under any government that concentrates enough power to govern a large territory: the power becomes sufficiently great for abuse. In proportion to its aggrandizement, furthermore, a temptation to this abuse grows.

This is what Jayber Crow had in mind about war. Waging war requires vast power and resources. To justify the use of such power and resources, the stakes of the conflict are often said to be existential or to center on the nature of the country's existence as it is. We have heard often that military expansion is performed in the service of the "American way of life." But for Crow, this explanation rings particularly hollow. The concrete community of which Crow is a member never started a war and could not possibly do so. Its very scale prevents this.

Over these objections, the Constitution was ratified. And some of its proponents would, in the coming years, praise the new arrangement for having so skillfully subsumed under a single umbrella so many disparate communities.[13] Some have seen a justification for imperialism scattered in the words of various American founders. But, as with previous moments in American history, perceptions of this kind have more to do with current politics than with the speakers' thinking. To take a representative example, Niall Ferguson sees the mere use of the word *empire* as indicating that George Washington, Alexander Hamilton, Thomas Jefferson, and James Madison had each endorsed the idea of an expansionist America from its beginning.[14] Of course, the words they spoke were not our words, since the meaning of terms like *empire* has changed over time.[15] Thus, an understanding of the policies and behavior of those speaking such words is necessary to form an adequate account of what is meant. When Jefferson and others wrote of an "empire of liberty," they did not mean the US would be an empire seeking territorial expansion and wealth. Walter McDougall asks and answers the relevant question: did the Founding Fathers embrace in foreign policy "none but idealistic ends sought by scrupulous means? Jefferson might have wished it were so, but even he bowed to reality in defense of the national interest. Did it mean that the United States would take up the cause of freedom everywhere and choose its friends on the basis of republican principles? Absolutely not . . . Foreign policy existed to defend, not define, what America was."[16] A foreign policy focused on trade and friendship, characterized by a truly defensive posture, was still the norm. Yet this is no longer the case. Changes in the way Americans think of themselves led to changes in the way its government acts.

More than any other event in American history, the Civil War recast in the American imagination the roles played by the local, state, and national governments. Successful prosecution of the war meant effecting a redefinition—or perhaps a final settlement of the question—of the terms and nature of American national unity. Whatever ambiguities characterized American politics and constitutionalism up to this point, the protracted bloody conflict resolved them in favor of a new and fundamental national union. The achievement was made possible by the violence of war. But the gains were solidified in its aftermath, when justifications for the war took on the character of the recently founded Republican Party. Though by no means alone in this influence, Abraham Lincoln's Gettysburg Address repainted the general picture of the American political tradition.[17] Though hard to imagine now, the speech was actually criticized at the time for attributing to the fallen soldiers motives they could not have had.[18] Nevertheless, today the hybrid "Gettysburg-Declaration" is a touchstone for one's own identity as an American.[19]

Few today could read the words of the Declaration about the "self-evident" rights of "Life, Liberty, and the Pursuit of Happiness" without simultaneously holding that America *just is* the country that, in all of world history, has sought to be "dedicated to the proposition that all men are created equal." Placing the war at the center of America's future prospects, subsequent generations have nodded along and adopted Lincoln's reading of America as, first and foremost, an idea or proposition. Glen Thurow persuasively argues that this rhetorical move was necessary in order for Lincoln to achieve his practical political end of perpetuating the Union.[20] I want to argue that, however necessary, this move has far-reaching implications. Before Lincoln's Gettysburg Address, it was common to think of the American states as somewhat distinct peoples with appropriately distinct republican institutions. Agrippa and other Anti-Federalists opposed the ratification of the Constitution on the grounds that the same laws could not possibly govern peoples as different as those in Georgia and Massachusetts. Even when Publius defends the notion of a robust union, he seems to suggest that the arrangement is feasible primarily because the federal government's power would be limited to very few objects.[21]

In the wake of the Civil War, that was no longer the case. To resolve the extreme of injustice, a power commensurate with that injustice was invoked. One side won the war; the other lost. And the victors wrote the history in principally Republican and Lincolnian terms, permanently altering Americans' self-image. In writing it, they came to emphasize the Declaration of Independence and its soaring eloquence. They made it possible to think of America as an idea. They encouraged the thought that the American idea is the thing that is truly American. Thus, Americans' self-conception was transformed from concrete to abstract. In Crow's terms, America was now a big idea.

As a big idea, America had now become exportable—something in the service of which power, leadership, talent, genius, and money would be justifiably employed. And as the twentieth century neared, Presidents McKinley and Theodore Roosevelt and their allies in the Senate spoke glowingly about the annexation and occupation of the Philippines. The treaty that ended the Spanish-American War ceded the islands to the United States, raising as a practical matter the question of their place in the American national order. In one side of the debate, the abstract account of American identity can be observed. On the floor of the US Senate, Albert Beveridge of Indiana argued, "Self-government is a method of liberty—the highest, simplest, best—and it is acquired only after centuries of study and struggle and experiment and instruction in all the elements of the progress of man. Self-government is no cheap boon, to be bestowed on the merely audacious."[23] Beveridge wished to argue that the only reasonable disposition of the Philippine Islands in the wake of the war was one of direct imperial rule by America. Rather than setting an example of republicanism and justice for the world, America, Beveridge claimed, must welcome the role that "our governing race" has long been called to play.[24] Yet, if the Declaration of Independence is constitutive of American identity, some of Beveridge's contemporaries wondered, would not its argument for the right to self-determination be near the top?[25] "No," Beveridge would say in answer, because that document and all those that lie at the heart of American politics have a common author. Even the dry text of the Constitution is inexplicable except in regard to race: "You can not interpret a constitution without understanding the race that wrote it."[26] With this, any deep commitment to republicanism as grounded in human nature is abandoned. The common humanity shared by Americans and far-flung others did not obligate America to respect the dignity of those nations. To the contrary,

Beveridge and his allies argued for the invasion of the Philippines, because in trying to govern the islands Americans will have gained a kind of laboratory of government. America will draw lessons from political experiments there that might apply to an evolved American self-government at home—all without the risk of incident there.[27]

Beveridge did not have the final word in the Senate. And he did not win the vote. In a stirring speech connecting the issue before them to the ultimate grounding of American politics itself, a senator from Delaware recalled,

> Mr. President, does not this cry for conquest take us back through the centuries until we find ourselves in that time of the Roman Republic, when by the ambition and greed of some of her sons was begun her conquest of the world—the beginning of her end? In that history can we not see ourselves and read our future? New territories were conquered and their people enslaved. Military governors were sent to rule over them. Strange laws were enacted for their government and alien judges sent to administer them. The religion and manners of the conquerors were enforced; in a word, all the miseries which follow in the train of the conqueror and oppressor came to the peoples to whom Rome brought the blessings of her civilization. Rome then thought herself trusted of the gods for the civilizing of mankind throughout the world, but soon was taught her mistake. In her struggle to destroy the liberties of others she lost her own. Man's unalienable rights—life, liberty, and the pursuit of happiness—then, as many times since, asserted itself [sic] and the conquered became the conquerors, the slave the master. And Rome, the mistress of the world, repudiated and despised, passed—a page in history. In imperialism she found her end.[28]

This and other arguments defeated Beveridge's effort in the Senate, but opponents of the annexation were left without the votes needed to halt executive action. The imperialism of the McKinley administration continued, committing America to the same course of action as other would-be world powers. America, like Spain, Germany, and other countries, sought opportunities to exert influence and control with little sensitivity to America's republican inheritance.

As in so many instances, arrival at a diagnosis also suggests a cure. What is missing and lost in the imperial stance of America is a sense of the concrete place in which everyday politics actually occurs. This alternative conception of "politics" calls for a very broad understanding of the term. Politics taken this way is not primarily about constitution-writing or parliamentary maneuvering. To the contrary, when constitutions are well ordered, they proceed—creatively and synthetically—from a preexisting political order that frames the institution-building. A constitution cannot write a politics into existence. It must in important ways ratify and structure existing lines of order, paying careful attention to gifts, dynamics, and realities on the ground. This is not a new idea. At least since Aristotle, political thinkers have noticed that political work is not reducible to mathematics-style formulae and solutions.

Citizens must work—as carpenters do—within the imperfect scenarios they are given and proceed from there to cultivate a good outcome. They must exist as part of a particular place, a "little place," in Crow's parlance. It is only when Crow, a wanderer for much of his youth, finds that he is rooted in and attached to Port William that much of the rest of his life makes sense to him.[25] Port William is a place, a "little place," and a nation is not. It is a place that can be loved because it can be known and possessed by its knower. A nation, because it is so big, cannot be one thing. It is so varied and multifarious that it cannot be known as a single thing. And so it cannot be known or loved. To love it requires reducing it to something static and knowable, something abstract, something that, if it had sufficient force behind it, might justify the projection of great power.

In seeking to understand war, Crow wonders: "And what caused it? It was caused, I thought, by people failing to love one another, failing to love their enemies." He keeps thinking: "Did I think that the great organizations of the world could love their enemies? I did not. I didn't think great organizations could love anything."[29] Crow is not making a long and sophisticated argument about the connection between the degree of power needed to run a nation on the scale of the United States. He does not argue that that political power necessarily tempts its possessors to abuse it. He does not argue that only a legislature responsible and responsive to a citizenry can carry out the legitimate work of government. But in arguing implicitly that the scale of our politics necessitates a lack of knowledge—a lack that in turn prevents good order and legitimate rule—he echoes once more a major theme in our political tradition and his. We might learn it somewhat abstractly by paying careful attention to our documentary heritage and gaining, therefore, a thorough understanding of the principles of our politics. Crow learned it by watching the ever-concrete work of farmers and reflecting on the nature of relationships in his community. Americans would do well to follow both paths back to their own little places.

NOTES

1. Wendell Berry, *Jayber Crow* (Washington, DC: Counterpoint Press, 2000), 142–43.

2. In 1764 English Prime Minister George Grenville was planning to institute a stamp tax to defray the costs of defending the colonies; a delay was undertaken to gauge the colonists' reaction and give them time to offer alternatives. See Edmund S. Morgan, ed., *Prologue to Revolution: Sources and Documents on the Stamp Act Crisis, 1764–1766*, (Chapel Hill, NC: University of North Carolina Press, 1959), 24–25.

3. "To the Representatives of Boston, September 18th, 1765," in *The Writings of Samuel Adams, Volume I: 1764–1769*, coll. and ed. Harry Alonzo Gushing (New York: G. P. Putnam's Sons, 1904), 8–9.

4. "The Declarations of the Stamp Act Congress," in *Prologue*, 62–63.

5. "The Declaratory Act, March 18, 1766" in *Prologue*, 155–56. Italics in original.

6. "Declaration and Resolves of the First Continental Congress, October 14, 1774," in *Documents Illustrative of the Formation of the Union of the American States*, ed. Charles C. Tansill (Washington, DC: Government Printing Office, 1927), 2 and 4.

7. "Declaration of the Causes and Necessity of Taking Up Arms, July 6, 1775" in *Documents Illustrative*, 16. Emphasis Added.

8. Indeed, some colonies refrained even from writing new constitutions, supposing their old colonial charters to suffice once references to the king were removed. See Donald S. Lutz, *The Origins of American Constitutionalism* (Baton Rouge, LA: Louisiana State University Press, 1988), 48–49.

9. Merrill Jensen has argued that, contemporaneous political wrangling and subsequent interpretation notwithstanding, "according to the constitution which united the thirteen states from 1781 to 1789, the several states were de facto and de jure sovereign." See Merrill Jensen, *The Articles of Confederation: An Interpretation of the Social-Constitutional History of the American Revolution, 1774–1781* (Madison: University of Wisconsin Press, 1959), 176. Jensen argues that the ambiguous arrangement in the Articles was a result of conflict between conservatives, who were the predecessors of later "States rights" advocates, and radical "nationalists," who wished to see the new Confederation Congress as a "superintending" power set above the states. The debates have been further obscured by the constitutional disputes that characterized the run up to the Civil War. See Articles of Confederation, 161–76.

10. Brutus, "Letter I," in *The Anti-Federalist: Writings by the Opponents of the Constitution*, edited by Herbert J. Storing, Selected by Murray Dry from *The Complete Anti-Federalist* (Chicago, IL: University of Chicago Press, 1981), 114.

11. Agrippa, "Letter IV," *The Anti-Federalist*, 235–36.

12. Brutus I, 115–16.

13. The "multiplicity and diversity of interests" seems to be the chief mechanism by which Publius's theory operates in Federalist No. 10.

14. Niall Ferguson, *Colossus: The Price of America's Empire* (New York: Penguin Press, 2004), 34. See also Kagan, *Dangerous Nation*, 38. Contemporary scholars are not the only ones to make this weak argument. In the contentious Senate debates on the invasion of the Philippines, Senator Caffery of Louisiana argues that the Supreme Court's use of the word *empire* amounts to that body's sanction of imperial policy. See *Congressional Record* 33 (Monday, February 5, 1900), 1495. Kagan, Ferguson, and Caffery alike put too much weight on the word and too little weight on its meaning in the context of the actions and documents they examine. *Empire* in the founding period is used synonymously with "large republic," "extended republic," and numerous other blanket terms—sometimes even "confederacy," although the authors of the Federalist famously use that term in a particular way. And, it should be noted, the matter of whether a large country could exist with a participatory core had still yet to be settled.

15. Forrest McDonald has pointed out the perils of basing historical arguments on specific words. See his *Novus Ordo Seclorum: The Economic Origins of the Constitution*, (Lawrence, KS: University Press of Kansas, 1985), x–xi.

16. Walter A. McDougall, *Promised Land, Crusader State: The American Encounter with the World Since 1776* (New York: Houghton Mifflin Co., 1997), 36–37.

17. Abraham Lincoln popularized this new picture of American identity as a proposition drawn from the Declaration of Independence, but he did not invent it. In the Republican Party's platform of 1856, the 1776 Declaration is conceived as a constitutional-type document with significant binding force on American principles and behavior. It begins as follows:

Resolved: That the maintenance of the principles promulgated in the Declaration of Independence, and embodied in the Federal Constitution are essential to the preservation of our Republican institutions, and that the Federal Constitution, the rights of the States, and the union of the States, must and shall be preserved.

Resolved: That, with our Republican fathers, we hold it to be a self-evident truth, that all men are endowed with the inalienable right to life, liberty, and the pursuit of happiness, and that the primary object and ulterior design of our Federal Government were to secure these rights to all persons under its exclusive jurisdiction . . ."

See Republican Party Platforms: "Republican Party Platform of 1856," June 18, 1856. Online by Gerhard Peters and John T. Woolley, *The American Presidency Project*. https://www.presidency.ucsb.edu/documents/republican-party-platform-1856. Accessed October 11, 2019.

18. David Herbert Donald, *Lincoln* (New York: Touchstone Books, 1995), 465–66. The *Chicago Times*, admittedly an opposition newspaper, wrote in an editorial on November 23, 1863, that parts of the address were "an insult at least to the memories of a part of the dead, whom he was there professedly to honor,—in its misstatement of the cause for which they died, it was a perversion of history so flagrant that the most extended charity cannot regard it as otherwise than willful."

19. I have made an argument similar to the points above and below in my *Twilight of the Republic: Empire and Exceptionalism in the American Political Tradition* (Lexington: University Press of Kentucky, 2013), chapter 4.

20. See Glen Thurow, "The Gettysburg Address and the Declaration of Independence," in *Abraham Lincoln, The Gettysburg Address and American Constitutionalism*, edited by Leo Paul S. de Alvarez (Irving, Texas: University of Dallas Press, 1976), 68–70.

21. See, for example, Federalist No. 39, where Publius argues that the extent of power wielded by the new government is not very great: "the proposed government cannot be deemed a *national* one; since its jurisdiction extends to certain enumerated objects only, and leaves to the several states, a residuary and inviolable sovereignty overall all other objects." (198, emphasis in original). See also Federalist No. 45, where Publius argues that the states "will retain, under the proposed constitution, a very extensive portion of active sovereignty" (239).

22. Albert Beveridge, "Our Philippine Policy," in *The Meaning of the Times and Other Speeches* (Indianapolis, IN: Bobbs-Merrill Co., 1908), 72.

23. Beveridge, 79.

24. Senator George Hoar of Massachusetts thought along just these lines. On April 17, 1900, Hoar says the following:

The confusion of the argument of our friends on the other side comes from confounding the statement in the Declaration of the rights of individuals with the statement of the rights of nations, or peoples, in dealing with one another. The whole Declaration is a statement of political rights and political relations and political duties. First. Every man is equal in political rights, including the right to life, liberty, and the pursuit of happiness, to every other. Second. No people can come under the government of any other people, or of any ruler, without its consent. The law of nature and of nature's God entitle every people to its separate and equal station among the powers of the earth. Our fathers were not dealing in this clause with the doctrine of the social compact; they were not considering the rights of minorities; they used the word "people" as equivalent to "nation," or "state," as an organized political being, and not as a mere aggregate of persons not collected or associated. They were not thinking of Robinson Crusoe in his desolate island, or of scattered settlers, still less of predatory bands roaming over vast regions they could neither own nor occupy. They were affirming the right of each of the thirteen colonies separately or of them all together to throw off the yoke of George III and to separate itself or themselves from Great Britain. Now, you must either admit that what they said was true, or you must affirm the contrary.

See *Congressional Record*, Vol. 33, 4384–85.

25. Beveridge, 84.
26. Beveridge, 77–78.
27. *Congressional Record*, Vol. 33, 1971 (January 20, 1900).
28. *Jayber Crow*. 144.
29. *Jayber Crow*, 142–43.

BIBLIOGRAPHY

Adams, Samuel. *The Writings of Samuel Adams, Vol. 1: 1764–1769*. Edited by Harry Alonzo Gushing. New York: G. P. Putnam's Sons, 1904.

de Alvarez, Leo Paul S., ed. *The Gettysburg Address and American Constitutionalism*. Dallas, TX: University of Dallas Press, 1976.

Berry, Wendell. *Jayber Crow*. Washington, DC: Counterpoint Press, 2000.

Beveridge, Albert. *The Meaning of the Times and Other Speeches*. Indianapolis, IN: Bobbs-Merrill Co., 1908.

Donald, David Herbert. *Lincoln*. New York: Touchstone Books, 1995.

Ferguson, Niall. *Colossus: The Price of America's Empire*. New York: Penguin, 2004.

Jensen, Merrill. *The Articles of Confederation: An Interpretation of the Social-Constitutional History of the American Revolution, 1774–781*. Madison: University of Wisconsin Press, 1959.

Kagan, Robert. *Dangerous Nation: America's Place in the World from Its Earliest Days to the Dawn of the Twentieth Century*. New York: Knopf Doubleday, 2009.

Litke, Justin B. *Twilight of the Republic: Empire and Exceptionalism in the American Political Tradition*. Lexington: University Press of Kentucky, 2013.

Lutz, Donald S. *The Origins of American Constitutionalism*. Baton Rouge: Louisiana State University Press, 1988.

McDonald, Forrest. *Novus Ordo Seclorum: The Economic Origins of the Constitution*. Lawrence: University Press of Kansas, 1985.

McDougall, Walter A. *Promised Land, Crusader State: The American Encounter with the World since 1776*. New York: Houghton Mifflin Co., 1997.

Morgan, Edmund S., ed. *Prologue to Revolution: Sources and Documents on the Stamp Act Crisis, 1764–1766*. Chapel Hill: University of North Carolina Press, 1959.

"Republican Party Platform of 1856, June 18, 1856." Gerhard Peters and John T. Wolley. *The American Presidency Project*. https://www.presidency.ucsb.edu/documents/republican-party-platform-1856. Accessed October 11, 2019.

Storing, Herbert, ed. *The Anti-Federalist: Writings by the Opponents of the Constitution*. Selected by Murray Dry from *The Complete Anti-Federalist*. Chicago, IL: University of Chicago Press, 1981.

Tansill, Charles C., ed. *Documents Illustrative of the Formation of the Union of the American States*. Washington, DC: Government Printing Office, 1927.

U.S. Congress. *Congressional Record*. 56th Congress, 1900. Vol. 33.

CHAPTER THIRTEEN

Resistance and Renewal

Irving Babbitt and China

Zhang Yuan and Justin D. Garrison

Critical reconsiderations of fundamental political and ethical issues are perhaps never more intensely felt than in times of cultural and constitutional crisis. One such crisis emerged in China, lasting from the early-nineteenth until the mid-twentieth century. There have been three major formative periods in China's long history. First, the Pre-Qin period (2100 BC–221 BC), that is to say, the Chinese "Classical Era," when China established its cultural identity. Second, the Wei-Jin period (AD 220–AD 589), which launched the splendid Chinese "Middle Ages" and paved way for the "Universal Empire" of the Tang Dynasty to assume cultural leadership in its known world. Third, the Modern period (1840–present), when China struggled with a cultural crisis "never experienced for thousands of years" and tried frantically to rebuild its identity. This last period consists of two stages. In the first stage (1840–1910s), China reacted passively to its encounters with various Western powers, clinging desperately to its past. In the second stage (1910s–present), Chinese intellectuals initiated the New Culture Movement (1915–1927), and it was during this period that China first began to deliberate over what if any Western resources it might wish to synthesize with and use to bolster a defense of its past. Such projects were often undertaken with the hope of transforming a dying Empire into a modern republic.

Into this exhilarating and volatile mixture of new ideas arrived an unlikely figure, the American humanist Irving Babbitt. Babbitt never visited China, but at Harvard he taught a number of students from Asia, especially from China and India, who sought out this American thinker because he was familiar with and admiring of Eastern religions and philosophies. In *Democracy and Leadership*, the essence of his attitude is captured when he writes, "Buddha and Confucius both managed to combine humility with self-reliance and a cultivation of the critical spirit. They may, therefore, be of help to those who wish to restore to their lives on modern lines the element for which Asia has stood in the past."[1] It was in part his belief that Western people had common ground with as well as things to learn from the East that attracted students from so far away. In this same spirit, Babbitt's brand of humanism itself has much to offer to Chinese intellectuals and the broader populace. Americans too can and should learn from Babbitt, especially now. Before delving into Babbitt's reception in China since the early twentieth century, a brief sense of the ideas and views that have been or could be most relevant to modernization efforts in China needs to be provided.

WHAT MIGHT BABBITT OFFER CHINA?

Perhaps one of Babbitt's greatest insights is that there is no need to choose between the past and the present, tradition and modernity. Animated by his historical sense, Babbitt argues persuasively that tradition endures to the extent that it can change. In holding such a view, he is of course not unique. Figures from the broader Western tradition, including Aristotle, Edmund Burke, Johann Wolfgang von Goethe, Charles Augustin Sainte-Beuve, Ernest Renan, and Matthew Arnold have similar attitudes. It should not be surprising that Babbitt crafts his historical consciousness in part out of the study of these and other like-minded scholars and statesmen, or, in the case of Confucius and Goethe, scholar-statesmen. Babbitt also brings his broad and deep knowledge of the past to bear on practical questions confronting the United States and the world in his own lifetime. His kind of humanism is not esoteric or detached from the broader culture that gives rise to his concerns. As will be shown below, the "Critical Review Group" attempts to use Babbitt himself to confront contemporary issues in China, but their achievements in these areas are mixed. Babbitt's particular understanding of the ways in which history shapes the present ultimately earned him the reputation in China as a traditional, that is, nonideological, American conservative.

Babbitt's historical mind shaped the way he thought about more discrete topics such as liberty, revolution, democracy, individualism, and education. As many readers of Babbitt know, he is often inclined to sharpen conceptual definitions of terms by creating dichotomies. When thinking about liberty, he sees it having two distinct and incompatible meanings. One type of liberty, which he finds laudable, he associates with Burke. This kind of liberty is one in which freedom and constraint cooperate in a way that makes the former genuine. To put this differently, a Burkean liberty is one in which subordination to a higher authority makes freedom possible. Another type of liberty, one that Babbitt sees as both popular and dangerous, he associates with Jean-Jacques Rousseau. This type of liberty is not moderated by any attachment to or belief in limitations on the exercise of free will. It is a gift of "nature."[2] For Rousseau and his admirers during the French Revolution, liberty becomes difficult to distinguish from aspirations for egalitarian utopia.[3] Babbitt believes that these two types of freedom are often present in a civil society. The Rousseauistic variety won out in France with the advent of Napoleon, in Babbitt's view. He also believes both have been present since the beginning of the American Republic. Even in his lifetime, he thought the question was open as to which would become predominant in American society.[4]

Babbitt's awareness of the formative power of the past also shapes his thinking about the foundations of politics and societies. Babbitt draws much from Burke's historically informed critique of the French Revolution to defend the difference he observes between regimes grounded in experience and those untethered from history. For Burke, the "old establishments" of politics and civil society in Britain "are not constructed after any theory; theories are rather drawn from them." Britain was not written up on paper before it existed; reflections on its principles of existence are possible because they are already embedded in concrete habits of living. In contrast to the British approach, the French formed a constitution based on "bad metaphysics" and thereby attempted "to destroy all vestiges of the ancient country, in religion, in polity, in laws, and in manners."[5] To Burke, the best *politeia* is a constitutional monarchy and he recommended to France reforms in this direction as more consistent with its organic society. Instead of following "the example of the British constitution," France embarked on an unprecedented experiment in total democracy. About such a regime, Burke remarked, "a perfect democracy is therefore the most shameless thing in the world."[6] Thus, the French Revolution was not a good idea badly implemented, as many interpreters of modern revolutions claim when confronted with the reality of objective failure and inhuman violence in pursuit of change. Its deliberate rejection of French traditions made it clear to Burke, and later to Babbitt, that it had no hope of success precisely because it was ill conceived and at odds with French tradition. Change is vital, but revolution is a cure worse than the disease.

Babbitt admires much about Burke and his criticisms of the French Revolution, but he has an appreciation of forms of individualism and self-government for which Burke does not have much enthusiasm. Like Burke, Babbitt rejects direct or unlimited democracy, but he has much to say in favor of what he calls constitutional democracy. If a "perfect democracy" is indeed "the most shameless thing in the world," Babbitt also argues "constitutional democracy" is probably "the best thing in the world."[7] Echoing Alexis de Tocqueville's claim that "it is because I am not an adversary of democracy, that I have sought to speak of democracy in all sincerity," Babbitt reconciles his defense and criticisms of modern democratic thought and practice by claiming that it is the humanist's aim "not to deny his age, but to complete it."[8] In the same spirit, Babbitt seeks to defend true modern individualism against its modern counterfeits. While Babbitt is attentive to the historical, he is no antiquarian. To be a true individualist in the modern world is to find the mean between the extremes of excessive traditionalism and excessive experimentation, to reconcile the needs for change and continuity. Burke is of course aware of this necessity and makes explicit reference to it in his *Reflections*. Babbitt may ultimately understand this issue more deeply than Burke because he articulates it in a more heterogeneous society, the United States, with a looser commitment to the ancestral when compared to its European cousins.

Babbitt believed that a central component of creatively defending or renewing a given traditional way of life was through humanistic (liberal) education. Genuine liberal education immersed students in the traditions of literature, science, philosophy, and religion that constituted the civilization they inhabited and would need to maintain and replenish through action. Following a figure such as Aristotle, Babbitt saw the purpose of such education as cultivating the mind and ethical character of students so that they might contribute to the vitality of their families, neighborhoods, and nation. At the time, Babbitt's vision stood in contrast in the US (and China) to the democratic educational theorizing of John Dewey. Here too the differences are rooted in incompatible understandings of liberty and equality. About Dewey, Russell Kirk claims that he "propounded a theory of education derived from Rousseau," "advocated a sentimental equalitarian collectivism," capped this "structure with Marxist economics," and looked for "the satisfaction of the masses." In a word, "every radicalism since 1789 found its place in John Dewey's system."⁹ To refer again to Aristotle, Babbitt wanted education to produce good people who could also be good citizens in the right society; Dewey was merely content to shape good democratic citizens. The differences between their views of education and its contributions to politics are irreconcilable.

BABBITTIAN HUMANISM IN CHINA: RECEPTION AND CONFRONTATION

Many of the ideas and problems that engaged Babbitt's mind were also of interest and concern to many in China. As was alluded to above, the weakness of the Qing Dynasty in the nineteenth century compelled a number of Chinese intellectuals to learn from the West while seeking to maintain China's distinct cultural identity and reclaim its pivotal role in world affairs. These needs to preserve and reestablish China took on increased urgency after the collapse of the Qing Dynasty in 1912. For Chinese intellectuals accustomed to living in a vast and respected country, the task of modernization, "saving the nation," in the twentieth century had two objectives. The first was to educate people so as to prepare them to be citizens in their new Republic. The second was to rehabilitate China's power so it could resume the role of cultural leader in Asia and beyond. In a number of instances, these goals came into conflict depending on which one received priority and how each was conceptualized as best achievable.

In the first stage of China's twentieth-century modernization, a prominent theory of "saving the nation" was *Zhongtixiyong*. As originally conceptualized, *Zhongtixiyong* meant adopting the Western way without changing the essence of China. The appeal of this particular approach was short-lived. As modernization during the New Culture Movement continued, "the Western way" blended with "the Chinese essence" to the extent that many people began to believe the differences between the two were apparent rather than real. This notion found concise expression in the idea of *ti yong bu er* the way *is* the essence and vice versa. Thus, in this period of time, it is ultimately insufficient to believe China saw the West merely as the "other."¹⁰ In reality, Western ideas and ideological movements made substantial contributions to the formation of China's modern cultural identity. After the failure of *Zhongtixiyong*, Chinese intellectuals increasingly interpreted themselves and their country through the various Western analytical lenses they embraced. Western readers should not be surprised to learn that many in China during this time began to identify as conservatives, liberals, and radicals. At the same time, these terms did not align with their American and Western equivalents at the time, and they do not fit with contemporary notions either. Thus, some sense of what these ideological identities meant in China in the early 1900s is needed to establish more clearly Babbitt's location in the broader landscape.

Out of the New Culture Movement, a number of so-called New Culture Groups and Anti–New Culture Groups emerged. Chinese liberals led by Hu Shih promoted the pragmatism of John Dewey and made up the "right wing" of the New Culture Groups. Li Dazhao and Chen Duxiu championed the ideas of Karl Marx and became the radicals at the forefront of the "left wing" of this movement. The liberals and the radicals fought bitter intellectual battles among themselves, as well as against the so-called conservatives who belonged to the Anti–New Culture Groups. The conservatives repaid the animosity of the liberals and the radicals with interest. Such tension is all the more peculiar when one recognizes that parts of the broader conservative coalition of political activists and scholars in this period were really a different kind of New Culture Group.

The composition of the Chinese conservatives at this time is more complicated than the other two camps of thought. One major faction consisted of the alleged "indigenous conservatives" who were preoccupied with what could be described as a reactionary commitment to preserving traditional Chinese culture. The other major group of conservatives within this broader movement, the "cultural conservatives," were more interested in integrating the best elements of Chinese culture with Western insights. Over time, the antiquarians ceded ground to the more creative conservatives who ultimately defined the movement, culminating in the establishment of the Critical Review Group. Led by Wu Mi, editor of the *Critical Review* magazine (1922–1933), it is this group that coalesced around Babbitt's humanist ideas. For over a decade, members of the Critical Review Group translated many of Babbitt's works into Chinese and tried to adapt Babbitt's central ideas to Chinese politics and culture.

Wu was one of the students who went to Harvard to learn from Babbitt. As the New Humanism Movement reached its peak in the United States during the 1920s, Wu and other like-minded intellectuals brought Babbitt and his brand of humanism to the attention of a broader Chinese audience, seeking to develop Babbitt's thought into an adequate response to the political and cultural challenges confronting China. The inclusion of Babbitt and American Humanism into the turbulent intellectual environment of early-twentieth-century China did not go unnoticed. Some were genuinely intrigued by the new possibilities opened up by Babbitt's ideas. At the same time, Wu and his colleagues became prime targets for ridicule from the liberals and radicals of the New Culture Groups. After 1949, charges of being "enemies" of China as well as "counterrevolutionaries" became much more serious, even life-threatening, for defenders of Babbitt and his humanistic philosophy.

The Critical Review Group made choices that did not always help their cause. The *Critical Review* magazine and the translations of Babbitt by the Critical Review Group were offered in plain classical Chinese. With similar political and cultural ideas as well as scholarly training, this seemed a common sense choice for the group. Unfortunately for them, this drew the ire of the Vernacular Movement, a subset of the liberal and radical side of the New Culture Movement. The Vernacular Movement was deeply hostile toward classical Chinese language, even in a modified, plain form. To write and publish in such a language, from their point of view, was intelligible only as a reactionary political statement. Theirs was a view with popular support. Many people in China had lived through and understood the last century of their history as a string of defeats and humiliations in the face of superior Western technology and, perhaps, society. For those who felt this way, maintaining the language and traditions associated with that period of decline was undesirable. Only the Critical Review Group and a few other conservatives thought traditional Chinese culture was not bankrupt. Furthermore, they believed this precisely because of the insights they achieved working with Babbitt's humanism. Hence, the traditionalism of the Critical Review Group became associated with Babbitt and inadvertently undermined some of his appeal in China at the time.

Some of Babbitt's followers began to recognize the practical problems associated with the interpretations provided by the Critical Review Group. Liang Shiqiu was a highly regarded man of letters and one of the central members of the "New Moon Group." Liang had taken classes with Wu and enrolled at Harvard in the 1920s. His encounters with Babbitt converted him from a passionate romantic into a steadfast classicist. He founded *The New Moon* magazine and became Babbitt's most prominent interpreter in the second generation of Babbitt scholarship in China. One of his first publication choices was to start publishing Babbitt in vernacular Chinese, thereby removing an unnecessary barrier for readers who might otherwise be receptive to his ideas. Liang's first critical essay, "The Romantic Tendency in Chinese Modern Literature," already indicated the strength of Babbitt's influence. After its publication, he continued to publish a large quantity of works in which he either rephrased or even copied passages from Babbitt. Based on Liang's successes, Wu approached Liang and the two coauthored the book *Babbitt and His Humanism* in 1929.[11]

1929 was the apex of Babbitt scholarship in China during this early period, but the same year also marked a decline of interest in the New Humanism Movement. To some extent, this outcome was a practical function of the global implications of the Great Depression. It was largely as a result of economic forces beyond its control that *Critical Review* ceased publication in 1933, which, coincidentally, was the year of Babbitt's death.[12] During the 1930s and 1940s, interest in Babbitt declined to the extent that it seemed as if he had not made a serious impression in China. The revolution of 1949 created unexpected opportunities and challenges for Babbitt scholars. Liang and many of his followers chose to settle in Taiwan, hoping Babbitt's humanism might contribute to the establishment of a humane society and politics on the island. The Critical Review Group chose to stay in the mainland. They suffered persecution from the new government.

In Taiwan, the New Moon Group did not realize its initial aspirations. Liang's students ended up taking the same approach to Babbitt as did their mentor a generation earlier. That is to say, Liang's followers restricted Babbitt's humanism to a type of literary criticism. Thus, Babbitt's social, ethical, and political ideas were generally ignored. This indifference to the full range of Babbitt's thoughts had the effect of reducing his wide-ranging social-cultural criticism to an academic interest far removed from the broader culture.[13] Something rather similar happened in the United States among Babbitt's followers during the mid-twentieth century. In the mainland, Chinese scholars with more conservative inclinations showed renewed interest in the Critical Review Group and their writings. Babbitt scholarship began to revive in 1989, and interest in the late American scholar extended far beyond literary criticism. Descendants of the New Culture Movement reemerged as well, reflecting renewed interest in figures such as Marx and Dewey. A new round of debates between these broad groups were held in the 1990s. While these debates were just as tense and combative as their early-twentieth-century ancestors, the indifference to such disputes that prevailed in Taiwan did not reach the mainland.

BABBITTIAN HUMANISM IN CHINA: ENDURING CHALLENGES

For those on the mainland interested in Babbitt, a twofold objective quickly emerged at the end of the twentieth century. Engaging in broader debates about the future of China became the primary goal, but this could be realized, in turn, only if mistranslations and misrepresentations of Babbitt were confronted and overcome. On this second point, in some instances figures such as Wu and Liang appropriated Babbitt to advance conceptions of politics and culture he would have found difficult to accept on the terms of his humanist philosophy. Perhaps the biggest challenge on this front was to decouple Babbitt's deep admiration for Confucius from the Confucianism promoted by members of the Critical Review Group. Prior to 1989, this task was essentially impossible. Access to Babbitt's primary sources was restricted, so knowledge of him was only possible through translations provided by Wu, Liang, and others.[14] This situation gave rise to the view, by no means appreciated by all in China, that Babbitt was a "Western Confucian" or "American Confucian." Even today, there are some who consider him the "Old Confucian."[15] As is tradition in China, translations are often assumed to be faithful representations of the original. On this topic, the tendency to take translations at face value compounded the problem of recovering the meaning of Babbitt's writings.

Of course, an honorific such as "Confucian" is about the highest praise a Westerner could ever receive in China. There is also a sense in which this is an accurate description of Babbitt. Like Confucius, Babbitt promoted an ethical philosophy that sought to live by the law of measure without primary dependence on a transcendently revealed account of how to achieve this end. At the same time, it seems as if early Babbitt translators put practical political concerns ahead of fidelity to his words. This continues to cause confusion over how to interpret Babbitt. By way of representative example, in 2002 Wang Qingjia published a well-received article in which reliance on *Critical Review* translations from Hu Xiansu led the author to claim, "Babbitt's humanism has much in common with ... Confucianism." This conclusion was derived from Hu's translations, which stated Babbitt claimed the following: "the way of Confucius is superior ... because Confucius clearly sees that in order to achieve *zhongyongzhidao* (the Doctrine of the Mean) one should *keji* (restrain oneself) and *zhiming* (resign oneself to fate)." All of this was alleged to have been written by Babbitt, but the sentence Hu claims to translate is much simpler and more general: "the law of measure itself is subject to the law of humility."[16]

Wu Mi did even more damage to Babbitt by distorting the American's meaning in an effort to make him more "Confucian." Babbitt was a proponent of sound individualism compatible with tradition and critical inquiry. In Babbitt's own words, a person who wants to be a sound individual should "retain one's hold on truths of the inner life," even if that means "breaking ... completely with the past"; "formerly the standards were supplied by tradition," but if the individualist "is to have standards, he must rely on the critical spirit in direct ratio to the completeness of his break with the traditional unifications of life."[17] In numerous articles, Wu gave a misleading sense of Babbitt's humanism by translating such statements in ways that made Babbitt appear to be deeply committed to promoting "Confucian Dogmas of Rites and Ethics." Wu drew this conclusion, in part, based on Babbitt's English language use of words such as "tradition" and "traditional" in laudable ways. In the *Critical Review*, for example, Wu translated the words immediately above as the following: "[the] inner life ... must defer to certain standards. In the past, these standards are [sic] provided by the Confucian Dogmas of Rites and Ethics ... but since today's individualists thoroughly destroy those old standards and hope to find new ones by themselves, the only thing they could rely on is their critical spirit."[18] Under Wu's influence, the Babbitt found in the *Critical Review* often speaks in highly technical Confucian terminology absent in Babbitt's writings. As a matter of fact, by rephrasing Babbitt's words in this manner, Wu pushes his mentor in a more traditional direction, putting him more at odds with modern individualists and making him more of a target of their criticism.

Babbitt is not the only American or Western scholar that Chinese scholars have interpreted as highly conversant with and supportive of Chinese philosophy. In various articles published in the *Critical Review*, Harvard professor Charles Grandgent; Katherine Fullerton Gerould; German scholar A. Reichwein; British classicist Gilbert Murray; and others were declared unqualified supporters of "Confucian Dogmas of Rites and Ethics." Such distortions were justified by those who created them as necessary to counter the revolutionary thinking found in competing publications such as *New Youth*, a Chinese radical publication, or publications associated with other left-wing coalitions in the New Culture Groups. In seeking to defend humanism and elements of Chinese tradition, Babbitt's supporters opened his thought to ridicule, then and now, through avoidable mischaracterizations and mistranslations.[19] Efforts to overcome this problem are growing stronger in the mainland.

BABBITTIAN HUMANISM, CHINA, AND AMERICA

Sound individualism, ordered liberty, historical consciousness, government that grows out of existing traditional structures, and humanistic education are all topics of thought in Babbitt's works that are deserving of renewed attention in China. In some instances, these ideas need to be reclaimed from past misrepresentations. In others, the ideas should be considered for the first time. The same can be said for the land of Babbitt's home, the United States. In some sense, the situation in the US might be more extreme. The signs of a post-constitutional society have been on display well before the 2016 presidential election. The prominence of Rousseauistic conceptions of liberty, equality, and democracy in the broader populace is equaled by the degree to which American education has followed the lead of Dewey and not Babbitt. Although the reasons given are numerous, there is a growing consensus that something is very wrong in America. For the United States to have a chance to rekindle the habits and ideas that make constitutionalism work in spirit as well as law, major changes are needed. To resume its place as an exemplar of ordered freedom for the world to admire and even emulate, America could do far worse than to consult the humanistic ideas of Irving Babbitt. With shared commitments to Babbitt scholarship and a broader humanistic outlook, relations between China and the US might even create unexpected and firm ground for meaningful relations and peace.

TABLE 13.1 Translations of Babbitt's Writings in the Critical Review (in Plain Classical Chinese)

1	Irving Babbitt, "Humanistic Education in China and in the West," *Chinese Students' Monthly* 17 (December 1922).	Translated by Hu Xiansu, *Critical Review* 3 (March 1923).
2	Louis Mercier: "L'Humanisme positiviste d'Irving Babbitt," *La Revue Hebdomadaire*, Trentieme annee VII (July 1921).	Translated by Wu Mi, *Critical Review* 19 (July 1923).
3	Irving Babbitt: "Introduction" to *Democracy and Leadership* (Boston and New York: Houghton Mifflin Company, 1924).	Translated by Wu Mi, *Critical Review* 32 (August 1924).
4	Irving Babbitt: "What's Humanism?," Chapter 1 of *Literature and the American College* (Boston and New York: Houghton Mifflin Company, 1908).	Translated by Xu Zhen'e, *Critical Review* 34 (October 1924).
5	Irving Babbitt: "Europe and Asia," chapter 5 of *Democracy and Leadership*, 1924.	Translated by Wu Mi, *Critical Review* 38 (February 1925).
6	Irving Babbitt: "Milton or Wordsworth?—Review of *The Cycle of Modern Poetry*," *Forum* 82 (October 1929).	Translated by Wu Mi, *Critical Review* 72 (November 1929).
7	Irving Babbitt: "Benda and French Ideas," *Saturday Review of Literature* 5 (1929).	Translated by Zhang Yinlin, *Critical Review* 74 (March 1931).

TABLE 13.2. Translations of Babbitt's Writings after the *Critical Review* (in Vernacular Chinese)

1	Irving Babbitt: "Romantic Morality: The Real," chapter 5 of *Rousseau and Romanticism* (Boston and New York: Houghton Mifflin Company, 1919).	Translated by Liang Shiqiu, *Selective American Literary Criticism* (Hong Kong: Nowadays World Press, 1961).
2	Irving Babbitt: "Humanistic Education in China and in the West," *The Chinese Students' Monthly* 17 (December 1922).	Translated by Hou Jian, *From Literary Revolution to Revolutionary Literature* (Taipei: Chinese and Foreign Literature Monthly Press, 1974). (Cf. the *Critical Review* version in 1922.)

Table 13.2 continued

3	Irving Babbitt: "The Critic and American Life," *Forum* (February 1928).	Translated by Wen Meihui, *Selective Western Literary Criticism of 20th Century* (Beijing, China: China Social Sciences Press, 1989).
4	Irving Babbitt and Wu Mi, Correspondence (Six Letters) 1921–1925	Translated by Wu Xuezhao, *Trans-Cultural Studies*, vol. 10 (Nanjing, China: Jiangsu People Press, 2002).
5	Irving Babbitt: *The Masters of Modern French Criticism* (Boston and New York: Houghton Mifflin Company, 1924).	Translated by Sun Yixue (Guilin, China: Guangxi Normal University Press, 2002).
6	Irving Babbitt, chapters 1, 2, and 3 of *Literature and the American College* (Boston and New York: Houghton Mifflin Company, 1908).	Translated by Wang Chen et al., *Humanitas: Rethinking It All* (Beijing, China: Sanlian Press, 2003). (Cf. the *Critical Review* version of chapter 1 in 1924.)
7	Irving Babbitt: *Rousseau and Romanticism* (Boston and New York: Houghton Mifflin Company, 1919).	Translated by Sun Yixue (Shijianzhuang, China: Hebei Education Press, 2003).
8	Irving Babbitt: *Literature and the American College* (Boston and New York: Houghton Mifflin Company, 1908).	Translated by Zhang Pei and Zhang Yuan (Beijing, China: Peking University Press, 2004).
9	Irving Babbitt: *Spanish Character and Others* (Boston and New York: Houghton Mifflin Company, 1940).	Translated by Sun Yixue (Shanghai, China: Shanghai Sanlian Press, 2010).
10	Irving Babbitt: *Democracy and Leadership* (Boston and New York: Houghton Mifflin Company, 1924).	Translated by Zhang Yuan and Zhang Pei (Beijing, China: Peking University Press, 2011). (Cf. the *Critical Review* version of Introduction in 1924 and chapter 5 in 1925.)
11	Irving Babbitt: *Collected Works*	Edited by Zhang Yuan (Beijing, China: The Commercial Press, forthcoming).

NOTES

1. Irving Babbitt, *Democracy and Leadership* (Indianapolis, IN: Liberty Fund, 1979), 209.
2. Irving Babbitt, *Democracy and Leadership* (New York: Houghton Mifflin, 1924), 295.
3. Babbitt, *Democracy and Leadership*, 108.
4. Babbitt, *Democracy and Leadership*, 127–28, 248, 312.
5. Edmund Burke, *Reflections on the Revolution in France* (New York: Rinehart & Co., 1959), 212–13, 225–26.
6. Burke, *Reflections on the Revolution in France*, 113, 152, 306.
7. Irving Babbitt, *On Being Creative and Other Essays* (New York: Houghton Mifflin Co., 1932), 206.
8. Alexis de Tocqueville, *Democracy in America*, trans. Henry Reeve (London: Oxford University Press, 1946), 292; Irving Babbitt, *Literature and the American College* (New York: Houghton Mifflin Co., 1908), 258–59.
9. Russell Kirk, *The Conservative Mind: From Burke to Eliot* (Chicago, IL: Regnery, 1960), 476.
10. Until the last decade of the twentieth century, several Chinese intellectuals still had to deal with the aftermath of the *ti yong bu er* generated in the first decade of the same century. For example, in the 1990s, fears over "aphasia" in literary theory spread to other disciplines and finally ended up with several acrimonious debates regarding "cultural aphasia." The sudden prevalence of worries about "aphasia" is itself an interesting cultural phenomenon, reflecting China's fin-de-siecle mood that after almost a century of self searching and building it is still anxiously on the way to finding its voice.
11. Liang Shiqiu, ed., Wu Mi et al., trans., *Babbitt and His Humanism*, Shanghai, New Moon Bookstore, 1929. This book is a collection of translations of Babbitt originally published in *The Critical Review* from 1922 to 1925. Wu saw Liang's willingness to be part of the publication as a friendly gesture in an environment increasingly hostile toward humanism.
12. Liang published five critical works elaborating Babbitt's humanism, namely, *The Romantic and the Classic*, Beiping: New Moon Bookstore, 1927; *The Discipline of Literature*, Shanghai, Shanghai Commercial Press, 1928; *The Moral Litterateurs*, Beiping: Zhonghua Book Company, 1934; *Collection of Prejudices*, Nanjing: Zhengzhong Bookstore, 1934; and *My Relation with Literature*, Taipei: Wenxing Bookstore, 1964. This last text is a collection of articles published after Liang fled to Taiwan.

13. Li Youcheng, "Babbitt in China," in *Chinese and Foreign Literature* 12 (1991): 64. Professor Li was a student of Hou Jian, and Hou was a student of Liang's. Hou was also a leading figure in the Babbitt revival in Taiwan in the 1970s. This intellectual heritage enhances the credibility of Li's observations.

14. Liang and Hou published revised translations in Hong Kong in 1961 and Taiwan in 1974, but such revised versions of Babbitt's works were inaccessible to mainland readers.

15. For a detailed treatment of this topic, see Zhang Yuan, "Irving Babbitt's Confucian Image In and After *The Critical Review*," *East Journal* 68 (2009): 82–94.

16. Wang Qingjia, "Babbitt and the Critical Review Group: A Comparative Study on the History of Academic Culture," *Collected Papers of Modern History Institution of Academia Sinica* 37 (2002): 68; Irving Babbitt, "Humanistic Education in China and in the West," *Chinese Students' Monthly* 17 (1922): 90. That Professor Wang, a highly regarded scholar at Rowan University, would continue to rely on mistranslations from the *Critical Review* period is evidence of how deeply rooted is this particular problem.

17. Babbitt, *Democracy and Leadership*, 8–9.

18. Wu Mi trans., "Irving Babbitt on Democracy and Leadership," *Critical Review* 32 (1924): 10.

19. Denunciations of Babbitt and the *Critical Review* often employed military imagery. For example, *New Youth* declared it would "launch the first round of a general offensive" in its "New Manifesto of the New Youth" (*New Youth*, vol. A, no. 2 [June 1923]). As for the "offensives" themselves, there are too many to discuss, but representative examples can be found in the following publications: Chen Duxiu, "Constitution and Confucianism," *New Youth* 2, no. 3 (November 1916); Chen Duxiu, "The Way of Confucius and Modern Life," *New Youth* 2, no. 4 (December 1916); Wu Yu, "Man-Eating and Confucian Dogma of Rites and Ethics," *New Youth* 2, no. 3 (November 1916).

BIBLIOGRAPHY

Babbitt, Irving. *Democracy and Leadership*. New York: Houghton Mifflin, 1924.
———. *Democracy and Leadership*. Indianapolis, IN: Liberty Fund, 1979.
———. *Literature and the American College*. New York: Houghton Mifflin, 1908.
———. *On Being Creative and Other Essays*. New York: Houghton Mifflin, 1932.
Burke, Edmund. *Reflections on the Revolution in France*. New York: Rinehart & Co., 1959.

Kirk, Russell. *The Conservative Mind: From Burke to Eliot*. Chicago, IL: Regnery, 1960.
Li Youcheng. "Babbitt in China." *Chinese and Foreign Literature* 12 (1991): 48–71.
Liang Shiqiu, ed. *Babbitt and His Humanism*. Shanghai, China: New Moon Bookstore, 1929.
Liang Shiqiu. *Collection of Prejudices*. Nanjing, China: Zhengzhong Bookstore, 1934.
———. *The Discipline of Literature*. Shanghai, China: Shanghai Commercial Press, 1928.
———. *The Moral Litterateurs*. Beiping, China: Zhonghua Book Company, 1934.
———. *My Relation with Literature*. Taipei, Taiwan: Wenxing Bookstore, 1964.
———. *The Romantic and the Classic*. Beiping, China: New Moon Bookstore, 1927.
de Tocqueville, Alexis. *Democracy in America*. Translated by Henry Reeve. London: Oxford University Press, 1946.
Wang Qingjia. "Babbitt and the Critical Review Group: A Comparative Study on the History of Academic Culture." *Collected Papers of Modern History Institution of Academia Sinica* 37 (2002): 41–92.
Zhang Yuan. "Irving Babbitt's Confucian Image in and after the *Critical Review*." *East Journal* 68 (2009): 82–94.

Conclusion

From among the diverse voices of this interdisciplinary dialogue there emerges a unity, a oneness within the many, in Babbittian terms, with regard to the cultural, moral, and political needs of Western civilization. There is, in short, a call for humanistic renewal. It may be observed that when examined etymologically, the word *renewal* is oxymoronic, insofar as it refers to that which is past or has already happened becoming novel, which in the strict sense must be impossible, since that which has come before is, by definition, no longer new. Conversely, one might understand *renewal* to refer to the return or coming again of the novel, which would also appear logically problematic. Yet, for the present authors, the compatibility of these concepts is not contradictory but an essential reality regarding the nature of human wisdom. Our knowledge of the past cannot be mere antiquarianism, but must involve bringing prior human experience to bear on the present. To do what is wise means making what was good in the past happen again, but in a way that is appropriate or fitting for the present and thus not identical with its previous occurrence. The humanistic renewal of the present volume refers to the past that must be made new again in this manner. Such rejuvenation is essential to human happiness in that it prioritizes the self-restraint or self-control that facilitates what has long been known as the life of proportion or measure. The call for humanistic renewal emphasizes cultural, moral, and political institutions that predispose human beings to this way of living. In other words, these scholars are concerned with the building up, or, to be more precise, the rebuilding of Western civilization. Even where these authors disagree or part company in their assessments of how this is to occur, they all share this fundamental concern.

The authors' collective orientation toward the role of intellectual reflection in such matters must be kept in full view here. It is important to note that the prescriptive nature of these contributions does not imply that the current volume is a theoretical blueprint or "road map" for future practice. Certainly, many of the essays engage in thinking that is theoretical or philosophical in nature. However, this need not indicate the imposition of an abstract model on concrete reality. Theory may be more or less closely tied to experience without, for that reason, being any more or less theoretical. In other words, conceptualizations may be based on romantic dreams as much as they may be based on human life as it is actually lived. What is attempted in the more philosophical of these essays is to conceptualize the concrete experience of human history, or some aspect of that experience, which may be contrasted with philosophy or theory that is precise and consistent in its use of terms but bears little correspondence to actual human experience.

For the advocates of such humanistic renewal, the wisdom contained within human history ought to inform reflection about culture, morality, and politics. They understand that these categories are not strict but pragmatic ways of distinguishing diverse areas of social life, which in reality are interconnected. It is for this reason that many of the essays, while primarily focusing on one of these areas, inevitably have spoken to the others. For example, Byrne's chapter, while principally focused on moral discourse and action, had much to say about the dispositions of character that are pre-formed by the imagination. Similarly, Frohnen's essay, concerned as it was with structures of governance and their relationship to civil associations, was certainly not silent on questions of virtue and the formation of "constitutional morality" among both citizens and legislators. The interpenetration of these three major subject areas, therefore, points toward a shared sense among the contributors that none are profitably viewed in isolation from the others. Such differences of focus are merely a function of what it is that the analytic intellect focuses on, not the concrete, experiential reality that is the subject of its examination.

Still, due to these differences of focus and often the disciplinary orientation of the particular scholar, these essays each in their own way put forth or suggest a potential way forward from our current predicament. As mentioned at the outset, there are resonances between these prescriptions for renewal, a harmony among the scholars' diverse perspectives; yet the viewpoints are not all sung in precisely the same key. They do not, as Aristotle says of Plato's *Republic*, "reduce concord to unison or rhythm to a single beat."[1] Thus, Birzer located the principal source of social order and stability in liberal education, suggesting that the process of reclaiming the highest of human truths entails, above all, an academy that promotes *humanitas*, in order to combat the "rampant egoism of the modern world." Alternatively, Holston argued that it is the Christian imagination that must be renewed along humanistic lines, whose institutional supports for resisting temptation must ultimately include "the family, the church, the neighborhood, and the community." Whereas, for Litke, it is a sense of place that must be restored and cultivated, and a return to the business of "everyday politics," in contrast to the present ideological ambitions of those who identify first and foremost with "the nation."

It is worth reiterating that what the essays here have proposed should be understood first and foremost as *ways forward*, not solutions, since it is true of the cultural, moral, and political alike that fixed models cannot meet the needs of changing circumstances. This is a key sensibility of those favorably disposed to historical consciousness or "the historical mind." Still, while this experiential variety demands humility regarding what human beings are capable of knowing, one cannot deny that history has much to teach us with respect to what is wise or prudent. Indeed, it would be anything but humble to turn one's back on what Goethe calls "the masses of universal history." There is, in short, a middle path or Aristotelian mean to be pursued, which demands neither absolute, objective knowledge with regard to historical truth, nor does it require ignorance or obliviousness with respect to the experience of previous generations. What must be recognized, in the end, is that in between these extremes of excess and deficiency lies an important mean or virtue—our continual openness and sensitivity to what it is that the past has to say.

NOTE

1. Aristotle, *The Politics*, trans. T. A. Sinclair, rev. trans. Trevor A. Saunders (1981; repr., New York: Penguin, 1992), 116.

BIBLIOGRAPHY

Aristotle. *The Politics*. Translated by T. A. Sinclair. 1962. Revised translation by Trevor A. Saunders. 1981. Reprint, New York: Penguin, 1992.

Contributors

IRVING BABBITT (1865–1933) was a professor of comparative literature at Harvard University. He was a leading figure in the American New Humanism movement in the early decades of the twentieth century. Babbitt drew students to Harvard from around the world, especially from India and China. He taught and had a significant influence on the Nobel Prize winning poet T. S. Eliot and was instrumental in the thinking of twentieth-century luminary Russell Kirk. In addition to publishing many articles, Babbitt's works include the following books: *Literature and the American College*, *The New Laokoön*, *The Masters of Modern French Criticism*, *Rousseau & Romanticism*, *Democracy and Leadership*, *On Being Creative*, and a posthumously published translation of the Buddhist holy text *The Dhammapada*. In 1960, Harvard established an endowed chair for the Irving Babbitt Professor in Comparative Literature.

CLAES G. RYN is professor of politics at The Catholic University of America in Washington, D.C. Born in Sweden, he earned his Ph.D. from Louisiana State University. His many books include *America the Virtuous: The Crisis of Democracy and the Quest for Empire*; *A Common Human Ground: Universality and Particularity in a Multicultural Age*; *Democracy and the Ethical Life: A Philosophy of Politics and Community*; *Will, Imagination and Reason: Babbitt, Croce and the Problem of Reality*; and the recent novel *A Desperate Man*. Ryn is editor of the scholarly journal *Humanitas*, and he is the founding director of the Center for the Study of Statesmanship. A frequent visitor to China, he gave the Distinguished Foreign Scholar Lectures at Peking University in 2000. In 2012, he was named Honorary Professor at Beijing Normal University. Three of his books and many of his articles have been translated and published in China.

BRADLEY J. BIRZER is Russell Amos Kirk Chair in American Studies and Professor of History at Hillsdale College. Though trained as an eighteenth- and nineteenth-century Americanist, he has focused his writings on Christian humanism, conservatism, and literature. He is also cofounder and editor at large of *The Imaginative Conservative*.

WILLIAM F. BYRNE is associate professor of government and politics at St. John's University (NY), where he teaches graduate and undergraduate courses in political theory and American government. A former congressional staff member, Byrne also spent several years in the private sector before entering academia. He holds a Ph.D. in politics from The Catholic University of America, an M.B.A. from George Mason University, and a B.A. in History from the University of Pennsylvania. He is the author of *Edmund Burke for Our Time: Moral Imagination, Meaning, and Politics*, as well as numerous scholarly articles.

MICHAEL P. FEDERICI is professor and chair of the Political Science and International Relations Department at Middle Tennessee State University. He received his B.S. in economics from Elizabethtown College and his M.A. and Ph.D. in politics from The Catholic University of America. He is the author of three books: *The Political Philosophy of Alexander Hamilton*, *Eric Voegelin: The Search for Order*, and *The Challenge of Populism*; he is also the editor of three volumes: *The Catholic Writings of Orestes Brownson*, *The Culture of Immodesty in American Life and Politics: The Modest Republic*, and *Rethinking the Teaching of American History*.

BRUCE P. FROHNEN is professor of law at Ohio Northern University's College of Law and senior fellow at the Russell Kirk Center for Cultural Renewal. He has authored or coauthored four books, including *Constitutional Morality and the Rise of Quasi-Law* (Harvard University Press, 2016, with the late George W. Carey) and *Coming Home: Reclaiming America's Conservative Soul* (Encounter Books, 2019, with Ted V. McAllister) and edited or coedited another eight. His articles have appeared in journals including *The American Journal of Jurisprudence*, *The Journal of Law and Politics*, and the *Harvard Journal of Law & Public Policy*.

RICHARD M. GAMBLE holds the Anna Margaret Ross Alexander Chair in History and Politics at Hillsdale College in Hillsdale, Michigan. His published works include *The War for Righteousness: Progressive Christianity, the Great War, and the Rise of the Messianic Nation* (ISI Books, 2003), *In Search of the City on a Hill: The Making and Unmaking of an American Myth* (Continuum, 2012), and *A Fiery Gospel: The Battle Hymn of the Republic and the Road to Righteous War* (Cornell University Press, 2019).

JUSTIN D. GARRISON is an associate professor of political science at Roanoke College in Salem, Virginia. He teaches courses on political theory, politics and literature, American politics, and American foreign policy. He is the author of *"An Empire of Ideals": The Chimeric Imagination of Ronald Reagan*, and he has published book chapters and journal articles on topics including the novels *Fight Club* and *All the King's Men*.

RYAN R. HOLSTON is professor of international studies and political science and Jonathan Myrick Daniels '61 Chair for Academic Excellence at Virginia Military Institute, where he teaches political theory. He is also an associate editor at the journal *Humanitas*. His published work has appeared in *Harvard Theological Review*, *History of Political Thought*, *Telos*, and other places. He is currently writing a monograph whose working title is *Tradition and the Deliberative Turn*.

ROBERT C. KOONS is a professor of philosophy at the University of Texas at Austin. He received his M.A. from Oxford University where he was a Marshall Scholar, and his Ph.D. from UCLA. He is the author or coauthor of four books, including: *Realism Regained* (Oxford University Press, 2000), and *The Atlas of Reality: A Comprehensive Guide to Metaphysics*, with Timothy H. Pickavance (Wiley-Blackwell, 2017). He is the coeditor (with George Bealer) of *The Waning of Materialism* (Oxford University Press, 2010), and coeditor (with Nicholas Teh and William Simpson) of *Neo-Aristotelian Perspectives on Contemporary Science* (Routledge, 2018).

JUSTIN B. LITKE is assistant professor of politics at The Catholic University of America and a fellow of the Center for the Study of Statesmanship. His book, *Twilight of the Republic: Empire and Exceptionalism in the American Political Tradition* (2013), explored the origins of the imperial strain of American exceptionalism through key moments in American history. His writing has also appeared in *Society*, *Anamnesis*, and *The Journal of Church and State*.

S. F. MCGUIRE is assistant professor in the Augustine and Culture Seminar Program at Villanova University. He has coedited *Concepts of Nature: Ancient and Modern*, *Subjectivity: Ancient and Modern*, and *Eric Voegelin and the Continental Tradition: Explorations in Modern Political Thought*.

ZHANG YUAN is an award-winning professor of comparative literature and executive director of *Renwen Yanjiusuo* (Humanities Institute) at Beijing Normal University. Her publications include *From Humanism to Conservatism: Irving Babbitt in the Critical Review* (2009), the edited volume *American Humanism: Tradition and Renewal* (2017), and various scholarly articles. She has translated many works into Chinese, including Thomas Paine's *Common Sense*, Irving Babbitt's *Democracy and Leadership* and *Literature and the American College*, and George Santayana's *Reason in Society*. She is currently completing translations for a forthcoming ten-volume collection titled *The Complete Works of Irving Babbitt*.

Index

Adams, John, xiii–xiv, xxiii–xxiv, xxviii, xxxvin34, 229, 231, 235
Adams, John Quincy, xxvii
Adams, Samuel, 242–243
Alighieri, Dante, 81–82
American Exceptionalism, xxxii, 222, 228, 232–233, 235, 237, 253n24
Aquinas, Thomas, 5, 132–133, 135, 138–139, 150, 177–178; and ethics, 131, 140, 152; and natural law, 84n20, 106, 127–130, 134–135, 153
Aristotle, xxxvn22, 16, 67, 105, 130–131, 133–134, 137, 140, 150, 153–154, 156, 177, 209, 250, 258, 260–261, 274; and ethics, 127–128, 136, 146, 152, 155
Augustine, 5, 11, 138, 177, 188

Babbitt, Irving, viii, xxxii, 2–3, 67–68, 77–78, 80–81, 84n20, 90–92, 94, 105, 107, 111–112, 114, 116, 127, 150, 156, 158, 159n5, 159n9, 159n11, 161n22, 162n30, 162n36, 163n38, 169–170, 178, 184, 190, 205, 216, 222–223; and culture, xv, xxxiii, 41–43, 47, 63, 161n17, 164n55, 175, 221, 258, 262–266; and democracy, xv–xvi, xxii, xxiv, xxv–xxvii, xxix, xxxviin42, 42, 161n17, 176, 181, 236, 259–260, 267; and *Democracy and Leadership*, xxviii, xxxviin42, 45, 49, 63, 161n17, 258; and education, 15–16, 52, 54, 82, 259–261, 267; and history, xix–xxi, xxix, xxxiii–xxxiv, xxxvn16, xxxvn20, 32, 49, 53, 258–259; and humanism, xv–xvii, xix, xxix, xxxi, xxxiii, xxxvn16, 1, 8, 11, 13–14, 49, 52–54, 63, 100, 106, 145–149, 151–155, 157, 160n13, 161n17, 161n18, 161n23, 163n39, 258, 262–266; and imagination, 9, 14–15; and *Literature and the American College*, xvi, 52; and *New Laokoon*, 74; and Kirk, Russell, xx, xxx, 42, 45–54, 55n4, 56n12, 132, 140, 260; and *Rousseau & Romanticism*, 1, 63, 73, 75, 164n52; and scientific naturalism, 43, 64–65, 69, 75, 79, 82–83
Bacon, Francis, 7, 61, 64, 66–76, 81–82
Bellamy, Edward, xxxii, 176–177, 180, 183, 185, 187–189, 195
Berry, Wendell, xxxii, 223, 241
Beveridge, Albert, 248–249

281

Bible, 228–231; and Daniel, 61; and Genesis, 91; and the Gospel, 151, 158, 236; and Matthew, 145; and Nehemiah, 227; and Romans, 165n63

Brownson, Orestes, xxvii

Buddha, xvii, xxxiii, 55n4, 67, 80, 147, 178, 258

Buddhism, xvii, 12, 146–147, 153–154, 160n13

Burke, Edmund, 8, 9, 32, 42, 46, 49–51, 54, 90, 106, 109–113, 115–120, 127, 130–132, 135, 140, 152, 184, 194, 258–260; and the French Revolution, 116, 259–260; and liberty, 259; and prejudice, 118; and wisdom, xxxiii, 51, 118–119, 184, 194

Bush, George W., xi–xiii, xxviii, xxx, xxxviin42, 33

Carey, George W., xxxii

China, xxxiii–xxxiv, 223, 226, 257–258, 260–267, 270n10

Christianity, xvi–xvii, xxxi, 6, 9, 11–12, 23, 29, 35, 50, 106–107, 121, 145–154, 157–158, 161n17, 162n30, 163n38, 164n52, 194, 229, 231, 236

Cicero, Marcus Tullius, xvi, 5, 46, 53, 127–129, 133–134, 138, 177–178, 184

communism, xxix, 29, 192, 195, 236

community, xxii, 2, 24, 41, 93, 97, 100, 105, 154, 158, 169, 177, 179, 191, 204–206, 209–210, 246, 250, 275

Confucius, xxxiii, 46, 67, 258, 265; and Confucianism, xvii, 154, 265

conservative, xxxiii, 7, 50–51, 128, 251n9, 258, 262–264

Croce, Benedetto, xvii, xxxvn16, 90, 140

Croly, Herbert, 176–177, 180–183, 189, 195

Dawson, Christopher, 46, 50–51

Declaration of Independence, xxiv, 244, 247–248, 252n17, 253n24

democracy, xv–xvi, xxii, xxiv–xxvii, xxix, xxxviin42, 3, 29, 31, 111, 113, 121, 170, 176–177, 181, 195, 201–207, 210, 212–213, 217n16, 221, 233, 236, 259–260, 267; and constitutional democracy, xxii–xxiii, xxv, xxix, 171, 204, 206–208, 210, 214–216, 260; and plebiscitary democracy, xxii, xxvi, xxxii, 171, 202–205, 208, 213–215

democratic peace theory, ix, xxxviin42

Dickinson, John, xxxvin34

diversity, xviii, xxv–xxvi, xxx, 111, 113, 245

education, xi, 5, 15–16, 41, 49, 52–54, 63, 71, 81–82, 114, 121, 185, 203, 214, 237, 259–261, 267, 274

Eliot, Thomas Sterns (T. S.), xxi, xxxi, 46, 49–51, 106, 145–148, 150–151, 154, 156–158, 159n5, 159n9, 159n11, 160n13, 161n17, 161n22

empire, xiii, xxvii–xxix, xxxii–xxxiii, xxxviin42, 70, 221, 232–233, 242, 244–246, 252n14, 257

Enlightenment, The, xvi, xxiv, xxxi, 29, 105–106, 109–111, 113–114, 116, 119, 122

epistemology, 91, 128, 130, 140

eudaimonia, xix, 2, 149, 152, 154–155

federalism, xxiii, 174–175, 190, 195, 215

Federalist, The, xxiii, 173, 179–180, 190, 193, 215, 252n14

foreign policy, xv, xxv–xxviii, xxxii, 20, 115, 221–222, 232, 234–236, 246–247

Founding, The, xi; 252

Framers, The, xiii, xxiv–xxv, 2–3, 19–20, 22, 34, 37, 169–170, 174, 176, 178–183, 189, 193, 195, 206

French Revolution, 29, 32, 50, 187, 196n7, 212, 259–260

von Goethe, Johann Wolfgang, xiii, 12, 258, 275

gnostic, 183–185, 189–192

higher will, xxxiii, 10, 12–15, 17, 146, 148, 152, 161n17, 161n22, 175, 178. *See also* inner check

history, vi, xi–xiii, xv, xxiv–xxv, xxix, xxxiii–xxxiv, 13, 16, 26, 28, 31–32, 43, 46, 48–49, 51–53, 80, 91, 93, 96, 99, 127, 131, 157, 173, 183, 188, 191, 194, 227–228, 231–232, 234–235, 237, 242, 246–249, 257, 259, 263, 274; and historical consciousness, xiv, xviii, xx–xxi, xxix, xxxvn22, 1, 41–42, 258, 267, 275; and historical sense, xvii, 258; and historicism, xix, xxxvn16, 92

Hobbes, Thomas, 21, 64, 71–75, 77–78, 82, 127

human law, 67–68, 73–75, 79–83, 84n20

human nature, xiii, xv–xvii, xx, xxiii, xxv, 1–3, 6, 10, 15, 19, 27, 31, 35, 64, 67–68, 72, 83, 131, 149, 152, 155, 162n30, 169–170, 173–176, 178, 180–182, 185, 189–191, 193, 195, 203, 206, 248

humanism, xv–xvii, xix, xxxi, xxxiii, xxxvn16, 1, 8, 11, 13–14, 42, 49, 52–54, 100, 106, 145–149, 151–155, 157, 160n13, 161n17, 161n18, 163n39, 164n52, 171, 258, 262–266; and American New Humanism, xv, xxix, xxxiii, 63, 145, 262, 264; and China, xxxiii, 258, 261–267

humanitarianism, xxv, xxviii, xxxiii, xxxviin42, 1–2, 7–9, 13, 70, 75, 79, 149, 178

ideology, xii, xiv, xxix, xxxi, 1, 54, 100, 115, 175, 177, 180, 183, 185, 189, 191–192, 194–195, 201–202, 204, 208, 215–216

imagination, xv, xx–xxii, xxix, xxxi–xxxii, 14–15, 23, 26–30, 32–34, 41–43, 50–51, 54, 62, 64, 78, 81, 89–101, 105–106, 111–113, 120, 128, 130–132, 134, 138, 140, 156–158, 170, 182, 185, 187, 192, 221–222, 231, 247, 274; and American imagination, xxv, 169, 226, 237, 247; and Christian imagination, 157–158, 188, 275; and creative imagination, 95, 98, 100; and diabolical imagination, 3; and idealistic imagination, 27, 29, 32, 112, 116, 122; and idyllic imagination, 3, 9, 32, 92, 94, 119, 157; and moral imagination, xx–xxiii, 43, 49, 90, 92, 94–95, 105–106, 119, 127–128, 130–132, 156, 222; and progressive imagination, 181, 183, 185, 188–189; and romantic imagination, xx–xxii, xxv, 29, 42, 116

imperialism, xxvi–xxix, xxxviin42, 16, 222–223, 226, 233, 236, 246, 249

inner check, 67, 146, 152, 156, 171, 183. *See also* higher will

Jacobins, 1, 29, 32–33, 202, 212–213

Jefferson, Thomas, xxiv–xxv, xxviii, 62, 204, 229–231, 235, 246–247

Jesus Christ, xvii, 67

Kagan, Robert, 234–236, 252n14

Kant, Immanuel, xxxviin42, 127, 130, 134

Kirk, Russell, xx, xxx, 42, 45–54, 55n4, 56n12, 132, 140, 260

Lewis, Clive Staples (C. S.), 56n12, 153, 164n53, 164n54, 164n55

liberalism, xxxii, xxxvii, 21, 51, 119, 171, 180, 209

Lincoln, Abraham, xxxiii, 222, 247, 252n17

literature, ix, xx, xxxiii, 5, 26–27, 46–47, 49, 63, 91, 96, 191, 260

Locke, John, 127

luminosity, 43, 93; and luminous, 43, 91, 94, 97, 99–100

Machiavelli, Niccolò, xvi, 73
Madison, James, xxiii, xxviii, 2, 173, 181, 228, 246, 251n9
Marx, Karl, 118, 262, 264
Mayflower Compact, 226, 229
McDougall, Walter, xxxii, 232, 234, 236, 246
McKinley, William, 248–249
metaphysics, 10, 73–74, 84n20, 115, 131, 160, 205, 259
metastatic faith, 185, 187, 190, 193
modernity, 25–26, 31, 37, 53, 116, 150, 258
moral universality, xix, xxxvn16, 152–153
morality, xxvi, xxxii, 20, 23–25, 29, 35, 37, 71–72, 75, 91, 106, 109, 111, 117–118, 128–129, 132–133, 138–139, 155, 171, 175, 221, 274; and constitutional morality, xxxii, 171, 202, 208–209, 213, 216, 274; and traditional morality, xxx–xxxi, 2, 6, 23, 33, 36, 73, 164; and Western morality, 23–24, 29
More, Paul Elmer, 45, 49

natural law, xxxi, 67, 74, 77, 84n20, 106, 127–135, 137–138, 153–154, 164n52, 164n53, 164n54, 178, 211
naturalism, 9, 43, 64–65, 69, 73, 75, 79–80, 82–83, 161n18, 175–177
neoconservatives, 20
Nietzsche, Friedrich, xviii, 51
Nisbet, Robert, 122

Oakeshott, Michael, 115–116, 118
Obama, Barack H., xi–xiii, xxviii, xxx, xxxviin42, 62–63, 81–82
original sin, 2, 13, 22, 148, 182, 188
originalism, 176, 178–179, 182–183, 190

Paine, Thomas, xvi, xxiv–xxv, 234
Plato, xvi, xix, xxix–xxx, xxxvn22, 15, 46, 91, 93, 95, 98–99, 131, 154, 177, 184–185, 274

post-constitutionalism, xiv–xv, xxix, 42, 170, 222, 267
progressivism, xxxii, 33, 169–171, 177–178, 180–183, 185–187, 189, 191, 195, 204, 213, 215–216, 223; and constitutionalism, 170, 176–178, 180, 183
Protestantism, 16, 49, 146, 162n30
prudence (*phronesis*), xxxi, 127–129, 136, 138, 146, 152, 155

rationalism, xvi, xviii, xxi, xxx, xxxvn22, 1, 14, 29, 48, 50, 106, 114, 116–119, 127, 156
Reagan, Ronald, xxvii–xxviii
relativism, xix–xx, 72, 79–80, 89
religion, xvi–xvii, xxii, xxvi, 1, 5, 8–13, 16, 20, 26, 48–49, 100, 109–110, 117, 147–149, 151, 153–154, 159n5, 160n13, 161n17, 161n18, 161n23, 162n36, 163n39, 227, 229–231, 234–236, 249, 258–260
republicanism, 121, 221–222, 229, 242, 248
Röepke, Wilhelm, 122
Roman Catholicism, 10, 24, 36, 49–50
romanticism, xiii, xviii, xxi–xxii, xxvi, xxx, xxxiii, 1, 9, 14, 29, 49–51, 54, 63, 69, 73, 75, 149–151, 158, 164n52, 175–176, 179, 183, 236, 263, 274
Roosevelt, Franklin, xxvii–xxviii
Roosevelt, Theodore, 180–181, 248
Rousseau, Jean-Jacques, 1–3, 5–7, 9–14, 26–30, 32, 37, 50, 63, 116, 170, 176, 180, 202–204, 259–260
Ryn, Claes, xxx, xxxiii, xxxvn22, 2, 23, 26–34, 41–42, 105–106, 109, 111–114, 116–118, 120, 130, 209, 222–223; and *America the Virtuous*, xxviii, 33, 202, 234; and democracy, xv, xxii, xxiv–xxv, xxxii, 3, 29, 31, 121, 161n17, 170–171, 201–208, 214–216, 217n16, 221, 236; and *Democracy and the Ethical Life*, xxii,

xxxii, 202; and ethical life, 216; and historicism, xix, xxxvn16, 92; and humanism, xv–xvii, xix, xxix, xxxi, xxxvn16, 1, 100, 164n52; and imagination, 23, 26–30, 32–34; and natural law, xxxi, 127–128, 132, 164n52; and peace, xix, xxvi, xxix, 29; and universality, xviii–xxi, xxxvn16, xxxvn20, 127, 131–132; and Voegelin, Eric, xxxi, 43, 89–101, 163n38, and *Will, Imagination and Reason*, 140, 163n38

scientism, xxxi, 48
Strauss, Leo, xxxvn22
Sumner, William Graham, xxxii, 232–234
Supreme Court, 178–179, 182–183, 189–190, 208, 226, 252n14

de Tocqueville, Alexis, 25, 36, 106, 121, 204, 207–208, 212, 229, 238n9, 260

U.S. Constitution, xiv, xxiii, 2, 19–20, 22, 25, 34, 37, 169, 174, 176–180, 182, 184, 190–193, 195, 206–208, 210, 214–215, 242, 245–248, 252n17; and American constitutionalism, xvi, xxviii, 2, 36–37, 170, 174–176, 180, 189, 191–192, 194–195

Voegelin, Eric, xxxi–xxxii, 42–43, 89–101, 163n38, 170, 173–176, 183–185, 189–194, 196n7

Warren, Robert Penn, xxxi, 42–43, 63–68, 74–76, 79–80, 82–83
Washington, George, xxvi, xxviii, 234, 238, 246
Webster, Daniel, 222, 225–226, 229–230, 237
Wilson, Woodrow, xxv, xxvii–xxviii, xxxii, 180–181, 212, 215, 222, 232–235, 238n9
Winthrop, John, 222, 227–228, 235–236

www.ingramcontent.com/pod-product-compliance
Ingram Content Group UK Ltd.
Pitfield, Milton Keynes, MK11 3LW, UK
UKHW041916140426
5217IPUK00013B/172